BASES OF
BOMBER COMMAND
THEN AND NOW

Gone are the trees and farmers' fruitful land,
Despoiled with concrete scars by war's cruel hand.
Those fellows lost and now among the dead,
Stood of their last upon this airfield spread.

Before each time a bombing raid is near
A cursed place sunk in our hidden fear.
If safe return, escaping personal grief
These blighted acres are our sweet relief.

And what of those unborn
Who will not have to fear the dusk and dawn?
What will be made of our today from their tomorrow?
Will they look back with pride or sorrow?

Will this place be a cherished spot
Or just forgot?

BASES OF BOMBER COMMAND

THEN AND NOW

By Roger A. Freeman

Credits

ISBN: 1 870067 35 5
© Roger Freeman/After the Battle, 2001
Reprinted 2003
Designed by Winston G. Ramsey,
Editor-in-Chief, *After the Battle*

PUBLISHERS
Battle of Britain International Limited,
Church House, Church Street,
London E15 3JA

PRINTERS
Printed in Slovenia for Compass Press Limited.

FRONT COVER
This well-known publicity shot of a Stirling of
No. 1651 Heavy Conversion Unit was taken
at Waterbeach in April 1942 (see page 171).

BACK COVER
Gathering hay near a north side dispersal at
Elvington in July 1943. This Halifax (DT807)
named *Rita*, belonging to No. 77 Squadron,
was lost on the night of October 3/4, 1943
during a raid on Kassel. There were two survivors out of the crew of seven.

FRONT ENDPAPER
Wellington T2470 BU-K of No. 214 Squadron being towed by a Fordson tractor into
the second hangar from the west at
Stradishall in October 1940. Type C hangars
were 300 feet long with ample room for three
Wellingtons.

REAR ENDPAPER
Destination Berlin! Stirlings of No. 90
Squadron lined up for take-off at dusk on
August 31, 1943. The photographer was
standing beside a Stirling parked on the
hardstanding north of runway head 31.

FRONTISPIECE
Linton-on-Ouse in No. 6 Group

MAPS
Map extracts are from the 1:50000 series published by Ordnance Survey. The extracts on
pages 20, 78, 123, 180, 220, 285 and 318 are
reproduced from Aeronautical Chart ICAO
1:500000 Edition 1951 with acknowledgement
to the Directorate of Military Survey. All maps
are Crown Copyright.

PHOTOGRAPHS
The following photographs are from the
author's collection: 36 top, 64 top, 65 top left, 72
top, 96 centre, 100 top, 105 top, 116 bottom left,
136 bottom left, 141 top, 161 top, 236 bottom,
244-245, 266 top, 328 top left, 338 top, 340 top.
    Others were either loaned or copies supplied
by various organisations, private collectors and
historians to whom the author is very grateful.
They are: **Barry Abraham** 38 top. Airfield
Research Group 38 top left. **David Appleby** 25
top left. **Eric Atkins** 92 top. **Ron Barrowcliffe via
Pat Otter** 196 top, middle left and middle right. **P.
Birch** 58 top. **Allan Bourne** 310 top. **Chaz Bowyer**
138 top. **Brentwood School** 122, **Ken Cothliff** 312
bottom left. **R. G. Davys** 26 top right, 62 bottom,
63 top left. **Flight International** 138 top, 150 top.
Garbett/Goulding Collection: C. Koder 54 top; **A.
R. Ashley** 174 top left; **J. H. Moutray** 225 top; **N.
D. Owen** 225 centre; **J. K. Aitken** 228 top; **D. F.
Cottier** 243 top; **G. E. G. Galletly** 253 top; **A. J.
Hart** 277 centre; **Public Archives of Canada** 322
top; **J. D. Garrick** 326 top left; **Mrs J. Aumann**
328 centre. **Jean Gardner** 249 top right. **P. H. T.
Green Collection: via Stewart Scott (Ron Taylor
photo)** 23 top right; via **Pat Otter** 35 top; **via N.
Franklin** 44 top; **via Ted Richardson** 272 centre.
F. E. Hay 146 centre. **M. Hodgson** 280 top, 292

top, 337 top. **Julian Horn** 85 middle, 116 top. **Hull
Daily Mirror (via D. F. Thompson)** 200 bottom
right. **Kerry Hutchinson** 184 centre, bottom left
and bottom right, 185 top, centre, bottom right,
186 bottom right, 187 bottom right, 349 bottom
right. **Imperial War Museum** front endpaper,
frontispiece, 2-3, 6 top, 11 top and bottom, 24 top
right, 31 top and bottom left, 46 top, 48 top, 69
middle, 70 top, 80 top, 81 top, 88 bottom, 111 top,
119 top, 130 top, 136 top, 145 bottom, 150 bottom,
153 top, 155 top, 158 top, 181 top, 184 top, 188
top, 199 top, 200 top, 202 top, 207 top, 208 top,
210 top and centre, 212 top, 213 top, 214 centre,
217 bottom left, 219, 222 top, 224 top, 239 top
right, 247 top and centre, 259 bottom, 264 top, 268
top, and centre, 272 top, 279 top left and centre,
298 top, 302 top, 303 top, 304 top, 314 bottom left,
324 top, 330 top, 332 top and middle, 334 top, 342
top, 346 top, rear endpaper, rear cover. **Christopher Jary** 316 top and bottom, 317 top, bottom
left and bottom right. **H. Kidney** 146 top left.
Laing Photographic Services 18 top. **A. S. Leslie**
232 top. **Julia Mills and Philip Shaw** 73 top left.
Barry Morse 37 top, 38 top. **D. S. Norton** 125 bottom, 139 top, 140 top, 154 bottom, 343 bottom.
Simon Parry 28 centre left, 52 top, 60 top, 64 centre, 133 top, 134 top, 192 bottom, 258 top, 260 top, 262
top. **Pooleys Flight Guide** 94 bottom, 214 top, 305
top. **Stephen Pope** 110 top. **RAF Museum** cover,
37 top, 71 top left, 86 top, 132 top, 149 top, 152
top, 171 top, 189 top, 217 top left, 238 top, 274 top.
Bruce Robertson 257 centre, 344 top. **Chris
Sheenan** 307 top left and middle, 308 top. **Sterling
Helicopters Ltd** 94-95. **Andy Thomas** 44 centre
right, 56 top, 98 top right, 109 top, 119 bottom left,
124 top, 165 top and bottom left, 168 top, 197 top,
282 top, 293 top, 295 top, 296 top, 299 top left, 309

bottom, 319 top. **David E. Thompson** 299 bottom,
300 top, 302 middle, 310 middle. **Alan Todd** 287
top left, centre left and bottom left, 288 top. **Peter
Usherwood** 196 centre and bottom left and right.
Wattisham Historical Society 114 top left.
    Contemporary aerial photographs taken by
the Royal Air Force are Crown Copyright and
were obtained either via the Royal Commission
for Historic Monuments, the Public Record
Office or from private sources. All present day
comparison photographs (unless otherwise stated) and aerials copyright *After the Battle*.

SOURCES
Much of the data used in these compilations was
extracted from Public Record Office files, princi-
pally the AIR 27 and 28 classes covering Bomber
Command squadrons and stations. Other records
used were in WORK, AIR 10 and AIR 20 classes,
notably AIR 10/4039 and AIR 20/7585-6. Publica-
tions consulted include: *RAF Bomber Command
Losses of the Second World War* by W. R. Chor-
ley (five volumes). *Bomber Squadrons of the
R.A.F.* by Philip Moyes. *The Bomber Command
War Diaries* by Martin Middlebrook and Chris
Everitt. *Action Stations No. 1* by Michael J. F.
Bowyer. *Action Stations Nos. 2 & 4* by Bruce B.
Halpenny. *The Airfields of Lincolnshire* by Ron
Blake, Mike Hodgson and Bill Taylor. *Royal Air
Force Stradishall* by Spencer Adams and Jock
Whitehouse. *Silksheen: The history of East Kirk-
by airfield. Strike Hard: A bomber airfield at war*
by John B. Hilling. Numerous issues of *Airfield
Review* which is published quarterly by the Air-
field Research Group, 35 Lyme Road, Hazel
Grove, Stockport SK7 6JX.

Acknowledgements

The author was very familiar with Bomber Command in the friendly sky during
the Second World War but few of its airfields were located in the area of his home.
Nevertheless the names of the bomber stations became familiar through an uncle
who started out as the adjutant of a very famous bomber squadron and by 1945 had
served in five bomber groups.
    In the past half-century most, if not all, of the bomber airfield sites have been vis-
ited but the detail required for this volume had, where possible, to be obtained
from the official archival records held by the Public Record Office and Royal Air
Force Museum. Even so, due to the very few documents extant that deal with actual development of individual airfields, it has been necessary to turn to people who
have made a detailed study of the subject. Foremost were members of the Airfield
Research Group who gave unstinting help in many quarters and its chairman Barry
Abraham was particularly active on my behalf in aiding the location of suitable
wartime photographs and proofing narratives. Any reader who is desirous of more
information on all aspects of airfields is highly recommended to join the Airfield
Research Group which publishes an excellent magazine devoted to the subject (see
below for address).
    Mike Garbett and Brian Goulding, whose knowledge of Lancaster squadrons is
unsurpassed, made available rare photographs and checked part of the text. Other
individuals who have provided information and material are: Ken Cothliff, Peter
Green, Ian Mactaggart, George Pennick and Andy Thomas.
    On the editorial side, Bruce Robertson, past editor of Service journals, has provid-
ed invaluable advice through vetting the text. Additional help was provided by Rod
Aspinell of the Airscene Museum Blake Hall, John Button, Frank Cheesman, Peter
Elliott and John Edwards of the RAF Museum, David O'Flanaghan, Wing Com-
mander Keith Hopkins, Julian Horn, Kerry Hutchinson, Christopher Jary, Wing
Commander John MacBean, Christopher Mace of Sterling Helicopters Ltd, Barry
Morse, D. S. Norton, Harold Panton of the Lincolnshire Aviation Heritage Centre,
Simon Parry, Stephen W. Pope, B.A(Hons), the staff of the Royal Commission for
Historic Monuments at Swindon, Mike Shilton, Jim Shortland, Len Taylor, Alan
Todd, David Thompson, Peter Usherwood, John Vivian and Marina Wingham. My
appreciation is extended to all who contributed to the present volume.
    We received tremendous help when visiting the airfields and my grateful thanks
to all those people and organisations who gave us facilities to take photographs,
particularly the Community Relations Officers at RAF Coningsby, RAF Cottesmore, RAF Leeming, RAF Linton-on-Ouse, RAF Marham, RAF Newton, RAF
Topcliffe, RAF Watton and RAF Wyton; the Army Air Corps at Dishforth and
Wattisham; the Ministry of Defence at West Tofts; the Defence School of Transport at Leconfield and Alconbury Developments PLC.

ROGER A. FREEMAN, 2001

Contents

No. 5 Group's 61 Squadron was based alternately at Syerston in Nottinghamshire and Skellingthorpe and Coningsby in Lincolnshire. This Lanc QR-W (DV397) was lost on the last major raid on Berlin on the night of March 24/25, 1944.

INTRODUCTION

This book covers 101 airfields used by operational Bomber Command squadrons during the Second World War. It does not cover those airfields occupied solely by the Command's operational training units and associated formations that on occasions undertook limited operations. Nor does it feature those airfields from which operations were carried out by bombers detached from home stations, as frequently occurred in the early war years. It would take a sizeable volume to record the full story of just a single airfield and for that reason the range of subjects in this volume is limited. The narrative does not include detailed squadron histories which, as the bibliography acknowledges, are well documented in other publications.

Concentration is on the layout and development of an airfield with acknowledgement of the Bomber Command units using it for operational purposes during hostilities. Unfortunately, few records of the Air Ministry Directorate of Works, primarily responsible for airfield design, construction and development, are to be found in any public archive and they were presumably destroyed during early post-war years. Thus there is a dearth of information on most aspects of airfield history apart from operational use. For this reason it has not always been possible to give precise dates for development stages. There was never a static period for wartime bomber airfields as they were being constantly developed and improved, albeit in minor ways when the desired Class A standard had been achieved.

RAF organisation was in area formations of groups under each command. Boundaries of group areas changed as the war progressed, some airfields passing from one group to another. The airfields in this book are presented, in general, by the groups they served in the later stages of the conflict.

The machines . . . and the men! This book was first conceived by ex-Sergeant Wilf Nicoll back in 1982 but he died before his idea could be brought to fruition.

A feature of *After the Battle*'s 'Then and Now' volumes is the matching of a wartime photograph with one taken from more or less the same spot today (2000 in this case). The RAF's preoccupation with security has meant that finding wartime photographs showing some identifiable landmark has been difficult and in a few cases not achieved. Tim Wingham visited all the airfields to take the comparison photographs, a task which took about 18 months and over 10,000 miles to complete. Tim says that 'it was a challenging but rewarding project and I feel privileged to have visited these often forgotten places where history was quite literally made. Sadly, though, with time, there inevitably becomes less and less physical evidence of wartime Bomber Command. Some of its airfields have virtually vanished, and yet, if you look hard enough something still remains of every one. An almost overwhelming air of sadness lingers over many of the airfields, disused or current: perhaps an invisible lasting testament to the 55,500 men who took the war to a former enemy . . . and paid the ultimate sacrifice.'

Left: **After the mammoth task of visiting the 101 airfields covered in this book, Tim Wingham (left) hands over the final pictures to** *After the Battle*'s **Editor-in-Chief, Winston Ramsey.** *Right:* **Editor Karel Margry then took over for the aerial photography.**

The aerial photographs were taken by Karel Margry, Editor of *After the Battle*. Flying from Sibson near Peterborough, he first photographed the airfields of Groups 1, 2, 3, 5 and 8 in the south before moving north to Sherburn-in-Elmet in Yorkshire to cover Groups 4 and 6. Karel's bird's eye view led him to marvel at the closeness of the airfields which did lead during the war to many collisions. 'Leaning out of the cockpit window, your head in the wind, you shoot off two or three frames. Turning backwards, you expose another two to make sure. As you pull back inside, the pilot sets course for the next airfield. Seconds later it already appears on the horizon. Imagine having to fly here in the dark on a 1,000-bomber raid! It certainly makes you admire the navigating abilities of the wartime aircrews and ground controllers.'

Karel took the majority of the aerial photos while flying from Sibson, then as now an airfield devoted to flying training. His pilot was John Nicholls *(left)*. Moving 100 miles north to cover Groups 4 and 6, Karel based himself at Sherburn-in-Elmet where he was flown by the CFI, Cas Smith *(right)*. During the war, Sherburn was a centre for aircraft research, manufacture and repair, a new factory being erected on the northern side for building the Fairey Swordfish by Blackburn Aircraft Ltd.

AIRFIELDS FOR BOMBERS

The nature of the flying machine called the aeroplane requires fast movement across a ground or water surface to gain sufficient lift from its wings to become airborne. Developments such as jets and rockets, able to thrust an aeroplane into the sky and achieve the desired forward motion without a surface run have proved too power consuming. A suitable airfield is as essential today as when man first undertook powered flight.

At first, aircraft were so light that any suitable large level meadow, devoid of boundary obstruction, sufficed. The First World War brought increased weight and size and more attention had to be paid to the nature of the land at any proposed airfield site. Free draining soil was desirable which accounts for many of the early airfields being established on sandy heathland. The war necessitated aircraft operating in all seasons but after heavy rainfall surfaces of even the most well drained meadows tend to 'mud up' at times prohibiting take-off. Tracks known as runways were reinforced with wood or compacted ballast at some installations to overcome this problem.

In the immediate post-war years the RAF's bomber arm was eventually reduced to a dozen regular squadrons at seven United Kingdom airfields, all concentrated in the Salisbury Plain area and East Anglia. Their strength was bolstered by a similar number of Reserve and Auxiliary squadrons with a bomber mission. Disquieting news from Germany brought some limited investment in airfield construction during the early 1930s, accelerated by the expansion programme announced in July 1934 whereby the RAF was to have 128 first-line squadrons Empire-wide by the summer of 1939, of which some 50 would be based in the UK. To this end, on July 14, 1936, a re-organised administrative structure was brought into being with the creation of the Bomber, Fighter, Coastal and Training Commands.

Initially, Bomber Command was organised into four groups: Nos. 1, 2, 3 and 6, the last being composed of Auxiliary units. As new squadrons were formed and new airfields became available there were several changes in group composition and Nos. 4 and 5 Groups were added while No. 6 was delegated to training. The group was an administrative, and

Linton-on-Ouse — then and now. A WAAF works on a pictorial map of the aerodrome when it only sported two runways.

later operational, headquarters between Bomber Command and the squadrons. Each was established to control bomber stations in a defined area and by the outbreak of war having squadrons flying the same bomber type. No. 1 the light Fairey Battle, No. 2 the Bristol Blenheim, No. 3 the Vickers Wellington medium, No. 4 the heavy category Armstrong Whitworth Whitley, and No. 5 Handley Page Hampdens rated as mediums. Following the creation of the Bomber Command roles were included in both group and squadron designations, for example No. 1 (Bomber Group), No. 51 (Bomber) Squadron. As role designations were later discontinued they are not used in this narrative.

Today the two pre-war runways are still in use but the third (18-36) can be seen now marked with the 'X' which denotes that it is disused. In September 2000, a nice line up of Tucano trainers could be seen on the enlarged apron in the south-eastern corner.

Linton-on-Ouse, some six miles or so north-west of York, was one of the earliest of the so-called 'Expansion airfields' designed to build up the strength of the RAF in the 1930s.

Officially opened in May 1937, its grass airfield occupied about 250 acres giving a maximum take-off distance of just over 1,000 yards. This shot was taken on September 12, 1938.

EXPANSION SCHEME AIRFIELDS

The new bomber airfields of the 1930s expansion programme had individual variations but were in general similar in layout and construction. All were grass-surfaced with the flying field occupying an area of approximately 250 acres, the actual extent usually decided by the acreage of the farm or farms purchased. The flying field was the first part of a new airfield to be developed in order to have a grass surface by the scheduled date of opening the station. The area developed contained a 1,100 yard diameter circle — known as the bombing circle — and so called because it was then usual for a squadron to drop practice bombs on a target set in the middle of its home airfield. This ensured a safeguarded area away from civilian life and property. Rectangular take-off and landing strips were established over the bombing circle, usually three with the main aligned to the prevailing wind, mostly south-west/north-east, and the others on headings west-east and north-west/south-east or thereabouts. The main strip was planned at 1,300 by 400 yards and the subsidiaries 1,000 by 200 yards, although in practice the width of the strips was often greater. At the end of each strip were clearance zones for flight approach at an angle of 1 in 15 from the horizontal, fanned out at a 15 degree angle. Extensive drainage schemes were installed to remove rainwater as quickly as possible with considerable under-drainage in more unstable soil conditions.

Outside the circumference of the bombing circle, four aeroplane sheds — the official term which later gave way to hangar — were erected in concave placement. By 1936 the standard was the Type C, steel framed with brick walls (later concrete), glazing and metal doors. The roof was hipped, 300 by 150 feet clear span and 35 feet high to eaves, although a later version had a height reduction of five feet. Annexes on each side of these hangars provided offices and stores. The crescent of Type C hangars remain the most telling fixture of an airfield originating in the 1930's expansion period. When the programme began it was still general practice to keep aircraft under cover and the four or five hangars provided storage for the complement of two squadrons, although with the arrival of the Wellington and Whitley this was no longer possible.

The hangars had side rooms providing office and store facilities. Directly behind the aeroplane sheds was the Technical Site with specialised buildings, workshops and stores. Backing the technical area was the camp with barracks and associated buildings, brick or concrete, flat-roofed and centrally-heated. The whole camp was neat and compact. It is surprising that in view of the growing prominence of aerial bombing in the late 1930s, no action was taken to disperse the installations, particularly barracks, or that, with the planned production of much heavier bombers, that earlier provision of hardened runways was not undertaken.

Linton was the first Bomber Command airfield in northern England to have hard runways laid down and the second in the whole of the Command. This picture was taken on April 25, 1941 just before the aerodrome was bombed by the Luftwaffe.

HARD RUNWAYS

Sod-surfaced bomber airfields gave no trouble in dry summers but when the British climate turned in a particularly wet year many flying fields became badly rutted, curtailing flying. This was the case in 1937. Hardened runways were the obvious answer and official vacillation was occasioned by the high cost of such provision. The Whitley and the Wellington had gross operating weights of approximately 32,000 lb, requiring ground runs of 650 and 520 yards respectively to become airborne. The new Short, Avro and Handley Page heavy bombers were expected to gross twice this figure, requiring ground runs of up to 900 yards. For all weather operation of these heavies hardened runways were imperative.

Surprisingly, the first programme of hardened runways for the RAF were for fighter stations. In Bomber Command the first hardened runways were born of necessity. At Stradishall, an expansion scheme airfield unwisely located on good Suffolk clay, it was found near impossible to conduct flying in winter weather. Two 1,000 feet concrete runways were approved and work commenced a few weeks before the outbreak of war. About the same time two 1,000 feet runways were also sanctioned for Linton-on-Ouse, an expansion scheme aerodrome in Yorkshire, similarly afflicted with water-logging.

Thereafter concrete runways became an accepted requirement for new airfields constructed for bomber use, and hard runways were also put down at existing sod-surfaced bomber airfields. The latter programme was long drawn out, principally because the airfield shortage created a lack of alternatives to which operational units could be moved while runways were laid. It was therefore necessary in many cases to close part of the area at some bomber stations while concrete was poured and to complete the provision of runways, taxi-

tracks and aircraft standings in sections, which naturally presented flying control difficulties. As with the first hard runways at Bomber Command stations, the next undertakings were also at problem sites; those with the more stable and free-draining soil continuing grass-surfaced in a few cases until as late as the autumn of 1943. Grass surfaces were preferred by many pilots as they considered them smoother, providing great allowance for 'swinging' during take-off and landings. Taxi-ing was also less restricted and time-saving.

The Halifax with higher tyre pressures than the Stirling was particularly prone to rutting turf and the first new airfields opened in No. 4 Group area had hard runways. This group was selected to operate the type, replacing its Whitleys. Meanwhile the first Stirling squadron had to operate from the large grass airfield at Oakington, presumably selected because the type when grossing 70,000 lb required a ground run of 900 yards and 1,400 yards to clear a boundary at 50 feet. Stirlings, assigned to No. 3 Group, were expected to replace the faithful Wellingtons. The third new 'heavy', the troublesome Manchester, went to No. 5 Group where it initially operated from grass.

With the expectation of attacks by the Luftwaffe on Bomber Command bases, action was taken to disperse aircraft around the boundaries of airfields. At some, hard tracks, usually compacted aggregate and tarred surfaces, were laid into adjoining properties, particularly where woodland or other suitable topography offered a measure of concealment. Such dispersal layouts were far from satisfactory creating servicing difficulties and were fuel and time consuming when getting aircraft back on the airfield for take-off. A more satisfactory solution was a satellite aerodrome a short road journey from the home station to which aircraft could be flown for dispersal.

While grass-surfaced aerodromes were able to support light bombers like this Bristol Blenheim (R3600 of the Wattisham-based No. 110 Squadron), which had a take-off weight of around six tons, later bomber types weighed over twice that and the four-engined heavies more than 30 tons. Hence the need for concrete runways to permit all-weather operations.

With the Lancasters take-off weight at 65,000lbs the aircraft would unstick at 105mph, or 120mph at 72,000lb, but in the latter case a hard runway had to be used. This Lanc, 'A'-Able of No. 106 Squadron, was pictured with its proud ground crew in December 1944 for an Air Ministry publicity picture as the machine had recently completed 100 sorties. JB663 went on to complete 111 sorties before it was retired in February 1945. No wonder the crew named it *King of the Air*!

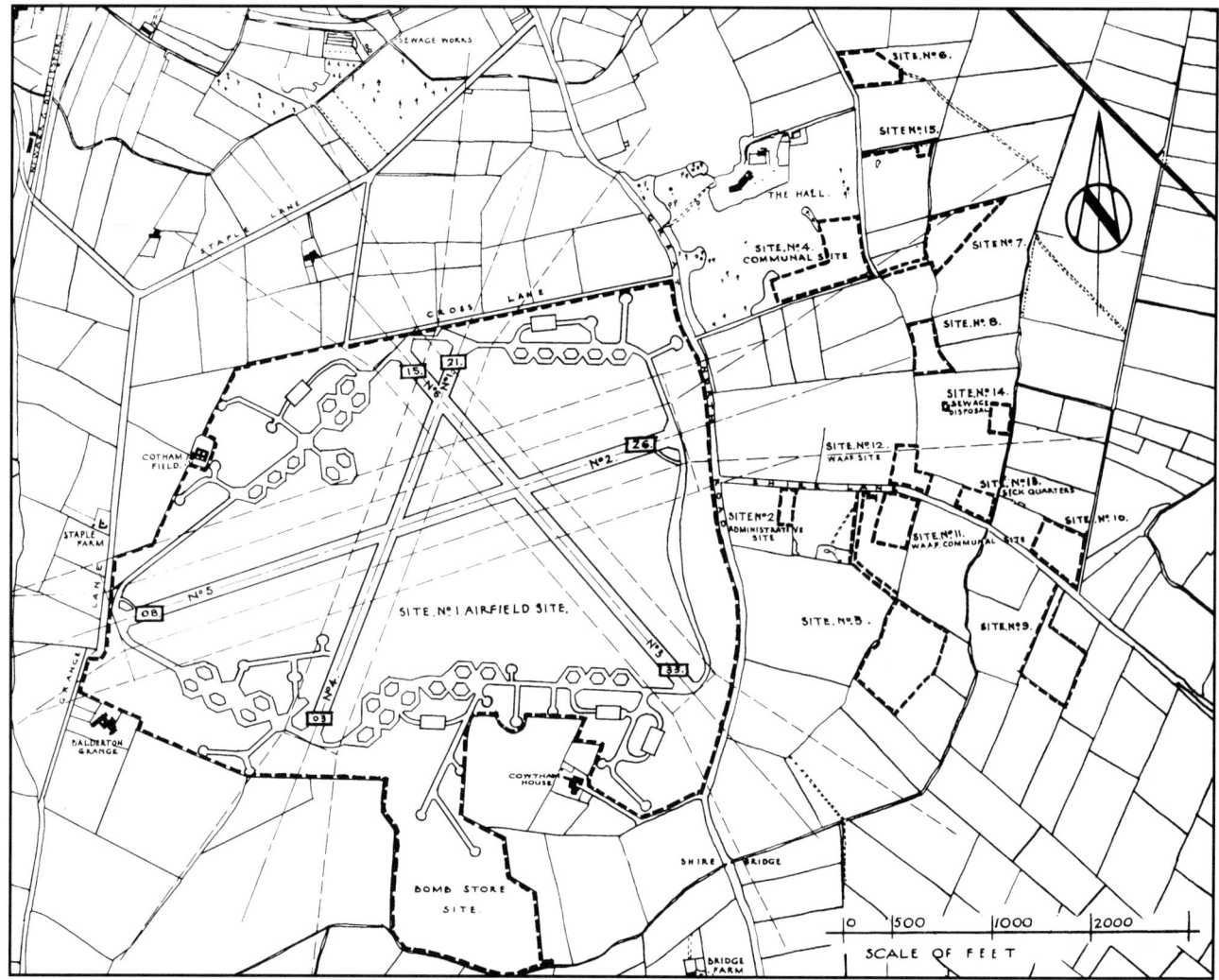

SCALE OF FEET
0 | 500 | 1000 | 2000

WARTIME DESIGN

By February 1940 the Air Ministry Directorate of Works had established guidelines for new bomber airfields with hard runways: three flight strips of a minimum 1,000 yards length as near 60 degrees to each other, intersecting to economise in land usage. The main cleared strip was to be 400 yards wide and the two subsidiaries 200 yards wide, with a hard runway along the centre of each strip 1,000 yards long by 50 yards wide. Allowance was made at new sites for the main runways to be extended to 1,400 yards and the subsidiaries to 1,100 yards. It was soon obvious that the original specification was inadequate for the new heavy bombers and by December 1940 the construction of hard runways at all bomber stations were to a Class A standard requiring a 1,400 yard main and 1,100 yard subsidiaries. Experience with fully-loaded Halifaxes and Stirlings showed that it was desirable to have even longer runways and a month later the requirement for the main was increased to 1,600 yards and allowance made for possible extension to 2,000 and 1,400 yards for the main and subsidiaries, respectively. At this time the approach funnels were revised to give more clearance for the main with 1 in 30 from the horizontal. By July 1941, a 2,000-yard main and 1,400-yard subsidiaries had been established as the ideal for all new airfields and in the following November all runways at bomber airfields were to be extended to these lengths where possible.

These requirements were incorporated in a revised Class A standard, to become the norm for an operational bomber airfield. There were detail changes during the next two years but the basic requirements remained the same. The massive building programme begun in 1941 was predominantly involved in producing airfields to Class A standard for both the RAF and USAAF. Existing bomber airfields were, wherever practicable, eventually brought up to this standard, the pattern of runway extensions being the most prominent indicator of this endeavour.

Balderton in No. 5 Group is typical of a simple satellite aerodrome which was later upgraded for the USAAF to what was called an 'A' Standard airfield. On this plan we see the runways numbered according to the pre-1943 system whereby each threshold was labelled from 1 to 6 in a clockwise direction. Identification by magnetic bearings was standard by 1943.

CLASS A STANDARD BOMBER AIRFIELD

The A Standard comprised a 2,000-yard main and two 1,400-yard subsidiary runways, all 50 yards wide with 100-yard cleared and prepared overshoots at all ends. In addition, cleared and levelled strips sown with grass were provided 175 yards wide either side of the main and 75 yards for the subsidiaries. A further 100-yards on either side of the prepared ground on main strips was levelled with all obstructions removed with the exception of light hedges not exceeding three feet in height. Maximum gradient allowed along a runway was 1 in 80 and 1 in 60 across a runway. In service, runways were first usually identified by a clockwise system — 1 to 6 for each threshold — but might also be referred to by the compass bearings or simply a number for the whole runway. By 1943 a standardised system had been adopted for both RAF and USAAF airfields. This used the first two digits of a runway's magnetic bearing relative to the direction of approach as the identification. For example, a true west-east runway aligned 090-270 degrees would be given as 09-27.

The perimeter track encircling the runway layout and giving access was 50 feet wide and averaged about three miles in length. Maximum gradient allowed was 1 in 40. A 10-yard levelling and clearance on both sides allowed for aircraft running off the track. No building or other obstructions were permitted within 50 yards of the centre of the perimeter track.

Aircraft hardstandings were sited immediately off the perimeter track or in clusters accessed by short 50-foot-wide tracks. At first these areas were of circular concrete design, 50 yards in diameter, and were known as the 'frying pan' type.

A far more practical loop type, popularly known as the 'spectacle', was introduced in 1942. From the spring of 1943 new bomber airfields were completed with a mixture of both types while later construction featured all spectacles, usually with the exception of the standing used to park aircraft for test firing at the stop-butt. The loops were 50 feet wide and the aircraft parking position centred a minimum of 50 yards from the centre of the perimeter track. RAF Bomber Command requirements were for 36 standings but as the USAAF intended to place from 40 to 70 bombers on a single airfield, hardstandings were increased to 50 and a few of these airfields came into RAF use.

About 400,000 cubic yards of concrete were used in the construction of a Class A standard airfield, the runway slab being from 9 to 12 inches thick.

Some of the early wartime airfields had Type J hangars which were prefabricated and featured a curved roof. Dimensions were similar to the pre-war Type C but much less costly to build. As first priority was to make the flying field available for use, the erection of hangars was sometimes not begun until after the airfield came into use. That adjacent to the main technical site was always the first to go up.

Hangar provision varied but by 1943 two prefabricated metal T2 type were usual on operational stations without special requirements or additional services. The common configuration of this steel-framed and corrugated iron-clad building was a 25 feet clear height, a span of 117 feet 6 inches, and a clear length of 239 feet 7 inches. Most bomber airfields later had an additional hangar for use by the civilian mechanics of the Ministry of Aircraft Production repair organisations. Of similar construction to the T2, but known as a Type B1, it was of MAP's own design and had lower eves and a higher apex.

Watch offices (control towers) also varied, particularly at the earlier stations, the most common type on late Class A airfields being to drawing No. 343/43. They were rectangular, flat-roofed and of brick and concrete construction, and frequently it was the only substantial building within the perimeter track. The main technical site backed one of the hangars and, apart from workshops and stores, included specialised buildings for synthetic training such as the Link trainer and bombing teacher.

On new stations, from 10 to 16 domestic, communal, hospital and sewage sites, were spread in the surrounding countryside. Domestic sites were usually composed of from 10 to 25 small prefabricated buildings, usual Nissen huts, the selection dependent on availability and other factors. In general, accommodation was provided for between 1,500 and 3,000 persons. One or two communal sites had mess halls and recreational facilities. In the event of disruption of local services, generating equipment was available and sufficient water storage on site.

A bomb store was, where possible, situated off the airfield boundary remote from the hangars and technical site. A series of bays between soil blast mounds was the common form of storage. Accessed by a vehicle road, wooded areas were preferred to reduce blast in the case of an accident. Usually combined or adjacent to the bomb stores was the armament store. Two or three sunken storage tank sites for aviation fuel were also placed outside the perimeter track, again, where possible, away from buildings. Total storage capacity was normally 72,000 Imperial gallons.

Total cost of a Class A bomber airfield was in the region of £1 million at 1940s values, and it has been estimated that one of these airfields built now would cost £100 million!

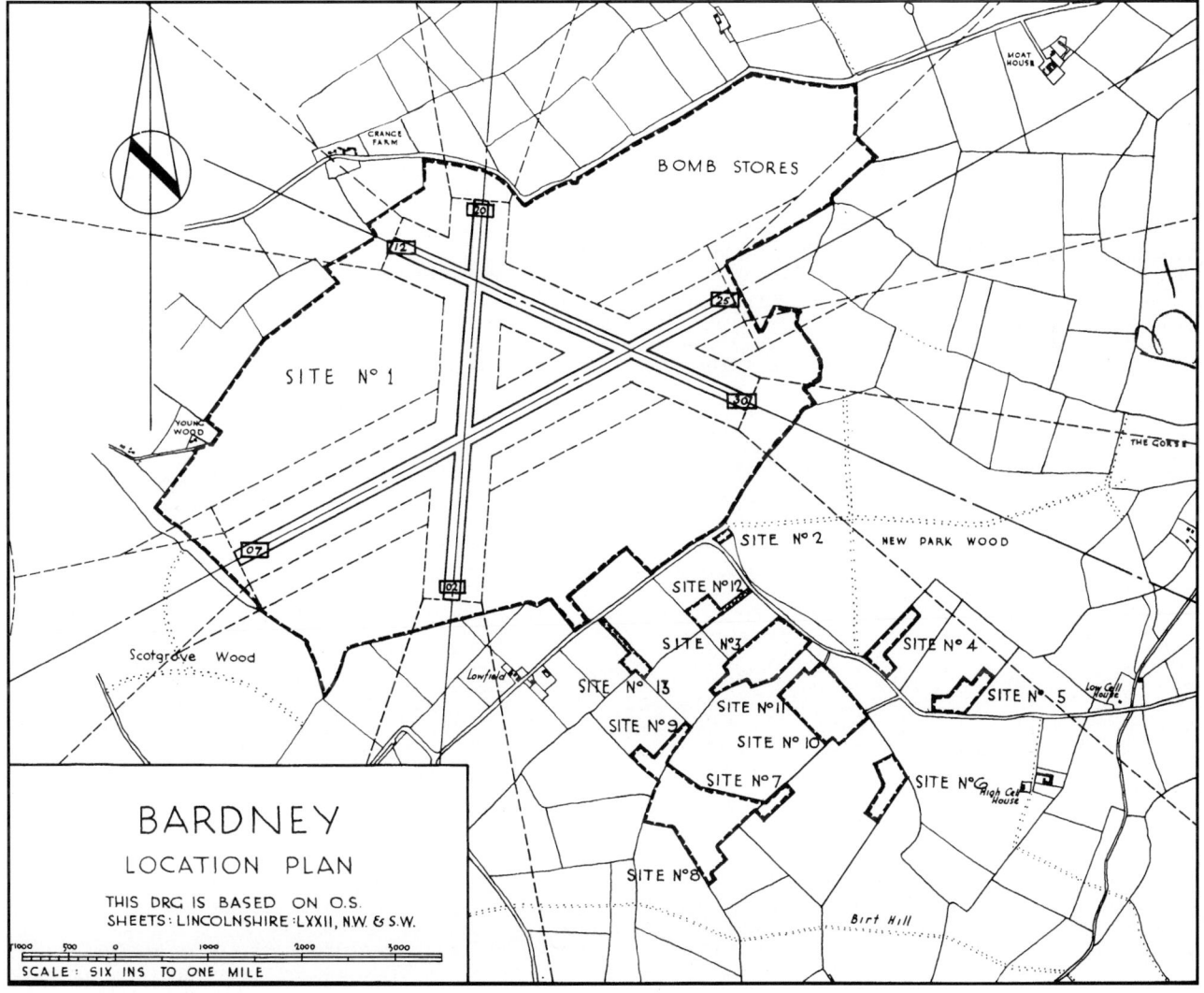

Bardney on the other hand, also in No. 5 Group, was built to class 'A' Standard from scratch with the main runway of 2,000 yards and the subsidiaries each of 1,400 yards, on this plan designated by their magnetic bearings.

HQ BOMBER COMMAND

Royal Air Force Bomber Command was formed on July 14, 1936, its first Air Officer Commanding-in-Chief being Sir John Steel, with its initial headquarters at Uxbridge, in west London. Just over a year later, in September 1937, command passed to Sir Edgar Ludlow-Hewitt who returned from India to take up the appointment while a permanent site was sought for a headquarters for the new command.

As one of the main RAF training depots, Uxbridge was required for the induction of new recruits, so Bomber Command found temporary accommodation in Bridge House in Richlings Park, Langley, Buckinghamshire, with additional space being found at the nearby Actors' Orphanage which was also requisitioned. Meanwhile, the search was on for a suitable site for a permanent headquarters.

'SOUTHDOWN'

The siting of the Bomber Command HQ at High Wycombe is supposed to have stemmed from a chance remark by Wing Commander Alan Oakeshott who was working at the Air Ministry when the search for a location was being undertaken. The Wing Commander had grown up in the village of Naphill, in the Chiltern Hills, where his father was a prominent local landowner, and he suggested that as the HQ had to be in southern England and well screened by trees, the wooded slopes of the Chilterns around Walters Ash would be ideal. Not only was the area remote, but it lacked significant features when observed from the air which would make it difficult for an enemy to spot. He backed up his suggestions with photographs and a decision was soon made by the Directorate of Works to build at Walters Ash. Work commenced in November 1938, the main contractors being John Laing & Son Ltd, although acquisition of all the land required was not finalised until 1940, the majority for the main sites being compulsorily purchased from Bradenham Manor.

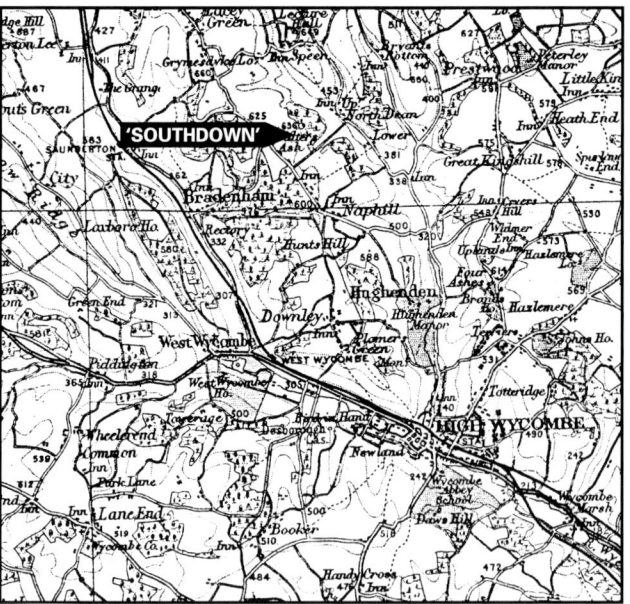

Before the Second World War, the Buckinghamshire town of High Wycombe, 30 miles north-west of London, was known mainly for its chair-making industry. This had become established in the area because of the extensive beech woods in the region, but the town's seclusion in the rolling Chiltern Hills also made it an attractive proposition when RAF Bomber Command began its search for a suitable location for its headquarters. A site was selected north of the town at Walter's Ash (more commonly spelt now as Walters Ash) where the road from Naphill runs beside Park Wood. This tree cover was maintained as far as possible during the building works which commenced in November 1938.

Although RAF Bomber Command existed for 32 years — from July 14, 1936 to April 30, 1968 — it is the tenure of its wartime chief, Sir Arthur Harris, with which the organisation is most remembered. Having taken over from Air Marshal Sir Richard Peirse who had held the appointment since October 1940, Harris assumed command in February 1942, and for the next three years he rigorously pursued the primary objective which had already been given to Bomber Command, which was to focus operations 'on the morale of the enemy civil population and, in particular, of the industrial workers'.

Left: **The guardroom shortly after its completion by John Laing and Son with its old-style telephone boxes.** *Right:* **The same view is now somewhat obscured by the erection in the early 1990s — as an increased security measure — of a** Yarnold Sangar, the circular prefabricated pillboxes named after the Squadron Leader from the RAF Regiment who hit on the idea of having them assembled from separate concrete segments.

Laings were instructed to complete the work, including the underground operations block, as soon as possible and a labour force some 500-strong moved in during 1938. Local rumour had it that it was a secret wartime site for the Houses of Parliament, one particular aspect of the work being the preservation of tree cover. Each tree was numbered so that every possible advantage could be gained from using natural camouflage, Any trees affected by the building work were supported, and several new coppices planted. Grim's Dyke, a ditched mound dating from around the 5th century which lay in the compound, was also preserved.

Site No. 1 was used for the command, administrative and office buildings, interconnected by underground tunnels which were also to act as service ducts. Nearly 29,000 cubic feet of spoil were excavated to construct the underground operations block, sited 50 feet below ground. It required the provision of 8,800 yards of waterproof concrete and 200 tons of reinforcement. The overhead protection was 20-foot-thick, comprising a 5ft 6in roof slab covered by a layer of ballast, then a second 2ft layer of concrete topped with a 4ft layer of earth. On top of this, a 5ft reinforced concrete 'burster' slab extended beyond the walls of the actual building to detonate a direct hit. The whole was covered with earth and grassed over. Armed guards patrolled the workings from January 1940.

Site No. 2 was located in a partial clearing between Yewtree Hill Plantation and Falconer's Hill Wood. A wide avenue, known as the Queen's Ride, crossed the area, which had been established to commemorate the visit of Queen Elizabeth I. Now, officers' married quarters were built together with a traditional pre-war-style officers' mess although this was adapted to look like a manor house standing in its own garden. The airmen's living quarters were grouped on Site No. 3, including the sick quarters and NAAFI.

The GPO began the installation of the communications equipment in October 1939, although extensive delays during the winter postponed a planned occupation date from the first week in February 1940 to March 12. The move from Richlings Park was completed by the afternoon of the 15th, the new code-name for the headquarters at Walters Ash being 'Southdown'. The first camp commandant was Wing Commander H. Dawes.

On April 3, Air Marshal Sir Charles Portal took over from Air Chief Marshal Ludlow-Hewitt as C-in-C Bomber Command. The new commander flew over the site to inspect its camouflage and promptly ordered that all the flat concrete roofs must be camouflaged. He was also concerned about the well-worn footpaths leading to the anti-aircraft emplacements sited nearby which would give the game away to an astute enemy photo-interpreter.

On the outbreak of war, on paper, Bomber Command consisted of 55 squadrons split into six groups, although there were no reserves and no training organisation. When ten squadrons were despatched to France, they became known as the Advanced Air Striking Force, comprising two wings of light bombers, mainly Blenheims and Battles. However, at that stage, British-based bombers were only permitted to drop propaganda leaflets or carry out restricted attacks on naval targets.

In August 1940, Air Marshal Sir Richard Peirse took over as AOC-in-C until illness forced his replacement by Air Marshal Arthur Harris on February 3, 1942 (who was knighted in June that year). Harris was a practical airman commanding No. 5 Group at the beginning of the war. Now, he was to mastermind the implementation of a new phase in air operations against Germany, the new AOC being instructed to focus his operations on the morale of the enemy civil population and, in particular, of the industrial workers. The new policy, adopted partly because of the difficulty of hitting pin-point targets at night, led to so-called 'area or carpet bombing' where whole towns were subjected to attack. Harris, himself, had had no part in the formulation of the new directive (from mid-1941 he had been in charge of the RAF delegation in Washington) yet misinformed public opinion has ever since labelled Harris as the instigator of the policy change which had already taken place when the new chief of Bomber Command arrived at High Wycombe. Nevertheless, he pursued his directive with ruthless efficiency.

Left: **The Air Staff Block on Site No. 1, today the headquarters of the Air Officer Administration** *above.*

15

This photo, taken by Laings during construction, conveys no idea of the huge area covered by the Operations Block.

The stairway leading down into the bowels of the earth to the nerve centre of Bomber Command.

The hub of Bomber Command headquarters was naturally the operations room, and the story is told that the staff below ground were always forewarned of the impending arrival of the AOC by the pre-arranged signal of sending a table-tennis ball down the Lamson pneumatic message tube!

At Southdown, a new building for the Operations Research Section was opened in February and, within three months, Air Marshal Harris had mounted the first 1,000-bomber raid. Then, in August, the Pathfinders were formed to direct the bomber formations into attacking the correct target and to try to improve bomb concentrations.

The Duke and Duchess of Gloucester visited the station on October 26, 1943, followed by His Majesty King George VI and Queen Elizabeth on February 7, 1944, when the workings of the Ops Room were explained to them.

Air Chief Marshal Harris remained in his post until September 1945 when he was replaced by Air Marshal Sir Norman Bottomley.

SITE No. 1

OPS BLOCK

SITE No. 4

SITE No. 3

PARK WOOD

SITE No. 2

WALTERS ASH

The 'Southdown' complex pictured soon after Bomber Command and Fighter Command merged into Strike Command.

The Air Officer Commander-in-Chief's office was located at the western end of the Air Staff Block.

Today the room is used by the Air Officer Admin for RAF High Wycombe.

Left: Air Marshal Sir Arthur Harris escorts the Duchess of Gloucester, centre, Air Chief Commandant of the Women's Auxiliary Air Force, on a visit to Bomber Command headquarters with the Senior WAAF Staff Officer, Group Officer

L. M. Crowther in October 1943. Right: In April 1968, Bomber and Fighter Command merged to become Strike Command when the office block on the right was constructed for an administrative HQ for the new command.

Left: The motor car parked outside the windows to his office is most probably Harris's. In this picture, he escorts the Duchess of Kent down the path leading to the underground operations block. Above: Our comparison deliberately takes in a wider view to show Sir Arthur's personal exit from his office through the door in the end of the block right alongside one of the ventilation shafts to the ops block.

The grass-covered mound shielding the underground Operations Block at 'Southdown'.

Bomber Command Organisation

The expansion and equipment of RAF Bomber Command to the premier destructive force it became took many months. In September 1939, No. 1 Group and its ten Battle squadrons were sent to France as the major part of the Advanced Air Striking Force. Until that time it had been based in the Salisbury Plain area with airfields at Abingdon, Bicester, Harwell, Benson and Boscombe Down. Although there were immediate plans to form another No. 1 Group, and a headquarters was established, this was soon disbanded. On the return of the battered Battle squadrons from France in June 1940 most of their former stations in the Salisbury Plain area were in use by other organisations and No. 1 Group was re-established with a headquarters at Hucknall and selected airfields in the Nottingham/North Lincolnshire area. A year later, the headquarters was moved to Bawtry in Yorkshire and airfields south of the Humber, mostly wrested from No. 4 Group in the north and No. 5 in the south, came under its control.

In September 1941, a new group, No. 8, was formed with headquarters at Brampton, Huntingdon, with the object of controlling new squadrons formed to handle the US heavies — Fortresses and Liberators — arriving for the RAF. New airfields being built in Huntingdonshire, Bedfordshire and Northamptonshire were tentatively earmarked for this group

In actual fact the Ops Block consisted of extensive office accommodation surrounding the nerve centre — the Operations Room itself. This painting shows it as it would have appeared during the war. (See also *After the Battle* No. 87.)

The wartime ops block remained in use until a new underground bunker was commenced in 1978 for Strike Command.

Later, Transport and Coastal Commands were merged into Strike to form a single multi-role organisation.

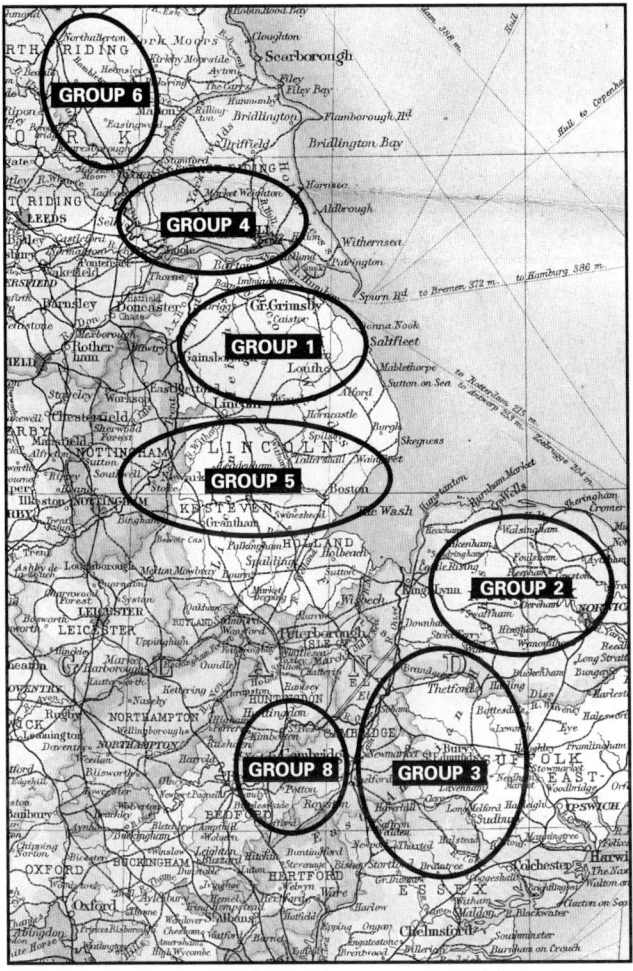

In the north, No. 4 Group had acquired Canadian-manned squadrons but in October 1942 an all-RCAF Group was formed — No. 6 — to take these and new squadrons coming from Canada. Eventually part Halifax and part Lancaster equipped, No. 6 Group had its headquarters at Allerton Park and stations in north Yorkshire and Durham. (The training organisation known as No. 6 Group in 1939 became an OTU organisation.) All Heavy Conversion Units, of which all appropriate groups had two or three, came under No. 7 Training Group in November 1944.

The popularity of satellite airfields with Bomber Command led to planning that each main airfield would have two satellites. The main base would have command and special facilities but the satellites would also be complete operational bases able to engage in operations independently if required. In 1943 the parent station became identified as a base and the satellites sub-bases, each base being identified by a two-digit number, the first digit being that of the group. A group area was planned for 12 or 15 airfields — four or five clutches of three. This same planning was also adopted by the USAAF when it arrived and was allocated five group areas which in its terminology became wing and eventually a divisional area.

RAF Bomber Command's use of airfields appears wasteful when compared with the Eighth Air Force. In the last year of war it was not uncommon to find 72 Fortresses or Liberators on an operational American air base while a few miles away no more than 20 Lancasters reposed on a similar-sized airfield. This stems in part from RAF bomber airfields having only 36 aircraft hardstandings through the policy that holding higher numbers of aircraft in one location put too much at risk from enemy air attack. A large number of aircraft launched from one airfield in darkness also brought difficulties in limiting the length of a bomber stream. Where two heavy bomber squadrons were based on one airfield they usually consisted of two flights each of ten aircraft.

When the USAAF planned to conduct B-29 operations from the UK, the Air Ministry took Lakenheath, Marham and Sculthorpe and in the spring of 1944 began enlarging each to have one 3,000-yard and two 2000-yard runways plus additional facilities. Most of the original airfield concrete was replaced with that of greater load-carrying capacity. However, the USAAF plan never materialised and work on the enlarged bases was not completed until 1945 at an average cost of near £2 million for each site. RAF Bomber Command then looked forward to having larger and heavier bombers and plans were made to upgrade other airfields to this new standard.

but only Polebrook became operational with Fortresses and then while still administered by No. 2 Group. The entry of the United States into the war and the arrival of the Eighth Air Force saw this area passed to its 1st Bombardment Wing and this first No. 8 Group was later disbanded.

Although No. 2 Group had headquarters at Huntingdon and entered hostilities with one of its four 'W' operational stations, at nearby Wyton, additions to its airfield list came increasingly in north Norfolk. Blenheims were replaced by Bostons, Mitchells, Venturas and Mosquitos, but not until May 1943 was the headquarters moved to Bylaugh Hall at East Dereham, shortly before Bomber Command lost No. 2 Group and its squadrons to the Second Tactical Air Force. When these moved to southern counties its north Norfolk area bases were passed to No. 100 Group which was formed late that year to support Bomber Command operations. Basically a force to counter and lessen enemy defences against Bomber Command raids, its squadrons had specialised tasks but some also engaged in bombing.

No. 3 Group maintained its presence in the Newmarket/Cambridge area throughout the war although, with the formation of the 'Pathfinder Force' at Wyton in August 1942 (which became the new No. 8 Group in the following January) No. 3's stations west of Cambridge were gradually claimed by the newcomer. No. 8 Group stations were mostly situated south and east of the US Eighth Air Force 1st Division's main base area and west of No. 3 Group's domain.

The Whitley squadrons concentrated on No. 4 Group's Yorkshire airfields converted to Halifaxes in 1941-42 remaining in that area to the end of hostilities.

No. 5 Group, having lost stations to No. 1 Group in the north, then acquired several to the south, including late in 1944 a few vacated by USAAF troop carrier units. Hampdens gave way to the unsuccessful Manchester, in small numbers, before the famous Lancaster came on stream. Its neighbour, No. 1 Group, also eventually shed its Wellingtons and became an all-Lancaster group. Likewise No. 3 Group shed its Stirlings and Wellingtons to operate only Lancaster squadrons.

	Sorties	Tonnage		Aircraft lost
		Bombs	Mines	
1939	591	31		40
1940	22,473	13,033	510	509
1941	32,012	31,704	707	985
1942	35,338 (1,088)	45,561	6,367	1,517 (26)
1943	65,068 (1,240)	157,457	9,136	2,457 (17)
1944	166,844	525,518	13,170	2,904
1945	67,483	181,740	3,373	708
	389,809 (2,328)	955,044	33,263	9,120 (43)
	392,137	988,307		9,163

BOMBER COMMAND OPERATIONS, 1939-45

The figures in brackets under sorties indicate operations by Bomber Command aircraft flying under the auspices of Coastal Command with the corresponding losses also in brackets.

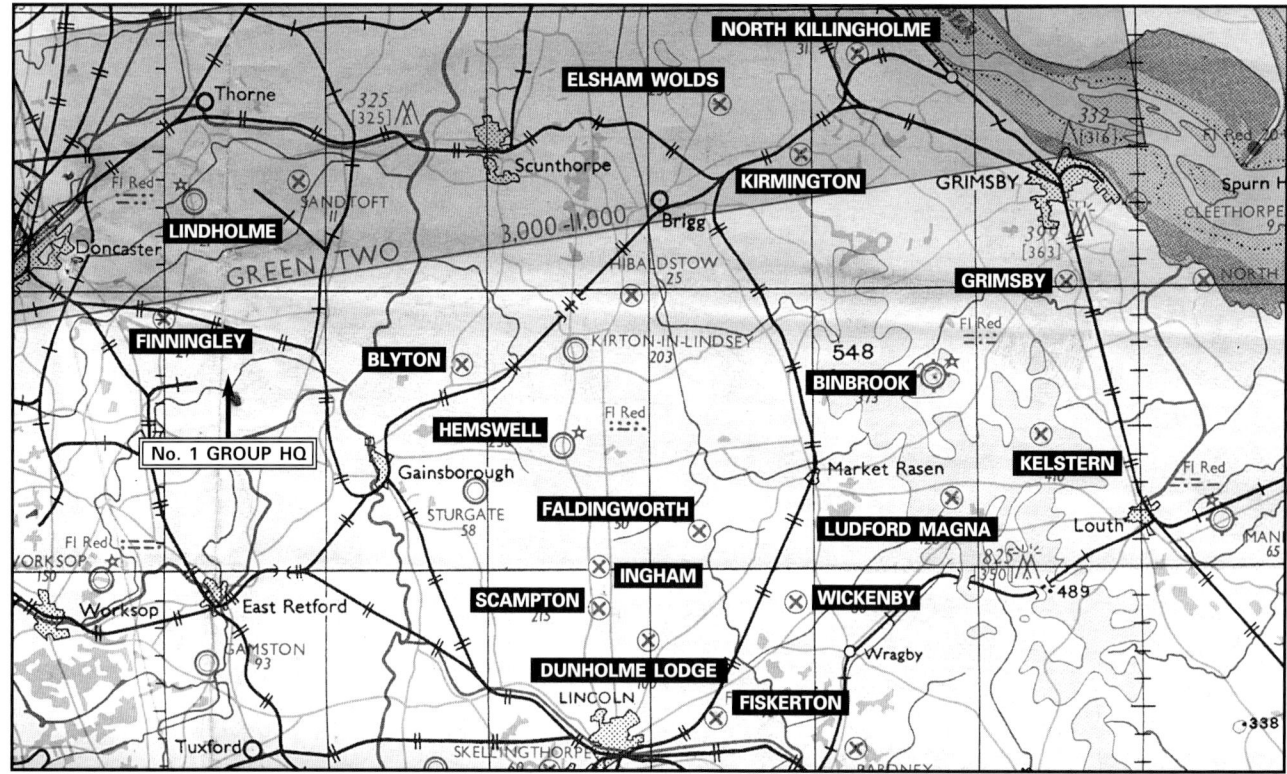

No. 1 GROUP HQ

After the Battle of France, No. 1 Group was re-formed on June 22, 1940 with head-quarters at Hucknall, Nottinghamshire. In July 1941 it moved to Bawtry Hall in Yorkshire.

With the introduction of the group and command organisations in 1936, No. 1 (Bomber) Group was formed on May 1 that year, in effect the redesignation of the RAF's Central Area HQ at Abingdon, Berkshire. Initially it controlled three light bomber airfield stations, Abingdon, Bircham Newton and Upper Heyford, with a total of ten squadrons all equipped with Hawker Hinds. Re-equipment with Battles and Blenheims followed and the group strength was expanded with additional squadrons and airfields. Shortly before the outbreak of war some of the units were reassigned to No. 6 (Pool) Group for operational training and No. 1

Group became the Advanced Air Striking Force being deployed in France with ten Battle squadrons for army support operations. A new No. 1 Group was formed in late September 1939 as an headquarters for a future deployment in France but this plan was dropped and the new organisation disbanded three months later.

With the return of the decimated battle squadrons from the continent in June 1940, a second reforming of No. 1 Group took place. The new headquarters was initially at Hucknall with airfields mostly to the east in south Yorkshire and north Lincolnshire. The Battles were replaced with Wellingtons

and by the summer of 1941 there were eight squadrons so equipped. In July 1941 the headquarters moved to a more central location, Bawtry Hall near Doncaster, where it was to remain until No. 1 Group was disbanded in the Cold War years. From the late summer of 1942 the first of the group's squadrons began to re-equip with Lancasters, building up to a maximum strength of 350 aircraft in 14 squadrons on 12 airfields by the end of hostilities. No. 1 Group's war record was 238,356 tons of bombs and 8,147 sea mines delivered in nearly 60,000 sorties. Some 9,000 airmen lost their lives during these operations.

Bawtry Hall is located some ten miles south-east of Doncaster.

The building remained the headquarters of No. 1 Group for the remainder of the war. Today it is privately owned and used as a training and conference facility.

We are very fortunate that the Station Commander at Hemswell was an amateur cinematographer who set out in 1942 to produce a film to enlighten newly-posted aircrew as to the extent of the operational planning in mounting a raid. Air Commodore (as he later became) Henry Cozens's unique film

Night Bombers was made without any official support and filmed in an opportunistic manner at Hemswell, Sturgate and, fortunately for us, at No. 1 Group HQ to which Cozens was posted as Senior Air Staff Officer (SASO). Here, we see a staff officer about to enter the Operations Room.

Two more stills lifted from the film which Cozens made using a second-hand clockwork Bell and Howell 16mm 'Filmo' 70DA camera. His intention was to show the whole sequence of a raid from the target being communicated from Bomber Command to Group; to show the efforts of the ground crews fuelling and arming the aircraft; and follow through on an

actual raid featuring a Lancaster, 'V'-Victor of No. 170 Squadron flown by Flight Lieutenant Bob Chandler. At Bawtry Hall he had to tread a fine line between recording actual events and staging them for his camera. Fortunately, Cozens was about to take a shot of the target announcement for that night just as the real target came in, springing everybody into action.

How many visitors would recognise the same room today . . . the ornate fireplace long gone in what is now the Peake Room.

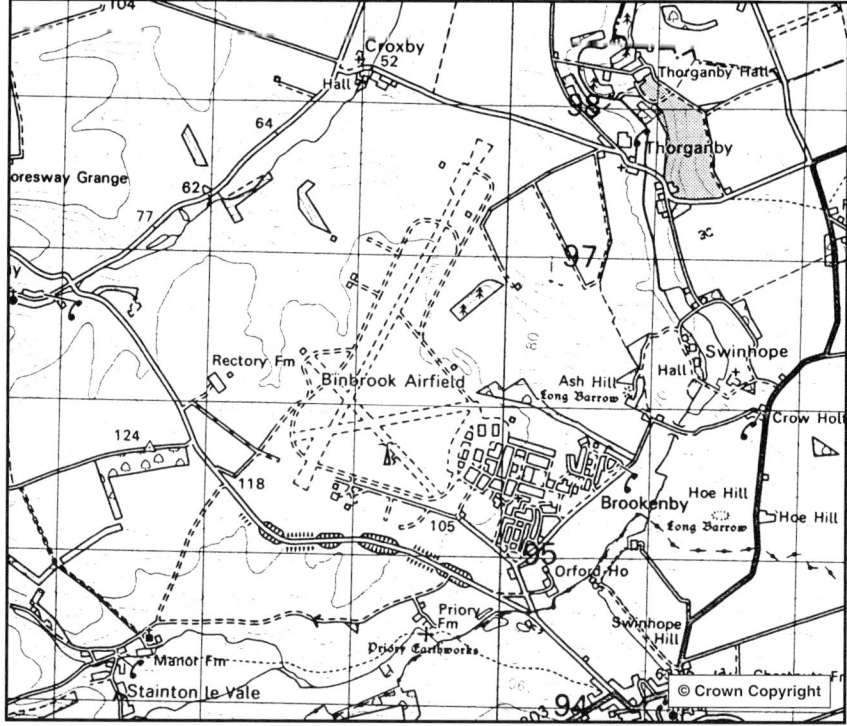

BINBROOK

One of the last batch of pre-war expansion scheme airfields, Binbrook was built on Ash Hill in the Lincolnshire Wolds, north-west of the village of Binbrook on the B1203 road, seven miles from Market Rasen. Construction did not begin until the spring of 1938 and was not completed until late 1940. The usual arrangement of the later Type C hangars, five in number, facing the bombing circle was backed by the administration, technical and barrack sites in close proximity. The flying area and basic operational facilities were ready by June 1940 and during the following month Nos. 12 and 142 Squadrons, decimated during service in France, arrived with a few Fairey Battles. However, their services were needed in the south and both squadrons moved their Battles down to Eastchurch to engage in attacks on French and Low Countries ports where invasion shipping was mustered. Returning to Binbrook in September they continued to fly night sorties over the Low Countries. The Battle being already obsolescent, the arrival of Wellingtons in November 1940 was welcomed but these bombers were in short supply due to the demands of other squadrons and it was the early spring before they first operated from Binbrook. During 1940 and 1941 a number of pan-shape aircraft hardstandings were put down round the airfield.

After a year at Binbrook No. 142 Squadron was transferred to the new satellite airfield at Waltham, officially named Grimsby. No. 12's Wellingtons pressed on with night bombing until September 1942 when the squadron was transferred to Wickenby as Binbrook was scheduled to have hard runways put down under a £200,000 contract. These were 04-22 of 2,000 yards, 09-27 of 1,415 yards and 15-33 of 1,429 yards. To obtain the required lengths it was necessary

Binbrook pictured on April 14, 1942 with No. 12 Squadron Wellingtons in residence. Two dozen pan hardstandings are visible and extensive pipe drainage work is in progress on the north side of the airfield. It is interesting to note that the NE-SW grass runway has been realigned further to the north-west almost on the line of the later 09-27 concrete runway laid down when Binbrook was uprated at the end of the year.

The present day Ordnance Survey map shows the final runway layout with the post-war extension to the 04-22 to the north. The plan also shows how the road to the south of the airfield had to be diverted and the lane to the west closed to accomodate the enlargements.

A Merlin-engined Wellington II of No. 12 Squadron about to be bombed up — incendiary canisters on the right — with the watch office, as control towers were originally called, beyond.

to extend the airfield boundaries in some areas which resulted in the main runway having a slope towards the valley at its 27 end. A perimeter track was also laid at this time and 19 loop hardstandings for aircraft were added to the 18 pan types that survived the runway building programme. With additional accomodation the station provided for a maximum of 2,298 male and 420 female personnel.

In May 1943, No. 460 Squadron, a Royal Australian Air Force unit, arrived from Breighton which was being transferred to No. 4 Group. Flying Lancasters, No. 460 remained the sole operational unit based at Binbrook for the rest of the war. It was developed to maintain three full flights and frequently had a complement of three dozen Lancasters. In consequence, the squadron is credited with delivering a higher bomb tonnage than any other in Bomber Command — in the region of 24,000 Imperial tons. However, Binbrook also sustained the highest casualties and losses in No. 1 Group with

In 1989, Binbrook sported two control towers in preparation for the remake of the wartime documentary *Memphis Belle*. *Left:* The modernised wartime building had a false wall added by the film company to hide the post-war glasshouse on the roof. *Right:* Meanwhile, an authentic copy of a 1939-45 watch office was built partly in brick in front of the northernmost hangar.

some 130 Lancasters lost on operations and another 30 written off in crashes. Additionally, on July 3, 1943, two Lancasters were destroyed and eight damaged on the airfield when incendiaries ignited during loading operations. All told 226 Bomber Command aircraft were lost on operations flying from this station, seven Battles, 79 Wellingtons and 140 Lancasters.

No. 460 Squadron was moved to East Kirkby in July 1945 and at the end of the summer Nos. 12 and 101 Squadrons moved from the utility buildings of their wartime bases to the permanent accommodation at Binbrook. The following year brought squadrons equipped with Lincolns, namely Nos. 9, 12 and 617. Canberra units first appeared in the summer of 1952 and at one time there were five squadrons with the type based at the station, Nos. 9, 101, 109, 139 and 617. Eventually all were moved or disbanded and at the end of 1959 Binbrook was put on care and maintenance status. The airfield then held appeal for Fighter Command which called for development work including the extension of the main runway by another 500 yards. Reopened for flying in June 1962 the first element of Fighter Command to take up station, was No. 64 Squadron with Javelins which stayed nearly three years.

The 'Memphis Belle' control tower was demolished soon after filming was completed but Tim Wingham was horrified to find that the other tower had also since been knocked down when he visited Binbrook in June 2000 The runways and taxiways are now going the same way.

Veteran Lancaster W4783 'G'-George of No. 460 Squadron pictured following its 90th raid on the night of April 20/21, 1944. This aircraft was later given to the Australian nation and is now housed in the war museum in Canberra. The view is north-east with the Type C hangar beyond runway 33.

No. 85 Squadron, with Meteors and Canberras for air fighting development duties, was at Binbrook for nearly nine years. Then in October 1965 English Electric Lightnings arrived for a re-born No. 5 Squadron joined by a second squadron, No. 11, in 1972. The Lightning squadrons remained until May 1988 — the last in RAF service.

The airfield was then surplus to RAF requirements and plans were made for its disposal. Before this occurred, Binbrook was selected for location filming of the Warner remake of *Memphis Belle* (see *After the Battle* No. 69). This took place in July 1989 with five B-17 Fortresses on hand, two of which had flown in from the United States and two from France. One of the latter suffered a take-off crash and was burnt out, fortunately without

The Type C hangars still survive and formed the backdrop to this scene from *Memphis Belle*. Two cut-out B-17s have been added as set dressing beside two genuine Fortresses.

loss of life. For the film it was necessary to erect a wartime-type control tower which was built by local labour in brick slightly in front of the post-war building. It was demolished after the filming was completed. The pan hardstandings on the west side of the airfield were used to park the B-17s, beyond which a fake church tower was erected in a farmer's field to simulate the opening sequence in William Wyler's original film.

The larger part of the airfield was put up for sale late in 1989, although the hangars were retained for military storage until 1998 when they too were sold. Only the flying field and runway are now retained by the Ministry of Defence. A memorial to No. 460 Squadron is to be seen in Binbrook village.

Looking north-west in September 2000. Some of the hangars are now used for grain storage

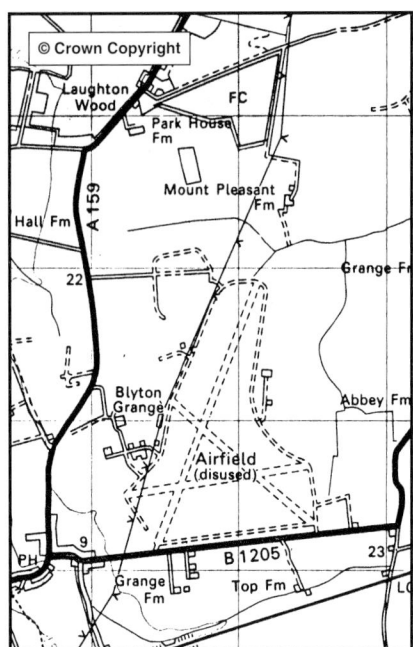

BLYTON

Blyton airfield was situated between the villages of Blyton and Northorpe, bordered by the B1205 in the south and the A159 through the camp sites on the west side. Built in 1942 , the main runway was 03-21 at 2,030 yards, the 14-32 runway at 1,400 yards and 11-29 at 1,430 yards. The usual 36 pan hardstandings were provided off the concrete perimeter track although one was lost on the east side to a T2 hangar erected north of Cold Harbour Farm. A B1 hangar was positioned south of Cold Harbour and a second T2 on the technical site situated south-west of the runway heads 03 and 11. Bomb stores were located in fields between runway heads 14 and 21. Six domestic, two WAAF, two communal and sick quarters sites were dispersed among fields north of Blyton village on either side of the A159. Total accommodation provided for 1,966 males and 389 females.

Allocated to No. 1 Group, Blyton was first used for flying in the spring of 1942 when 'B' Flight of No. 18 (Polish) Operational Training Unit brought in Wellingtons from Bramcote, remaining until February 1943. No. 199 Squadron was reformed at Blyton in early November 1942 and equipped with Wellingtons, the squadron undertaking its first operation on the night of December 6/7 when six aircraft were sent to bomb

A Halifax of No. 1662 Heavy Conversion Unit on its dispersal hardstanding at Blyton — for over two years a specialised training base. The first Heavy Conversion Units (HCU) were formed in 1941 with the specific purpose of providing crew training for Stirling, Halifax and, later, Lancaster four-engined bombers. Each newly established crew spent a variable period in gaining experience on the type they were to fly operationally before being posted to a squadron. To swell the numbers, HCUs were occasionally called upon to provide crews and aircraft to participate in operations with Bomber Command Main Force, totalling 167 sorties. Thirteen HCU aircraft failed to return from operations although not all the losses were due to enemy action. During the last two years of hostilities, HCUs were sometimes required to fly diversionary sweeps over the North Sea to attract attention from enemy defences.

Mannheim. After four weeks of operations the squadron received orders to transfer to Ingham, leaving Blyton on February 1, 1943, having flown 119 sorties with only one aircraft lost (on the night of December 11/12) with but a single fatality among its crew. The reason for the move was the need for an airfield with long hard runways to take four-engined heavies — Lancasters and Halifaxes — of No. 1662 Heavy Conversion Unit (Ingham was a grass field unsuitable for heavy bombers.)

Although No. 1 Group was to be an all-Lancaster formation, production could not keep up with the increasing demand and towards the end of 1943 all the Lancs were withdrawn from Blyton and No. 1662 HCU was left with some 30 Halifaxes. This remained the situation for a year until the station was transferred from No. 1 to No. 7 (Training Group) in November 1944 when Lancaster production finally allowed the

Halifaxes to be retired. No. 1662 HCU resided at Blyton for 26 months losing over 50 aircraft in crashes. By the end of March 1945, the demand for specialised operational training was being more than met and the unit disbanded early in April.

From late 1943 the runways and taxiways at Blyton had often needed repair and by the spring of 1945 these surfaces were generally in a poor state. As a result, no further RAF flying units were based on the airfield which, after a period of care and maintenance, was left to decay. In the 'fifties it appeared that the Cold War would give the station a new lease of life as it was allocated to the USAF for refurbishment as a reserve airfield. However, no renovation is known to have been carried out and the USAF party soon withdrew. The following two decades brought sale of the hangars and land and the inevitable removal of runway concrete for hard core.

Left: **Much of the concrete has now been removed, the main remaining sections of runway and perimeter track being at the** northern end. *Right:* **The picket post at the entrance from the B1205 to the old fuel installation at the south-eastern corner.**

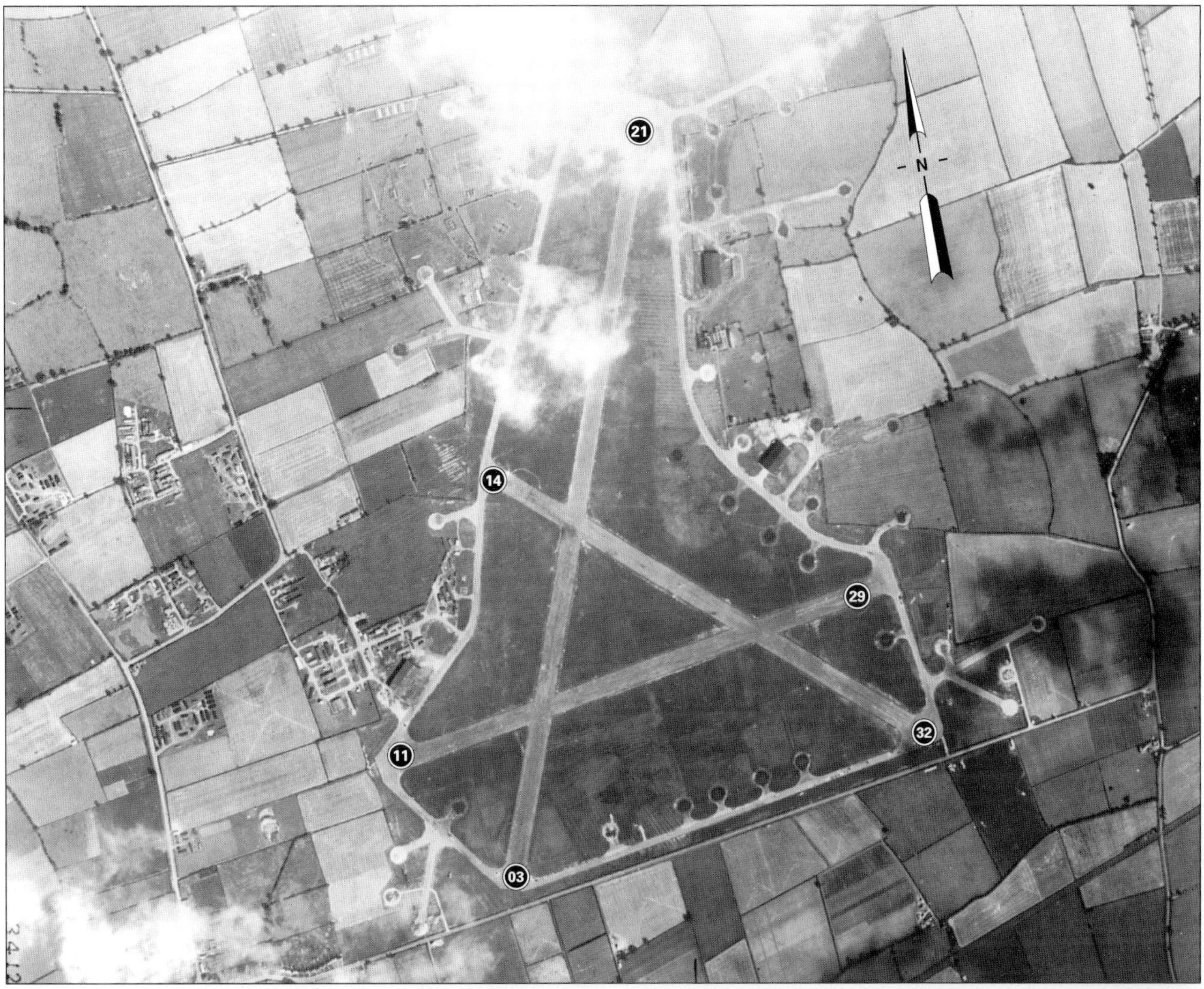

Above: The airfield was deserted when a No. 541 Squadron Spitfire took this vertical on August 26, 1945. The bomb stores on the north-western corner are partially hidden by the cloud.

Below: The extant north-western corner is the most intact — now used by stock cars, hot-rods and bangers. Picture taken 55 years later, almost to the day.

DUNHOLME LODGE

A wartime development, Dunholme Lodge was located in the parishes of Welton and Dunholme on the north-west side of the A46, 3½ miles outside Lincoln, the name being taken from a large country house a mile from the village that was requisitioned for accommodation. The site was first acquired for a Scampton satellite in 1941 and Hampdens were occasionally dispersed there from the parent station. Horncastle Lane crossing the site was closed. A number of pan-type hardstandings were put down round the flying field which was grass-surfaced. Fuelling and arming facillities were available. However, there are no records of operations being carried out during the 1941-42 period apart from a target-towing flight which was stationed on the airfield from August to late October 1942.

Scheduled for development to Class A standard, work began on runway construction in September 1942 with Wimpey as a major contractor. The three runways were 04-22 of 2,000 yards, 16-34 at 1,400 yards and 10-28 at 1,300 yards. However, this last was extended to 1,700 yards by No. 5002 Airfield Construction Unit in February-April 1944. Twenty-five pan hardstandings and 14 loop type were provided along the perimeter track, another three of the original pans being isolated and not linked to taxiways. The technical site was north-east between runway heads 22 and 34 near the Lodge. One T2 hangar stood on the technical site, a

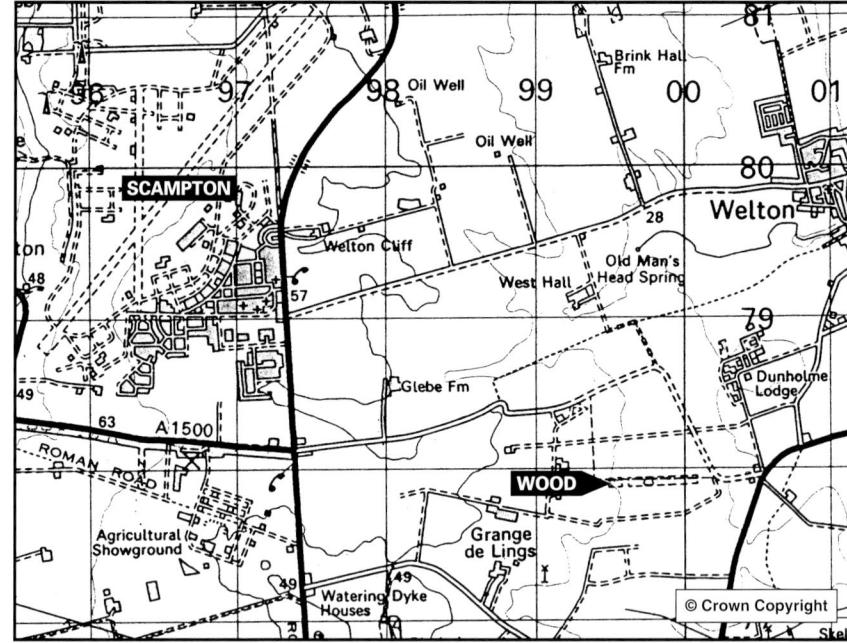

The close proximity of so many of the bomber airfields to each other is graphically demonstrated at Dunholme Lodge just a couple of miles south-west of Scampton for which it was originally built as a satellite. Not a lot remains to orient the present-day Ordnance Survey map with this vertical taken post-war *(opposite)* at a time when hundreds of redundant airfields littered the British countryside. One identifying feature is the trees running east to west between the 10-28 runway and the southernmost T2.

Another crew that made it! A picture with the ground personnel of ND578 KM-Y on April 18, 1944. This veteran Lancaster went on to complete 121 sorties by May 1945. The hardstanding is near the T2 hangar on the south side of the airfield.

second further south between heads 04 and 34, near the bomb stores, and a B1 between heads 04 and 10. Dispersed in the countryside around Welton were seven domestic, two communal and the sick quarters providing for a maximum 1,637 males and 468 females.

Dunholme Lodge was re-opened in May 1943 in No. 5 Group and it became the home for the veteran No. 44 Squadron removed from its long association with Waddington. No. 44's Lancasters were not joined by another squadron until April the following year when No. 619 moved in from Coningsby. In September 1944, the station was re-allocated to No. 1 Group and both Lancaster squadrons moved out, to Spilsby and Strubby respectively. The following month No. 170 Squadron, recently re-formed as a Lancaster squadron at Kelstern, took up station but its stay was little more than a month before it was moved to Hemswell. Unconfirmed reports state that the airfield was vacated to reduce local night congestion, there being several other stations close by with overlapping circuits. This may be true as the airfield was then used mostly for daylight traffic, namely the reception, storage and delivery of Hamilcar gliders. During Bomber Command's offensive operations from Dunholme Lodge 120 Lancasters either failed to return or were destroyed in crashes.

Sugar beet flourishes where once was concrete, but the pan dispersal is still visible as a slight depression in the ground. Representing the two families that now farm the former airfield are, left to right, Simon Ranshaw, Hugh Wykes, Bernard Ranshaw and Brian Wykes. The Wykes family were the owners of Dunholme Lodge when the airfield was built. Note the tree line in the background (see map above).

Wartime cover of Dunholme Lodge is poor — this shot taken from 16,400 feet by No. 58 Squadron on April 16, 1947 is much better.

So little remains of Dunholme Lodge that it is difficult to orient the old runways, hence we have dotted them in on this September 2000 shot taken looking south-east. However the line of trees is still a prominent reference point.

Like many other wartime-built airfields, its utility accommodation soon saw the station abandoned once peace came. It was, however, given a brief return to military use in 1959 when it was selected as a site for a Bloodhound ground-to-air missile deployment. The operating unit, No. 141 Squadron, disbanded when the missiles were withdrawn in 1964. The area reverted to agriculture and by the 1990s most of its concrete and buildings had disappeared. The B1 hangar still survived for commercial storage in 1999. A memorial plaque to No. 44 Squadron is to be found in Dunholme church.

Simon Renshaw points to where one of the workers laying the runways had marked the date, '23/2/43' in the wet concrete. This is on the southern end of a small section of runway 34 retained for agricultural storage.

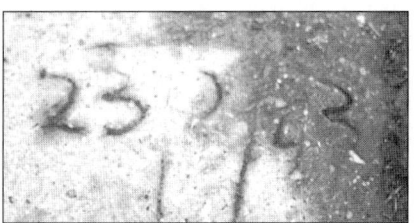

One of the few surviving wartime buildings carries the notice 'Automatic Discharge Section' and probably relates to the Bloodhound days.

ELSHAM WOLDS

The wide expanse of grazing pasture on Elsham Wolds, lying some nine miles south of Hull on the Lincolnshire side of the Humber, was first utilised as an airfield in 1916 when No. 33 Squadron, RFC, with its FE2b and FE2d biplanes was deployed between Hull and Lincoln to counter the Zeppelins coming in over the Lincolnshire coast during their night raids on the Midlands. While Gainsborough served as an headquarters, the limited endurance of the FE2s necessitated No. 33's complement being split into three flights and placed at suitable locations roughly 12 miles apart in a line between the two cities. Elsham Wolds served 'C' Flight which arrived in December 1916 and stayed until June 1918, flying many sorties to try to counter the Zeppelin raids but without success. Wooden huts and a small aircraft shed were erected but had been demolished by 1919 when the wold was returned to cattle and sheep.

Above: **The crew about to board a No. 103 Squadron Lancaster in the summer of 1943.** *Below:* **Fifty-seven years later the dispersal has gone from the north perimeter but the farmhouse still stands little changed.**

Left: **An attack on a military camp at Mailly-le-Camp on the night of May 3/4, 1944 cost Bomber Command 42 Lancasters in one of the most successful interceptions by Luftwaffe nightfighters. Fortunate to escape was this Lancaster of No. 576 Squadron which Pilot Officer R. R. Reed managed to bring back to base despite severe damage from a Ju 88's gun-fire. The tail gunner, Sergeant Alf Hodson, was killed in the attack.**

Right: **Hard to believe that this is the same location with a new road, fencing and street lighting. Only the J-type hangar tells that this was once the location of a bomber airfield. Its door runner can just be seen above the port tailplane of the crippled Lancaster in the wartime photograph. Buildings of the industrial estate now cover the exact spot where the Lanc stood in May 1944.**

31

The extensions to the original runways can be seen in this rather poor photograph taken in April 1942 when No. 103 Squadron was in residence.

In the late 1930s, with the threat of another war, there was a requirement to find new airfield sites for RAF expansion. The 1914-1918 locations were some of the first reviewed but at Elsham Wolds an area to the west of the earlier site was found more suitable. Preparations did not begin until the winter of 1939-1940 and were not completed until the summer of 1941 owing to the decision to put down hard runways before the station was opened and these were then extended: the main 14-32 at 2,000 yards and subsidiaries 02-20 to 1,400 yards and 08-26 to 1,600 yards. Initially 27 hardstandings were provided, later increased to 36 which comprised three loops and the rest pans. The technical site with one Type J hangar and two T2s was built on the east side of the airfield. Three Type T2s were erected early in 1944 to serve No. 13 Base Maintenance. These were on a spur that ran to the edge of the First World War aerodrome site, south of runway head 28. Domestic sites for up to 2,068 males and 493 females were dispersed in adjoining farmland to the south-east. Bomb stores were located off the north-east side of the airfield.

In July 1941 No. 103 Squadron and its Wellingtons arrived from Newton for operations, the first sorties from Elsham Wolds being flown on the night of the 24th. In the following spring the squadron began conversion to Halifaxes. However, this association was brief for no sooner had No. 103 taken the Halifax to battle in July 1942, than No. 1 Group embarked on all-Lancaster re-equip-ment and by October the Halifaxes had been withdrawn. In November 1943, No. 103 shed its 'C' Flight which expanded to become No. 576 Squadron. The new squadron and its Lancasters remained until October 1944 when they moved to Fiskerton, that station being transferred from No. 5 Group. No. 100 Squadron's Lancasters were moved in from Grimsby during the last month of the war, supposedly due to deterioration of that air-field's runways.

Only one other Bomber Command squadron had a longer association with one airfield during wartime than No. 103 for it remained at Elsham Wolds until six months after VE-Day. No. 103 is credited with more operational sorties than any other No. 1 Group squadron but consequently it suffered the group's highest losses and of the 248 bombers lost on operations while flying from Elsham Wolds, 198 were from No. 103 Squadron. Of the 248 total, 28 comprised Wellingtons, 12 Halifaxes and 208 Lancasters. One Elsham Wolds Lancaster, ED888, which served with both Nos. 103 and 576, held the Bomber Command record for operational sorties having completed 140 between May 1943 and December 1944.

The Lancaster squadrons departed for Scampton's permanent and more comfortable camp in December 1945, No. 103 having been re-numbered No. 57 in one of those insensitive number-juggling exercises in

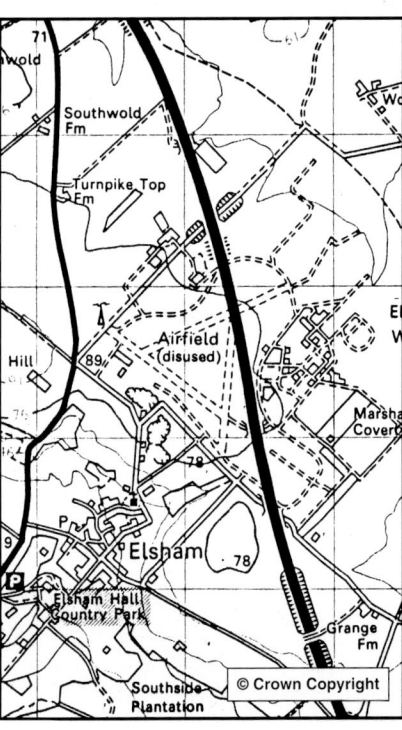

© Crown Copyright

which the Air Ministry frequently indulged. Their place at Elsham was taken by No. 21 Heavy Glider Conversion Unit of Transport Command which exercised with Halifax and Albemarle tugs and Horsa gliders for nearly a year, before its personnel too were given superior accommodation at North Luffenham. This marked the end of Elsham Wolds

Now a trunk road scythes its way through the airfield leaving the old technical site divorced from the flying field. *Above:* **Looking west and below north-west.**

as a military airfield, the land soon being returned to agriculture and many of the buildings employed for commercial enterprises. In 1970s, the new A15 dual carriageway road linking the M180 with the Humber

Bridge was taken across the old airfield site. During the same period a water treatment works was built near the A15. The control tower, visible from this road for many years, was reputed to be haunted!

FALDINGWORTH

Faldingworth was constructed on an isolated area of farmland covering three parishes south-east of the River Ancholme, 4½ miles from Market Rasen. The contractors involved were Tarmac Ltd and J. Cryer & Sons Ltd, with work totalling £810,000.

Site clearance of woodland and hedges began in July 1942 and runway laying was completed by the following summer. Built to Class A standard, the runway lengths were 08-26 at 2,000 yards, and 1,400 yards for each of the subsidiaries, 01-19 and 13-31. Thirty-six hardstandings, all loops, and two T2 and a single B1 hangar were provided. The dispersed camp sites were towards Newton by Toft in the north-east, giving accommodation for up to 1,957 males and 281 females.

No. 1667 Heavy Conversion Unit arrived in August 1943 flying Halifaxes and Lancasters, losing several in crashes before being moved to Sandtoft in February 1944. This was to allow No. 300 Squadron a more suitable airfield from which to operate Lancasters, conversion from Wellingtons taking place when the squadron arrived at Faldingworth from Ingham's grass surface. No. 300 was the veteran Polish-manned bomber unit and it was to remain at this station until disbanded in October 1945. During its operations a total of 37 Lancasters were lost flying from Faldingworth, 32 of which were classified as failing to return.

The birth pangs of an aerodrome. It is interesting to see that the main runway at Faldingworth was laid out first . . . by October 1942 when the picture was taken.

The same month . . . but six years later. Its intended use as a bomber station over, the airfield awaits its next assignment.

Overflying Faldingworth — then and now. *Above:* **A formation of Lancasters from No. 300 Squadron cross the airfield from** **west to east. The bomb dump is just out of the picture to the right beyond the threshhold of runway 13.**

After the war the station became a holding camp for Polish forces with No. 305 Squadron flying its Mosquitos in from the Continent prior to dispersal and eventual disbandment.

Although no further use was made of the airfield as an RAF flying station, it was kept in a state of care and maintenance for some years. In the early 1950s its comparatively isolated position in the Lincolnshire country-side saw the airfield selected for development as one of the major stores for nuclear weapons. Underground bunkers were built in western part of the former flying field and surrounded by high fences, with guard

The bomb dump now. After the war, Faldingworth became a nuclear weapons store under No. 92 Maintenance Unit, the secure area later being taken over by Royal Ordnance which **still has a presence on the site in the foreground. The impression in the grass of the large loop dispersal behind the Lancasters can be seen in front of the old bomb dump on the left.**

No. 300 'Masovian' Squadron was the first Polish bomber unit to be formed in the RAF. It was born on July 1, 1940 at Bramcote in Warwickshire, equipped with Battles, and ended its days at Faldingworth on October 11, 1946. Its arrival in March 1944 was to permit its conversion from its Wellingtons (BH-V is pictured *right*) to Lancasters which necessitated concrete runways.

towers to afford tight security. For much of the next two decade the main controlling agency was No. 92 Maintenance Unit. In the early 1970s this central store was no longer required by the RAF and the site was eventually taken over by an armaments manufacturer associated with Royal Ordnance. This organisation used Faldingworth for secure armament storage and experimentation until 1996 when this facility was put up for sale. Royal Ordnance still retains part of Faldingworth, security being maintained. In 1999 the main runway remains intact and a single B1 hangar also survives. The major area of the airfield, some 470 acres, was sold for agricultural use in 1998.

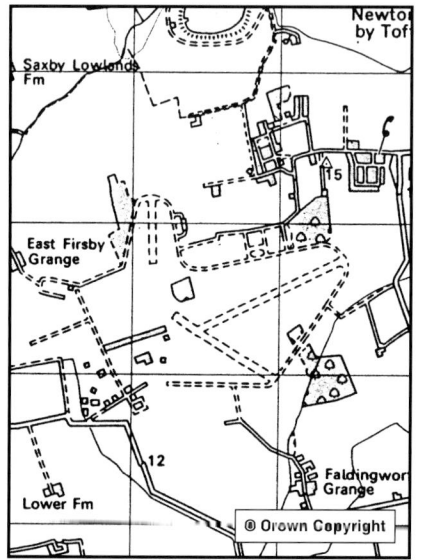

Above: **A difficult shot to match, Tim Wingham believes that it could have been taken on this dispersal — the rough grass showing where the concrete has been lifted. It lies off the south-eastern peri-track (on the right in the aerial *below*) where a hedge — albeit now run wild — still forms a backdrop.**

FINNINGLEY

Pilots and Wellesleys of No. 76 Squadron on parade for the camera outside the westernmost hangar at Finningley in 1937. Camp housing can be seen in the background.

Finningley's participation in Bomber Command's offensive may have been short but the station played a vital part in finishing crews with operational training for the bombing role. An early pre-war expansion scheme airfield the site, farmland in a well-wooded locality four miles south-east of Doncaster was acquired in the summer of 1935. The Gainsborough-Doncaster LNER line ran a quarter mile to the north and Finningley village lay a similar distance to the east. The flying field covered around 250 acres with the camp area situated to the north-west between Mare Flats Plantation and the A638 road. Four Type C hangars were erected in the usual crescent layout facing the bombing circle, with a fifth directly behind the southernmost of the line. Administration and technical site buildings were immediately to the rear of the hangars.

Nos. 7 and 102 Squadrons moved in during August 1936 from Worthy Down with Handley Page Heyfords, this being prior to the official opening date given in station records of September 3. In the following year, No. 7 Squadron begat No. 76 and No. 102 similarly divided to produce No. 77, the latter two soon being moved south to Honington. No. 7 Squadron converted to Whitleys in March and April 1938 while No. 76 continued to operate Wellesleys, the type it had been formed to fly. By the end of that year No. 5 Group completed its acquisition of No. 3 Group stations north of the Wash and, under its control, Finningley squadrons started conversion to the Handley Page Hampden, with Ansons to fill out strength until more of this new type were available from production.

The need to establish units devoted to training crews on the new bomber types resulted in the setting up of so-called pool squadrons during the summer of 1939. A revision of this arrangement brought the designated pool squadrons into operational training units and, shortly after war was declared, both the Finningley squadrons moved to Upper Heyford to form one of these organisations.

Finningley was to continue in a training role for No. 106 Squadron which brought its Hampdens in from Cottesmore in October. Also classed as a reserve squadron, No. 106 continued the operational training role for No. 5 Group that the previous occupants had started to provide. By August 1940 the critical war situation caused No. 106 to be placed on operational call. Most of its early sorties were to drop mines in the approaches to French Channel ports thought to be harbouring invasion barges. There was still need for a

Over 60 years later, with the concrete extended, the married quarters beyond the poplars and the hangar remain.

Lancaster DV200 of Bomber Command's Instructors' School parked near the railway line on the airfield's northern boundary. Finningley station can be seen on the extreme right. This aircraft dispersal area was outside the original boundary and was reached by crossing the public road.

Although the railway track is now obscured by the greenery, a tie-down midst the grass confirmed the position of the dispersal.

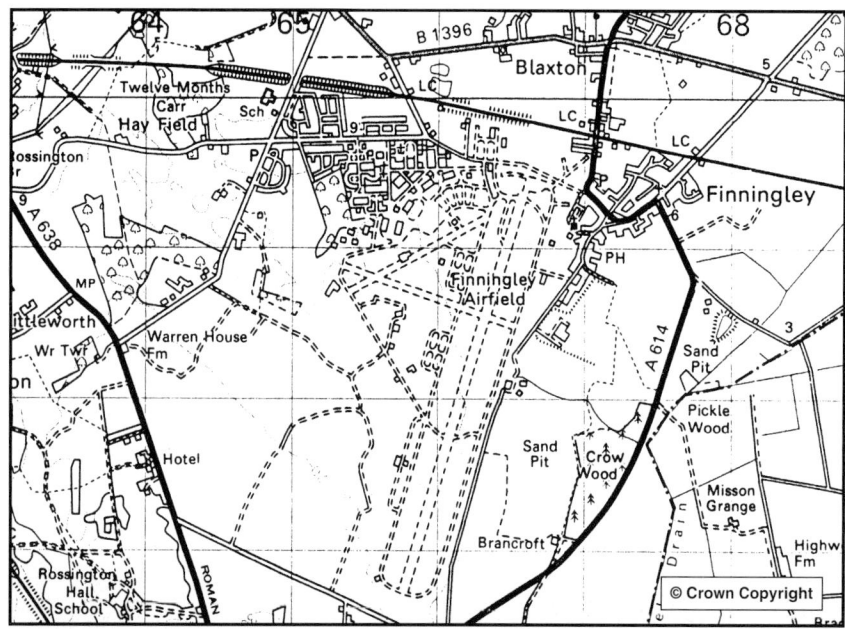

Being one of the RAF's major bases, it remained active after the war — the picture right being taken in September 1948. In 1955 it was earmarked as a V-bomber station in 1955 when the main runway was extended to the south by 1,000 yards.

final polish for new Hampden crews and in February 1941 No. 106 left its 'C' Flight at Finningley to continue with this task while the rest of the squadron moved to Coningsby for full offensive operations. While flying from Finningley, six Hampdens had failed to return. In March the former No. 106 'C' Flight metamorphosised into No. 25 OTU, initially continuing to train with Hampdens and Ansons. A few Manchesters arrived in the spring of 1941, and the unit was later bolstered with Wellingtons.

Early in 1942 Finningley passed to No. 1 Group and with no further need for Hampdens or Manchesters No. 25 OTU concentrated on Wellingtons, nine of which were lost when the station was called upon to participate in Bomber Command operations. No. 25 OTU was disbanded in February 1943 and in March No. 18 OTU moved in from Bramcote and began using Bircotes and Worksop as satellites. In November the Wellingtons were moved to these satellites as hard runways were to be laid at Finningley. These were put down during the winter of 1943-44, the main 03-21 being 2,000 yards, 07-25 1,400 yards and 12-30 1,400 yards. A concrete perimeter track had been laid in 1942 and asphalt pan-type hardstandings constructed in 1940-41 linked to it, two of the original clusters crossing the A614 road between Finningley village and Bawtry. A single loop-type standing was added to bring the total to 36. Some additional domestic accommodation was provided to cater for a maximum 1,592 males and 459 females. The bomb store was in Finningley Big Wood.

The station re-opened for flying in May 1944 when No. 18 OTU returned from Bramcote. By the end of the year requirements for operational training had reduced and in January 1945 the OTU was disbanded and the Wellingtons removed.

The Bomber Command Instructors' School had been established at Finningley in December 1944 and this organisation, with a variety of bomber types, saw out the remaining months of the war at this station and did not depart until the spring of 1947. From 1946 to 1954 a number of different training units were stationed at Finningley with a variety of aircraft types. The last of these units withdrew in 1954 leaving only the Meteors of No. 616 Squadron, Royal Auxiliary Air Force, manned largely by part-time personnel, but their days at Finningley were numbered for in May 1955 the squadron moved to Worksop. The reason was that Finningley was about to be given a new lease of life as a V-bomber station and during the next two years work was carried out to relay and extend the main runway to approximately 3,000 yards. Unit stores for atomic weapons were also constructed. Re-opened in the spring of 1957, No. 101 Squadron was re-formed in October that year to operate Vulcans. A year later No. 18 Squadron with ECM Valiants was also established at Finningley. In 1961, No. 101 Squadron took its Vulcans to Waddington changing places with the Vulcan training organisation, No. 230 Operational Conversion Unit. Two years later, with the Valiant having seen its day, No. 18 Squadron was disbanded.

Victors were added to the Finningley scene in later years before Strike Command (the amalgamation of Bomber and Fighter Commands on April 30, 1968) moved its units out and Training Command took over the station in May 1970. Navigational training was the main objective of No. 6 Flying Training School, first using Varsity and later Dominie aircraft. Although Finningley passed to Support Command in 1977, its training role continued throughout in the next decade before RAF activity was terminated. However, the station remained intact and well kept and in 1998 Peel Holdings Plc announced that they were planning to develop the airfield as Doncaster Finningley airport.

The Station Headquarters still bears the faint traces of its wartime camouflage. . . .

. . . and the old Operations Block also still stands. Now it is planned to give Finningley a new lease of life as a civil airport.

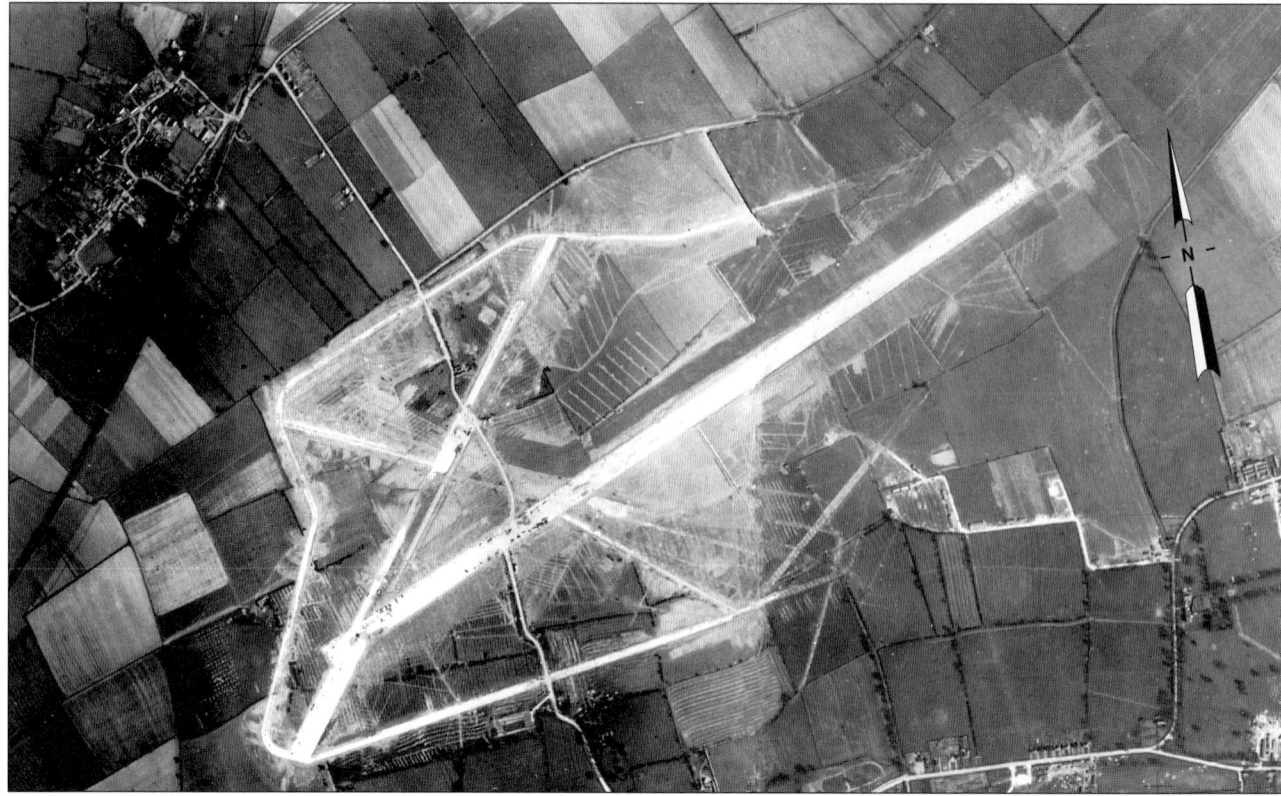

Fiskerton under construction in 1942 — this picture being taken on April 14 by No. 1 Photographic Reconnaissance Unit. Many airfields required the closure of minor roads and the route of the one from Fiskerton village to Reepham (top left) is plainly visible crossing the airfield. Some of the 15 or so dispersed sites which had to be built at all the wartime-expediency airfields to cater for messing and service facilities, can be seen taking shape to the south-east.

FISKERTON

Only 4½ miles east of the city of Lincoln, this bomber airfield was constructed to Class A standard on the west side of Fiskerton Moor, south-east of the LNER line from Lincoln to Market Rasen. At the same time the road from Fiskerton village to Reepham had to be closed. The concrete runways were 08-26 at 2,000 yards and the subsidiaries, 05-23 and 13-31, both 1,400 yards in length. The normal 36 hardstandings were provided, all of the pan type, but one was lost with the erection of a T2 hangar on the north side between runway heads 23 and 26. Another

T2 and a B1 were put up near the technical site on the east side between runway heads 26 and 31, the B1 being the southernmost. The bomb stores were to the north between runway heads 13 and 23. Most of the domestic sites were dispersed in fields close to the Fiskerton village to Stainfield road, comprising seven domestic, two communal, one WAAF and sick quarters. Maximum accom-

modation was put at 2,016 males and 297 females. F. G. Mintee Ltd and Constable Hart & Co. Ltd were involved in the later stages of construction.

Built in 1942 and assigned to No. 5 Group, the airfield was ready for occupation by the end of the year and No. 49 Squadron brought its Lancasters in from Scampton in January 1943. During runway repairs effected during

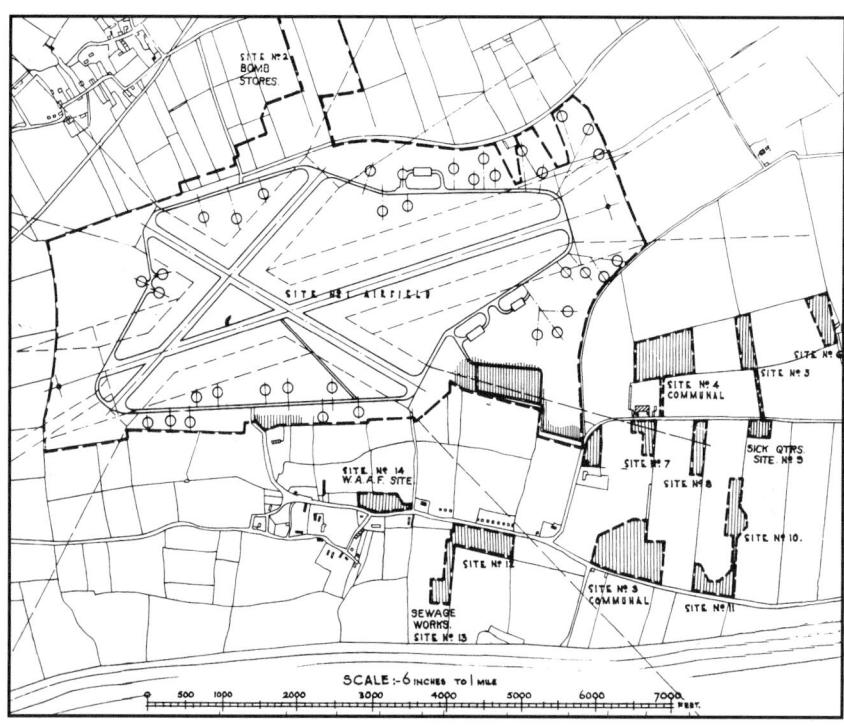

Comparative plans: *left* as completed in 1944 and *right* as it remains today.

NO. 3 COMMUNAL SITE

175	Officers' Mess
176	Sergeants' Mess
177	Institute
178	Dining Room
179	A/M Ablutions Showers & Change
180	A/M Latrines
181	Ration Store
182	M. & E. Plinth
183	Picket Post
184	Decontamination Centre
185	Store, Shoemakers & Barber's Shop
186	Post Room
187	Grocery & Local Produce Store
188	Medical Inspection Block
189	Sergeants' Showers
190	Fuel Compound
191	Stand by Sgt House
192	Sergeants' Latrines
193	Officers' Baths & Latrines
194	C.O's Quarters
195-9	A/WKS Barracks & Ablutions
200	Squash Courts
201	Post Office

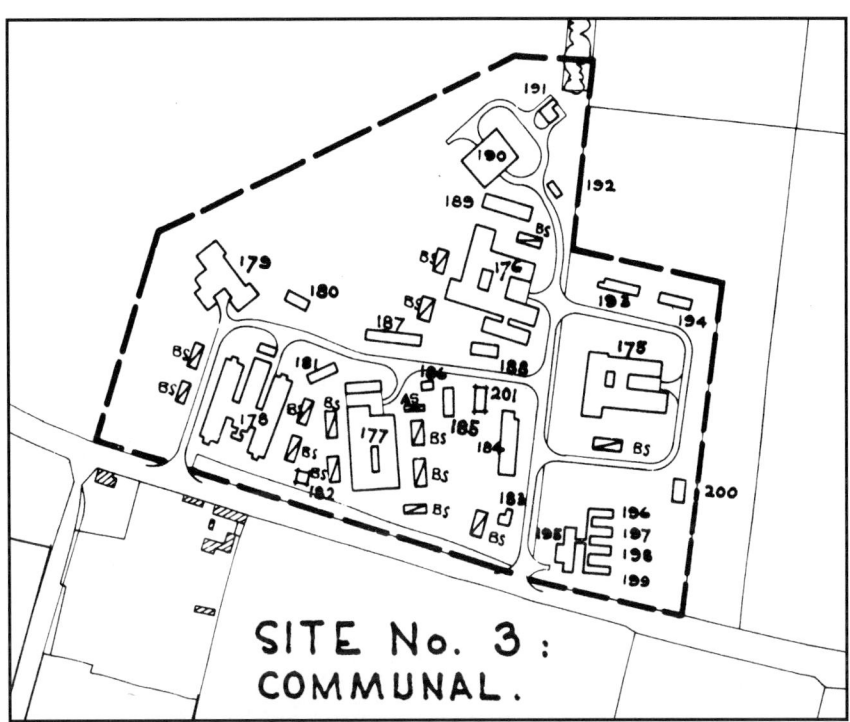

SITE No. 3: COMMUNAL.

Generally, an airfield had two messing or communal sites, a sick bay, WAAF site and half-a-dozen quarters' sites, althogh there was no hard and fast layout — apart from being spaced out to minimise casualties in the face of a bombing attack.

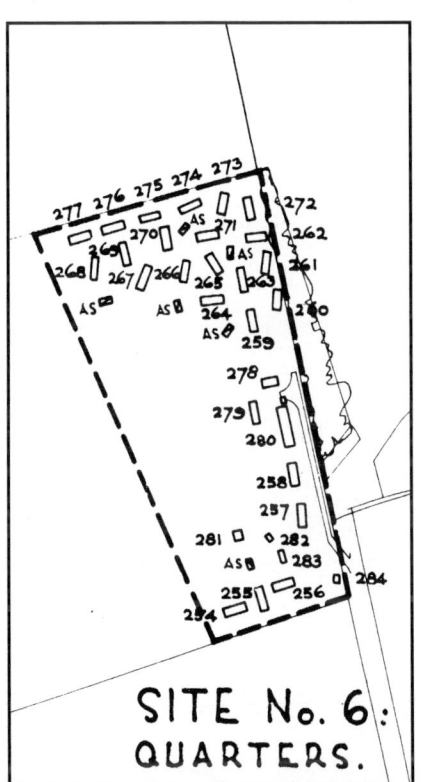

SITE No. 6: QUARTERS.

NO. 6 QUARTERS SITE

254	Officers' & Servants' Quarters
255	Officers' & Servants' Quarters
256	Officers' Quarters
257-8	Sergeants' Quarters
259-77	Airmens' Barracks
278	Drying Room
279	Sergeants' & Airmens' Latrine
280	Sergeants' & Airmens' Ablutions
281	Pump House (Sewage)
282	Officers' Latrine
283	Officers' Ablution
284	Picket Post

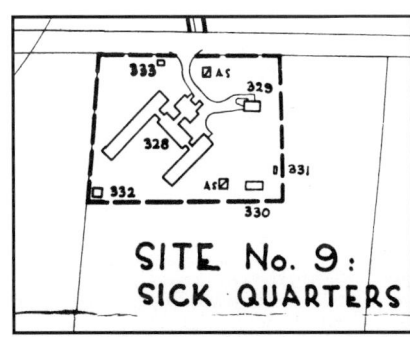

SITE No. 9: SICK QUARTERS

NO. 9 SICK QUARTERS SITE

328	Sick Quarters & Annexe
329	Ambulance Garage & Mortuary
330	Sergeants' & Orderlies' Quarters
331	Ablutions, Latrines & Drying Room
332	M. & E. Plinth
333	Picket Post

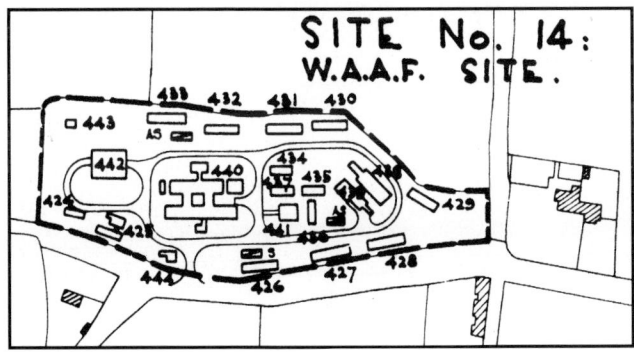

SITE No. 14: W.A.A.F. SITE.

NO. 14 W.A.A.F. SITE

424	Officers' Quarters
425	Officers' Quarters & Bath House
426-33	Airwomens' Barracks
434-7	Airwomens' Barracks
438-39	Ablutions, Baths, Latrines & Decontamination Centre & Hairdressing
440	Mess & Institute
441	Static Water Tank
442	Fuel Compound
443	M. & E. Plinth
444	Picket Post & Detention Room

Lancaster UL-C of No. 576 Squadron about to touch down on runway 31 with the technical site in the background.

September and October 1944, the opportunity was taken to install the fog dispersal system called FIDO. While this work was carried out No. 49's Lancasters operated from Dunholme Lodge. No. 49 remained in residence until October 1944 when a re-allocation of airfields in the area put Fiskerton into No. 1 Group's control and No. 49 moved to Fulbeck, recently vacated by the USAAF. At the end of the same month, No. 1 Group brought in No. 576 Squadron to give more space at Elsham Wolds. At around the same date 'C' Flight of No. 550 Squadron was detached and sent to Fiskerton to become the nucleus of a re-formed No. 150 Squadron but within a few days No. 1 Group had a change of plan and the emergent squadron was moved to Hemswell which had also been acquired from No. 5 Group.

No. 576 Squadron stayed at Fiskerton until the end of the war, thereafter gradually reducing in both personnel and equipment to be officially disbanded in September 1945. During hostilities, 117 Lancasters of the two squadrons were lost in the course of operations from this station. Before the end of the year the base was put on care and maintenance but as there was no further need for the flying field it was returned to agriculture. In the 1950s, a protected Royal Observer Corps group headquarters control room was built adjacent to the former technical site

Not all landings were as straightforward. Here, a machine of No. 49 Squadron runs off the concrete on August 11, 1943. This particular Lancaster, ED805 EA-S, was lost in the Baltic during the August 17/18, 1943 raid on the Peenemünde V-weapon experimental station. Squadron Leader Richard Nevil Todd-White and his crew all perished.

and it remained in use until the Corps was disbanded in September 1991. Only small areas of runway concrete and the odd building ruin remain in 2000. A memorial to Nos. 49 and 576 Squadrons is on the roadside near the old main runway.

Landings in poor visibility were even more dangerous and many crews returned from an operation only to find their airfield fogbound. Early in 1942, Churchill had instructed the Petroleum Warfare Department to investigate methods of dispersing fog at airfields and the result was FIDO (Fog Investigation and Dispersal Operation). The system involved the installation of pipes on either side of the main runway, carrying petrol burners which were ignited — the tremendous heat generated burning a path of visibility which was a welcome safety beacon to a tired crew returning after a long trip. After initial experiments were carried out at Graveley (No. 8 Group) and Lakenheath (No. 3 Group), Fiskerton became the first airfield to receive a full-scale trial — only to alert the Lincoln Fire Brigade which feared a major catastrophe. Arriving at the airfield to the

cheers of the airmen, the firemen were astonished to see the flames extinguished at a stroke! In all, 15 airfields had FIDO installed enabling nearly 2,500 aircraft to land safely . . . albeit at an overall expenditure of 100,000 tons of petrol! *Left:* When Air Commodore Cozens at Hemswell wanted to include a FIDO shot in his *Night Bombers* film, he persuaded the works department at Sturgate — a non-operational station to the south-west — to test its new installation while he filmed it. The sequence shows a Lancaster landing amidst the flames in a never-to-be-forgotten experience because it nearly ran down Cozens as the noise of its engine had been drowned out by the roar of the burning petrol. *Right.* FIDO supply pipes removed from beside the main runway at Fiskerton during agricultural operations.

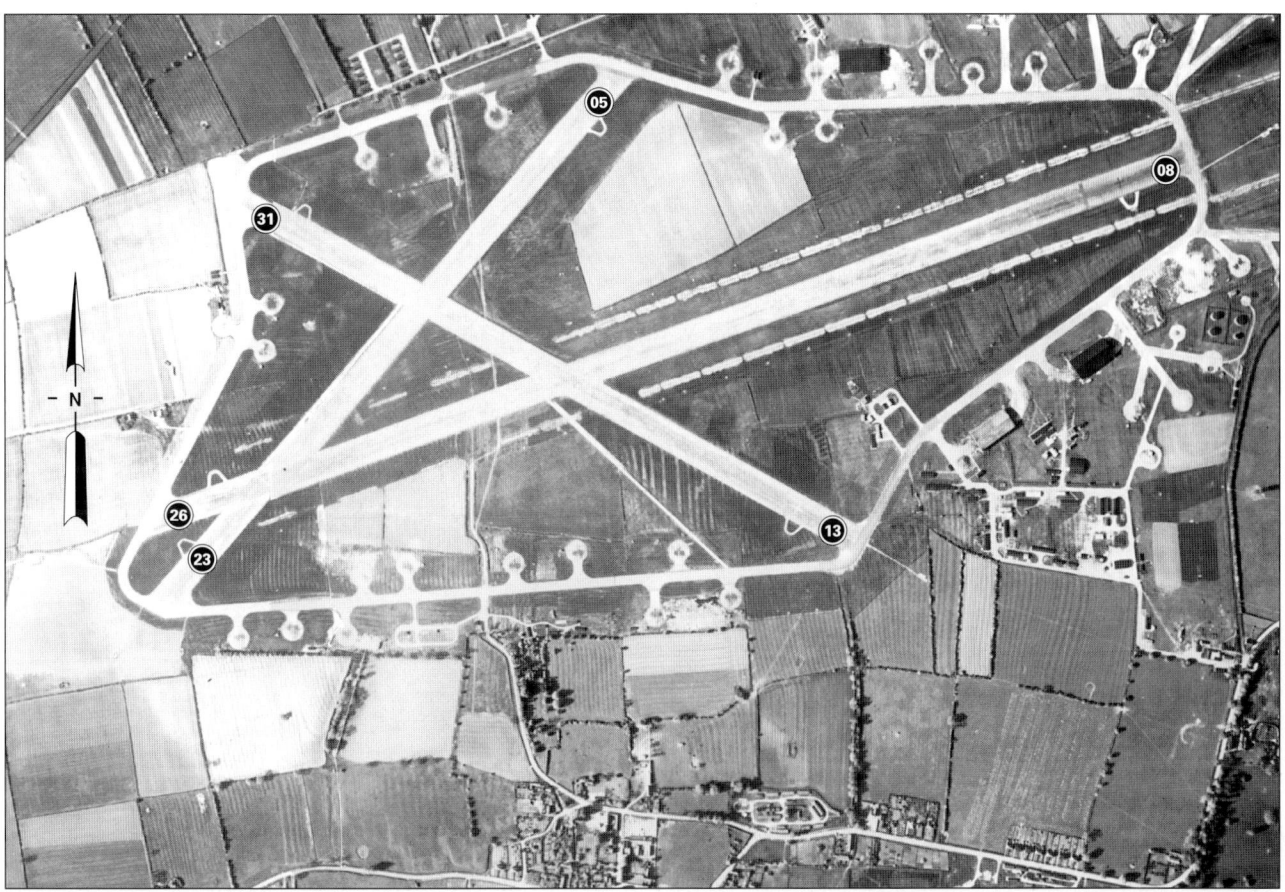

This 1946 aerial taken by No. 138 Squadron clearly shows the line of FIDO burners along each side of the 08-26 runway.

September 2000. In the foreground the restored road between Fiskerton and Reepham. Where it crosses the old main runway a memorial has been sited honouring Fiskerton's wartime occupants (see page 350). Picture taken looking north-east.

45

GRIMSBY (Waltham)

Flight Lieutenant H. G. Topliss and crew with No. 100 Squadron veteran ND644 HW-N on a pan hardstanding in the north-east corner of the airfield with the B1 hangar in the background. This Lancaster was lost on its 115th raid, being shot down near Nuremberg on the night of March 16/17, 1945. Only two of the crew members survived.

A private flying club started by enthusiasts in the Grimsby area during the early 1930s was based on meadowland three miles from the town in the parish of Waltham. The Lincolnshire Aero Club had a club house and two wooden hangars but a larger, more substantial hangar was built in 1937. In 1938, Waltham aerodrome was selected for establishing one of the Elementary and Reserve Flying Training Schools set up by the Air Ministry and run under civilian contracts to provide instruction for would-be RAF pilots. A variety of training aircraft types were used by the school during 14 months of activity but the principal type was the Tiger Moth. Apart from an occasional visitor, the airfield was devoid of flying tenants from September 1939 and late the following year was temporarily closed, the site having been surveyed and found suitable for development. Work began in the winter of 1940-41 to extend the flying field into the parish of

Holton-le-Clay, taking in part of the A16 Louth to Grimsby road on the north-east side. The three runways were 18-36 at 1,200 yards, 06-24 at 1,400 and 12-30 at 1,100 yards. Pan hardstandings, 36 in number, were built off the encircling perimeter track. Two T2 and one B1 hangar were eventually provided.

Initially opened as a satellite for Binbrook in November 1941, the new station was officially named Grimsby although the local name Waltham persisted among locals and servicemen on the station. This may have led to some confusion elsewhere as there already was a White Waltham airfield near Maidenhead.

No. 142 Squadron's Wellingtons arrived from Binbrook in November 1941 and carried out bombing operations from Grimsby

until December 1942. With an urgent need for more night bombers to support the 'Torch' invasion, No. 142 was split, half going to North Africa and the remainder moving to Kirmington where it was used as the basis to form another squadron in the New Year. With the break-up of No. 142 Squadron, No. 1 Group used Grimsby to add a new Lancaster unit to its strength and No. 100 Squadron (reformed in mid-December), commenced operations on the night of March 8/9, 1943. From early 1942, Gee, Walker & Slater Ltd were involved in extending runways 18-36 to 2,000 yards and 12-30 to 1,400 yards across the A16. During this work some 19 hard standings were lost and replaced with loops. Additional domestic sites gave a maximum of accommodation for 2,203 males and 254 females.

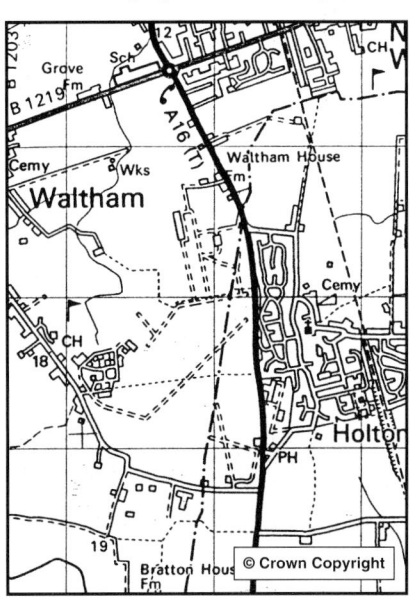

© Crown Copyright

Viewed from the perimeter track, looking towards the dispersal beyond where the Lancaster was parked, the B1 hangar remains in a good state of preservation.

In November 1943, No. 100 Squadron's 'C' Flight became No. 550 Squadron but by mid-January its growth brought a move to North Killingholme. No. 100, however, made Grimsby its home until April 2, 1945 when, owing to deterioration of the runways, a move was made to Elsham Wolds. This marked the end of Bomber Command flying units at the station. Operations from Grimsby cost 164 bombers missing in action or crashing in the UK, 48 being Wellingtons and 116 Lancasters.

In the immediate post-war years the hangars were used by No. 35 MU for storage and the flying field reverted to agricultural use. In later years improvements to the A16, with a bypass for Holton-le-Clay, reclaimed part of the eastern side where a memorial to the men of No. 100 Squadron can be seen. At the end of the 1990s, many airfield buildings still survive for commercial use, including the B1 and a T2 hangar.

Some of No. 142 Squadron's Wellingtons can be seen on pan hardstandings in April 1942 when work was in hand on extending the main runway.

The memorial at the junction of the Holton-le-Clay road with the A16.

About to 'land' on the E-W runway in September 2000. The hangar near where the Lanc was parked is top right.

HEMSWELL

October 15, 1940. Hampdens leave Hemswell at twilight bound for Germany. Six months earlier, No. 61 Squadron had dropped the first RAF bombs on German soil.

One of many airfields close by the A15 — the Roman Ermine Street that runs north through Lincolnshire to the Humber — this site was first used for flying in the First World War. Late in 1916, a broad pasture, on the north-east side of the junction of what were to become the B1398 and A631 at the village of Harpswell, was requisitioned for the Royal Flying Corps for a night landing ground. In 1918, Nos. 199 and 200 Training Squadrons were established at Hemswell and by the end of hostilities several buildings, including four hangars, had been erected on the eastern side. However, these units and the aerodrome had but a brief existence and within a year cattle were again in residence.

In the early 1930s, the site became a candidate for an expansion scheme airfield for the RAF, the land being compulsorily purchased with construction beginning in 1935. To the standard requirements of the time, half the 400 acres acquired were for the flying field and the remainder, on the south-eastern side close to the delightfully named A15 hamlet Spital-in-the-Street, to build the camp. Four Type C hangars fronted the bombing circle with the administrative, technical and barrack sites in close proximity to the rear. Officially named Hemswell after the large village on the western boundary beyond the B1398, the station was opened in January 1937 with Nos. 61 and 144 Squadrons being installed as the resident units the following month. During the next two years, the squadrons shed the Hawker Audax biplanes with which they had arrived, and moved through Ansons and Blenheims to Hampdens, the type on which No. 5 Group was standardising. Both squadrons remained at Hemswell until the station was transferred to No. 1 Group in July 1941 when they moved to North Luffenham.

No. 61 Squadron's Hampdens are credited with being the first Bomber Command aircraft to drop bombs on German soil. This occurred on the night of March 19, 1940 when the seaplane base at Hörnum was attacked. During Hampden operations from Hemswell, some 300 raids were undertaken and 45 aircraft failed to return with another 38 lost in operational crashes. A Manchester was also lost on the night of June 26/27, 1941, one of the few that the squadron had on strength at that time.

With its acquisition of Hemswell, No. 1 Group moved in No. 300 Squadron — the Polish unit based at Ingham where the turf needed refurbishment. No. 301, another Polish-manned squadron, came in from Swinderby so that the language communica-

This vertical of Hemswell taken on April 12, 1942 shows the extensive network of pan hardstandings on the north side. Eleven were destroyed or isolated when the airfield was extended northwards.

With Hemswell, we are very fortunate that it was here that Air Commodore Cozens shot most of his film depicting life on a wartime bomber station. *Above:* **Arriving at the main gate . . . then and now.**

tion difficulties were concentrated at one location. A third, No. 305, joined the other Polish squadrons in July 1942. By 1943, the numbers of Polish crews available had dropped to a point where a decision had to be taken to reduce the active bomber units. The axe fell on No. 301 and it was disbanded in April that year, some personnel remaining on the station to join No. 300. In June, No. 300 had to switch back to its old base at Ingham, again taking No. 305 with it, so that work could begin on laying concrete runways at Hemswell to bring the airfield up to Class A standard. The main runway 17-35 was to be 2,000 yards long, 06-24 1,550 yards and 10-28 1,500 yards. The ends of 24 and 28 were both extended to 1,700 yards, apparently before the station was re-opened. Some 36 asphalt pan hardstandings had been put down in the 1940-1941 period but during runway and perimeter track construction at least four were destroyed. Another six on the south side were compromised by being directly in front of runway 35. Sixteen of the surviving pans were on the other side of the A631 accessed by long taxiways. Evidently several of the original hardstandings were no longer held as suitable for aircraft parking for 17 loop-type standings were added along the perimeter track. Also it is evident that some extra work was done to the bomb store situated north-east of the camp. Additional domestic accommodation resulted in a total of 2,807 male and 298 female places at the station. The runway construction was carried out by J. McGeoch and Son Ltd and the other work by B. Pumfrey and Sons Ltd.

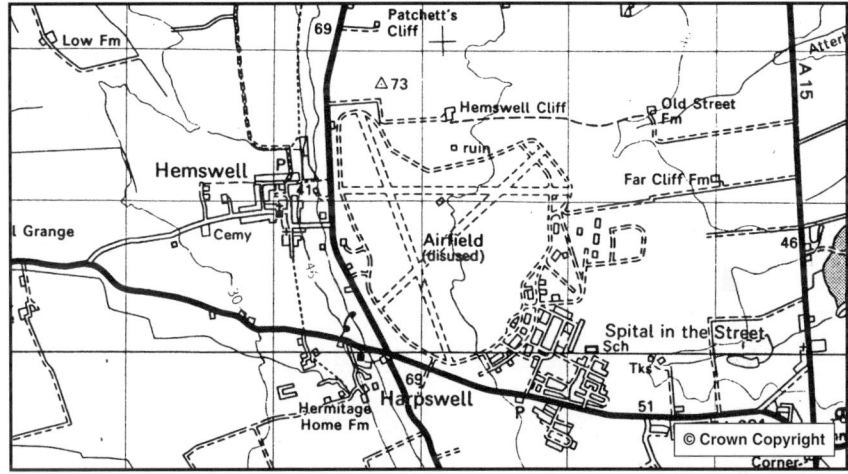

When the airfield was re-opened in January 1944 it was used by No. 1 Lancaster Finishing School which remained until November. Hemswell then became a satellite or sub-base of Scampton receiving two recently re-formed squadrons, Nos. 150 and 170. No. 150 flew its first operational sorties from Hemswell but No. 170 had already started raids from Kirmington. Both these Lancaster squadrons remained at Hemswell until disbanded in November 1945. During the war a total of 122 bombers were lost while on operations from Hemswell, 38 Hampdens, 62 Wellingtons and 22 Lancasters.

In the immediate post-war years, Hemswell played host to a number of RAF units. Mosquitos of Nos. 109 and 139 Squadrons stayed briefly in 1946 and in November that year Nos. 83, 97 and 100 Squadrons brought in Lincolns, a type present for nine years as squadrons came and went. Nos. 109 and 139 returned with their Mosquitos in 1950, converting to Canberras in 1952-53. They left in January 1956 — the last flying units based at the station. No. 97 Squadron returned in another guise when three Thor medium range missiles were located on part of the base but the squadron was gone in 1963, the

Left: **Flight Lieutenant Bob Chandler (called Harris in the film in honour of Bomber Command's chief) with his puppy dog. In the background the central heating plant (Building 67)** stands on the left with the MT shed (Building 66) on the right. *Right:* **Both still survive today. Note how Tim has even managed to include a dog in his comparison!**

Bombing up. The bomb train transfers its deadly charges from the store on the north-eastern corner of the aerodrome.

weapon being already obsolete. For three years, the camp area then housed No. 7 School of Recruit Training, the barrack area being retained thereafter for overflow married quarters for Scampton and later as a staging area for displaced Ugandan refugees. The hangars were used for intervention grain storage, a T2 being erected to provide further capacity.

Hemswell was put up for sale in the early 1980s, the buildings now serving many purposes: markets, antique restorations and, most notably, the old Officers Mess being converted into an hotel. The runways were removed for hard core in the 1980s but fortunately Hemswell's substantial buildings of the pre-war camp site have endured into the next century.

Above: **Classic shot of the Lancasters taxiing around the peri-track towards the threshold of the main runway.** *Below:* **Then the hangar door was open but now it is sealed and in use as an intervention grain store.**

Turning round the south-eastern corner of the perimeter, the Lancs line up on runway 35 ready for take-off.

INGHAM (Cammeringham)

The site of this airfield was apparently considered for an expansion scheme airfield in the mid-1930s but was passed over for more favourable grounds. Nevertheless, with the proposed growth of Bomber Command, Ingham was resurrected early in 1940 and developed as a satellite for Hemswell.

Sandwiched between the A15 and B1398, east of Ingham village, gradients restricted the size of the flying field making it unsuitable for the hard three-runway configuration then seen as the necessary standard for a bomber airfield. A total of 24 pan-type aircraft standings were put down and in the spring of 1942 a complete perimeter track with 12 extra dispersals. Plans also called for the extension of the grass runway across the road on the southern boundary but this work does not appear to have been carried out. The technical site with a T2 hangar bordered the B1398. A second T2 was erected near the eastern boundary alongside the A15.

Apart from the occasional dispersal of aircraft from Hemswell, Ingham was little used until May 1942 when the Wellingtons of No. 300 Squadron arrived. The squadron operated from Ingham until January when No. 1 Group decided to concentrate Polish bomber squadrons at Hemswell. The Wellingtons of No. 199 Squadron (ex-Blyton) arrived soon after the Poles left, only to be transferred, less aircraft, south to No. 3 Group in June 1943. In the same month, the Poles of No. 300 returned, plus No. 305 Squadron, to avoid the runway laying at Hemswell. Extra

Although Ingham was a satellite for Hemswell it was much nearer to Scampton which lay just two miles to the south. It was squeezed into a restricted area hemmed in by two roads and with a farmhouse right in the middle. This view was taken looking across Ingham's turf from the technical site in September 1941. The Wellington in the foreground, Z1407 BH-Z of No. 300 Squadron, lost most of its rear fuselage fabric through battle damage sustained on September 4/5 when raiding Bremen.

buildings were put up by Wates Ltd in early 1943, presumably to accommodate two squadrons. The Poles continued operating with Wellingtons until September when No. 305 was transferred to the Second Tactical Air Force to become a Mitchell-equipped bomber unit. No. 300 soldiered on alone until March 1944 when it was scheduled to be re-equipped with Lancasters and moved to Faldingworth. A total of 35 Wellingtons had been lost in the course of operations flown from Ingham.

Ingham had remained a sod-surface airfield, unsuitable for the operation by four-engine heavy bombers due to the limitations of the grass runways, and for the rest of 1944 the station was home to bomber defence training units, Nos. 1481 and 1687 Flights, charged with target-towing and bomber interception practice using mainly Martinets and Hurricanes.

On November 24, 1944, notice was given that the name of the station had been changed to Cammeringham. This was to avoid confusion with villages of the same name in Suffolk and Norfolk although why it took four years for officialdom to decide this was necessary is puzzling. In any case, by January 1945 the surface of the airfield had deteriorated to a point where it was no longer considered suitable for flying and was put in the hands of a holding party until closure shortly before the end of hostilities.

Today it is difficult to realise there ever was an airfield at Ingham.

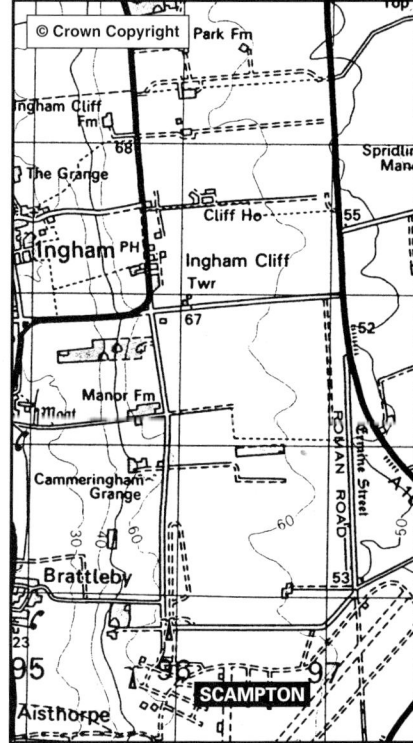

The control tower, its windows unseeing eyes to former glories, still surveys the aerodrome which was later renamed Cammeringham.

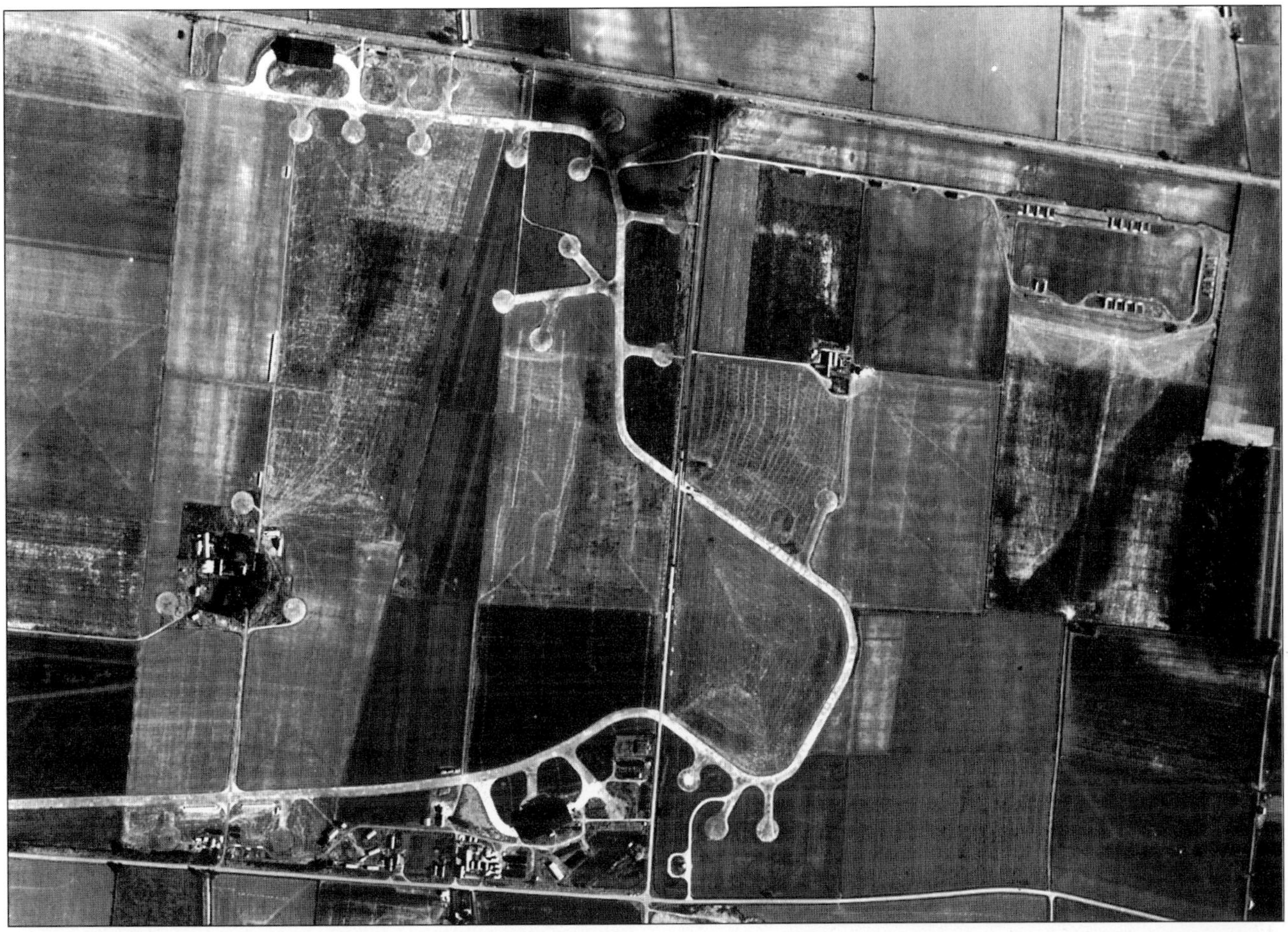

Cliff House Farm, surrounded by the three grass runways, was taken over by the RAF and used for messing facilities. Because so little remains to trace the airfield's wartime face, we have dotted in the line of the runways on this September 2000 shot looking just north of east. Cliff House still sits isolated amidst the fields.

CLIFF HOUSE

KELSTERN

Bleak Kelstern, January 1945. Lancaster BIII PB736 CF-G of No. 625 Squadron sits on its snow-covered dispersal point. Beyond is the northern T2 hangar.

Located only four miles from both Binbrook and Ludford Magna airfields on the Lincolnshire Wolds, Kelstern was a half a mile north-east of a First World War night landing ground established in 1917 near Mill Farm. Intended as a refuge for No. 33 Squadron Zeppelin hunters running low on fuel, it was little used, the RAF departing in March 1919, yet it was to return to the fold 24 years later.

In total, some 400 acres of farmland was acquired and in July 1942 construction commenced on a £810,000 contract to build an airfield to Class A standard. The minor road from Binbrook to South Ellington running across the centre of the site was closed. Three intersecting concrete runways were the main 06-24 at 2,000 yards and the subsidiaries, 01-19 and 13-31, both 1,400 yards each. The 36 hardstandings were all the loop type. A T2 hangar was placed on the technical site on the north-west side of the airfield between the 13 and 06 runway heads, a second T2 between runway heads 01 and 31 and a third on the north side between 19 and 24. The bomb store was off the south-east side of the airfield. where the camp sites were dispersed in fields to the north-west. The buildings largely the work of George Wimpey & Co. Ltd and provided for 1,585 males and 346 females.

Opened as a sub-base for Binbrook, No. 625 Squadron formed at the station as of October 1, 1943, its nucleus being 'C' Flight of No. 100 Squadron which arrived from Grimsby. The first sorties were flown on the night of October 18/19 and Kelstern was to remain No. 625's home through all but five raids of its operational period. During these 17½ months, 88 operations were undertaken and 66 Lancasters failed to return. A year after its arrival at Kelstern, No. 625 Squadron gave birth to a re-formed No. 170 Squadron but after flying its first raid on the night of October 19/20, 1944, the new squadron moved out to Dunholme Lodge two days later.

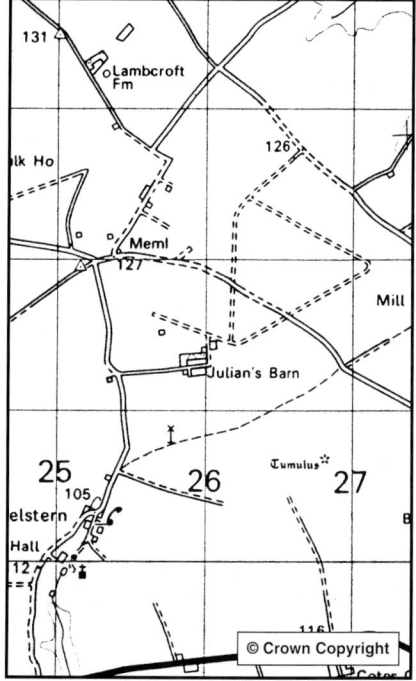

The aerodrome pictured by No. 540 Squadron as it appeared in July 1948. Compare with this present-day Ordnance Survey plan on which only the southern ends of the two subsidiary runways and the south-eastern peri-track remain.

A winding road . . . a field of grain . . . this is Kelstern in September 2000.

In April 1945, No. 1 Group shifted a number of units and found room at Scampton for No. 625 Squadron which took its Lancasters there on the 5th of that month. It appears probable that the close proximity of other airfields and the risk of collisions through the overlapping circuits was behind this move as thereafter no other flying units were based at Kelstern. A total of 70 Lancasters failed to return or were lost in crashes during operations from the airfield.

The holding party withdrew in the summer of 1945 and the property returned or was sold to the landowners in 1965-66. The country roads across the airfield which had been closed were reopened and eventually much of the concrete was broken up and removed. The hangars were sold and dismantled. A memorial to No. 625 Squadron is to be seen at the junction of two roads near the village.

Left: **One of the few remaining buildings is the Operations Block not far off what was the main entrance on the Binbrook** **to South Ellington road.** *Right:* **A memorial honouring No. 625 Squadron stands at the roadside.**

KIRMINGTON

This Class A airfield, on which work begun late in 1941, was completed the following summer. Located directly south-west of Kirmington village on the A18 Scunthorpe to Grimsby road, the airfield conformed to the standard of the time with three concrete runways, the main, 04-22, being originally 1,450 yards long, 15-33 1,150 yards, and 09-27 1,100 yards. However, it appears that extension of the runways was carried out before the station was opened and this involved the closure and diversion of the A18 just west of Kirmington village, and also the closure of the minor road running north to the village on the east side of the airfield. When extended the runways lengths were 04-22 at 2,000 yards and the others both 1,400 yards. Of the original 36 pan-type hardstandings two were lost by perimeter track and hangar taxiway extensions. Two loop-type standings were added as replacements. A T2 hangar was located on the main technical site between runway heads 22 and 27 and another on the maintenance site near Kirmington Villa with another T2 and a B1 a little to the north.

On a hardstanding near the entrance to the airfield by the technical site, Lancaster NN770 AS-R of No. 166 Squadron reposes in the first days of peace in May 1945. The main workshops on the technical site can be seen in the background.

No. 166 Squadron Lancasters rest on many of Kirmington's hardstandings on a fine day in the summer of 1945. That on which Lancaster NN770 stands can be clearly seen in the technical site area near the top of the photograph.

The old technical site today. The terminal buildings for what is now Humberside Airport are located on the opposite side of the airfield where the second two T2 hangars were once sited.

Two blister hangars were erected on pan hardstandings adjacent to the technical site T2. The bomb store was off the south side of the airfield and 11 camp sites, of which seven were domestic, were dispersed around Kirmington village and further to the east, allowing for 2,177 males and 345 females.

Kirmington was first used by No. 15 (Pilots) Advanced Flying School from March 1942, but on October 23 that year the station was transferred to No. 1 Group, Bomber Command when No. 150 Squadron and its Wellingtons arrived from Snaith preparatory to having half of its strength despatched to

North Africa. The remaining crews continued on operations and were joined in December by part of No. 170 Squadron from Grimsby which had suffered a similar fate. Instead of re-building both squadrons, a decision was taken by Bomber Command to amalgamate both under another designation. Thus, on January 27, 1943, No. 166 Squadron was re-born, having last existed as a Handley Page V/1500 heavy bomber squadron in the First World War. No. 166 flew Wellingtons until September 1943 and then converted to Lancasters. As Bomber Command continued to expand, No. 166 lost its 'C' Flight in

October 1944 for the re-forming of No. 153 Squadron. It flew its first raid on October 7 but, as was common practice, as soon as the new unit was fully established it was transferred to a station where more room was available. Thus by the middle of the month it had moved to Scampton. During operations from Kirmington, a total 178 bombers either failed to return or were destroyed in crashes, 51 being Wellingtons and 127 Lancasters.

Kirmington continued as home for No. 166 Squadron until November 1945 when, along with several other bomber squadrons, it was disbanded. From February 1946 the station was put on care and maintenance until relinquished by the Air Ministry to the Ministry of Agriculture in 1953. Some private crop-spraying and commercial flying with light aircraft took place over the next few years, use being made of wartime buildings by the operators. From summer 1967, a small charter company started regular flying from the airfield and its activities gradually expanded. In 1970 Kirmington was selected as the best location for a regional airport serving the Hull, Grimsby and Scunthorpe localities. By this time the A18 had been restored and took in part of the northern end of runway 22, but the others were in good order although a minor road had been reopened across the flying field. In furtherance of the project, the airfield was purchased by Lindsey County Council for a reported £85,000, a further £170,000 being invested in refurbishing the runways, building a new terminal and control tower. Opened in March 1974, Kirmington eventually became Humberside Airport and home to small charter airlines. It has since been acquired by Manchester Airport PLC. A memorial plaque to the men of No. 166 Squadron is to be found in Kirmington village church.

The same runways which once launched a thousand machines of war now perform a similar task for more peaceful purposes. The main runway (now re-numbered 03-21) has now been extended a further 400 yards to cater for the requirements of an international airport while the old 15-33 runway has virtually disappeared. This shot was taken looking north in September 2000.

A parade of Polish personnel at Lindholme in the spring of 1942 photographed from the top of the watch office looking south between the hangars. Wellington W5590 SM-A of No. 305 Squadron was hit by flak over the Elbe on the night of May 3/4 that year and ditched in the North Sea. All the crew were rescued by an MTB.

LINDHOLME (Hatfield Woodhouse)

An expansion scheme aerodrome built on the wide expanse of Hatfield moors, some five miles east of Doncaster, the site, to the east of the A614 Trone to Bawtry road, was a mile south of the small village of Hatfield Woodhouse, the name first selected for the new station. Work began in the spring of 1938 taking in approximately 250 acres of pasture for the airfield itself and a further 150 for the camp and support facilities. Three Type C hangars fronted the south-west side of the bombing circle, with a fourth and fifth behind the two outer hangars. The administration, technical and barrack area lay along-side the A614. As common with these expansion scheme airfields, the construction of buildings took place over several months and the pace was only quickened by the outbreak of war. Officially opened in June 1940 under No. 5 Group, No. 50 Squadron and its Hampdens arrived the following month. Two and a half months after its official opening, notification was received on August 18 that the station name was to be changed to Lindholme, the reason being possible confusion with Hatfield airfield in Hertfordshire. Lindholme was a country house and hamlet on the eastern boundary of the airfield.

In August 1985 it was announced that RAF Lindholme had been sold to the Home Office to become a closed adult training prison housing prisoners in security Catagory C — those whose escape would not be a danger to the public. Even so, the authorities denied *After the Battle* access; thus a comparison photograph from the same location could not be obtained. The wartime watch office (seen on the left of this picture) was modified after the war — circa 1955. The C type hangars endure and this is the front one of the west side pair, photographed from outside the wire. *Right:* Lincolns and Lancasters at Lindholme in September 1948.

Wellingtons of No. 304 Squadron parked near the hangar line in the spring of 1942. Photographed from the top of the watch office looking north — another shot we could not match up. According to legend, Lindholme is haunted by 'Willy', believed to be a Polish airman who lost his life when his aircraft crashed into Hatfield Moor — the huge peat bog surrounding the airfield. The story goes that the Wellington (or Lancaster, depending on which version one believes) sank in the bog but surfaces every few years before sinking again. Each time the aircraft appears, so does Willy.

No. 50 was the sole resident at Lindholme until June 1941 when a new Canadian-manned bomber squadron was raised there. No. 408 Squadron was equipped with Hampdens and, once having found its feet, it was moved to Syerston to begin operations in July. The following month, Lindholme was one of a number of No. 5 Group stations handed over to No. 1 Group, as a result of which No. 5 Group moved its No. 50 Squadron to Swinderby. From Syerston, No. 1 Group moved in two of the Polish squadrons under its charge — Nos. 304 and 305 — both flying Wellingtons. These two squadrons, having been operational since April, continued their contribution to Bomber Command's offensive from the new station throughout the following winter. In May 1942, No. 304 Squadron was detached to assist Coastal Command but the detachment soon became an assignment and did not return to Bomber Command. Two months

later No. 305 was transferred to Hemswell to concentrate Polish-manned bomber squadrons on one station.

During the first two years of war, a bomb store had been constructed on the far side of the A614 as had a taxi spur with three pan hardstandings. A perimeter track and over 30 pan hardstandings had also been built during this period. By 1942 Lindholme was due for upgrading and the construction of concrete runways was put in hand. However, extension of the airfield was somewhat restricted by the Hatfield Moor Drain on the eastern boundary but more land was acquired to the north necessitating the closure of two roads, one to the hamlet of Lindholme. Because of these physical restrictions, only two runways were built, 14-32 and 05-23, both of which were extended to 1,400 and 2,000 yards respectively. A new bomb store was fashioned on land to the north of the station which resulted in obstruction of seven

pan dispersal points. Two others were lost due to the construction of a new perimeter track. Even so, the station ended up with 41 pans and one loop type. A few additional camp sites were added to the south of the main area giving the station maximum accommodation for 2,192 men and 365 females.

Re-opened for flying in late October 1942, No. 1656 Heavy Conversion Unit moved in with a few Lancasters and Manchesters from Breighton to serve No. 1 Group's conversion to the former type. Now an operational training base, over the next two years, Lindholme was host to other units with an instructional mission. Both Lancaster and Halifax crews were tutored here with No. 1667 HCU being established on the airfield here in June 1943, moving out to Faldingworth in October. In November the same year, No. 1 Lancaster Finishing School was activated using existing flights with a similar mission. On November

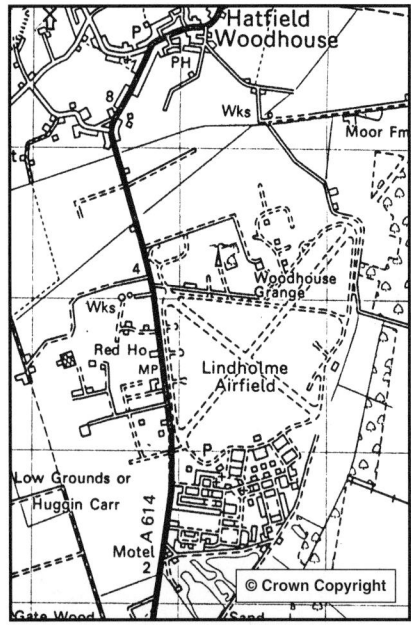

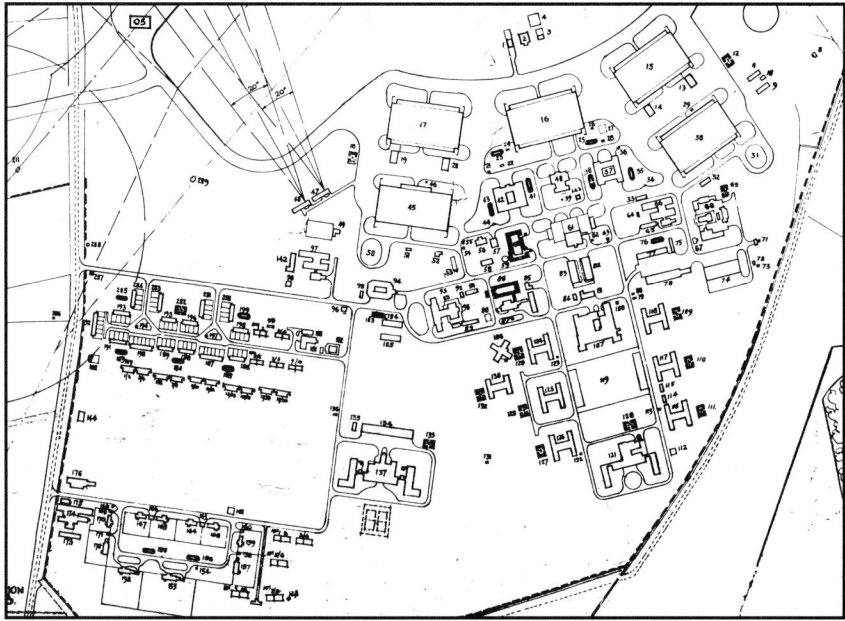

Left: On this 1986 Ordnance Survey map (1:50000 Sheet 111), the prison has not yet been built. *Right:* The layout of the technical site — compare this with the aerial views opposite to see how the prison and its facilities now occupy this corner of Lindholme.

3, 1944, the station became No. 71 Base under the new training organisation — No. 7 Group. Meanwhile, No. 1656 HCU remained at Lindholme until November 1945 when many Bomber Command units were disbanded. During the war, a total of 76 bombers were lost on operations flying from this airfield: 40 Hampdens, 35 Wellingtons and a single Lancaster.

The immediate post-war years found Nos. 57 and 100 Squadrons with their Lincolns in residence from May to September 1946. Thereafter the station went back to a training role, the longest resident being the Bomber Command Bombing School which had become the Strike Command Bombing School by the time it moved out in 1972. Hangars were used for storage by a USAF detachment during the height of the Cold War and later various RAF ground units, including Northern Radar, occupied the camp area. By 1980 Lindholme had been reduced to the status of a relief landing ground and in 1985 the whole camp was sold and turned into a prison. Much new building took place to effect the jail although most of the original permanent camp buildings still survive. The last RAF connection, an automatic routing installation, was closed in March 1996.

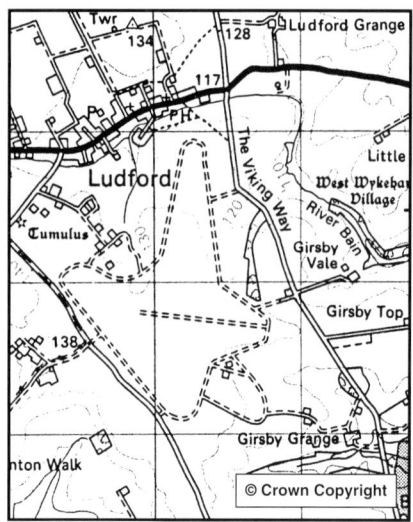

LUDFORD MAGNA

A wartime airfield built to Class A standard, Ludford Magna was commenced in June 1942 and completed early in 1943 with George Wimpey as the main contractor on a £803,000 project. Located five miles east of Market Rasen directly south of the A631 and the village for which it was named, the site took over land in two other parishes. The three concrete runways were 02-20 at 1,950 yards, 11-29 at 1,430 yards and 15-33 at 1,400 yards. The usual 36 hardstandings adjoined the perimeter track and all but one were pans. Two other pans were lost due to the erection of four T2 hangars off the southwest perimeter in the technical area. A lone T2 was located on the east side of the airfield and a B1 and T2 on the station technical site near Ludford Magna village, between the heads of runways 15 and 20. A road on the west side from the A631 to A 157 was crossed by dispersals in this area. Domestic and communal sites were dispersed in farm-

Runway and perimeter track construction was nearing completion at Ludford Magna when this vertical was taken from 14,000 feet on October 11, 1942.

Mid-upper gunner Sergeant 'Dusty' Miller and bomb aimer Flight Sergeant 'Taxi' Walters, RCAF, with their No. 101 Squadron Lanc before operations on the night of May 27/28, 1943.

W4275 SR-C flown by Pilot Officer W. Ager was shot down on the night of July 8/9, 1943 when only three survived of the seven-man crew.

Left: **Flying Officer Jefferies' Lanc ED422 SR-E2 on Ludford Magna's east dispersal area in July 1943.** *Left:* **This machine was lost in a training accident four months later with another crew.**

Right: **Only the perimeter track remains alongside the strip of woodland that backed No. 101 Squadron dispersals during the war.**

land to the north of the airfield. There were seven domestic, two mess, a communal site and sick quarters. Maximum accommodation was given as 1,953 male and 305 female.

Opened in June 1943, it was to be the home of the veteran No. 101 Squadron which had served three different groups in Bomber Command. As well as being part of the main force, the squadron was given the additional and unique role operating radio-countermeasures employing the ABC device to jam enemy transmissions. In this battle with Luftwaffe night fighter control, German-speaking operators were carried in some of its Lancasters to intrude on enemy voice transmissions. During operations from Ludford Magna, 113 Lancasters failed to return or crashed.

No. 101 Squadron was moved to the domestic comforts of nearby Binbrook in October 1945 thus ending Ludford Magna's use by flying units. The establishment was eventually returned to civil use and gradual decay. However, in 1958 it was selected as one of the sites for Thor missiles, three separate launch pads and stores being construct-ed in the centre of the airfield. No. 104 Squadron, the designated operating unit, was in residence from July 1959 to May 1963 when the unit was disbanded following the removal of the missiles. Thereafter Ludford Magna gradually returned to agricultural use, the land being sold in 1965-66. The hangars were sold and dismantled, although many buildings survive for small business use. The most poignant reminder of its existence is the memorial to No. 101 Squadron dead erected in 1978 in Ludford Magna village.

The airfield viewed from the south-east in September 2000. Prominent in the centre are the three missile launch pads constructed in the late 1950s for the American Thor. The Thor was America's first Intermediate Range Ballistic Missile (IRBM) fuelled by liquid oxygen and kerosene (paraffin). The rocket began life in 1957 with a thrust of 150,000lb and was thereafter developed as a first stage launcher in various space missions for the Delta series. By the end of 1972 more than 450 Thors had been successfully launched. The RAF formed its first Thor squadron in August 1958 and subsequently expanded its force to comprise 20 squadrons each.

The force was organised as four main launch sites each with four satellite bases utilising abandoned Second World War airfields, each with three launch pads. One squadron was at the main base (in capitals) and one at each satellite as follows: FELTWELL, Mepal, North Pickenham, Tuddenham and Shepherds Grove. HEMSWELL, Ludford Magna, Bardney, Coleby Grange and Caistor. DRIFFIELD, Carnaby, Catfoss, Breighton and Full Sutton. NORTH LUFFENHAM, Folkingham, Polebrook, Harrington and Melton Mowbray. Thors were only in place for five years, the last of the 60 missiles being withdrawn in August 1963.

NORTH KILLINGHOLME

Close by the Lincolnshire side of the Humber estuary, North Killingholme airfield was situated to the west of the village of that name on a low-lying area of farmland, and a mile from the site of the First World War seaplane base used in 1918 by the US Navy. The western boundary was the waterway known as Skitter Beck and the LNER Ulceby to Immingham line ran close to the south-east side, making it a somewhat confined site for a bomber station.

Built to Class A standard, work started in August 1942 with John Laing & Son Ltd as the main contractor with this £810,000 project. The three runways were 04-22 at 2,000 yards and 09-27 and 15-33 both at 1,400 yards. The 36 hardstandings were all loop type. A T2 hangar stood by the technical site, south of runway head 22, close to North Killingholme village. A second T2 was on the south-west side of the airfield, between runway heads 04 and 33. A B1 hangar was erected later for the Ministry of Aircraft Production contractor engineer's use.

Bomb stores were close to Skitter Beck between runway heads 15 and 09. The camp was to the east, between the village and that of Bass Garth, and consisted of single mess, communal, WAAF sites, six domestic and sick quarters, all dispersed in farmland. Accommodation availability was put at 1,939 males and 325 females.

This Lancaster of No. 550 Squadron — EE139 — which survived until the end of the war having flown 121 sorties, was aptly named *Phantom of the Ruhr*.

It is sad that such an illustrious machine with its elaborate nose artwork should be unceremoniously scrapped in February 1946. The B1 hangar on the northern side of the airfield can be seen beyond the crew.

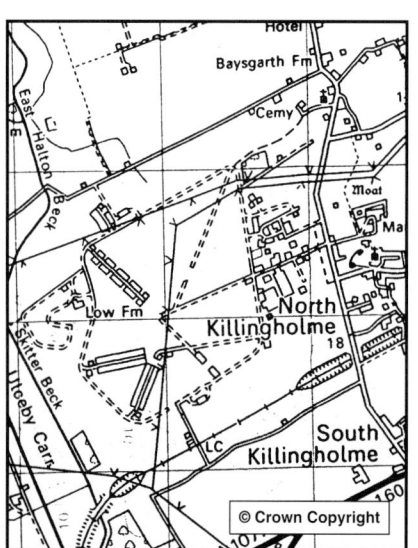

© Crown Copyright

The technical site has now found a new lease of life as a combined vehicle park and storage depot for the nearby port of Immingham. The B1 hangar still stands in the distance.

Left: Compared to the US Eighth Air Force, which was attacking European targets by day from airfields in East Anglia (see *Airfields of the Eighth Then and Now*), nose art was not a widespread feature on Bomber Command aircraft during the early years of the war. Neither was it common to name individual machines so No. 550's artistic efforts on NG287 *Try This for Size* was another nice touch. BQ-Q had completed 30 ops at the time this photo was taken and she was eventually lost on the night of March 15/16, 1945 during an attack on Misburg just east of Hannover. *Right:* The same B1 is visible beyond.

An early post-war vertical of North Killingholme airfield shows how it was penned in by water courses, rail lines and villages.

Allocated for No. 1 Group use, the airfield was occupied by No. 550 Squadron which, six weeks after its formation, transferred from Grimsby early in January 1944. No. 550 was to be the only squadron associated with North Killingholme, the station's mud and mists being its home until the squadron was disbanded at the end of October 1945. During 14 months of operations from this station, No. 550 flew some 190 raids with 58 Lancasters failing to return and another four destroyed in crashes.

No further use was made of this airfield by the RAF although it remained in a reasonably complete state for the next 30 years. The hangars and many of the buildings were taken over for light industry and storage, mostly associated with the nearby port of Immingham. Runways provide container parks and also support poultry houses.

The runways remain in a remarkably good state of repair forming ideal dispersed sites for poultry houses, spaced out to reduce the risk of disease.

SCAMPTON

Probably most well-known of all Bomber Command stations, Scampton is located partly on the site of a First World War landing ground known as Brattleby or Brattleby Cliff. Located four miles north of Lincoln, the first of several airfields built on the rise known as the Lincoln Cliff running north on the west side of the A15, the original station opened in 1916. A number of timber administration and barrack huts were erected and six large wooden hangars. Reserve squadrons were the first residents, soon joined by a flight of No. 33 Squadron's FE2bs for home defence. By the spring of 1917 Brattleby, then known as Scampton, had become a training establishment supporting No. 60 Training Squadron. No. 81 Training Squadron was formed at the station in the summer and a third training squadron, No. 11, arrived from Grantham in September. In July 1918 these squadrons were incorporated in No. 34 Training Depot Station which endured until April 1919, although its activities were severely reduced during the last four months of its existence. The landing ground was relinquished in January 1920 and within the next five years all buildings, including six hangars, were removed leaving little trace of wartime usage.

Scampton as it was during the First World War. It does not seem possible that the whole of this technical site — hangars, workshops and barrack huts — was totally swept away in the post-war rundown of the RAF. Virtually nothing was left to mark the site until work began again in 1935 to establish a new airfield beside Ermine Street, the old Roman road seen running from left to right in the background.

No. 4 hangar (nearest the camera) now approximately occupies the spot where the farm with its duckpond lay. Even on this oblique taken from the same angle in September 2000 — 80 years later — the faint trace of Pollyplatt Lane is still visible, the road itself having been incorporated within the camp. The bombing circle lay close to the end of the disused runway (01-19).

Left: **October 2, 1936. No. 9 Squadron arrive with their Handley Page Heyfords to find the aerodrome still incomplete. The Type C hangars were still being built and some accommodation was still under canvas as seen by the marquee on the right.**

Right: **Over six decades later the boarded up hangars present a sad sight. In the foreground, fenced off to deter latter-day body snatchers, lies the grave of the most famous RAF 'mascot' of all: Wing Commander Guy Gibson's black labrador, Nigger.**

With the expansion of the RAF to meet developments in Germany during the 1930s, the Air Ministry turned first to abandoned First World War landing grounds when looking to build the required new airfields. The Scampton aerodrome site proved suitable although a larger acreage was required taking in farmland to the south in the parish of Scampton, a village to the west of the B1398. Compulsorily purchased in 1935, work took the best part of two years and the RAF appeared before completion. The camp area was placed in the south-east corner and accessed from the A15 which formed the eastern border of the station. Substantial flat-roofed, brick buildings predominated and four Type C hangars were erected. The weapons stores were further north on the eastern side of the airfield.

By October 1936, No. 9 Squadron and its Heyfords and No. 214 with Virginias arrived from Northern Ireland with No. 3 Group administering the station. No. 214 converted to Harrows early in 1937 only to be transferred south to Feltwell in April. In June, 'C' Flight of No. 9 Squadron became the re-formed No. 148 Squadron, flying Audax biplanes for two months while awaiting Wellesley monoplanes. In March 1938, the recently-formed No. 5 Group was given bomber stations in Lincolnshire so Nos. 9 and 148 Squadrons moved south to No. 3 Group's new station at Stradishall. Their place was taken by Nos. 49 and 83 Squadrons, ex-Worthy Down and Turnhouse respectively. Both surrendered their Hawker Hinds for Handley Page Hampdens later in the year.

With the outbreak of war, the most frequent operational commitment of the Hampdens was minelaying approaches to the enemy's ports. The first two Bomber Command VCs went to men from the Scampton squadrons. On August 12, 1940, Flight Lieutenant Roderick Learoyd's No. 49 Squadron Hampden was badly damaged by ground fire when he pressed home a low-level attack on the Dortmund-Ems canal. The award was made for his conduct in this action and bringing the badly mauled bomber safely back to base. Sergeant John Hannah was a wireless operator/air gunner in a No. 83 Squadron Hampden which was set on fire from a direct flak hit in the bomb-bay while attacking invasion barges on September 15, 1940. Sergeant Hannah could have baled out but he stayed and fought the fire which enabled his Canadian pilot to fly the crippled machine back to Scampton. Sergeant Hannah was the youngest recipient of the VC for aerial operations during the war.

No. 49 Squadron Hampdens wait to be loaded with 250lb HE bombs in the summer of 1940. Part of the camp housing can be seen in the distance. The aircraft nearest the camera was lost on the night of August 16/17 the same year though all the crew survived to be taken prisoner. The far Hampden, P1347 EA-D made a forced landing in France on the night of September 4, 1940 but again all the crew survived as prisoners. However, the pilot Flying Officer L. M. Hodges and Sergeant J. H. Wyatt managed to escape and reach Gibraltar.

In 1990 it was announced that Scampton — the most famous of all Bomber Commands bases — was to close. A high profile 'Save our Scampton' campaign was in by the *Lincolnshire Echo* but all to no avail and the sad day came in November 1995. As it was hoped to dispose of the airfield including the hangars and non-housing buildings, the quarters seen in the background were fenced off from the airfield which was still used every flying day during the winter months for practice by the Red Arrows based at Cranwell, some 20 miles to the south, to avoid the crowded airspace over the Central Flying School.

Lancaster R5669 OL-E of No. 83 Squadron at the head of runway 01 in the summer of 1942.

In December 1941, No. 83 Squadron began to receive Avro Manchesters with No. 49 using the type the following April. This troublesome aircraft had limited operational use before it was gradually phased out (starting in May 1942) in favour of its four-engined successor, the Lancaster. No sooner had No. 83 converted to the Lancaster than it was selected as one of the squadrons for the new Pathfinder Force and departed to Wyton. Its replacement was No. 57 Squadron from Feltwell. In fact, this former No. 3 Group Wellington squadron was re-built with Lancaster crews and aircraft, becoming operational in October. Early the following month, No. 467 Squadron, an Royal Australian Air Force-manned unit, was formed at Scampton to fly Lancasters in No. 5 Group. As was current practice, once in being it was transferred to another station, in this instance Bottesford. Then in January 1943, No. 49 Squadron was moved from its home of near five years to the new Scampton satellite at Fiskerton, apparently to allow both squadrons to expand to three flights and 30 Lancasters each.

On March 15, 1943, a bomb accidentally released from a No. 57 Squadron Lancaster detonated and destroyed this and four visiting No. 50 Squadron aircraft parked nearby. Six days later No. 617 Squadron was formed at Scampton for the task of attacking Ruhr dams with the Barnes Wallis's rotating mine. The raid, carried out on the night of May 16/17, 1943, brought No. 617's leader, the legendary Wing Commander Guy Gibson, the station's third Victoria Cross.

At the end of August 1943, No. 57 Squadron moved to East Kirkby and No. 617 to Coningsby so that Scampton could be upgraded with concrete runways. In the early

Scampton as it appeared in October 1942. Pollyplatt Lane (at the bottom of the photo) still forms the southern boundary. That same month No. 57 Squadron arrived with its Lancasters to join the long-time resident No. 49.

Looking towards the same hangar line and technical area, as seen in the top photo, in the summer of 2000.

Left: Gibson's specially converted Lancaster with its Upkeep mine, launched against the Ruhr dams by No. 617 Squadron on the night of May 16/17, 1943. *Right:* **A sad end. The squadron's old hangar is now empty and boarded up awaiting disposal.**

war years, 36 asphalt hardstandings had been built round the airfield and several of these were lost when the hard runways were added. These were 05-23 at 2,000 yards, 01-19 at 1,500 yards and 11-29 at 1,400 yards. A total of 11 loop hardstandings were laid down along the perimeter track to replace those lost or isolated by the construction. New bomb stores were fashioned on land north of the north-west corner of the airfield and a T2 erected nearby. Total accommodatiuon available at Scampton at this time was given as 1,844 males and 268 females.

Work was not completed until the summer when a fighter affiliation unit, No. 1690 Flight, moved in to conduct exercises for bomber defence training. As of October 1944, Scampton passed to No. 1 Group which immediately moved in the newly re-formed No. 153 Squadron with its Lancasters. No. 1687 Bomber Defence Training Flight took up station in December 1944 to perform much the same duties for No. 1 Group as No. 1690 BDT Flt had done for No. 5 Group. At the end of March this unit moved to Hemswell and Scampton once again had two operational bomber squadrons when No. 625 arrived from Kelstern. The two Lancaster squadrons undertook their last bombing raids from Scampton on April 25, 1945 when

they mounted an attack on Hitler's mountain retreat at Obersalzberg. During the war the total losses of all squadrons operating from Scampton was 266 aircraft. Of these 155 were Hampdens, 15 Manchesters and 95 Lancasters.

In the weeks following the last bombing raid, Nos. 153 and 625 participated in food drops and the ferrying of POWs and displaced persons before both units were disbanded in the early autumn. Within a month, however, No. 57 Squadron returned and No. 100 joined it early in December. Both units were flying Lancasters but No. 57 prepared to convert to Lincolns and had just done so when both were transferred to Lindholme in May 1946. As with many other former bomber stations, Scampton then became host to training organisations, Bomber Command Instructors' School appearing in January 1947 and remaining for the next six years. From July 1947 to April the following year runway strengthening and other upgrading was carried out.

Between July 1948 and February 1949 Scampton played host to 30 B-29 Superfortresses of the 28th Bomb Group of the US Strategic Air Command, being relieved by the 301st Bomb Group with a similar strength. This was because Scampton was one

of the few stations with runways long and strong enough to sustain these large aircraft. When Strategic Air Command had no further use for Scampton, it became the home of No. 230 Operational Conversion Unit, specialising in Lincolns. In 1953 the station once again supported regular bomber squadrons, Nos. 10, 18, 21 and 27, all Canberra equipped, but by June 1955 all had been moved elsewhere so that Scampton could be redeveloped for heavy jet bomber use. The main runway was re-laid to Class 1 standard and extended to 3,000 yards necessitating a diversion of the A15. On completion of this work, No. 617 Squadron was re-formed at Scampton in May 1958 to fly Vulcans, joined in 1960 by another former resident, No. 83 Squadron, also on Vulcans. The latter squadron was disbanded in 1969. No. 230 OCU appeared again that year, its task being the preparation of Vulcan crews, and in 1973 a second regular Vulcan squadron was again added to the station complement when No. 27 was re-formed. Two years latter a third Vulcan squadron appeared-No. 35. The V-bomber force remained in being until 1982 from when Scampton again reverted to a training role, the Central Flying School taking up station in September 1984 and remaining until 1996 when the station was closed.

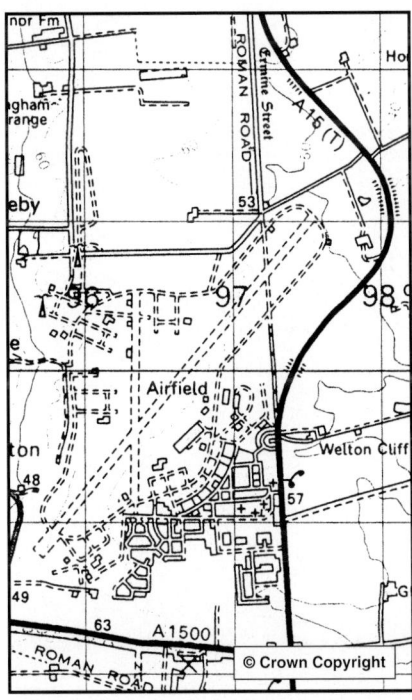

When the main runway was extended northwards, the A15 on the old Roman road had to be diverted to the east.

After having been devoid of permanent flying units for five years, in 2000 Scampton became a detached operations base under RAF Cranwell and the RAF's aerobatic display team, the Red Arrows, moved in to hangar No. 4 in December.

WICKENBY

Ten miles north-east of Lincoln, between the village of Wickenby and the north-west side of the B1399, this Class A bomber airfield was begun by McAlpine in late 1941. The site took in land in the parishes of Snelland and Holton necessitating the closure of the road between these two villages. The concrete runways were, 09-27 at 2,000 yards and 04-22 and 16-34 both at 1,400 yards long.

Thirty-six pan types hardstandings were provided with one neutralised by a T2 hangar adjacent to the technical site on the north-east side and a lone B1 at the opposite extremity of the flying field near the end of south-western runway. Domestic sites, mostly Nissen huts, were dispersed in fields on the eastern side of the B1399. Available accommodation was put at 1,788 male and 287 female. Additional construction work on the airfield was carried out by Laings in early 1943.

On completion of the main facilities, No. 12 Squadron with its Wellingtons arrived from Binbrook in September 1942 and stayed for three years. Conversion to Lancasters took place in November-December and a year later 'C' Flight was taken out to form No. 626 Squadron. However, unlike most newly-formed squadrons, No. 626 was not moved to another base, spending its whole existence at Wickenby. During hostilities, over 300 operations were flown from the airfield with 166 bombers missing, all but six

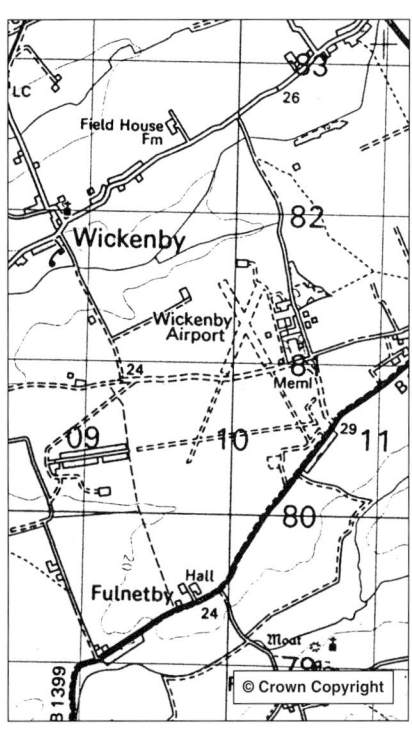

More than a thousand airmen — possibly including this unidentified crew *(top)* of 'Q'-Queenie — of No. 12 Squadron — gave their lives flying from Wickenby. Their memory is commemorated in stone by this memorial at the side of the B1399 near the end of the main runway and actively by a visitor's centre which has been established in the old control tower seen on the right.

Julia Mills and Philip Shaw have established a collection of memorabilia relating to the airfield's wartime history in the beautifully restored control tower which also serves as the clubhouse for Lincoln Aviation. *Left:* Here they stand in for two long-forgotten 'Raf' types in the same corner *(right)* of flying control.

being Lancasters. Another 30 aircraft were lost in operational crashes.

After VE-Day, No. 12 Squadron moved to Binbrook in September 1945 and No. 626 disbanded at Wickenby in October. No. 109 Squadron's Mosquitos were there for a few weeks following the departure of the Lancasters but they too were gone in late November when flying ceased. The next occupant, No. 93 Maintenance Unit, collected ordnance from other disused stations and stored it on the runways to await disposal. They remained in residence until 1952 when No. 92 MU took over, staying until 1956. During 1964-66, the airfield was cleared and the land returned, where possible, to the former civilian owners or sold. At the same time the road from Snelland to Holton-cum-Beckering, closed to construct the airfield, was reinstated. From the mid-1960s private flying took place on the northern part of the airfield at what is now Wickenby Airport. Several wartime buildings survive in good condition including a T2 hangar.

Looking west from the tower, the skyline is little changed from the day in 1943 when the famous photograph *(overleaf)* was taken of Wickenby's personnel with their machines drawn up for a publicity shot to depict the might of Bomber Command.

The set-up for the press photographers involved 21 Lancasters from Nos. 12 and 626 Squadrons and 16 crews. The date was January 20, 1944 and that night most of these men and aircraft took part in a raid on Berlin.

In October 1948, when this vertical was taken from 16,600 feet, Wickenby's runways were lined with cylindrical blast bombs of 4,000lb and larger, neatly spaced for safety. These had been removed from the bomb dumps at other surplus airfields.

From Wickenby then . . . to Wickenby now . . . and the end of our survey of No. 1 Group airfields.

You may remember in the film Target for Tonight *a young airman goes around telling the crews where he thinks they're going. When asked how he could possibly know, he says, 'I get around. I get the 'Gen'. Two days before we attacked the power-house near Cologne, everybody on our station was getting around, getting the 'Gen'. We knew there was something big in the air, but no one was quite certain what it was. In fact, no one had the faintest idea.*

We were keyed up when we went into the briefing-room at 6.45 on the morning of the raid, and the Station Commander's opening remarks did nothing to lessen the tension. He started off by saying, 'You are going on the biggest and most ambitious operation ever undertaken by the RAF.' Then he told us what it was. Cologne, in daylight. One hundred and fifty odd miles across Germany at tree-top height and then — the power-house. We were given the course to follow, the rendezvous with other squadrons of bombers, and the rendezvous with fighters. We were given the parting point for the fighters and the moment at which certain flights would peel off the formation for the attack on the second power-house, and then — in formation across Germany. Our orders were to destroy our objectives at all costs.

Over Holland we saw fields planted out in the pattern of the Dutch flag. People everywhere waved us on, there was a remarkable amount of red, white and blue washing about the place. I saw one Storm Trooper standing over a group of workers, and when he saw us he ran like a weazel. Near the frontier they did not wave they just watched us. In Germany itself men scuttled off for shelters. During the whole of our trip we saw no motor transport of any kind.

I was sitting in the rear turret and I didn't know we were over the target until I saw the power-house chimneys above me — four on one side, eight on the other. Then the observer called out, 'Bombs gone,' and as I felt the doors swinging to, the pilot yelled, 'Machine gun!' I burst in all I could as we turned away to starboard. Three miles off I had a good view of the place. We had used delayed action bombs, and banks of black smoke and scalding steam were gushing out. Debris was rocketing into the air, and I thought of those turbine blades ricocheting around the building.

On the way back we kept sufficiently good formation to worry attacking Me 109's. The first I knew of them was the leading air gunner calling out: 'Tally-ho! Tally-ho! Snappers to port beam.

'Six squadrons of Blenheims of Bomber Command penetrated into the Rhineland this morning to attack the great Cologne power stations at Quadrath and Knapsack. Fighters accompanied the bombers as far as Antwerp. The bombers went on alone, often flying at less than 100 feet, on their 150 miles penetration of the German defence system. Both power stations were attacked at 11.30 a.m. at point-blank range. A great number of bombs scored direct hits and the targets were left in flames.' Air Ministry Communiqué, August 12, 1941.**

While pilots an observers were getting all they could from the weather man, we rear gunners gathered round the signals officer for identification signs and then hurried out to get ready. Someone said, 'What a trip' and got the answer, 'Yes, but what a target!'

Knapsack, we were told, was the biggest steam power plant in Europe, producing hundreds of thousands of kilowatts to supply a vital industrial area. If we got it, it would be as good as getting hold of a dozen large factories.

One of the pilots on the raid was in civil life a mains engineer for the County of London Electricity Supply. He came away rubbing his hands and explained to us that, with turbines setting up about 3,000 revolutions a minute, blades were likely to fly off in all directions at astronomical speeds, smashing everything and everyone as they went.

We crossed a fairly choppy sea to the mouth of the Scheldt, flying in probably the biggest formation of bombers ever to deliver a low-level attack. It was grand to see them. Even while we were attacking we knew that other bombers and squadrons of fighters were penetrating deep into the Pas de Calais.

Up five hundred.' The attack went on for eight minutes until they broke off and another formation of twelve enemy snappers came into action. They left us when they saw our own chaps coming out to meet us.

Some odd things happened on this raid. One draughty hole in a front perspex was stopped by the gallant observer sticking his seat in it to keep out the gale. Over Holland we flew into hosts of seagulls, and some aircraft brought back specimens stuck in their engine cowling, so giving rise to the suggested Dutch communiqué, 'And from these operations five of our seagulls failed to return.' Twelve ducks also failed to return; one of our aircraft came back with them inside it, all of them dead. But I should think the oddest things of all must have happened inside that power-house at Knapsack.

When we got back we astonished a few people on our station when we told them where we had been. Sometimes we get around too. We also get the 'Gen', and we certainly got the target.

ANONYMOUS, BBC BROADCAST

Introducing No. 2 Group with a spectacular low-level attacks by 54 Blenheims of Nos. 18, 21, 82, 114, 139 and 226 Squadrons.

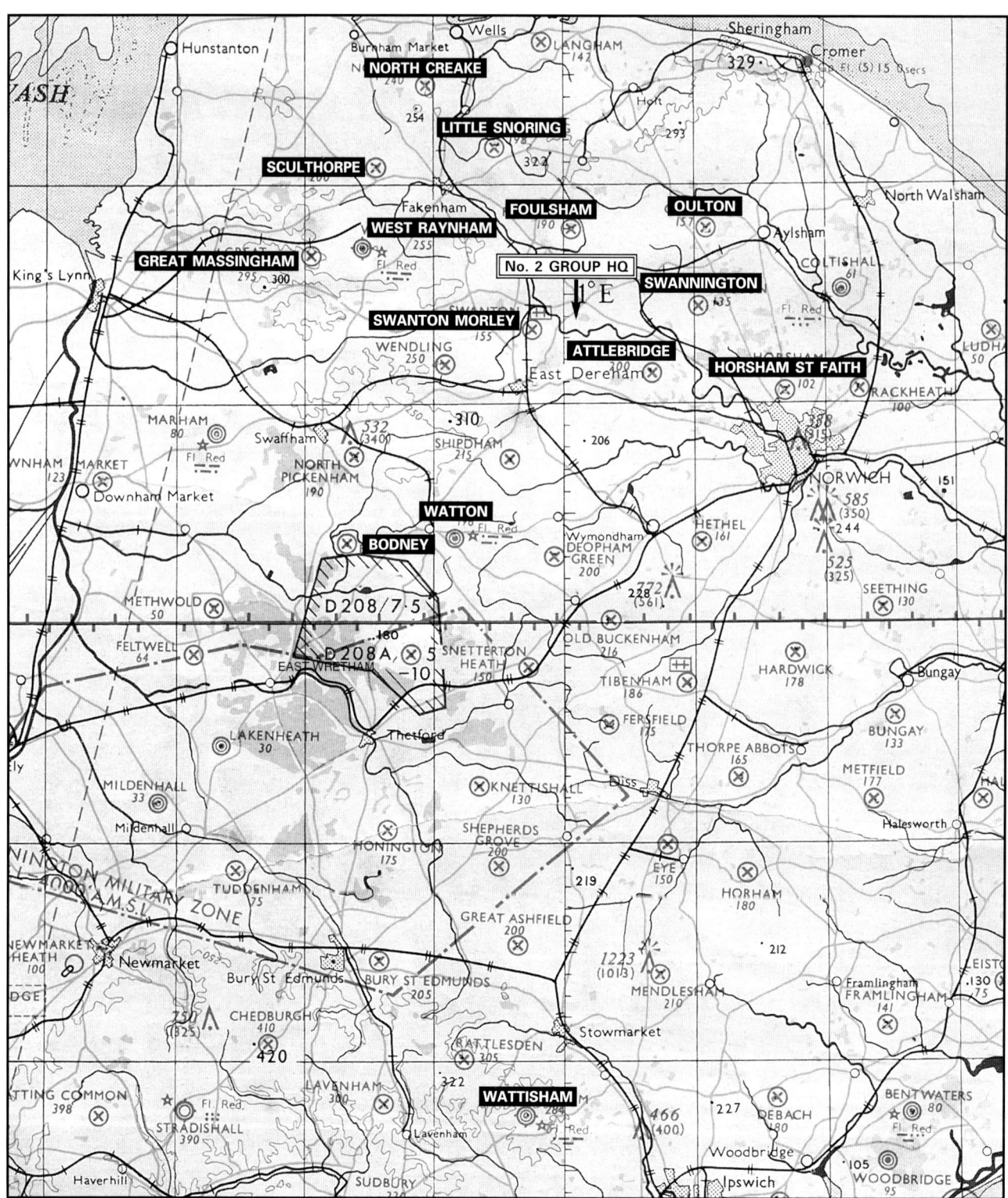

No. 2 GROUP & No. 100 GROUP HQ

Formed on March 20 1936, No. 2 Group HQ was based at Abingdon until the following January when it was moved to Andover. In May 1938 the headquarters moved again, this time to Wyton where it remained until shortly after the outbreak of war. Like No. 1 Group, No. 2 was allocated mostly light bomber squadrons equipped with Hinds, eventually being chosen to be an all-Blenheim group. At the outbreak of war, the group had seven squadrons at four stations with 80 aircraft.

In October 1939 headquarters moved from its airfield location at Wyton to a large house in nearby Huntingdon where it remained until May 1943, despite its operational airfields eventually all being located in north Norfolk.

When a move to a more central location was made — to Bylaugh Hall near East Dereham — the group and its squadrons were scheduled for transfer from Bomber Command to the Second Tactical Air Force, which was to be the RAF's commitment to the forthcoming cross-Channel invasion of the Continent. At the date of the transfer, No. 2 Group had 10 squadrons, two with Mosquitos, two with Bostons, three with Mitchells and three with Venturas. Aircraft total was 190 deployed on seven airfields.

No. 100 Group was a specialist organisation formed on November 11, 1943 to counter enemy defences against Bomber Command operations. When No. 2 Group moved its headquarters south to Mongewell Park House in Berkshire in January 1944, No. 100 Group HQ took over Bylaugh Hall. As No. 2 Group squadrons vacated airfields in north Norfolk these also came under No. 100 Group control as did several newly-built airfields in the area. Eventually the group controlled eight airfields with 260 aircraft, 140 of which were various marks of Mosquito night fighter intruders and the remainder 80 Halifaxes, 20 Fortresses and 20 Liberators carrying electronic jamming equipment.

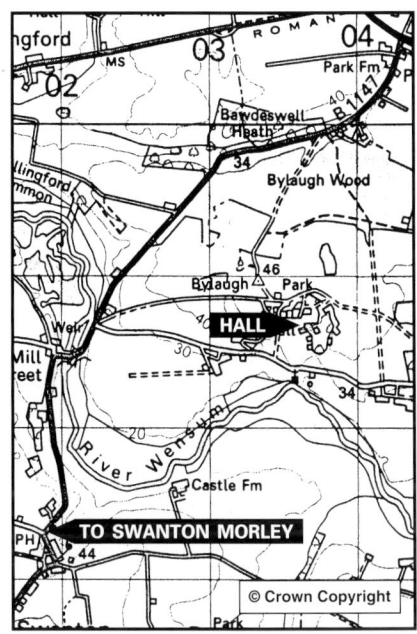

This was not really a No. 2 Group head-quarters while with RAF Bomber Command, only when it was transferred to the Second Tactical Air Force. Stately homes were often a financial burden for their owners during the first half of the 20th century and the Second World War found many providing a new lease of life as headquarters for the military. Bylaugh Hall, under a mile east of RAF Swanton Morley, became the headquarters for No. 2 Group from late May to December 1943 when it was then taken over by No. 100 Group which inherited most of No. 2's stations. Relinquished by the Air Ministry soon after the war, it fell in disrepair and was partly demolished. Several temporary buildings erected to provide additional working space for the staff during the war still survive, albeit with nature reinstating itself by smothering most with vegetation. The hall itself remains a shell and the locals imply that it is not a safe place to in be after dark!

ATTLEBRIDGE

About to touch down on runway 22, a Blenheim IV of No. 105 Squadron returns to Attlebridge, July 1941. The photograph was taken looking south near the junction of runways 04-22 and 09-27, the latter appearing to have been still under construction.

In furtherance of the programme of providing each principal operational station with a satellite, early in 1941 a pasture at Hungate Common, just south of the village of Weston Longville, was requisitioned for use as an airfield to serve Swanton Morley. At first exceedingly rudimentary with a few huts and farm buildings as cover, it was then developed as a full-size airfield with hard runways laid during the spring of that year. The lengths were 09-27 at 1,220 yards, 14-32 at 1,120 yards and 04-22 at 1,080 yards. Thirty-six pan-type hardstandings were placed on access lanes off the perimeter track. In June 1941 the airfield was used to disperse Blenheims of No. 105 Squadron, the crews returning to quarters at Swanton Morley or requisitioned local accommodation. Facilities were hastily developed and in August No. 88 Squadron moved in from Swanton Morley to become the first full tenants. In October the squadron exchanged its Blenheims for Bostons, the first bomber squadron to do so. Anti-shipping strikes were the predominant role for much of the time No. 88 was resident.

Early in 1942, Attlebridge was earmarked for development as a bomber base for the US Eighth Air Force with the necessary upgrading to Class A status. In the late summer of 1942, a sudden requirement for airfields to hold American units destined for Operation 'Torch', the Allies invasion of North Africa, caused No. 88 Squadron to be transferred to Oulton at the end of September so that Attlebridge could take two squadrons of B-26 Marauders fresh from the USA. These were part of the 319th Bomb Group, the first Marauder-equipped group to come to Britain and not without much misfortune during the passage via Greenland and Iceland.

In November the Marauders left to fly on to North Africa whereupon Costain began work to enlarge the airfield and lengthen the runways, 09-27 being extended to 2,000 yards, and both 04-22 and 14-32 to 1,400 yards. This work was completed by March 1943. Thirty-four loop hardstandings were added during the course of this construction, 12 of the existing pans being lost or neutralised. Additional stretches of taxiway also

had to be provided and two T2 hangars were erected, one on the main south technical site, the other being located on the north side of the airfield. Accommodation for 2,894 personnel was provided on eight dispersed domestic sites to the south.

Although it took until October 1943 to complete all the additional building work, from March 1943 No. 2 Group loaned the airfield, moving in No. 320 Squadron, a Dutch-manned unit that was giving up Hudsons and its Coastal Command assignment in order to fly Mitchells.

With the restricted use of Attlebridge due to the reconstruction, it was not until August that No. 320 undertook its first bombing operation by which time No. 2 Group had left Bomber Command and been placed under the Second Tactical Air Force. In early September the Dutchmen took their Mitchells to Lasham and at the end of the year the airfield was returned to the USAAF. While No. 2 Group was under Bomber Command, six Blenheims and six Bostons were lost during operations flown from Attlebridge.

Most of the runways survive at Attlebridge thanks to their use as ideal foundations for Bernard Matthews' turkey sheds.

Boston III, RH-J of No. 88 Squadron, basks in the spring sunshine as two members of the ground staff seek shade from a substantial oak. The aircraft has 22 raid symbols on the side of the nose.

The oak endures but the hardstanding has given way to wild vegetation. The location is the east side of the airfield with the site of the bomb store beyond. Access to the airfield is restricted due to bio-security regulations.

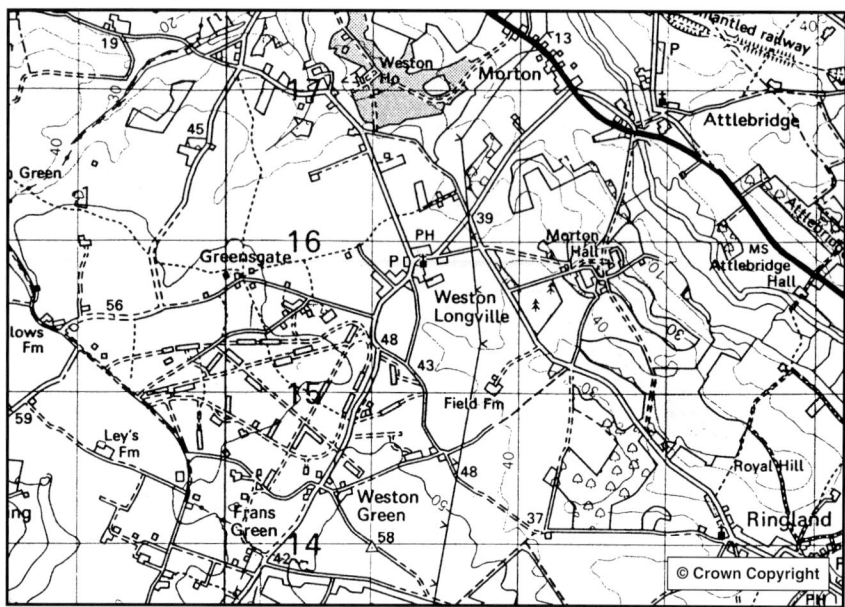

During the winter of 1943-44, the Eighth Air Force temporarily had a surplus of airfields as several units to be assigned were still completing training in the USA. Thus it was early March 1944 before the 466th Bomb Group and its four squadrons arrived at Attlebridge with 64 B-24 Liberators. The group started operations on the 22nd of that month with a mission to Berlin and flew another 260 missions before its last on April 25, 1945. The Americans had left by early July and on the 15th the airfield reverted to RAF administration. No further flying units operated from Attlebridge and in 1959 the airfield was sold. The runways were retained to support what was called 'the largest turkey farm in the world', the poultry sheds thereon being afforded a high degree of isolation for these birds are highly susceptible to disease. At one time more than 300,000 turkeys were held on this site. The Bernard Matthews company also built modern factory buildings there for processing and took over the control tower for use as offices.

Above: **Attlebridge in April 1946;** *right* **in September 2000.**

BODNEY

Above: Grass-surfaced Bodney with the outline of the three runways faintly visible on this vertical taken in July 1946. Below: The tree-lines which now cross the site are not indicative of the line of the runways — see plan opposite.

ROSE COTTAGE

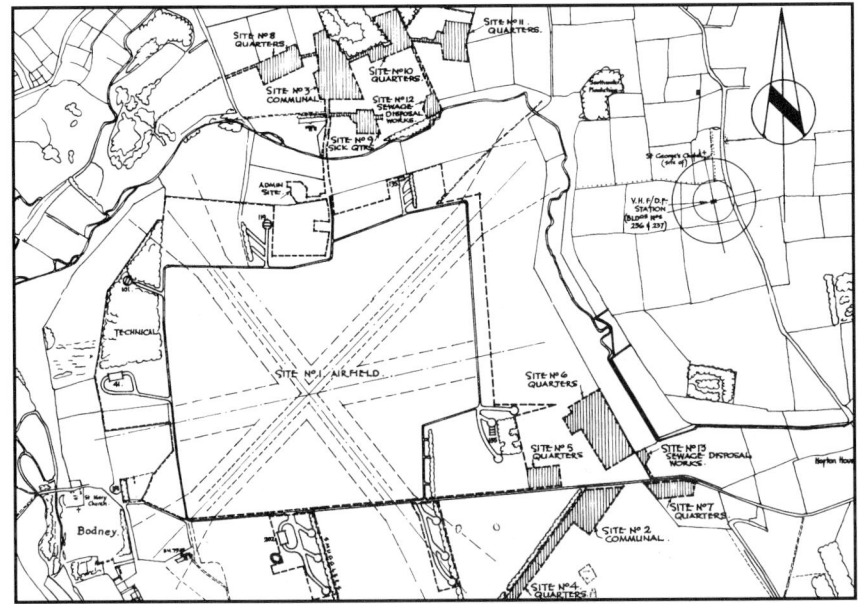

Wissey. The camp was in two areas: to the south-east where one communal and four domestic sites were dispersed, and to the north along the road to Little Cressingham where there were three domestic, a communal site and sick quarters. Total accommodation allowed for 1,709 persons.

The reason for the move of the Venturas was Bodney's allocation to the USAAF for development into a Class A standard bomber station. Meanwhile the airfield was used as a relief landing ground for training aircraft from Watton until the unit involved moved out in May 1943. However, the airfield was not developed as a bomber station and in June it was allocated to the USAAF as a fighter base. Occupied in July by the three squadrons of the 352nd Fighter Group, initially flying P-47s, converting to P-51s in April 1944, the group remained at Bodney until the autumn of 1945. After the base was officially returned to the RAF on November 8 that year, the airfield was closed to flying and following some government use of the domestic sites these were gradually demolished. In later years the site was absorbed into the nearby Stanford battle training area for use by the army.

The desirability of establishing satellite airfields for bomber stations led to the investigation of many possible sites in the winter of 1939-40. For Watton, an open stretch of Breckland seven miles south-west from that station was acquired. Some woodland had to be removed and Bodney came into use during the spring of 1940 as a dispersal for Blenheims of Nos. 21 and 82 Squadrons from their parent station. A number of huts were erected on the northern side of the airfield for administration and technical services and some local housing was requisitioned for barrack use. The first operation flown from the airfield appears to have taken place on May 14, 1940 when No. 21 Squadron flew to attack enemy forces in the Ardennes. Two Blenheims were lost while another was so badly shot up that it crashed on return to Bodney. Later in the year both Watton squadrons alternated between parent and satellite for periods of several weeks.

Throughout 1941, Bodney continued to be used by Watton's units but in early March the following year No. 21 Squadron was reformed at the station. The squadron had been sent to Malta and disbanded there, its revival finding it flying Bodney Blenheims again prior to receiving the first Venturas with which it was proposed to equip three squadrons in No. 2 Group for daylight operations. During operations from Bodney between May 1940 and March 1942, 34 Blenheims were missing in action, 27 of which came from No. 82 Squadron. Additionally, 10 Blenheims were lost in operational crashes.

The first deliveries of Venturas were made at the end of May but No. 21 never took them into battle before being moved to Methwold in September. During this period of RAF occupation the airfield was gradually improved. Five blister hangars were erected followed by two T2s, one on the technical site in a wood on the west side and the other on a dispersal spur on southern side. Aircraft dispersals were 15 large pans and squares grouped in threes, eight small pans and four blind strips, all asphalt, placed round the airfield, some on long access lanes. The grass surface runways were NE-SW 1,000 yards long, NW-SE and E-W, both 900 yards long. Bomb stores were located three quarters of a mile south of the airfield by the River

The land around Rose Cottage was developed as the technical site but the building fell into disrepair and was eventually demolished. Dense woodland now covers the area and only the foundations of the cottage can be traced.

When Bodney was first taken for use as the Watton satellite, a requisitioned house served as a temporary HQ. Known as Rose Cottage, it is seen in this snap of Corporals Claude Rennie and Eddie Bolton, Aircraftmen McCann and 'Det' Terry taking a break.

FOULSHAM

Mitchells of No. 180 Squadron lined up for review on the end of the main runway for a press review on July 28, 1943. Mitchell FL684 (EV-S) in the foreground had a charmed life and survived hostilities.

Work commenced in 1941 on this airfield, situated 15 miles north-west of Norwich in the parishes of Wood Norton and Foulsham, and a half mile north of the latter village. Laid out with three concrete runways, 01-19 of 1,900 yards, 08-26 of 1,400 yards and 15-33 of 1,350 yards, it had 37 hardstandings of the pan type spaced along an encircling perimeter track. The main technical area, between runway heads 26 and 33 on the east side of the airfield, eventually had seven hangars, all T2s except the most northerly which was a B1. There was another T2 on the south-west side, between runways 01 and 15 near Wades Farm, and two more T2s on the south-east corner between 01 and 33 by Mill-hill Farm. Five of the nine hangars were built during 1943-44 for use by No. 12 Maintenance Unit for assembling and storing Horsa gliders, a surprising use for a planned operational bomber station. Domestic sites, for 2,135 males and 355 females were dispersed in farmland south of the Skitfield road to the east of the airfield, and the bomb stores were off the south-west side. Kirk & Kirk Ltd are believed to have been responsible for erection of many of the buildings.

Construction work was fairly complete by the late summer of 1942. In October, Foulsham became the operational base of the

first two RAF squadrons equipped with the North American Mitchell, Nos. 98 and 180. No. 98 had a previous existence in the First World War but No. 180 was a new birth when both units were given substance at West Raynham a few weeks before the move into Foulsham. It took three months to work up on these aircraft and the first operation from Foulsham — an attack on an oil storage plant in Belgium — conducted on January 22, 1943, met stiff opposition from ground fire and fighters. Of the 12 aircraft involved, three were missing, including that of the CO of No. 180 Squadron. This operation had been conducted at low-level, a form of attack that changed to bombing from medium altitudes at an optimum 10,000 feet. With No. 2 Group's transfer to the Second Tactical Air Force on June 1, 1943, the Mitchell's days at Foulsham were numbered and in mid-August they moved south to Dunsfold. The station then came under No. 3 Group administration. During service with Bomber Command, ten Mitchells from Foulsham were lost during operations.

Foulsham was then used during No. 3 Group's switch from Stirlings to Lancasters. In September, No. 514 Squadron formed at the station and No. 1678 Heavy Conversion Flight arrived to supply crews. The squadron

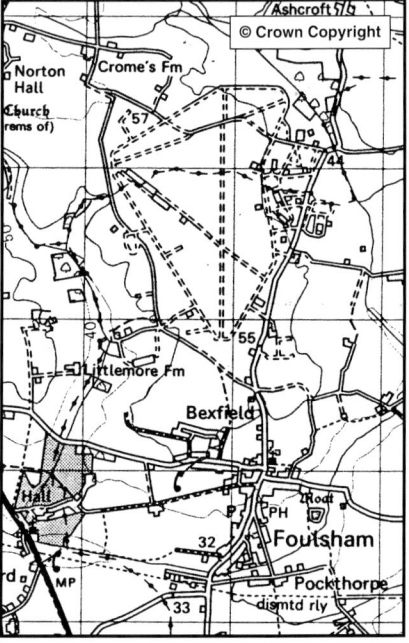

The same runway, now reduced to a single vehicle width strip of concrete.

The Mitchells moved out of Foulsham in August 1943, this vertical being taken that December by the US 7th Photo Group.

became active on the night of November 3, 1943, but flew only six raids before the Lancasters moved to Waterbeach later the same month. The reason was the formation of No. 100 Group and its deployment in the area once the domain of No. 2 Group. The electronic surveillance unit, No. 192 Squadron, then moved in from Feltwell with a mixture of Wellingtons, Mosquitos and the odd Halifax. The squadron plus a specialist flight were the only tenants at Foulsham until December 1944 when No. 462 Squadron with Halifaxes was moved from No. 4 to No. 100 Group to increase its capability.

In 1944 Foulsham was selected to have the FIDO fog-dispersal system installed on its main runway, the only airfield in Norfolk county so endowed. This resulted in many visitors from other stations arriving during periods of fog or poor visibility.

A total of 45 Bomber Command aircraft failed to return or were lost in crashes during operations flown from Foulsham; ten being Mitchells, two Wellingtons, 26 Halifaxes, five Mosquitos and two Lancasters. Nos. 192 and 462 Squadrons were disbanded at the station in August and September 1945 respectively. At first, the airfield was retained on a care and maintenance basis and after the RAF personnel were withdrawn it was kept intact on reserve status. During the early 'fifties it was used by USAF ground units and it was not disposed of until the 1980s at which time it was still reasonably intact. One of the T2 hangars has been used to hold bulk grain for an agricultural merchant; another is used by the Department of the Environment to store equipment and yet another by a warehousing company. The control tower has been demolished but portions of the taxiway are used by light aircraft.

Fifty-seven years later, Karel Margry pictured the airfield looking eastwards towards the technical site.

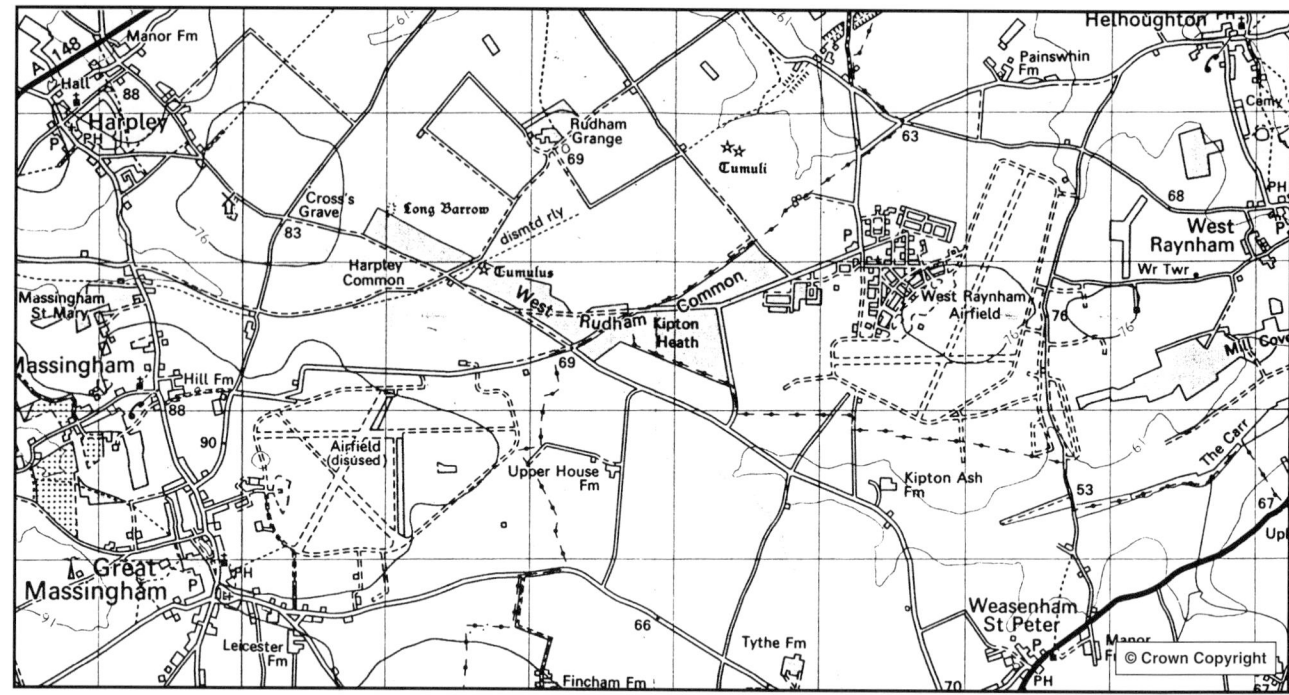

GREAT MASSINGHAM

Only two miles separated West Raynham from the farmland taken in 1940 for its satellite aerodrome. The site directly adjacent to Great Massingham village was first used to disperse West Raynham's Blenheims but when sufficient facilities were constructed and requisitioned to maintain a squadron, No. 18 transferred from the parent station in September having sustained appalling attrition during the Battle of France. The squadron stayed until mid-April the following year when it was moved a few miles to Oulton, another satellite airfield.

A month later No. 107 Squadron, another Blenheim unit, was posted to Great Massingham from Scotland where it had been loaned to Coastal Command, and a few days after that the Fortress Is of No. 90 Squadron arrived. It was thought that Great Massingham offered more space for these then-giant aircraft but it was obvious that the type was better suited to operating from hard runways and the few Fortresses available were soon moved over to Polebrook. No. 107 remained until mid-August 1943, longest resident squadron at this station, although in the late summer of 1941 the aircraft were flown off to Malta and the detachment disbanded.

Back at Great Massingham, the squadron was re-built this time to fly the Douglas Boston the first example arriving soon after New Year's Day 1942. No. 107's Bostons went into action on March 8, 1942 with a medium altitude attack on Abbeville rail yards. Raids at both medium and low-level were carried out during the ensuing months from Great Massingham, the former eventually being the norm. However, by the time No. 2 Group was transferred to the Second Tactical Air Force, No. 107 had suffered the highest loss rate of all its squadrons although it is said to have flown the highest number of sorties. In operations from Massingham, 11 Blenheims and 26 Bostons were lost in some one hundred raids. In July 1943, shortly before No. 2 Group vacated the airfield, No. 342 Squadron, a French-manned Boston

The Press Day for the Bostons of No. 107 Squadron, believed to have been held on April 9, 1942. At this time the airfield was still grass surfaced. The trees of West Rudham Common appear on the horizon and conceal the hangars of West Raynham which, as the Ordnance Survey plan shows, were only two and a half miles distant.

A vertical by an F-5 Lightning of the 7th Photo Group on March 28, 1944 shows the work to provide hard runways nearing completion. The additional T2 hangars were erected to store Horsa gliders, a dozen of which can be seen parked outside.

unit, was moved in from Sculthorpe although it remained only a few weeks before moving to Hartford Bridge to where No. 107 had preceded them.

Soon after, the station was relinquished by No. 2 Group for the Unit Construction Company Ltd to lay hard runways. In doing this the area of the airfield was extended to the west so that the distance from West Raynham was reduced to 1½ miles resulting in an overlap when aircraft were circling to land. The runways were the main 10-28 at 2,000 yards and the 04-22 and 15-33, both 1,400 yards. Only 16 of the existing pan hardstandings remained after the runway and perimeter track building programme, so 20 loop types were added to make the number up to 36. Four T2 hangars had been erected in previous years, two on the east side of the airfield north of the village and two on the north-east side between runway heads 22 and 28. A single B1 hangar was located south-east between runway heads 28 and 33. Bomb stores were to the north between runway heads 15 and 22. The camp, north-west of the village, eventually consisted of dispersed sites, two communal. two WAAF, five domestic and sick quarters. Accommodation catered for 1,778 males and 431 females.

At the beginning of the 21st century, wheat clothes the former flying field in our comparison, now taken at ground level due to the absence of the control tower. West Rudham Common is even more wooded and only the skyline to the north remains much the same as in 1942. The grove prominent in the wartime photograph was removed when runways were laid.

The station was re-opened in late April 1944 under No. 100 Group, the first operational squadron to be based at the rejuvenated airfield being No. 169, equipped with Mosquitos from Little Snoring. Also present was No.1692 Flight, a bomber support training unit with Beaufighters and Mosquitos. No. 169's main effort was night Ranger and later Serrate sorties to seek out any night fighters operating against Bomber Command main force operations. The last sorties from Great Massingham were flown on the night of May 2, 1945. During hostilities a total of 52 Bomber Command aircraft were lost in operations from station: 11 Blenheims, 28 Bostons and 13 Mosquitos.

No. 1692 Flight was disbanded in June 1945 and No. 169 Squadron two months later.

In August 1945 Great Massingham came under the auspices of Fighter Command but its proximity to West Raynham seems to have precluded further use as a base for flying units, although the station was retained as satellite. The hangars were used for storage for some years but in the late 1950s the whole station was sold.

Great Massingham's basic outline remains remarkably intact save for a short section of perimeter track which has been lifted on the north-eastern corner.

HORSHAM ST FAITH

In 1938, an area of farmland to the east of the A140, between the villages of Horsham St Faith in the north and Catton in the south, was selected for building a permanent RAF station. Being only two miles from the centre of Norwich this development was not welcomed by many in the city. Before work began the main A140 road from Norwich to Aylsham was diverted to the west. Construction began in earnest in 1939, the camp being at the Catton end with the usual flat-roofed brick buildings for administration and barrack purposes. Three of the later Type C hangars fronted the bombing circle with a fourth and fifth backing the two end hangars. The area of the flying field was approximately 1,700 yards by 1,500 yards and this was available for use late in 1939 and used for dispersal of aircraft from other stations. The station officially opened on June 1, 1940 although the buildings were not completed until the late summer.

Following severe losses during the Battle of France, Nos. 114 and 139 Squadrons received new crews and Blenheim IVs at Horsham St Faith in June and July 1940. When deemed ready for operations again, No. 114 Squadron moved to Horsham's satellite field at Oulton while No. 139 stayed at the main base until July the following year and then moved to the satellite, changing places with No. 18 Squadron which had replaced No. 114 when this unit went to

Three Blenheims of No. 139 Squadron make a low pass over the north-west side of the airfield. In the foreground is the roadside hedge of the A140 which was crossed by a number of tracks to aircraft dispersals. The main highway from Norwich to Cromer, it was eventually closed and a new section put down circumnavigating the airfield to Horsham St Faith village. The eastern Type C hangars can be seen in the distance below the high tree line of the horizon. No. 139 did not go operational with the Blenheim V, instead becoming the second squadron to receive the Mosquito IV.

The hangars still stand with several new buildings of busy Norwich Airport. A view from the ramp in front of Sterling Helicopters premises that are located on the north-west side of the airfield.

Coastal Command in Scotland. In September that year, No. 139 Squadron moved back to Horsham for two months before again moving to Oulton. No. 18 Squadron also returned to Oulton in November 1941, this toing and froing being deemed necessary to ensure the mobility of operational squadrons. During 1940-41 at least 24 pan-shaped hardstandings were put down, some with long access tracks.

Horsham St Faith was then chosen as the

station at which the first two de Havilland Mosquito-equipped light bomber squadrons were to be formed. The first, No. 105, shed its Blenheims at Swanton Morley before arriving at Horsham early in December 1941. The supply of Mosquitos was agonisingly slow and, when No. 139 Squadron was reformed in June 1942, its crews had to use No. 105's aircraft on operations. Before both squadrons were transferred to Marham in

From aerodrome . . . to airfield . . . to airport! Norwich began life as a grass-surfaced flying field, seen here in August 1941.

When Horsham St Faith was assigned to the US Eighth Air Force in 1942, plans were made to upgrade the airfield with hard runways for heavy bomber use. The early beginnings of that work can be seen in this shot which, although undated, must have been taken around August 1943. By comparing with the picture below taken in 1946, one can see that the strip running east-west across the grass, is the first beginnings of the 10-28 runway.

September, a few Blenheims were acquired for training. The Mosquito attrition was high, 18 failing to return from 52 raids between May 31 and September 25 while at Horsham. All told, 51 aircraft failed to return or were destroyed in crashes during Bomber Command operations from the station (32 Blenheims and 19 Mosquitos).

Horsham St Faith had been earmarked for use by the US Eighth Air Force and scheduled for upgrading to Class A standard bomber station. In October 1942, the 319th Bomb Group, arrived with B-26 Marauders, having been assigned to the newly-activated Twelfth Air Force destined for Operation 'Torch' and North Africa. While the 319th

BG Headquarters remained at Horsham, the B-26s were mostly based at Attlebridge where the hard runways were safer for operating this bomber with its high wing loading which necessitated long take-off and landing runs. The Marauders and 319th personnel were gone by December and the airfield was little used until April 1943 when the P-47s of

All runway designations — then as now — are based on magnetic bearings to the nearest 10 degrees but abbreviated by omitting the third figure. Nominally, to land on runway 28 for example, the main at Horsham St Faith, the designation would indicate that the aircraft should fly on a heading of 280 degrees magnetic to line up with the correct runway, but in practice the bearing can be up to 10 degrees out. This is because any bearing between 275 degrees and 284 degrees will be expressed as '28', either rounding up or down as appropriate. Runway headings decrease in true terms as magnetic north slowly changes. For example, the wartime 05-23 runway has now become runway 04-22. The variation changes in different parts of the country, magnetic north being 10 degrees west of true north in 1944, whereas today it is nearer 5 degrees west. Also note that the north arrows added by us to the vertical photographs indicate *grid north* to assist readers in aligning them with the extracts from the Ordnance Survey maps. Grid north varies from magnetic north with true north lying somewhere in between!

the 56th Fighter Group arrived. By July, contractors were ready to develop the station into the planned bomber airfield whereupon the 56th FG moved out to Halesworth. The three new intersecting runways constructed were 05-23 at 2,000 yards, 10-28 at 1,400 yards, and 17-35 at 1,400 yards. Fifty loop hardstandings were provided, several of the existing hard pans being destroyed in the process. Two new domestic sites with Nissen buildings were built in Catton and the total accommodation at the station raised to 2,972 persons.

The 458th Bomb Group with its four B-24 Liberator-equipped squadrons were based on the rebuilt airfield from March 1944 to July 1945, operating as part of the US Eighth Air Force's 2nd Air Division. Returned to the RAF on July 15, 1945, Horsham came under Fighter Command control first with Mosquitos, then Hornets, Meteors and Hunters before the RAF finally quit the station in 1960. The airfield then came into use for private flying and commercial operations, eventually being established as Norwich Airport.

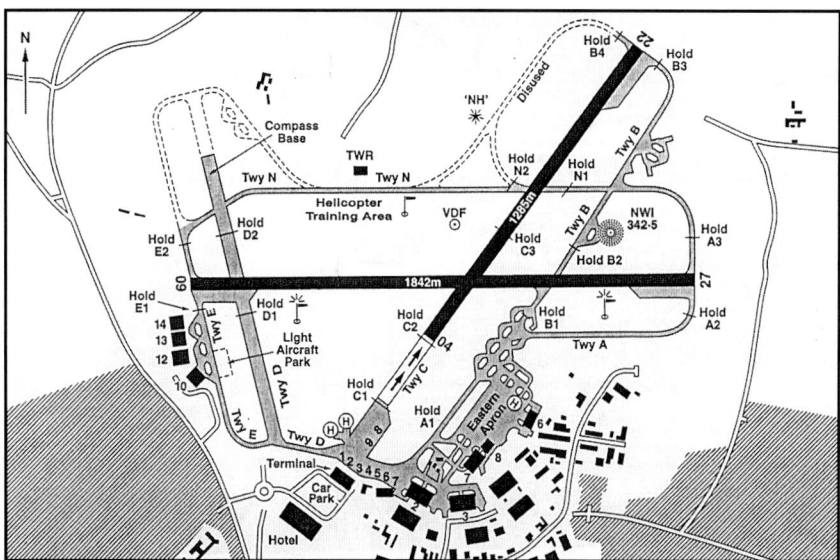

As this plan from the 2000 edition of *Pooleys Flight Guide* shows, the wartime 17-35 runway is no longer in use. *Right:* Lined up on runway 22 at Norwich Airport in August 2001 — a photo by Sterling Helicopters Ltd.

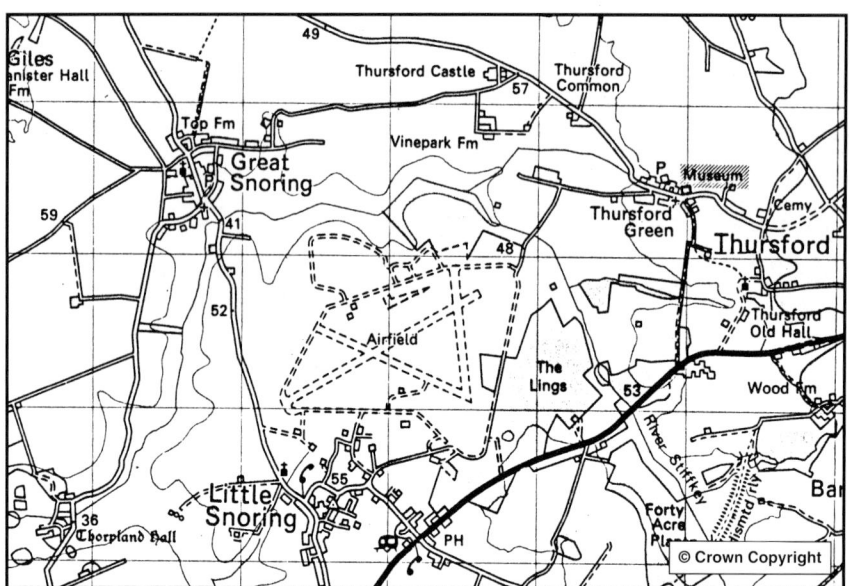
© Crown Copyright

LITTLE SNORING

Located north of the A148 and east of the Little to Great Snoring road, this airfield was begun by Taylor Woodrow in September 1942, being built in the No. 2 Group area to Class A standard. The three runways were 01-19 at 1,400 yards, 07-25 at 2,000 yards and 13-31 at 1,400 yards. All 36 hardstandings were loop-type and, owing to the gradients of adjacent land, several of these were on a loop taxiway off the north side of the perimeter track. It was necessary to close a road from Thursford to Little Snoring when construction began as this crossed the site. Two T2 hangars were placed adjacent to the main technical site in the south, between runway heads 07 and 01, and another two T2s lay on the north side, between 19 and 13. A single B1 was situated between runways heads 01 and 25 off the south-east perimeter. Two of the T2s were for Horsa glider storage. The bomb store area was to the north of the airfield. The camp, dispersed around Little Snoring village towards the A148 road, consisted of eight domestic, two mess and one communal site for 1,807 males and 361 females.

By the time Little Snoring was available for use in the summer of 1943, No. 2 Group was in the process of moving its units south and the airfields in north Norfolk were available to No. 3 Group. In August No. 115 Squadron with its radial-engined Lancaster IIs moved in from East Wretham which was to become an American fighter base. In the same month No. 3 Group's Lancaster conversion unit, No. 1678 HC Flight, also removed from East Wretham to Little Snoring for a few weeks before moving on to Foulsham. However No. 3 Group's extended domain was soon reduced with the proposed formation of the Bomber Support Group, No. 100.

In November 1943, No. 115 moved back west to Witchford having lost three Lancasters in operations from Little Snoring. Early in December No. 169 Squadron arrived from Ayr and a week later it was joined by No. 515 from Hunsdon. No. 169, a recently re-formed unit training on Mosquitos for the Serrate role, flew its first sorties seeking enemy night fighters during the Bomber Command raid to Berlin on January 20/21, 1944. No. 515 Squadron was equipped with Beaufighters on its arrival, but it started to convert to Mosquitos in February, undertaking its first sorties from Little Snoring in early April 1944. In June, No. 169 was moved to Great Massingham and No. 23 Squadron, newly

returned from the Mediterranean area, took its place to practice No. 100 Group techniques. Nos. 23 and 515 Squadrons remained in residence to the end of hostilities, the lat-

ter disbanding in June 1945 and No. 23 in September. Another Mosquito squadron, No. 141, was moved in from West Raynham in July 1945 preparatory to disbandment two months later. A total of 55 Bomber Command aircraft were lost in operations flown from Little Snoring: 12 Lancasters and 43 Mosquitos.

In the immediate post-war period Little Snoring was used to store aircraft, mainly Mosquitos. It was then on care and maintenance until an anti-aircraft co-operation unit on civilian contract operated from the airfield over the Wash ranges for several years during the 1950s. Spitfires, the main type employed, gave way to Vampires before the unit was disbanded in 1958 and thereafter the airfield became redundant. The road to Thursford was reopened in the 1960s using part of the eastern perimeter track as the new route. Local flying interest, sustained by the Cushing family who owned much of the land taken for the airfield, ensured that Little Snoring was maintained for club and private flying over the next three decades. The eastern and southern parts of all three runways have been removed but the remainder is retained for flying. Memorial plaques to the No. 100 Group squadrons – recording that they claimed 66 enemy aircraft destroyed and 75 damaged – are to be found in Little Snoring church.

Above: **Mosquito FB III RS566 (3P-F) of No. 515 Squadron parked near the technical site at Little Snoring. An entrance to an air raid shelter can be seen on the left and southernmost T2 hangar is in the background on the right. This particular aircraft was passed to the French Armée de l'Air in 1947.** *Below:* **Another, older, de Havilland — a Hornet Moth — was using the dispersal in 2000.**

Above: **Only 13 Mosquitos were to be seen when a No. 542 Squadron Spitfire took this vertical on June 18, 1945.** *Below:* **Still used for flying, only 540 yards of the original 2,000 yard main runway is now serviceable at the western (07) end. A secondary runway (10-28) utilises the southern perimeter track with a grass area provided in front for taildraggers.**

NORTH CREAKE

Five miles north-west of Fakenham and two miles east of North Creake village, this was another Class A airfield, construction starting in October 1942. Taylor Woodrow built the flying field on a £331,000 contract and W. Lawrence & Son Ltd put up the buildings for £336,000. The site was on an area of farmland known as Bunker's Hill with the camp on the east side. The road from Burnham Thorpe to Little Walsingham running across the airfield site was closed. The technical and administrative sites bordered the unclassified country roads that ran from Wells to Fakenham and domestic sites for 2,951 males and 411 females were dispersed in farmland to the east. The three intersecting runways were 04-24 at 2,000 yards and 01-19 and 13-31 both at 1,400 yards. All 36 hardstandings were the loop type, six on the east side of the Egmere Wells to Crabbe's Castle road which was closed to civilian traffic. Hangarage was the standard two T2 and a single B1.

Originally intended for No. 2 Group, North Creake passed to No. 3 and then, in December 1943, to No. 100. It was not immediately occupied as it was tentatively selected for upgrading to very heavy bomber standard. However, apparently after further survey work had taken place, the airfield fell from favour and Sculthorpe took its place.

Reverting to usage by No. 100 Group, in May 1944 the Stirlings of No. 199 Squadron were transferred from No. 3 Group and Lakenheath to engage in Window and Mandrel sorties against enemy radar tracking of Bomber Command raids. In September 1944, No. 199's 'C' Flight was used to re-form a squadron, No. 171, and boost No. 100 Group's radio counter-measures capability.

One can count 46 Halifaxes dispersed around the airfield when this shot was taken on June 8, 1945.

Halifaxes of No. 171 Squadron (this is *I'm Easy* MZ971 6Y-E) at North Creake and. . .

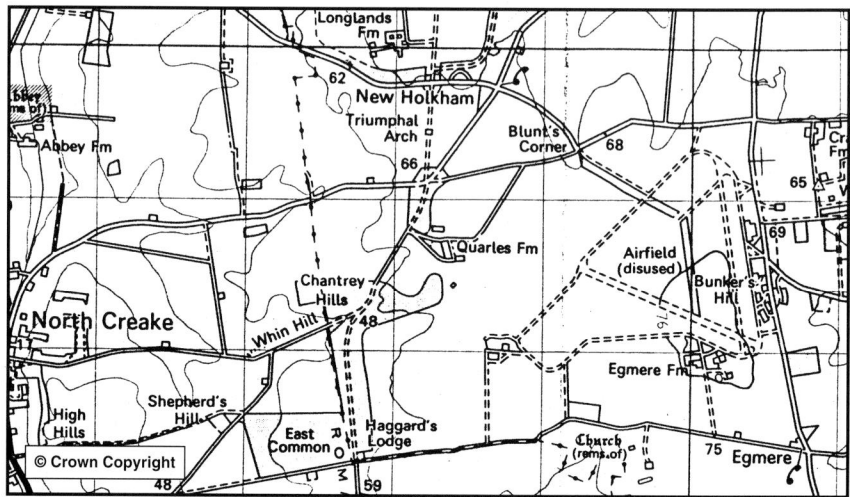

© Crown Copyright

Initially equipped with Stirlings, No. 171 converted to Halifaxes before the end of the year, No. 199 following suite in March 1945 — the last Bomber Command squadron still with Stirlings. The final sorties of the war from North Creake were flown on the night on May 2. The two squadrons had lost a total of 17 aircraft during operations from the airfield, eight Stirling and nine Halifaxes.

Three months later both squadrons had been disbanded and the airfield was being pressed into use for aircraft storage, mainly for Mosquitos. The RAF finally relinquished North Creake in the autumn of 1947 whereupon the flying field was returned to agriculture and the runways eventually removed apart from narrow strips used as farm roads. The former technical site buildings were used for a number of years by an animal feedstuff company. The control tower has now been converted into a house. In 1999 the site was proposed as a tourist facility, mainly for caravans.

. . . Stirlings of No. 199 — the last squadron in Bomber Command to operate the type.

The control tower is now a private dwelling, ironically occupied by an ex-RAF type and his wife.

Oblique taken in September 2000 looking almost directly due south.

A Fortress III BU-N of No. 214 Squadron with her crew. Crew numbers varied according to the equipment carried, two being electronic operatives. The deep bomb bay of the Fortress could hold the large Jostle jamming device.

OULTON

Oulton airfield started life as one of the hastily acquired satellite landing grounds on which aircraft from a main station could be dispersed to lessen the risk of loss through air attack. In this case the main station was Horsham St Faith and it was to Oulton that the Blenheims of No. 114 Squadron were sent in August 1940.

The site to the east of the B1149 Norwich to Holt road lay largely in the parish of Oulton Street, had been requisitioned earlier that year and the majority of the aircrews were initially accomodated in civilian property, including the historic Blickling Hall. No. 114 conducted its operations from Oulton until March 1941 when it was sent to Thornaby to

aid Coastal Command, seven of the squadron's Blenheims failing to return from operations while at the airfield. No. 2 Group then moved No. 18 Squadron's Blenheims to Oulton from Great Massingham in April 1941 and out to Horsham St Faith in July. No. 18 returned in November for a few weeks before returning once more to Horsham. In

With the taxiway and hardstanding gone, the view towards the former technical site in the last of the 20th century shows only the derelict control tower and night flying equipment sheds from wartime days. The T2 hangar was removed soon after the site was returned to civilian use and a farm building later erected on the former perimeter track.

In April 1942 Oulton was still a grass field with 15 pan hardstandings and a lone blister hangar.

The derelict control tower photographed in the summer of 1999. It was considered unsafe, and was demolished that December.

ADDITIONAL BOMB STORE

MANOR HOUSE

12

RAILWAY LINE

07

The airfield was closed in September 1942 to bring the airfield up to Class A standard. This picture was taken on April 20, 1944.

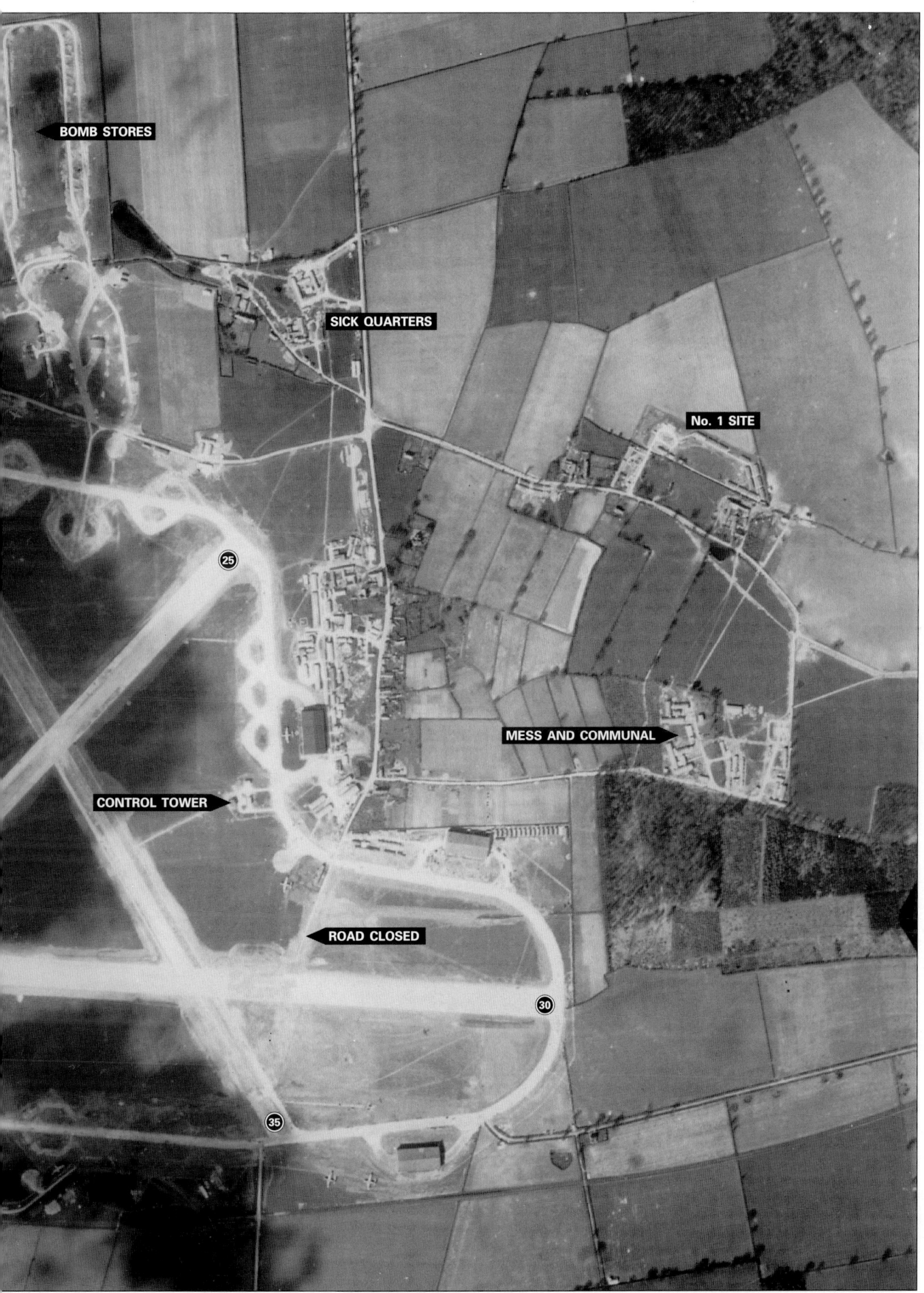

The runways have now been completed and a sprinkling of Horsas can be seen dotted around the airfield.

December, No. 139 Squadron appeared with Lockheed Hudsons on which it trained before being shipped to the Far East. The Hudsons lingered on at Oulton for a while in the hands of No. 1428 Flight that had been formed to provide conversion training.

During the summer of 1942, Oulton was loaned to Coastal Command which placed a Beaufighter shipping strike squadron — No. 236 — on the station which arrived in July and stayed for a little over two months. In September, No. 2 Group transferred in the Bostons of No. 88 Squadron from Attlebridge. On the last day of October, a 250lb high explosive bomb that had failed to release from a Boston during a sortie, exploded while being removed killing six ground crew airmen.

Only limited operations were undertaken during the winter of 1942-43 as the squadron was hampered by a shortage of aircraft. It was moved to Swanton Morley in March and its place at Oulton taken by No. 21 Squadron which had to move from Methwold when that station was returned to No. 3 Group. Ventura-equipped, No. 21 conducted operations from Oulton until September by which time No. 2 Group came under the Second Tactical Air Force. No. 2 Group's airfields in Norfolk were then transferred to No. 3 Group control, Oulton being one although it never received any of that group's squadrons.

In September 1942, work began on bringing the airfield up to Class A standard. This involved closing the Oulton Street to Cawston road across which the main runway was extended. The three runways were 12-30 at 2,000 yards and 07-25 and 17-35, both 1,400 yards long. The 36 hardstanding consisted of 32 loop type and 11 pans. Three of the pans put down in earlier years on the south side near the old railway line were isolated and another four incorporated in the new bomb

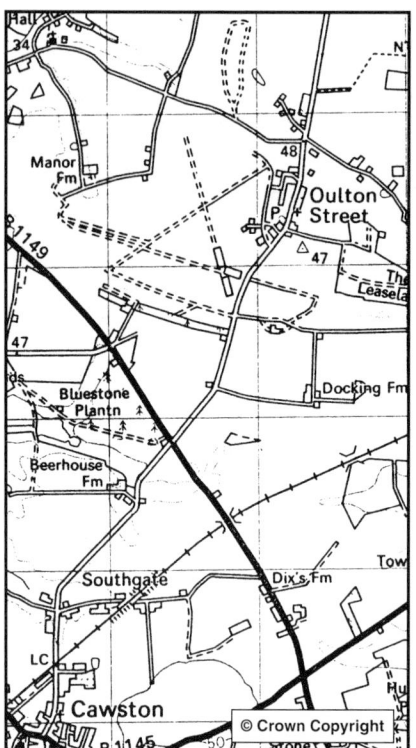

The Oulton Street to Cawston road now bisects the old airfield.

dump off the north-west side between runway heads 12 and 17. Two T2 hangars were on the technical site on the east side between runway heads 25 an 30 near Oulton Street.

Another T2 was located between runway heads 30 and 35, and a fourth T2 north of runway head 12 near the Manor House. Two of these T2s were for housing gliders. Prestige & Co Ltd were involved in the construction of buildings. The early camp was around Blickling Hall where there were four domestic sites, but additional sites — three domestic, a communal and sick quarters — were located nearer the east side of the airfield. Total accommodation was provided for 1,532 males and 250 females.

Re-opened in May 1944 under No. 100 Group, No. 214 Squadron was moved in from Sculthorpe which was closing for major reconstruction. No. 214 was one of the few RAF squadrons equipped with Fortress aircraft, this type chosen for its deep bomb-bay capable of taking special equipment necessary for radio counter-measure operations, and for a while the squadron tutored a USAAF provisional squadron at Oulton in this role. In August 1944 No. 223 Squadron re-formed at Oulton to fly Liberators with Mandrel electronic detection equipment, and thereafter both squadrons continued RCM activities until the end of the war. A total of 56 Bomber Command aircraft were lost flying in operations from Oulton: 34 Blenheims, two Bostons, a Ventura, 16 Fortresses and three Liberators.

No. 100 Group's presence at Oulton came to an end in late July 1945 when both the resident squadrons were disbanded. Later that year the station came under No. 274 Maintenance Unit's administration and was another site for the collection of surplus Mosquitos. By 1948 the RAF had departed and the road between Cawston and Oulton Street was re-opened. While much of the land was reclaimed for agriculture the runways remained and were used for locating poultry houses in isolation.

Oulton in September 2000 looking south-west across the old technical site.

SCULTHORPE

This Fortress, AN520, was used as a trainer at Sculthorpe and arrived in the white livery of its previous service with Coastal Command. It was the last of the 20 B-17s received by the RAF in 1941 to remain in service.

Originally built to Class A standard, Sculthorpe was situated between the village of that name and Syderstone to the west, north of the A148 Fakenham to King's Lynn road. Its construction involved the closure of two country roads. The runway lengths were 06-24 at 2,000 yards and 1,400 yards for the two subsidiaries, 00-18 and 13-31. The usual 36 hardstandings were provided, all loops, while the technical area with two T2 hangars lay on the west side of the airfield, with two communal and seven domestic dispersed sites, for 1,773 males and 409 females further to the west. There were two more T2s, one on the south-east side, one between the thresholds of the 24 and 31 runways, and the other on the north-east side between the 18 and 24 runway heads. Bomb stores were south of the technical site. The contractors were Bovis Ltd and Constable Hart & Co. Ltd which had completed the station by October 1943.

The first operational unit to take up residence was No. 342 Squadron, recently formed at West Raynham with French personnel. Flying Bostons, the squadron spent its first weeks at Scunthorpe continuing training and flew its first sorties on June 12, 1943 when three of its Bostons were part of a force sent to attack a power station at Rouen by which time No. 2 Group was no longer part of Bomber Command. The Frenchmen

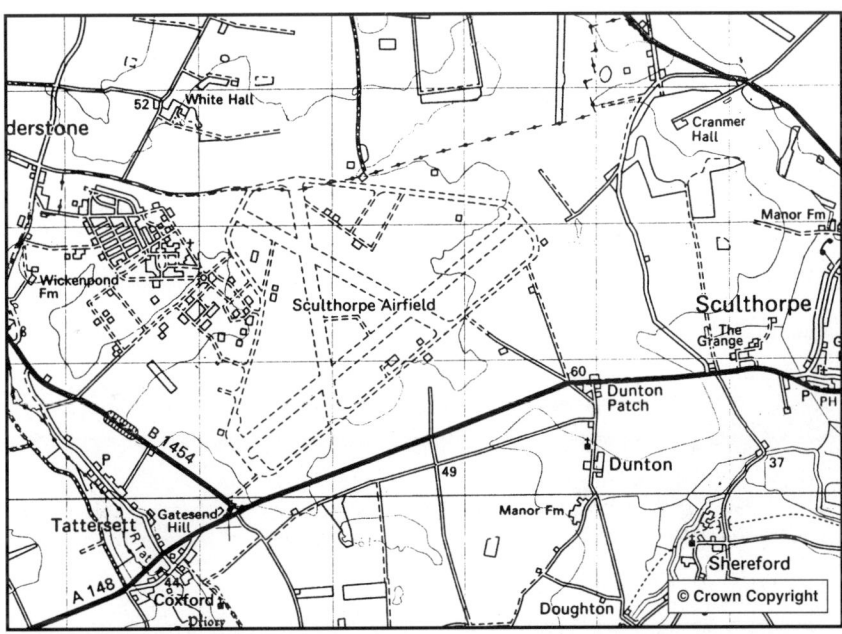

Greatly expanded when it was turned into a 'Very Heavy Bomber' base in 1944-45, Sculthorpe was further enlarged by the USAF after it took up residence in 1951.

In 2000 the grass around the concrete was unkempt. The distinctive house on the skyline is believed to have been lost when the airfield was rebuilt post-war but this is thought to be the approximate location of the wartime photograph.

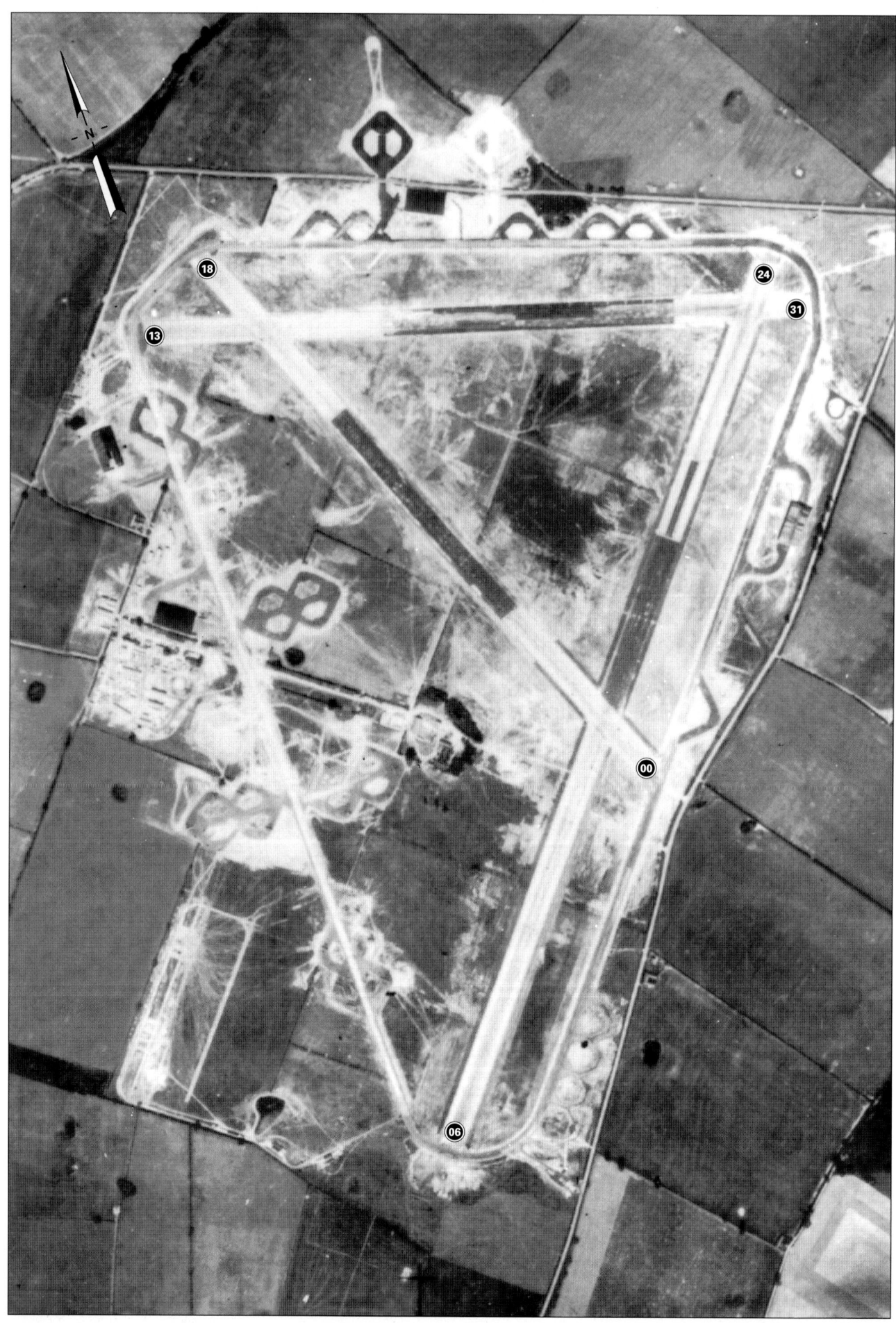

Sculthorpe as it appeared on July 16, 1943 with Venturas on its aircraft dispersal points.

moved to Great Massingham in July, their place being taken by Nos. 464 and 487 Squadrons from Methwold with Venturas. Pleasant aircraft that the Ventura was to fly, it proved far too slow and vulnerable for daylight operations as conducted by No. 2 Group, which began converting both squadrons to Mosquitos at Sculthorpe. They were soon joined by the remaining Ventura squadron — No. 21 — also converted to Mosquitos, commencing operations in October.

Sculthorpe was retained by No. 2 Group longer than any of its Norfolk bases, the three squadrons not moving south until the end of the year, although during operations they had used advanced airfields to lessen the distance to their targets. No. 100 Group was the new custodian of Sculthorpe and moved in No. 214 Squadron which it had gained from No. 3 Group at Downham Market. The squadron's Stirlings gave way to Boeing Fortresses modified for electronic counter-measures with highly secret equipment. The conversion took some weeks and RCM work did not begin in earnest until April 1944. At this juncture, No. 214 was alerted to be ready for another move as Sculthorpe was to be closed for reconstruction.

As far as is known, no aircraft of the squadron or of any other Bomber Command unit were lost in operations flown from this station. The Fortresses left for Oulton in early May and the contractors moved in to turn Sculthorpe into a 'Very Heavy Bomber' base. All the original runways were torn up, two more country roads closed, and new 300-foot-wide and substantially stronger runways laid down. The main 00-18 was 3,000 yards long and the others both 2,000 yards. Major reconstruction work was not completed before the end of the war and thereafter some facilities still had to be finished. Not until 1949 was the airfield brought back into regular use when B-29 Superfortresses (for which the wartime restructuring was carried out) arrived to counter the Berlin crisis threat. Thereafter, Sculthorpe was used for

Above: **The post-war tower, vacant in 2000 but still in good condition.** *Below:* **Sculthorpe pictured looking north-east along the 3,000-yard main runway. The airfield site has been retained and the runway maintained by the Ministry of Defence for use in conjunction with the Stanford Training Area (STANTA).**

three years for temporary duty assignments by the USAF Strategic Air Command with a succession of B-29 and B-50 units resident, usually for three months at a time. The USAF formerly took over the station as tenant in January 1951 and a substantial building programme took place over the next few years, providing both service and domestic accommodation.

In May 1952, the 47th Bomb Wing arrived as a true resident with B-45 Tornado tactical bombers. The three squadrons of the group were joined by a fourth flying the RB-45

reconnaissance version in 1954. Conversion to B-66 and RB-66 Destroyers took place in 1958 but as tactical fighters were by then able to perform the NATO mission more economically, the wing was inactivated in June 1962. Thereafter Sculthorpe became a stand-by base occasional hosting visiting USAF units particularly during exercises.

The USAF withdrew and the base closed at the end of 1992. The housing, mostly bungalows, built for USAF personnel, and now known as Wicken Green Village, was sold in the mid-1990s.

Today Swannington is almost invisible amidst the patchwork quilt of the Norfolk countryside.

SWANNINGTON

Located eight miles north-west of the centre of Norwich, this airfield was built east of the Swannington village to Brandiston road which was closed. The Cawston to Horsford road was also cut south of St Nicholas's church. The main contractor was Kent & Sussex Construction Co. Ltd which started work on the £882,000 contract in October 1942. Built to Class A standard, the three intersecting runways were 10-28 at 2,000 yards and 05-23 and 14-32 both 1,400 yards long. The usual 36 hardstandings were of the loop type. Two T2 hangars were positioned on the technical site between runway heads 23 and 28. A B1 hangar was located just west of the bomb stores which were situated west of runway 32 between Moegoes Plantation and Crimea Covert. The camp was dispersed between the airfield and Hall Farm, mostly in the park of Haveringland Hall. There was one communal, one WAAF, four domestic and a sick quarters site. The officers' mess was in the Hall which had been requisitioned. Total accommodation was put at 1,956 male and 450 female.

Although construction began in 1942, the airfield was not completed until early in 1944. Under No. 100 Group administration, it became home to two Mosquito fighter squadrons, No. 85 from West Malling and No. 157 from Valley, both to be committed to bomber support operations over enemy territory. However, the V-1 onslaught saw both units move to West Malling for several weeks returning to Swannington in late August. The Mosquitos then flew bomber support operations right up to the end of the war, their last sorties being made on the night of May 2, 1945. During the course of operations from the station the two squadrons had lost a total of 19 Mosquitos. In late June, No. 85 Squadron moved south to Castle Camps while No. 157 disbanded on August 16, 1945. The following month No. 100 Group relinquished control and Swannington became the headquarters station of No. 274 Maintenance Unit which received and stored surplus Mosquitos at this and other airfields in the region.

The RAF withdrew from Swannington in November 1947 although the airfield was kept intact until sold ten years later. It then reverted to agricultural use with much of the concrete broken up for hardcore. A seed packing firm acquired the technical site, first using two hangars before erecting new units.

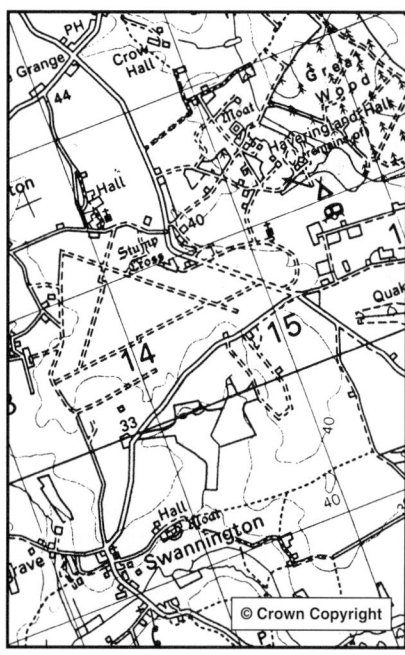

© Crown Copyright

How sad to see the old control tower — once the scene of high drama — now having fallen almost into oblivion.

It wasn't always so. The winter of 1944-45 produced some hard weather with heavy snowfalls in the New Year. RS-J, Mosquito NF XIX (MM654) of No. 157 Squadron, pictured on the snowy north-east side of the technical area, had suffered an undercarriage collapse when it swung on take-off at West Malling the previous July but had soon been repaired.

Although a Class A airfield, Swannington was quickly run down at the end of the war and no aircraft at all are visible on this shot taken in July 1946, and by the following year the RAF had pulled out altogether. Note the parkland surrounding Haveringland Hall to the east of the airfield where the station camp was located.

SWANTON MORLEY

Last respects for a fallen comrade. This picture was taken from the roof of the guardroom. The same location in 2000 shows the earthen blast wall on the right having been replaced by an extension to Station HQ.

Situated 2½ miles north-north-east of East Dereham, overlooking the south side of the Wensum valley, Swanton Morley was an expansion scheme airfield that was never completed to the usual standard. With the outbreak of war a far more utility station resulted, devoid of the familiar Type C hangars. The camp was built by Richard Costain & Co. Ltd near Mill Street on the eastern side of the aerodrome. The area taken involved the closure of country roads, notably that between the villages of Worthing and Swanton Morley.

This grass surface airfield was first occupied by No. 105 Squadron Blenheims in October 1940, by which time a single Type J hangar had been erected on the technical site. Over the following months a number of tarmac hardstandings were put down round the airfield, work there by Costain eventually totalling £490,000. As with most Blenheim squadrons, No. 105 took heavy losses during 1940-41 but its CO, Wing Commander Hughie Edwards, was awarded a VC for his conduct in leading an attack on Bremen on July 4, 1941. No. 105 remained at Swanton Morley until December 1941 when it was transferred to Horsham St Faith to become the first squadron to convert to the Mosquito IV bomber. Their first two Mosquitos were received before the move to Horsham. No. 105's replacement was No. 226 Squadron with Blenheims, which it soon shed in favour

of Bostons. The squadron's first use of the Boston as a bomber was on March 8, 1942 when it flew from a forward airfield in the south to raid a factory near Paris. In the spring No. 226 tutored the USAAF's 15th

Bomb Squadron and led it on that unit's first raid, which took place on July 4, 1942. In May 1943, No. 226 converted to Mitchells, shortly before No. 2 Group left Bomber Command.

Swanton Morley photographed in April 1946 shows 12 Wellingtons, 9 Ansons and two unidentified types near the technical site.

Unlike most other No. 2 Group squadrons, No. 226 was not moved south during the summer and autumn of 1943 but remained at Swanton Morley until February 1944. Another squadron equipped with Mitchells at Swanton Morley was the Polish-manned No. 305 which cast off its Wellingtons at Ingham in September 1943 only to leave Swanton two months later for Lasham to retrain yet again, this time on Mosquitos.

During March 1944, No. 98 Squadron Mitchells moved back to Norfolk from Dunsfold and carried out operations until October that year when it moved to liberated Belgium. In fact, Swanton Morley was the only Norfolk airfield retained by No. 2 Group which, at the beginning of April 1944, formed No. 2 Group Support Unit at the station. This body was primarily a holding unit for aircrew and other personnel to make good losses in No. 2 Group's squadrons during the forthcoming cross-Channel invasion.

At some time between 1941 and 1943, four T2 hangars were erected on the airfield, 31 loop hardstandings and a perimeter track put down. Other work involved utility buildings for barracks with the station's total accommodation raised to 1,968 males and 390 females.

A beautiful piece of Bomber Command history — an original wartime aerodrome still surfaced with grass and not agriculturalised.

In response to No. 100 Group's need of an additional airfield near its HQ, in December 1944 No. 2 Group had finally to relinquish Swanton Morley. The support unit moved to Fersfield, an airfield in south Norfolk just vacated by the USAAF. Thereupon No. 100 Group established its Bomber Support Development Unit on the airfield, carrying out a number of experimental operational flights. The group's communications flight was also based at Swanton. Operations launched from Swanton Morley while under Bomber Command incurred a loss of 39 aircraft — 21 Blenheims and 18 Bostons.

With the demise of No. 100 Group in the summer of 1945, little use was made of the station until December 1946 when No. 4 Radio School moved in. Flying Proctors, Prentices and Ansons, the school changed its name to No. 1 Air Signallers, then Air Elec-tronic School, remaining in residence until late 1957. Thereafter, the airfield, still turf-surfaced, was little used for RAF flying although the camp continued to serve for ground units until September 1995. A flying club flourished for several years. In 1996 the camp and much of the landing ground was taken over by the Army for Robertson Barracks, the J and T2 hangars being demolished for new AFV buildings.

Now in the hands of the British Army and renamed Robertson Barracks after Field-Marshal Sir William Robertson (1860-1933).

Pictures taken at Wattisham during Bomber Command's tenure are very hard to come by as the squadrons based there in the early part of the war were often dispersed to other airfields to avoid possible bombing attacks. *Left:* This picture kindly supplied by the Wattisham Airfield Historical Society is genuine of the period and shows Sergeant Robson and Flight Lieutenant Berman outside No. 110 Squadron's offices in early 1940. *Right:* Chris Hunn stands in outside No. 2 Hangar.

WATTISHAM

One of the four 'W' stations which hosted No. 2 Group's squadrons at the beginning of the war, Wattisham was an expansion scheme project on which work began in 1937.

Located in the parishes of Wattisham, Ringshall and Great Bricett, two miles northeast of the little Suffolk town of Bildeston, the main contractor involved in construction was John Laing & Son Ltd. It was not an easy site to work due to the high clay content of the soil that required much underdraining. The camp of permanent buildings lay near the village of Great Bricett and its construction brought about the closure of the road to Ringshall. A road from Bricett to Wattisham that ran across the landing ground was also closed and eliminated. Four Type C hangars formed an arc adjacent to the bombing circle.

Officially opened in March 1939, the station received Nos. 107 and 110 Squadrons from Harwell and Waddington respectively. These resident squadrons were in action on the second day of hostilities losing half the Blenheims despatched in an attempt to sink enemy warships near Wilhelmshaven. As with most Blenheim stations, the attrition rate were very heavy during the spring and summer of 1940 and a total of 61 aircraft were lost by Nos. 107 and 110 while flying from Wattisham.

No. 107 left in May 1941 when sent north to Leuchars to aid Coastal Command. Its place was taken by No. 226 Squadron which had left its Battles in Northern Ireland and was retrained to fly Blenheims. No. 226 left in December for Swanton Morley where it was to convert to Bostons, its Blenheims being taken over by a re-formed No. 18 Squadron. The remaining original Wattisham squadron, No. 110, left its Blenheims at Wattisham when its personnel were sent to the Far East in March 1942. No. 18 Squadron was disbanded in March only to reappear from Scotland in May but in August it was packed off to West Raynham preparatory to leaving for North Africa. This marked the end of Bomber Command operations from Wattisham which had seen 118 Blenheims fail to return or crash, the highest loss of Blenheims from any station.

During the 1940-41 period, at least 30 asphalt pan hardstandings were put down on the west and north sides of the airfield. On June 4, 1942, Wattisham was listed for upgrading to Class A standard as a USAAF bomber base and work started on laying runways and in October it was also identified as the site of an air depot. However, a crisis in the airfield building programme saw work temporarily halted on the runways. In the event, this work was not restarted as the airfield was now not required for a bomber station, ultimately housing a USAAF fighter group, the 479th, equipped first with P-38s and then P-51s, while the depot was utilised for fighter servicing, modification and repair. The three runways eventually laid down at Wattisham were 11-29 at 1,400 yards, all concrete, and 16-34 comprising 350 yards of concrete and 1,050 yards of turf. The main 06-24 had a mixture of 567 yards of concrete and 1,433 yard of steel matting. A concrete perimeter track was linked to 19 existing hard pans to which 39 loops were added. Other pan hardstandings were destroyed during development of the airfield. Additional domestic sites with Nissen huts were constructed in Great Bricett parish giving accommodation for up to 1,709 men. The depot area, official name Hitcham, was built in Nedging Tye on the south side of the airfield during 1943, its access track having 17 loop hardstandings. There were four T2 hangars.

Wattisham began life as one of the expansion period aerodromes with the standard for Type C hangars in a crescent bordering the grass airfield. This rather poor shot dates from March 1943 when the RAF was about to relinquish the base to the USAAF.

During American tenure, major expansion took place with the establishment of a fighter servicing and repair base just off the southern perimeter (in the right foreground). This shot from the 1970s shows how the main 06-24 runway was extended for use by post-war jet-powered aircraft with only a short stub of the secondary 16-34 remaining at its eastern end.

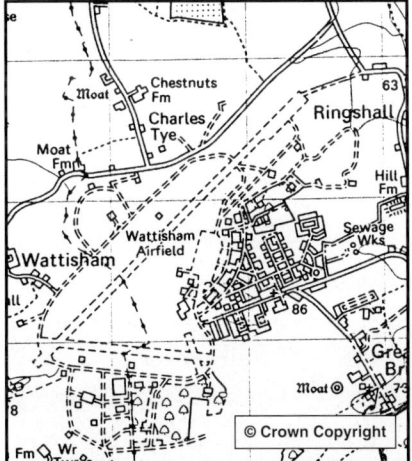

© Crown Copyright

Wattisham was handed back to the RAF on December 15, 1945. The station was in care and maintenance for a time until it was taken over by Fighter Command in October 1946 which based Meteor squadrons there for a few months. In April 1947, the station was again closed for flying while hard runways were completed and other building work undertaken. Fighter squadrons did not return until October 1950, Meteors giving way to Hunters in 1954 followed by Javelins and Lightnings. Wattisham's final days as a fighter base were with agile if noisy Phantoms. The RAF vacated the station in 1992 and after much additional building work the Army made Wattisham its major helicopter base with as many as seven squadrons in residence at any one

The RAF left Wattisham in 1993 when the base was transferred to the Army. At the time the picture below was taken the airfield housed 3 and 4 Regiments, Army Air Corps, with their Lynx and Gazelle helicopters and 7 Battalion, REME. Also a small RAF Search and Rescue detachment (B Flight 22(SAR) Squadron) with Sea Kings. Careful comparison between the two aerial shots reveals the new hangarage and also the hardened aircraft shelters on the old USAAF Hitcham technical side.

WATTON

Above: **The C-type hangars, which were a feature of many of the 'expansion period' airfields, under construction at Watton in the late 1930s.** *Below:* **The same location today with the hangar partially masked by later buildings.**

Another of the four operational expansion scheme airfields under No. 2 Group when war was declared, Watton was built on free-draining soil between the B1108 and B111 roads just to the east of the small town of Watton. Permanent buildings included four Type C hangars in a crescent fronting the bombing circle of the 250-acre grass aerodrome. The main contractor was John Laing & Son Ltd.

The usual practice followed of placing two squadrons on the station as soon as it was ready for occupation, this being in March 1939 when No. 21 Squadron brought its Blenheims from Eastchurch and No. 34 came with the same type from Upper Heyford. No. 34's association with Watton only lasted six months, the squadron being sent out to Singapore whereupon No. 82 Squadron moved in from Cranfield. From June to October 1940, No. 21 Squadron was loaned to Coastal Command operating out of Lossiemouth, thus largely escaping the slaughter that befell most Blenheim bomber squadrons during that summer. No. 105 Squadron arrived in July 1940 to be re-equipped with Blenheims after its mauling with Battles during the German Blitzkrieg in France. No. 82 Squadron carried out most of the offensive tasks for Watton's Blenheims, flying more raids than any other Blenheim squadron in No. 2 Group. However, it also suffered by far the heaviest losses and between September 27, 1939 and March 1942 when it was posted to Malta, 62 Blenheims were missing in action with another 25 lost in operational accidents, many of these losses occurring flying from

Bodney — Watton's satellite — or Lossiemouth. All told, 100 Blenheims were lost by Nos. 21 and 82 Squadrons while flying from Watton.

No. 21 Squadron had been sent to Malta in December 1941 but was disbanded there and re-formed at Bodney the following March. During 1941 several concrete pan hardstandings were constructed on well-dispersed sites around the airfield totalling, it is believed, 24.

In January 1942, No. 17 (Pilots) Advanced Flying Unit was formed at Watton to provide refresher courses. Equipped mainly with Miles Masters, this organisation became the sole resident of Watton after No. 82 Squadron left. The reason for a training unit occupying a front line operational airfield is believed to be due to a shortage of airfields for flying training. It continued in residence until May 1943.

Loss of hydraulic pressure caused the pilot of this Blenheim to make a 'wheels up' landing with YH-J at Watton on July 6, 1941. The engine fire was soon extinguished but Z7432 was beyond repair.

The tower of Griston church seen in the distance still looks on from the south-west but the popularity of poplars in the late 20th century are in stark contrast to the more traditional Norfolk skyline.

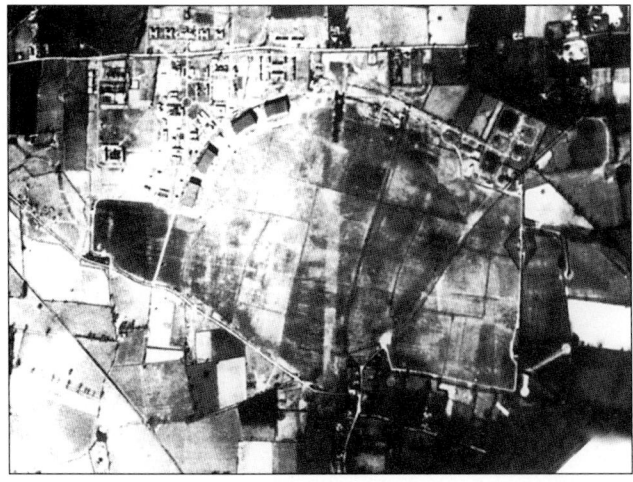

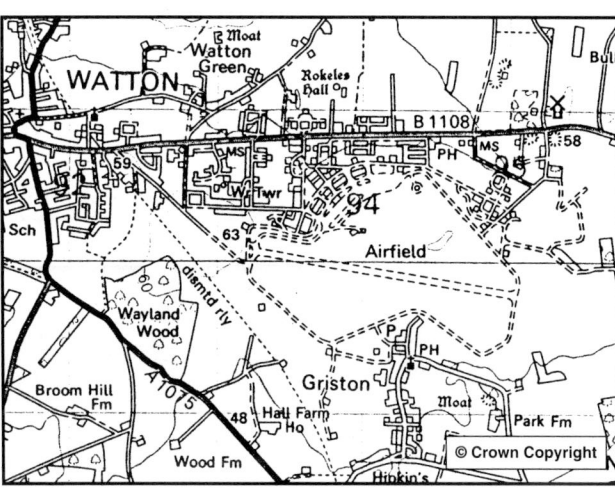

A pre-take-over survey photograph taken by the Americans prior to the airfield becoming operational with the Eighth Air Force in March 1943. Watton lies just east of the town of that name.

In August 1942 Watton had been allocated to the USAAF as a bomber base and two months later it was, in addition, scheduled for an air depot. By the spring of 1943 the overloaded airfield building programme resulted in a decision not to put down hard runways on any more of the existing grass-surface airfields, Watton being re-allocated for use as a fighter station. The Americans arrived in August 1943 with air service groups maintaining the B-24 Liberators of the 2nd Bomb Division, Watton officially transferring to the USAAF on October 4, 1943.

Construction of the air depot, officially known as Neaton but actually built on the opposite side of the airfield at Griston, consisted of 24 loop hardstandings, three grouped T2 hangars and numerous Nissen-type workshops. Early in 1944 a provisional reconnaissance unit was established becoming the 802nd (P) Reconnaissance Group in April and the 25th Bomb Group (R) in August. Two squadrons operated Mosquitos and the third B-24s before converting to B-17s.

During the winter of 1943-44 the grass runways were reinforced with steel mat but in July 1944 the 899th Engineer Battalion, US Army, laid a 2,000-yard concrete runway on the axis 11-29. A concrete perimeter track with 41 loops was also put down linking with 14 of the existing pan hardstandings.

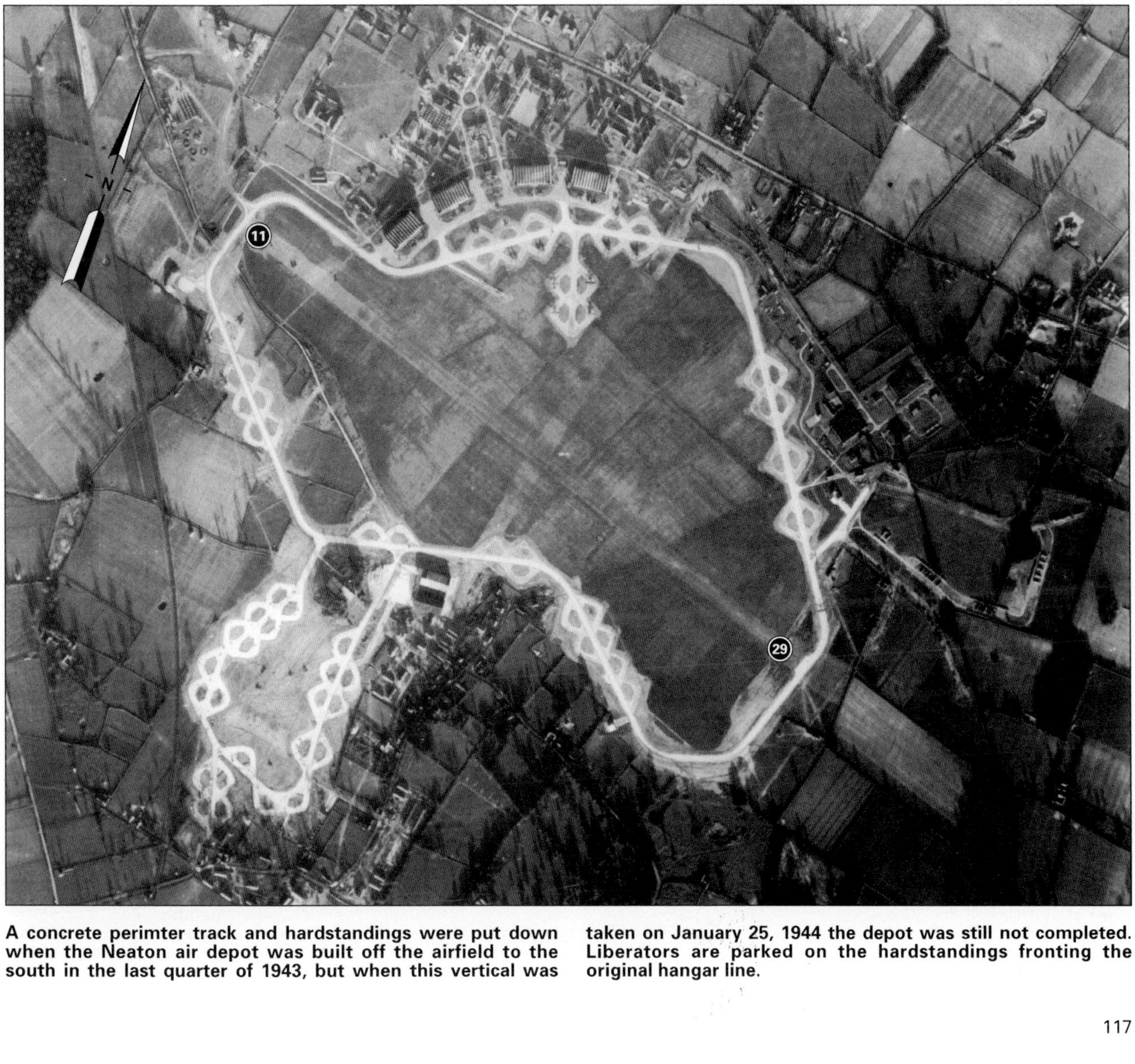

A concrete perimter track and hardstandings were put down when the Neaton air depot was built off the airfield to the south in the last quarter of 1943, but when this vertical was taken on January 25, 1944 the depot was still not completed. Liberators are parked on the hardstandings fronting the original hangar line.

Watton was returned to the RAF on August 15, 1945 when the station became the home of the Radio Warfare Establishment, later re-titled the Central Signals Establishment. The composition of this organisation varied over the next two decades. Following the departure of the CSE regular flying from Watton ceased but it continued as a major air traffic control centre with Eastern Radar until the 1980s. Then in the 1990s, the airfield

One of the striking features of Watton today is the stands of trees which have been planted as part of its new role as a battle training area. *Above:* **Looking east down the single main runway (originally built by US Army engineers), and** *(below)* **northwards towards the hangar line.**

came into use by the Army in connection with the nearby Stanford Training Area. Part of the camp put up for sale in 1995 was sold to a developer for the creation of a new housing estate. Three of the type C hangars

have been used for grain stores for some years when the Griston depot became a prison where various memorials to wartime activities can be inspected, possibly under the vigilant eye of CCTV!

WEST RAYNHAM

An unmistakeable silhouette on an equally historic day! The Prime Minister watches a Halifax being put through its paces . . . on June 6 . . . only this is 1941 at West Raynham . . . not Normandy in 1944!

This aerodrome was an expansion scheme airfield located five miles south-west of Fakenham and two miles west of West Raynham village. The camp was situated to the north-west of the landing ground with the standard Type C hangars arranged in an arc fronting the bombing circle. Permanent buildings backed up against the Coxford to Kipton Ash road which was eventually closed to public use. Built 1938-39, No. 2 Group moved in No. 101 Squadron and its Blenheims from Bicester in May 1939. No. 101 had the station all to itself as the reserve squadron of No. 2 Group until a target-towing flight was formed in February 1940. In April No. 76 Squadron was reformed with the prospect of becoming a second operational Blenheim unit but the crisis in France brought about a hasty disbandment after only three weeks. A victim of the Blitzkrieg, No. 139 Squadron came to recuperate for eleven days and, after its departure for Horsham St Faith, No. 18 Squadron, which had similarly suffered, arrived on June13.

No. 101's Blenheims went into action for the first time on July 4, 1940, single aircraft attempting to attack oil storage tanks in German ports. It continued to fly sorties from West Raynham for a year during which time

it lost 15 Blenheims in some 610 sorties. The attrition in Blenheim squadrons was said to be behind Bomber Command's decision to move one of No. 2 Group's squadrons to No. 3 Group and convert it to Wellingtons, No. 101 being selected for this transfer which entailed saying goodbye to West Raynham and moving to Oakington. No. 2 Group was then able to retrieve No. 114 Squadron from Leuchars where it had been on loan to Coastal Command. The squadron moved its Blenheims into West Raynham, where they remained for over a year before being sent to North Africa following the 'Torch' invasion. While based at West Raynham, No. 114, like all other No. 2 Group Blenheim squadrons, was often detached to other stations for bombing or shipping strike activities. The squadron ceased operations in August 1942 to convert to the Blenheim V which it was to use in North Africa. No. 18 Squadron returned to West Raynham during that month to be similarly re-equipped for the North African venture.

While the Blenheim squadrons were thus engaged with new aircraft, No. 180 Squadron was formed to fly Mitchells which were flown from the larger airfield at Great Massingham, Raynham's satellite. No. 342 Squadron,

French-manned to fly Bostons, was also formed at West Raynham in the spring of 1943 before moving on to Sculthorpe for operations.

Hard runways were then put down but, in contrast to most bomber airfields, there were only two and to build these it was necessary to extend the boundaries of the station, notably to the west where a country road was closed. The runways, built from May-November 1943, were 04-22 at 2,000 yards and 10-28 at 1,400 yards. During 1940-41, 36 pan-type standings had been put down although only 23 of these remained useable after the runways and perimeter track were built. Fourteen loop-type standings were added during the refurbishment programme, Allnott Ltd being involved in this construction programme. The bomb stores were off the south-east corner of the airfield. Additional accommodation raised the station's faccilities to 2,456 for males and 658 for females.

No. 100 Group took over the station in December 1943 bringing in two Mosquito-equipped night fighter squadrons to pursue bomber support operations in enemy air space. These were Nos. 141 and 239 which flew Serrate patrols and Ranger sorties until the end of hostilities. No. 141 then trans-

Mosquito NT362 from No. 239 Squadron (HB-S) stands near one of the Type C hangars during the period when No. 100 Group used the airfield for bomber support operations.

The screening trees had reached a substantial height by the turn of the century and a post-war concrete apron has replaced the wartime turf. This is the northernmost hangar.

West Raynham's satellite Great Massingham lay just a mile to the west (see page 84).

ferred to Little Snoring in July 1945 while No. 239 was disbanded at West Raynham the same month. Bomber Command operations carried out from this station during the war claimed 86 aircraft: 56 Blenheims, 29 Mosquitos and a Beaufighter.

After the war, West Raynham was first home to the Central Fighter Establishment, concerned with tactics and trials involving several small units, which flourished at the station until 1962. (In January 1950 the land which had been taken for hardstandings across the eastern side of the public road had been relinquished and sold.) From August 1960 the station also hosted fighter squadrons, Javelins and then Hunters, the later under No. 38 Group. After the Hunters left in the summer of 1969, Canberras appeared and remained until the end of 1975 when West Raynham was finally closed for flying. Bloodhound missiles for air-to air defence were then sited on the station to defend East Anglian military installations. These were removed in 1991 and West Raynham went the way of so many surplus RAF installations being closed in July 1994.

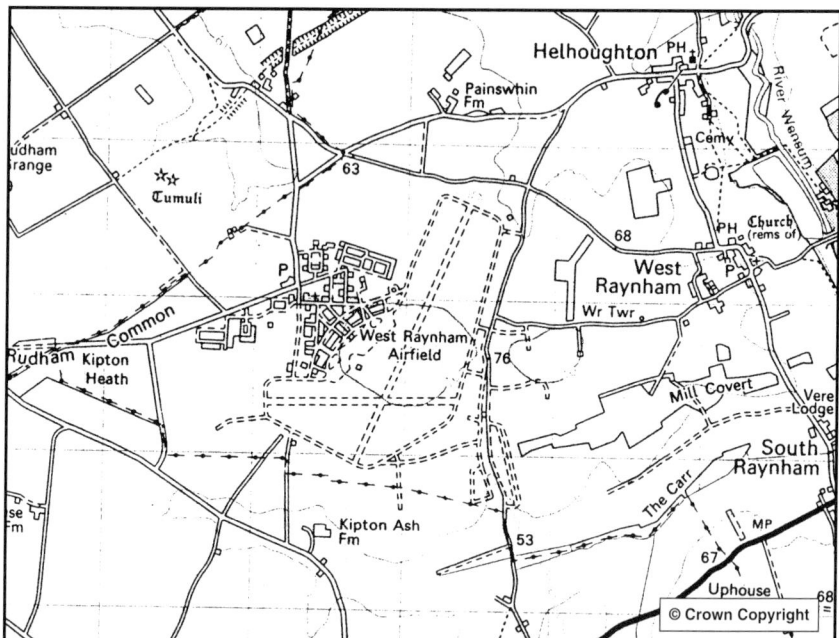

© Crown Copyright

The original three marked grass runways show clearly in this vertical of West Raynham taken on June 26, 1942. (Only the 04-22 and 10-28 were later hardened.) Interestingly, No. 114 Squadron chose not to park its Blenheims on the pan hardstandings, possibly because they were widely dispersed outside the airfield boundaries and mostly reached by long access tracks.

Above: **Approaching West Raynham from the north-west in September 2000.** *Below:* **The airfield closed in 1994 but a circuit** of the aerodrome reveals that, save for the missing aircraft, it still bears all the hallmarks of a front-line RAF base.

THE TIMES

AN AIRMAN'S LETTER

Dearest Mother,

Though I feel no premonition at all, events are moving rapidly, and I have instructed that this letter be forwarded to you should I fail to return from one of the raids which we shall shortly be called upon to undertake. You must hope on for a month, but at end of that time you must accept the fact that I have handed my task over to the extremely capable hands of my comrades of the Royal Air Forces, as so many splendid fellows have already done.

First, it will comfort you to know that my role in this war has been of the greatest importance. Our patrols far out over the North Sea have helped to keep the trade routes clear for our convoys and supply ships, and on one occasion our information was instrumental in saving the lives of the men in a crippled lighthouse relief ship. Though it will be difficult for you, you will disappoint me if you do not at least try to accept the facts dispassionately, for I shall have done my duty to the utmost of my ability. No man can do more, and no one calling himself a man could do less.

I have always admired your amazing courage in the face of continual setbacks; in a way you have given me as good an education and background as anyone in the country; and always kept up appearances without ever losing faith in the future. My death would not mean that your struggle has been in vain. Far from it. It means that your sacrifice is as great as mine. Those who serve England must expect nothing from her; we debase ourselves if we regard our country as merely a place in which to eat and sleep.

History resounds with illustrious names who have given all, yet their sacrifice has resulted in the British Empire, where there is a measure of peace, justice, and freedom for all, and where a higher standard of civilization has evolved, and is still evolving, than anywhere else. But this is not only concerning our own land. Today we are faced with the greatest organized challenge to Christianity and civilization that the world has ever seen, and I count myself lucky and

honoured to be the right age and fully trained to throw my weight into the scale. For this I have to thank you. Yet there is more work for you to do. The home front will still have to stand united for years after the war is won. For all that can be said against it, I still maintain that this war is a very good thing; every individual is having the chance to live and dare all for his principles like the martyrs of old. However long the time may be, one thing can never be altered — I shall have lived and died an Englishman. Nothing else matters one jot nor can anything ever change it.

You must not grieve for me, for if you really believe in religion and all that it entails that would be hypocrisy. I have no fear of death; only a queer elation . . . I would have it no other way. The universe is so vast and so ageless that the life of one man can only be justified by the measure of his sacrifice. We are sent to this world to acquire a personality and a character to take with us that can never be taken from us. Those who just eat and sleep, prosper and procreate, are no better than animals if all their lives they are at peace.

I firmly and absolutely believe that evil things are sent into the world to try us; they are sent deliberately by our Creator to test our metal because He knows what is good for us. The Bible is full of cases where the easy way out has been discarded for moral principles.

I count myself fortunate in that I have seen the whole country and known men of every calling. But with the final test of war I consider my character fully developed. Thus at my early age my earthly mission is already fulfilled and I am prepared to die with just one regret, and one only — that I could not devote myself to making your declining years more happy by being with you; but you will live in peace and freedom and I shall have directly contributed to that, so here again my life will not have been in vain.

Your loving Son.

On June 18, 1940, *The Times* published this moving letter written by a young RAF bomber pilot. It had been left unsealed with his station commander with the wish that it be sent to his mother should he be killed. He failed to return on May 30, 1940 during a night raid to Diksmuide in Belgium in support of the retreat of the British Expeditionary Force to the coast. When his CO read the letter before sending it on (as he was obliged to do in compliance with security procedures), the spirit in which it had been written prompted him to ask the pilot's mother if it could be published — completely anonymously — as a marvellous example of the esprit de corps then prevailing in the Royal Air Force. The letter appeared in *The Times* two weeks later and within a month of publication the newspaper had received over half a million requests for a copy. Yet the identity of the young airman remained unknown throughout the war and it was not until February 18, 1981, when a correspondent contributed an obituary notice to *The Times* for a Mrs Lillian Rosewarne, that the identity of the writer was revealed: her only son Vivian. Flying Officer Vivian Rosewarne was serving with No. 38 Squadron based at Marham in Norfolk where his Wellington (R3162 HD-H) was brought down at Veurne, 25 kilometres south-west of Ostend. He was killed together with his entire crew: Pilot Officer Roy Baynes, Sergeant John Knight, Sergeant Dennis Spencer, AC2 James Adams and Sergeant John Dolan. All were buried in the extension to Veurne Communal Cemetery which was established by the Germans for the many British casualties suffered during the evacuation, Flying Officer Rosewarne being buried in Grave No. 1 in Row B. Sixty years after he penned his memorable letter, his name is also remembered in a most unlikely place: on the Roll of Honour of the British Union of Fascists founded by Sir Oswald Mosley in 1932. Over 1,000 members of the BUF are believed to have been killed on active service in the Second World War.

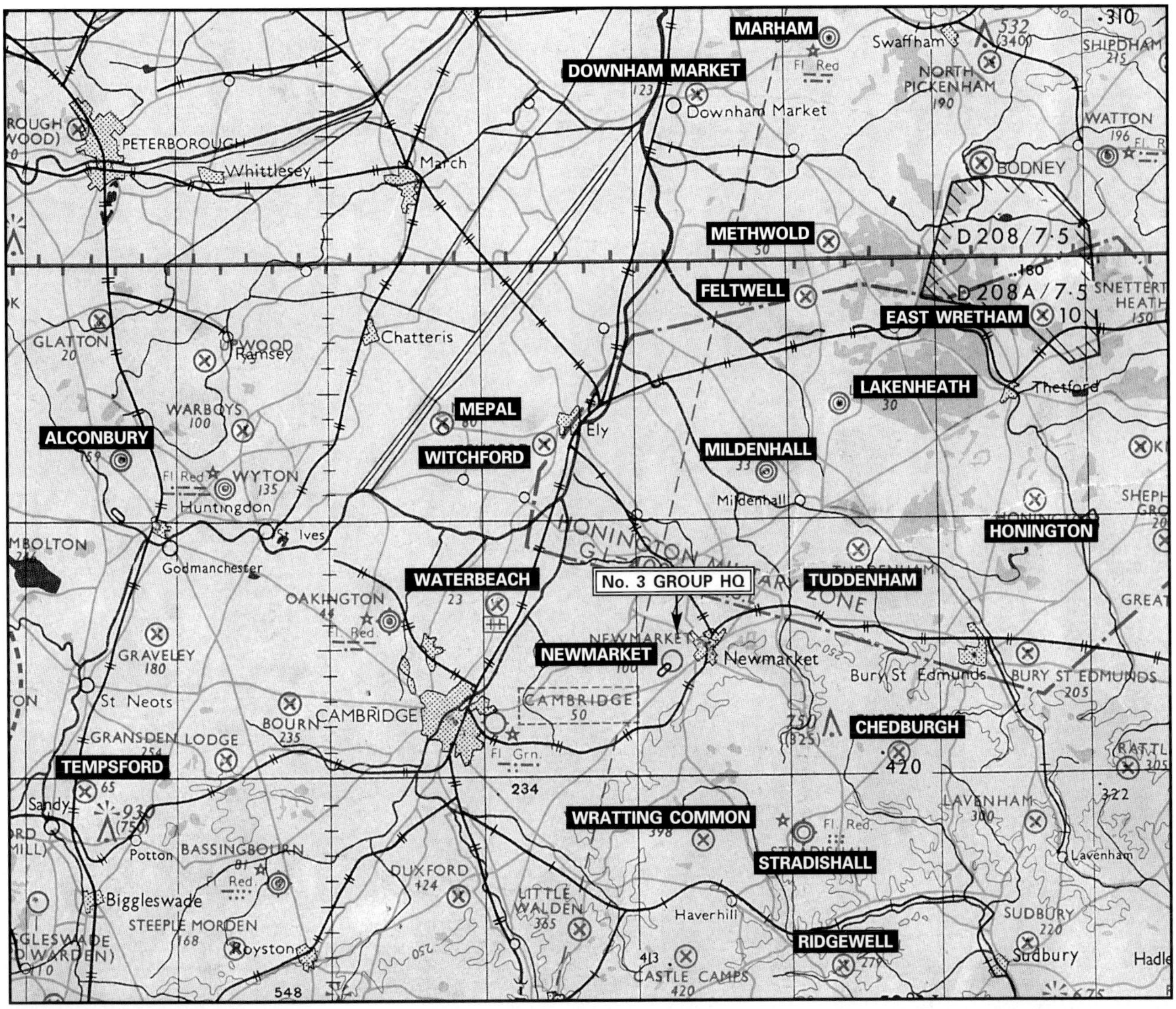

No. 3 GROUP HQ

Scheduled to control the RAF medium/heavy bomber squadrons, No. 3 Group HQ came into being at Andover on May 1, 1936 and soon gathered 14 squadrons spread far and wide with a collection of types, chiefly Heyfords and Virginias. However, a planned reorganisation and formation of two more bomber groups saw No. 3 Group

HQ moved to Mildenhall, Suffolk, in January 1937 and selected to operate the new Wellington medium bomber, the first of which arrived in autumn 1938. A year later it commenced operations with an all-Wellington force of over 100 in eight squadrons at five East Anglia airfields.

In March 1941 the group headquarters was moved to the mansion in Exning, near Newmarket, where it remained for the rest of the war. By the end of 1941 its strength had increased to more than 200 bombers and 14

squadrons, three of which were equipped with the Stirling four-engine heavy. Plans to make No. 3 an all-Stirling group were discontinued when the limitations of this type became clear and by early 1943 the last of the Wellington squadrons commenced conversion to Lancasters. Seven Stirling squadrons were gradually converted to the Lancaster during the following months, the group's last operation with the type being in September 1944. By May 1945 No. 3 Group had 330 Lancasters in 11 squadrons on nine airfields.

Exning House, standing in park grounds on the east side of the village, was acquired by the Air Ministry in the 1930s for use as the headquarters for the newly formed No. 3 Group. Returned to private ownership in the 1950s, it was scheduled for conversion into flats when we took this picture at the end of the century.

ALCONBURY

Before hard dispersals were laid, bombers were often parked on a runway not in use if there was a risk of bogging down in the rain-soaked turf. R1647 BL-R survived operational service to serve with two OTUs before being scrapped.

In 1937 some consideration was given to dispersal of Bomber Command aircraft in the event of air raids on its stations. Despite efforts to keep new airfield sites and measures to camouflage them secret, there was little doubt that the potential enemy knew exactly where they were and would have little difficulty in finding them from the air. Satellite aerodromes were considered one answer to this threat — a landing ground within reasonable road travel distance of the parent airfield to which aircraft could be diverted if the home station was bombed or likely to be attacked. If need be operations could be conducted from the satellite field with fuel and munitions delivered by road. Thus, in the spring of 1938, the Air Ministry acquired some 150 acres of open meadowland at Alconbury Hill, Huntingdonshire, expressly for use as a satellite airfield. The exact location was adjacent to the ancient Roman road Ermine Street, north-west of Little Stukeley village, near to the junction where Ermine Street became A1 instead of A14. After only a minimum of preparation, it was put to the test in May 1938 when No. 63 Squadron, the first to be equipped with the Fairey Battle light bomber, flew in from its home station of Upwood five miles away. This was a two-day training exercise and other squadrons were to follow over the next 15 months. During this period, accommodation was limited to a few wooden huts but plans were afoot to provide both refuelling and rearmament facilities.

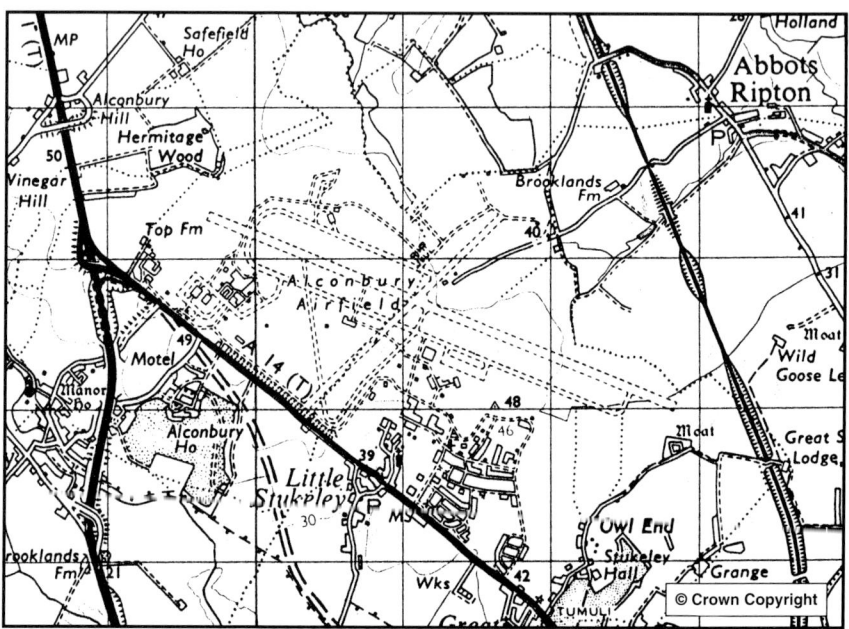

For nearly six decades, Alconbury remained one of Britain's front line bases, first under the auspices of RAF Bomber Command from 1938 to 1941, then the United States Army Air Force between 1941-1945, and from 1953 to 1995 by the United States Air Force. During that time the facilities were greatly enlarged, the main runway being more than doubled in length.

Then the main runway at Alconbury hosted the war machines of No. 40 Squadron . . . now replaced by a lone security vehicle.

New hangars and hardened shelters erected during the USAF era have drastically changed the Alconbury skyline.

Soon after war was declared, Upwood squadrons were given operational training roles and Alconbury became Wyton's satellite under No. 2 Group. That station's resident squadrons during the 'Phoney War', Nos. 12, 40 and 139, frequently deployed to Alconbury, No. 139 being the first to be actually stationed there, if only for nine days. Nos. 15 and 40 Squadrons converted from Battles to Blenheims but did not take part in bombing raids with the new type until the German Blitzkrieg was unleashed in May 1940. No. 15 Squadron took up residence on April 14, when additonal requisitioned accomodation was available. It flew its first raid of the war on May 10 against a German-occupied airfield near Rotterdam, all eight aircraft returning, some with flak damage. A following operation, an attempt to break the Albert Canal at Maastricht, was disastrous as half the 12-plane force despatched failed to return. The remnants of No. 15 then moved back to Wyton and Alconbury reverted to satellite use by both Wyton squadrons. In the autumn of 1940 these decimated units were scheduled to be converted to Wellingtons and on November 1, Wyton and Alconbury came under the control of No. 3 Group.

Alconbury was then upgraded to bomber airfield status, W & C French Ltd being the main contractor. A main concrete runway bearing 00-18 was built 1,375 yards long, the ancillaries 06-24 being 1,240 yards and 12-30

Alconbury 'airdrome' pictured by the US Eighth Air Force on March 12, 1943.

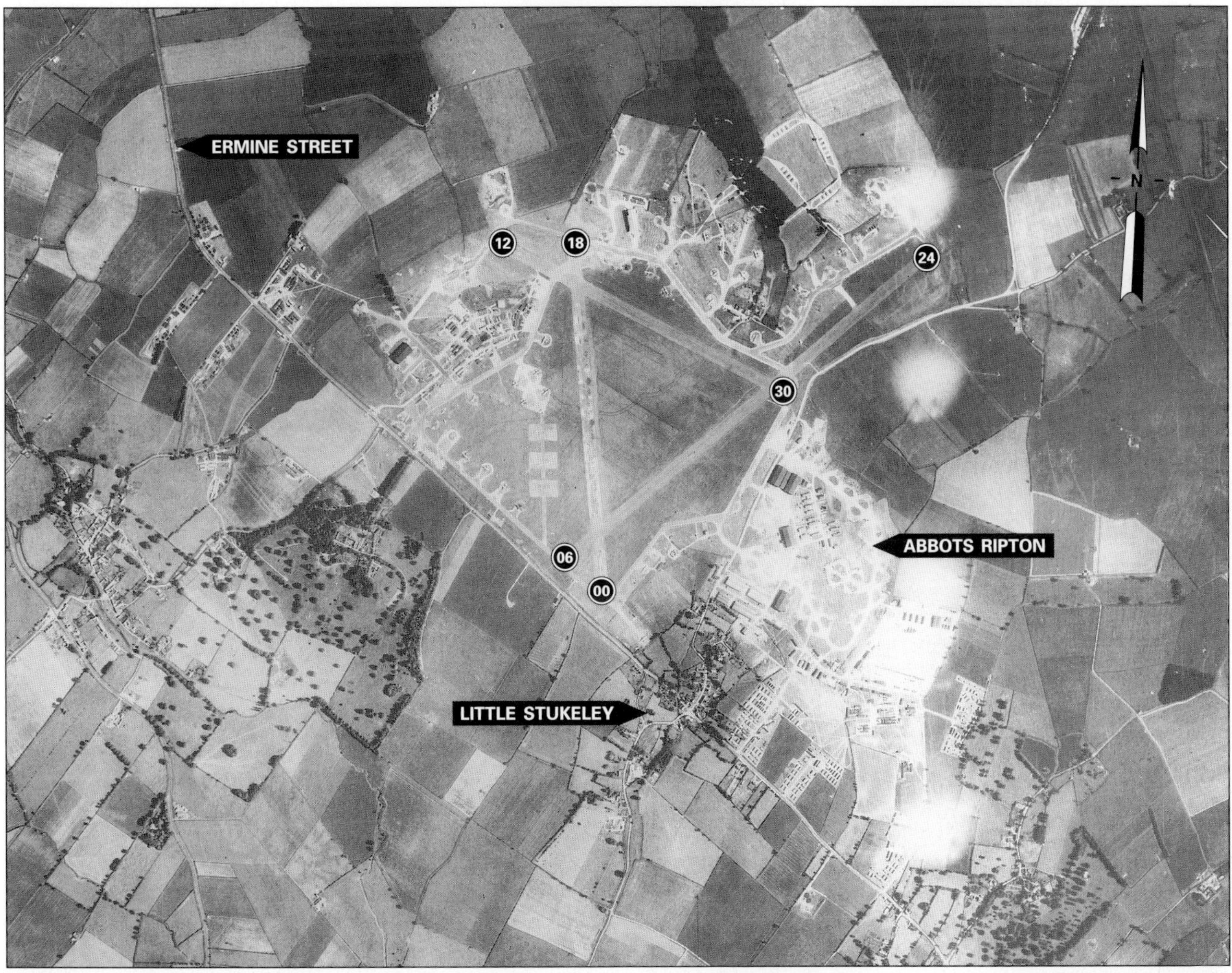

ERMINE STREET

LITTLE STUKELEY

ABBOTS RIPTON

The main runways for propeller-driven aircraft were always laid down to take advantage of the prevailing wind — westerly or south-westerly in Britain — so the 06-24 runway, aligned north-east to south-west, was designated the primary at Alconbury. This was increased from 1,240 yards to 2,000 yards in 1942 when the airfield was upgraded to Class A standard for heavy bomber use. However the ever-longer runways demanded for the operation of jet-powered aircraft (where wind direction is not of the essence), led to the secondary runway 12-30 becoming the main. This was extended to 3,000 yards in the early 1950s for the Strategic Air Command when the airfield was handed over to the USAF. A major factor in the choice of Alconbury as a base was the servicing and repair complex which had been established during the war off the south-eastern corner as a separate station — No. 547 — Abbots Ripton.

Empty since the USAF vacated the airfield in 1995, Alconbury Developments Limited — a joint venture between the British Airports Authority (BAA Lynton plc) and ProLogis Kingspark Developments Limited — are conscious of the long link with military aviation and they have announced that a heritage centre will be set up once development is underway 'to honour the memory of the people in the armed forces who have worked on this former RAF site over the years'. The oblique taken in September 2000 shows rows of vehicles parked on the western end of the main runway.

at 1,110 yards, all 50 yards wide. The encircling perimeter track served 30 pan type hardstandings, most leading off of five long access tracks on the northern side of the airfield. The technical site on the north-west side was expanded where a single T2 hangar was also erected. A second T2 was sited adjacent to the hardstanding complex east of the threshold of runway 18. Personnel accommodation was provided to the south-west side of the A14, around Alconbury House which had been requisitioned earlier.

While this work was in progress, No. 40 Squadron brought its Wellingtons to Alconbury in February 1941 and operated on night raids until the autumn. In October two of its flights with 16 Wellingtons were dispatched to operate from Malta, supposedly on an emergency detachment. The residue of No. 40 soldiered on but never had more than eight aircraft on strength. By February 1942 it was evident that the major section of No. 40 would not be returning from the Mediterranean area and on St Valentine's Day 1942 the Alconbury element formed into No. 156 Squadron. Operations with No. 3 Group continued until August when No. 156 was chosen to become one of the special Pathfinder Force units, moving to Warboys early that month. This was the end of RAF Bomber Command's association with Alconbury as earlier that year the airfield had been included in the group area planned for the first US Eighth Air Force Bombardment Wing with headquarters at Brampton Grange. This was currently the domain of the non-operational No. 8 Group which was acting as caretaker for the 15 existing and planned airfields in this area. A total of 67 bombers had been lost in RAF Bomber Command operations flown from Alconbury, eight were Blenheims and 59 Wellingtons.

USAAF personnel arrived in August 1942 and the following month the 93rd Bomb Group flew in with the first B-24 Liberators to join the Eighth Air Force. Runway lengthening was then underway to bring the airfield up to Class A standard: 06-24 to 2,000 yards and subsidiaries both to 1,400 yards. The work was completed by the end of the year when the B-24s left but additional hardstandings, all loops, were not ready until April 1943 when the B-17s arrived. At first, Alconbury was the home of the four squadrons of the 92nd Bomb Group, but later in the year the special pathfinder organisation, the 482nd Bomb Group, was built up at Alconbury. This organisation provided pathfinder leads with both H2S and H2X radar-equipped B-17s and B-24s for Eighth Air Force missions, although from the spring of 1944 to the end of hostilities, its role was primarily training. During the latter part of 1943, an air depot facility was added at the Little Stukely end of the airfield occupied by the 2nd Strategic Air Depot tasked with the major repair, servicing and modification of B-17s of the 1st Division.

Alconbury was handed back to the RAF on November 26, 1945 and remained on care and maintenance status for 7½ years but the threat from the USSR brought the Ameri-

These are the two T2s bordering the taxiway at the south-eastern end.

cans back to Alconbury, officially on June 1, 1953. The airfield had been selected for further upgrading with strengthening and extension of runway 12-30 to 3,000 by 67 yards. New aircraft standings, access tracks together with an on-going programme of service and domestic building continued for some years. First USAF flying unit based on the rejuvenated Alconbury was the 85th Bomb Squadron with B-45 Tornado jet bombers. This unit converted to B-66B Destroyers before departing in August 1959. The 10th Tactical Reconnaissance Wing arrived from France later that month flying RB-66s, the reconnaissance version, retained until 1965 when the two squadrons of the wing converted to the RF-4C Phantom. The 527th Tactical Fighter Training Squadron with Northrop F-5Es replaced one of the Phantom squadrons in April 1976 and eventually a version of the U-2 'spy plane', the TR-1, replaced the other Phantoms. A-10s and other types operated from Alconbury before the USAF withdrew in 1995. Sold to British Airports Authority for commercial development in 1997, the runway and hardened aircraft shelters were to be retained for ten years, yet Alconbury's long term future as an airfield is unlikely.

Original flight control buildings just off the taxiway at the western end.

127

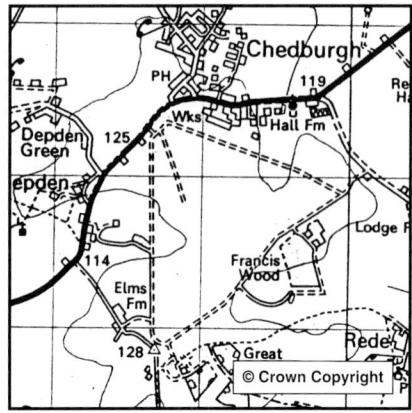

© Crown Copyright

CHEDBURGH

Planned as a subsidiary station serving Stradishall, Chedburgh was built on farmland directly south of the village of that name, located on the A143 road six miles from Bury St Edmunds. Major construction work was carried out by John Laing & Son Ltd during the first nine months of 1942 with an official opening of the station in No. 3 Group on September 7 that year. Built to Class A standard, the airfield had three concrete runways, 05-23 at 2,000 yards and 12-30 and 17-35 both at 1,400 yards. Around the concrete perimeter track were 34 pan and two loop hardstandings. Two T2 and a B1 hangar were positioned on the sub-technical site near Rookery Farm, the B1 westernmost. Later two more B1s were erected for glider storage near Brush Wood, east of runway head 05, and a single T2 for the same purpose just south of runway head 30. The technical site was on the north side between runway heads 12 and 23, close to Chedburgh Hall and church. Dispersed domestic sites for 1,862 males and 238 females were also north of the airfield. The bomb stores were located off to the south-east between runway heads 30 and 35, near Rede Hole.

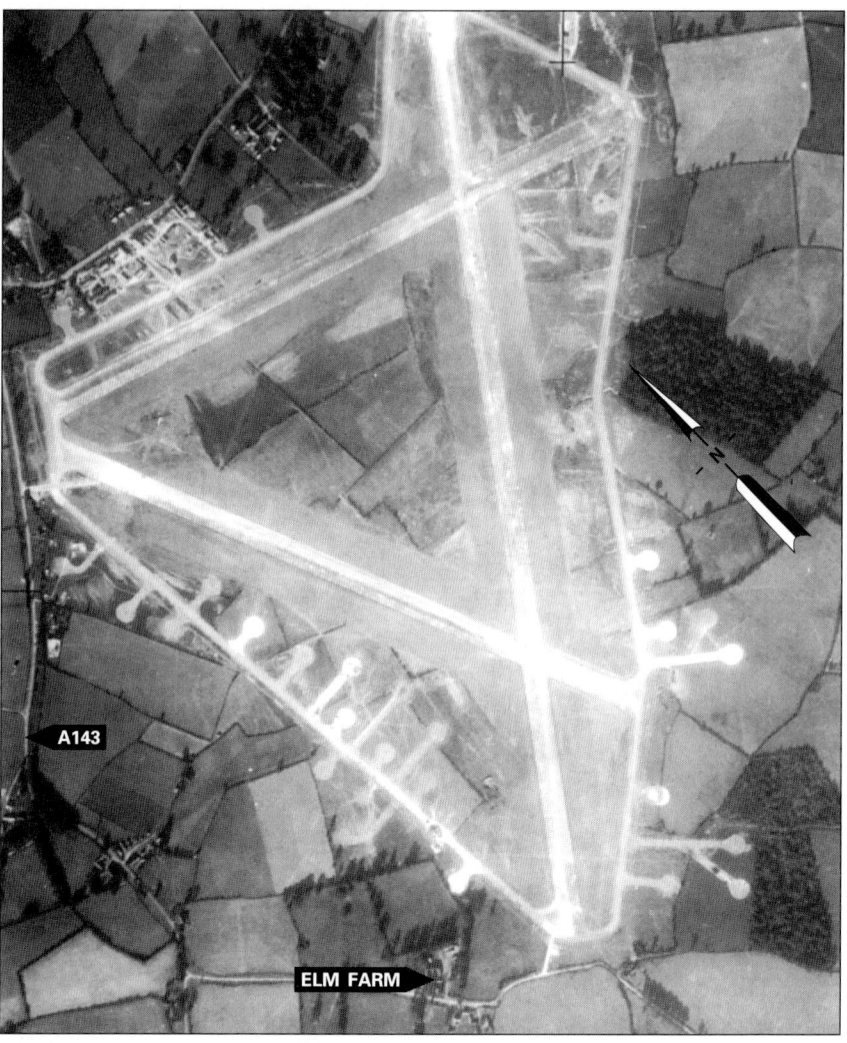

A143

ELM FARM

A bright scar across the landscape, this picture was taken the day after Chedburg opened for business in September 1942.

Back under the plough. With Elm Farm in the foreground, the airfield — having served its purpose — has returned to agriculture.

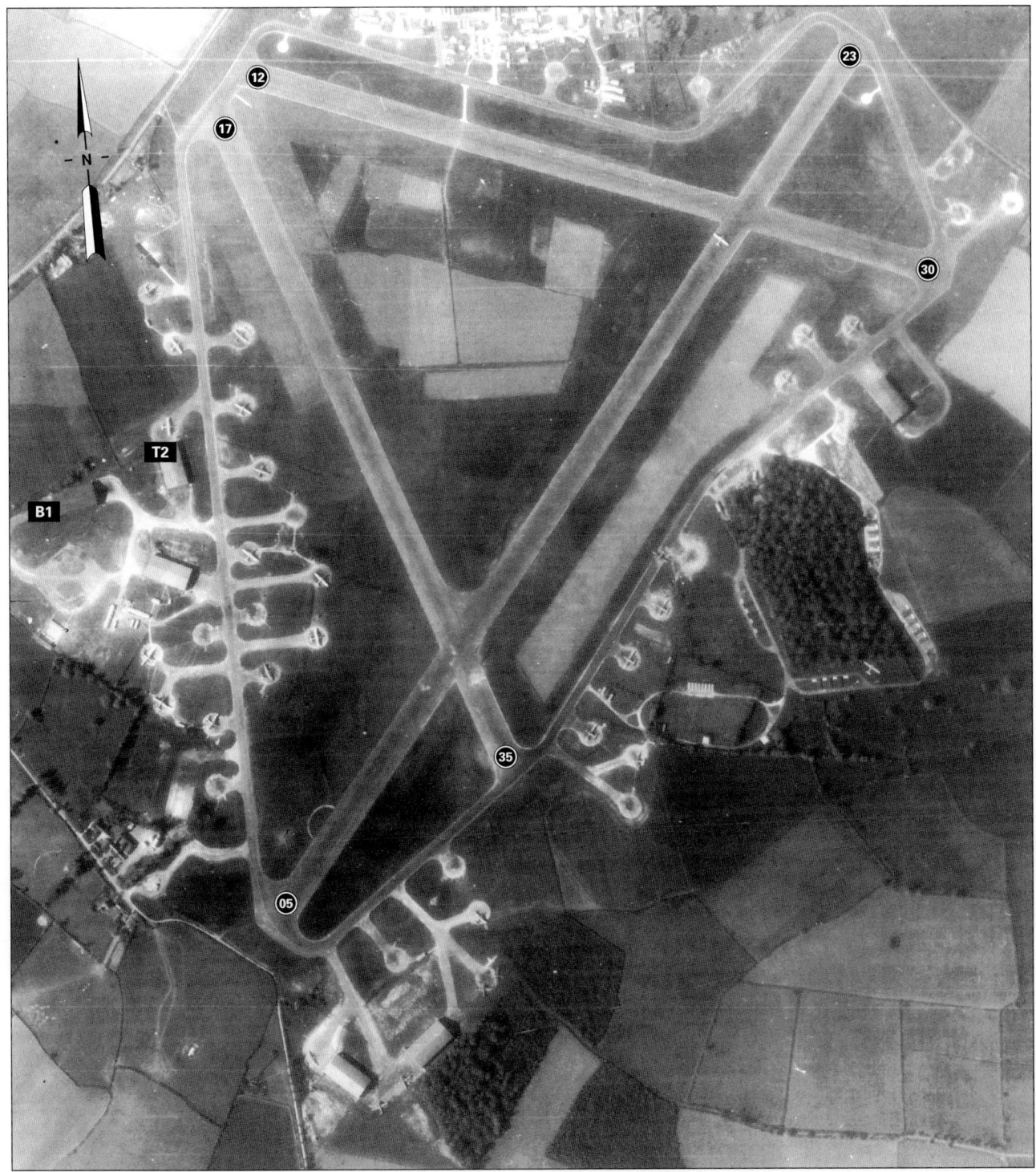

Hostilities have ended and Warwicks and Halifaxes of RAF Transport Command are now dispersed on the aerodrome which was then (May 9, 1946) occupied by Nos. 301 and 304 Polish Squadrons. The B1 and T2 hangars depicted overleaf are marked.

The first operational squadron to be based at Chedburgh, No. 214, moved in October 1942 from Stradishall where it had converted from Wellingtons to Stirlings a few months earlier. During its fourteen months at Chedburgh, the squadron lost more than 50 Stirlings on operations and in crashes. Built up to a strength of 24 aircraft in the spring of 1943, its 'C' Flight, and that from No. 149 Squadron at Lakenheath, became the nucleus of No. 620 Squadron, formed on June 17 and put immediately on operational status. No. 620 added another 25 Stirlings to Chedbrugh's crippling losses before the squadron was transferred to Transport Command and moved out to Leicester East on November 27, 1943. By this date No. 3 Group was going over to the Lancaster and the following

month No. 214 Squadron moved to Downham Market, preparatory to joining No. 100 Group for bomber support operations flying Fortress IIIs. However, Chedburgh retained Stirlings and No. 1653 Heavy Conversion Unit formed here officially on November 21. Still linked to Stradishall, which under Bomber Command identification of main stations became No. 31 Base in the spring of 1943, Chedburgh provided 'polish' for Stirling crews going to No. 3 Group's squadrons still operating the type. Nevertheless, the days of the Stirling as a bomber were over and in December 1944 No. 1653 HCU moved out to North Luffenham to serve Transport Command requirements. Lancasters of No. 218 Squadron moved in during the first week of December 1944 as No. 31 Base became

operational again, eventually building up to a strength of 30 aircraft.

No. 218 Squadron stayed until the end of hostilities, participating in an increasing number of daylight raids, mostly to the Ruhr. Its Lancasters continued to occupy Chedburgh for a several weeks following VE-Day until the unit was disbanded on August 10. During hostilities 83 bombers were lost flying from Chedburgh, 71 being Stirlings and 12 Lancasters. The station was then transferred to Transport Command and in September 1945 two Polish-manned squadrons, Nos. 301 and 304, arrived. Flying a mixture of Wellingtons and Warwicks, replaced by Halifax VIIIs the following year, these units operated long-range transport flights on a diminishing scale until disbandment in December 1946.

Mechanics work on *Edith* (LM577 HA-Q) of No. 218 Squadron on a pan hardstanding (No. 37). The B1 hangar is in the left background with the T2 on the right. The work of the ground crews is often unsung but on a typical bomber airfield with a complement of 2,000 they outnumbered flying personnel ten to one. Altogether there were five trade groups covering more than 50 crafts. Group 1 included airfield controllers, airframe, engine and armourer fitters, wireless and radar (RDF-radio direction finding) mechanics, instrument technicians, draughtsmen, electricians and carpenters. Group II included RDF and wireless operators, photographers, meteorologists, interpreters, bomb disposal as well as a variety of maintenance trades. Group III covered such trades as shoemaker, tailoring and cooking while Group IV could be claimed as covering the administrative side of running an RAF station. Group V included barbers, batmen, drivers, motor cyclists, musicians, PT instructors, police and telephonists and Group M the medical side such as nursing, optician and dental practices. Rates of pay varied according to the rank held from the lowest Aircraftman 2nd Class at 3/- per day to a Warrant Officer at 17/6.

Thereafter Chedburgh, like so many former bomber airfields, remained intact but deserted for some time until the flying field was returned to agriculture and the technical site used for various civilian businesses. Eventually, however, most of the runways fell under the crushing machinery of the St Ives Sand and Gravel Company for the production of hardcore.

The B1, re-clad, survives on the west side of the airfield, but the T2 has gone as has the majority of the concrete.

CRIMPLESHAM

REINSTATED ROAD

It does not look much like a battlefield now . . . but 60 years ago Downham Market aerodrome launched over 300 operations against enemy targets . . . operations which resulted in the loss of 170 aircraft . . . and the award of two Victoria Cross-

es. This oblique, taken in September 2000, looks east down the line of the old main runway which has now been completely expunged from the map. The reinstated subsidiary road from Crimplesham to Wimbotsham can be seen on the left.

DOWNHAM MARKET

Opened in the summer of 1942, Downham Market was built to Class A specification, initially to serve as a satellite for Marham. The airfield site was directly north-east of the small town of the same name, between the A10 and A1122 roads as existed at that time, with the usual technical and operational buildings adjacent to the former. The public road from Wimbotsham to Crimplesham across the north of the site was closed. Messrs W & C French were the main contractors. The lengths of the three concrete runways were 09-27 at 1,900 yards and 16-34 and 03-21 both at 1,400 yards. The 36 pan hardstandings were put down but two were lost when a B1 hangar was built in the north-west corner of the airfield, west of runway head 16. Six T2 hangars were erected during 1942-43, three being for glider storage. Two were off the north side between runway heads 21 and 27; two were on the west side between 09 and 16 and south of the B1 hangar; a single T2 lay to the south-east between runway heads 27 and 34, and another on the technical site between runway heads 03 and 34 alongside the Downham Market road. The bomb stores were in Lough Covert. The dispersed camp, consisting of seven domestic and two communal sites for 1,719 males and 326 females was to the south of Bexwell Hall, requisitioned at an early date for an officers' mess.

The first operational squadron to be stationed at Downham Market was No. 218 equipped with Stirlings which moved in from Marham in July 1942 when this airfield was transferred to the expanding No. 2 Group. This squadron remained in residence for approximately 20 months. As with many other No. 3 Group squadrons, its expanded 'C' Flight was used as a nucleus for a new squadron, No. 623, forming at Downham on August 10, 1943, and flying its first raid that night. The Stirling's vulnerability to enemy

This vertical cover was taken by No. 1 Photographic Reconnaissance Unit (PRU) on April 13, 1942 when the end of the 03-21 runway was yet to be completed. Parts of the perimeter track and all the hardstandings also still had to be laid.

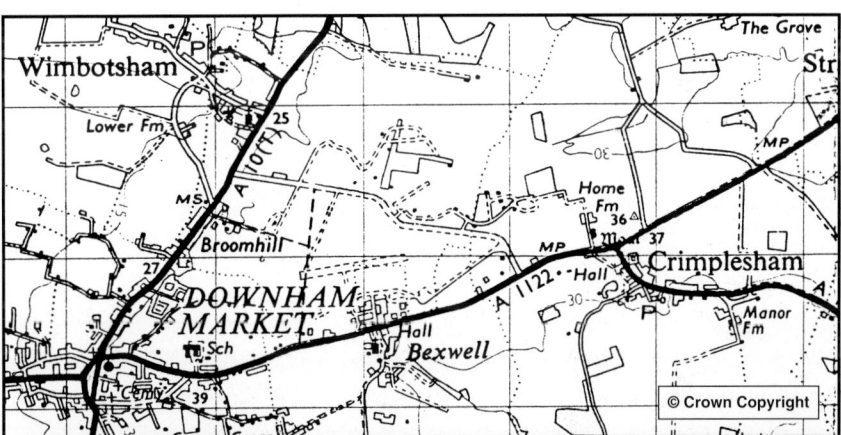

© Crown Copyright

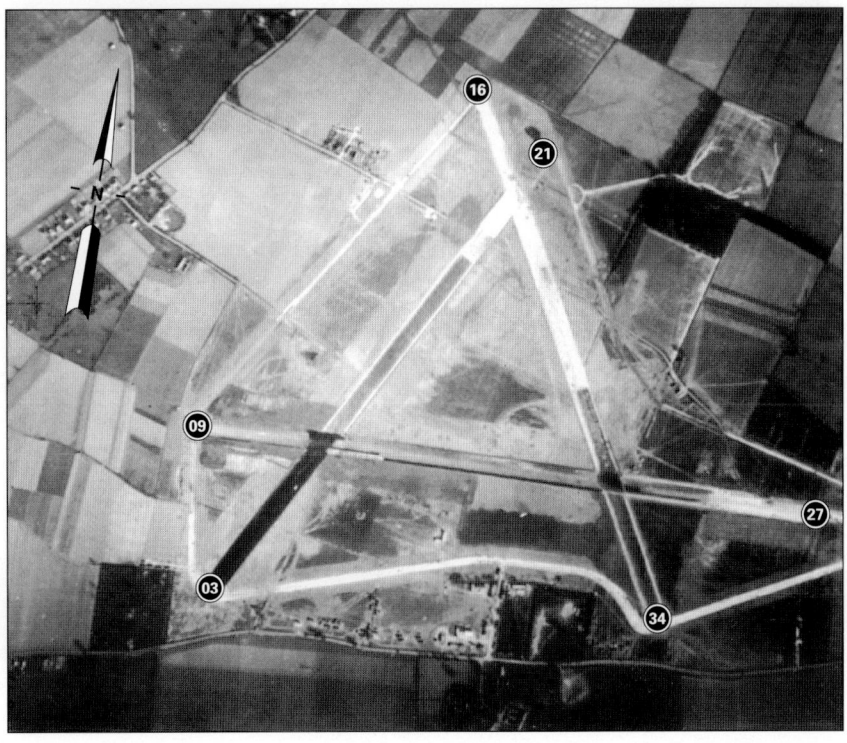

defences, chiefly through its inability to operate at high altitudes, brought a decision to re-equip No. 3 Group with Lancasters. While Stirling squadrons were employed on less exposed duties, notably minelaying, a few were transferred to Transport Command. In No. 623's case, never having been built up to full strength, it was disbanded in early December having existed for less than four months. In 39 operations flying 150 sorties No. 623 lost ten Stirlings while at Downham.

Nos. 218 and 623 Squadron Stirlings were involved in some 300 operations from Downham Market in the course of which over 100 of their aircraft failed to return or were destroyed in crashes. On the night of August 12/13, 1943, during a raid on Turin, Stirling EF452 HA-O was shot up by a night fighter. Despite horrific wounds, the captain, Flight Sergeant Arthur Aaron, aided the crews efforts to fly and crash-land at a North African base where he died a few hours later, an exploit which brought him a posthumous Victoria Cross.

In October 1943, the airfield became the second to have a FIDO installation to disperse fog brought into operation.

In March 1944, Downham Market passed to No. 8 Group and No. 218 Squadron moved out to Woolfox Lodge. No. 8 Group immediately took steps to form another Lancaster squadron, using the 'C' Flights of Nos. 35 and 97 Squadrons from its other stations. As a result, No. 635 Squadron became operational on the night of March 22/23, 1944. In April 1944 a Mosquito squadron was formed

No. 218 Squadron Stirlings make a low pass over Downham Market in the summer of 1942. The photographer was standing near the control tower, the concrete road to the main runway being visible in the lower right-hand corner. A T2 hangar can be seen on the far side of the airfield and the houses at Upper Farm are further to the right. At this time a second T2 had yet to be erected close to that in the photograph. The Stirling, introduced in February 1941, was the first of Bomber Command's four-engined heavy bombers. It was much maligned for its inability to reach its operational height with a full bomb-load and achieved a reputation of being difficult to fly yet it could take considerable punishment due to its robust construction. However the altitude problem led to it being very vulnerable to night fighters as it flew lower than the main bomber stream and the Stirling suffered grievous losses during the first weeks of the Battle of Berlin which began in August 1943. By the third week of November the Stirling squadrons — which equipped most of No. 3 Group's squadrons — had lost 109 aircraft. Also, as the maximum bomb-load of the Stirling — 14,000 lbs — was less than that of the Lancaster and Halifax, the attrition rate of 6.4 per cent was deemed unacceptable and the aircraft was withdrawn from front-line operations the same month. This led to No. 3 Group being relegated to a secondary role until it re-equipped with the Lancaster.

at Downham, No. 571, but it moved the same month to Oakington. Not until August that year was No. 8 Group in a position to follow its general policy of placing one Mosquito and one Lancaster squadron on each station. No. 608 Squadron was re-formed in August and equipped with Canadian-built Mosquitos, operating as part of the Light Night Striking Force five days after its rebirth.

A second Victoria Cross was awarded posthumously to a Downham Market airman for the heroic action by Squadron Leader Ian Bazalgette of No. 635 Squadron on a sortie to Trossy-St-Maxim in France on the night of August 4, 1944.

No. 608 and 635 continued to operate from Downham to the end of the war, both being

disbanded in late summer of 1945. Bomber Command lost 170 aircraft which either failed to return or crashed during the operations launched from this station, the total comprising 109 Stirlings, 40 Lancasters and 21 Mosquitos.

Although the station was retained by the RAF for another year, little flying took place. Closed in October 1946, like many of the surplus airfields it stagnated for a few years before finally being disposed of in 1957. Farming reclaimed the land and the technical site was developed as an industrial estate including a heavy goods vehicle testing centre and depots for Anglia Water and Norfolk Highways. An unmanned radio-relay tower stands in one corner.

Acres of wheat now cover the flying field with the houses at Upper Farm visible in the far distance.

EAST WRETHAM

An area of Breckland heath six miles north-east of Thetford, south-west of East Wretham village, came into use as a satellite for Honington in 1940. As with most hurriedly acquired sites for satellite aerodromes, East Wretham started out with requisitioned properties and a few hastily-erected huts and even tents. Eventually, two grass runways were developed, NE-SW, measuring 1,880 yards and NNE-SSE at 1,400 yards. Over the next two years, 24 Macadam hardstandings with long access tracks were put down, and a technical site erected on the west side, with two Bellman and six Blister hangars at various points round the perimeter. The dispersed camp sites were north-west and north-east of the airfield and consisted of eight domestic, a communal and sick quarters. Wretham Hall was requisitioned and used as an officers' mess.

The station first came into use during the spring of 1940 as a dispersal for Honington's Wellingtons. In later months a more economic policy developed whereby a squadron from the parent station would be moved into the satellite and in mid-September 1941 this was No. 311 Squadron which had started operations earlier in the month from Honington which was the first and only Czech-manned squadron in Bomber Command. It flew from East Wretham until April 1942 when it was permanently transferred to Coastal Command, departing for Northern Ireland. During its stay at East Wretham, its Wellingtons had participated in some 145 raids with a loss of 20 aircraft. A Wellington-equipped training unit for the Czechs, No. 1429 Operational Training Flight, was called upon to participate in two of the Thousand Bomber raids before it left in July.

In June 1942, East Wretham was allocated to the USAAF for development into a bomber station to Class A standard. This work was delayed and when runway laying commenced at Mildenhall when No. 115 Squadron was moved into East Wretham with its Wellingtons. One of the virtues of

Personnel from the Czech Air Force who had fought in France and escaped to Britain were mustered in four Czechoslovak squadrons. Nos. 310, 311, 312 and 313. All but No. 311 served in RAF Fighter Command, the latter being established at Honington in July 1940 equipped with Wellingtons, moving to the satellite at East Wretham in mid-September that year. This machine, (R1598) coded KX-C stands on a freshly laid hard-core dispersal on the western side of the aerodrome.

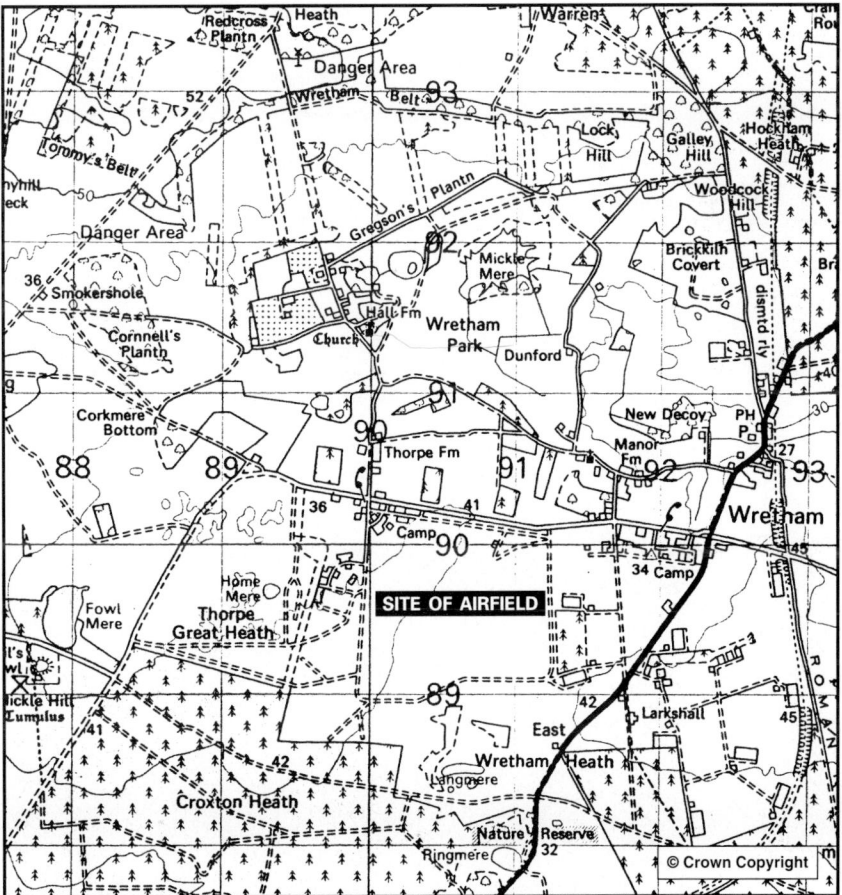

Today the airfield lies within the Stanford Training Area (STANTA).

133

the airfield was the free-draining nature of its sandy soil and no problems were anticipated when No. 115 was converted to the radial-powered Lancaster II in March 1943 and a conversion unit formed with this mark in the same month. The first Lancaster operation from East Wretham was flown on March 20, 1943. In June the plan to turn East Wretham into a Class A standard airfield was abandoned and instead the station was re-allocated to the USAAF for fighter use. No. 115 Squadron took its Lancasters to Little Snoring in August, there being no other suitable stations available in the traditional area of No. 3 Group. This was the end of RAF Bomber Command's association with the airfield which had seen 60 aircraft lost: 39 Wellingtons and 21 Lancasters.

Officially transferred to the US Eighth Air Force in September 1943, the 359th Fighter Group and its three squadrons arrived in October and went into action in December flying P-47 Thunderbolts. The group converted to Mustangs the following spring and remained in occupation until the late autumn of 1945. East Wretham was officially returned to the RAF on November 1, 1945.

No further flying units were based at the station which was retained in a care and maintenance state under three different commands during the early post-war years. The camp was used to house Polish veterans and their families in the late 'forties. Although parts of the site were sold off in the 1950s, several of the camp sites were retained for use by the Army. Later still, a large part of the old airfield was incorporated into the adjoining Stanford Training Area.

Another Czech Wellington (R1804) pictured in a sorry state by the north-west boundary of the airfield close to the Wretham-Croxton Heath road. This was the result of colliding with a steam roller which was made of tougher stuff! Another Wellington can be seen in the distance.

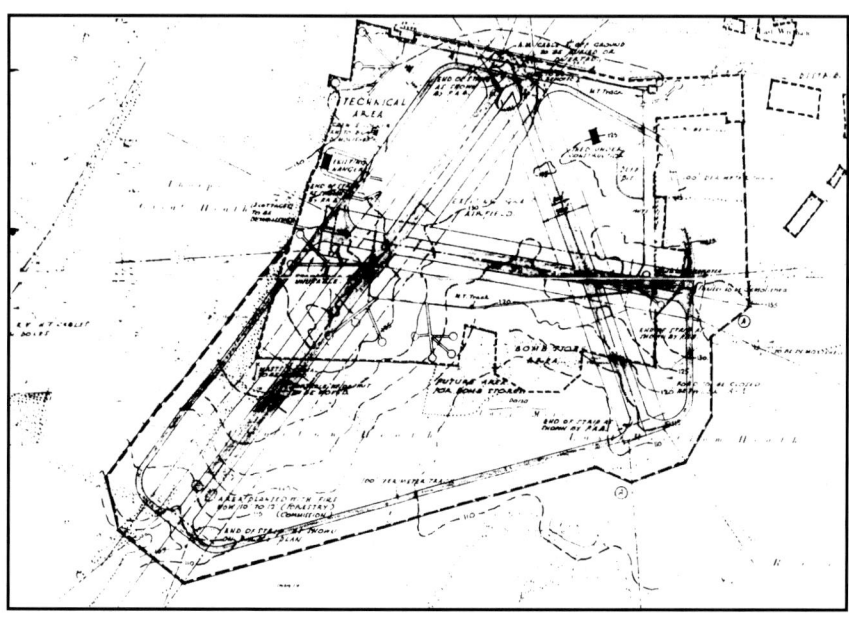

In June 1942, East Wretham was earmarked for transfer to the USAAF as a bomber base to Class A standard. Plans were drawn up but abandoned the following year when it was designated as a fighter station for which hard runways were not considered necessary.

Military buildings now encroach on the area where the Wellington accident occurred. This view had to be taken further away among ripening wheat. The telegraph poles still stand and tree line is little altered. Several of the buildings on the wartime domestic sites near East Wretham village still stand.

Then . . . and now. *Above:* East Wretham looking north-east in February 1942 and from the same angle *below* in September 2000.

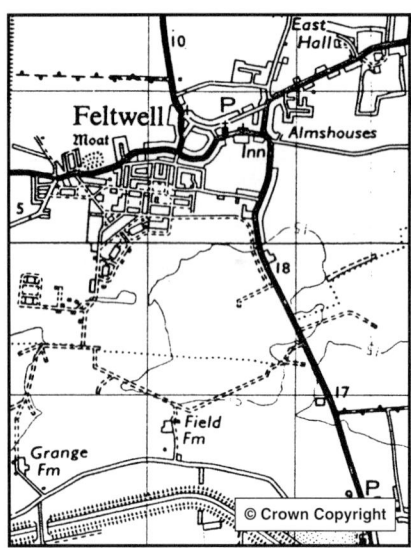
© Crown Copyright

Aircrew of No. 75 (New Zealand) Squadron in the south-west dispersal area. At the time this photograph was taken, early spring 1941, asphalt taxiways and standings were being laid, hard core for which can be seen near the hedge beyond the Wellington.

FELTWELL

The corny RAF joke 'I was stationed at Feltwell but felt bloody awful' could well have had a ring of truth during the early years of the Second World War as on more than one occasion the squadrons operating from this airfield sustained crippling losses which must have had a demoralising effect on survivors.

An expansion scheme airfield, construction began in 1936 on open farmland directly south of Feltwell village on the edge of the fens. Four Type C hangars were placed outside the north-west curve of the bombing circle, with a fifth Type C behind the one furthest north. The hangars were backed by the administrative, technical and barrack area and the adjacent B1386 road. Bomb stores were on the west side of the airfield.

Opened in No. 3 Group, the Handley Page Harrow equipped No. 214 Squadron, which had been building up at Scampton, arrived in April 1937. Bomber Command planned that each of its new airfields would support two squadrons and no sooner had the squadron settled in than one flight was used as a nucleus for No. 37 Squadron which re-formed at Feltwell the same month. Both Nos. 37 and 214 operated Harrows from Feltwell for the next two years, until Wellingtons started to arrive as replacements in May 1939. When war came, Bomber Command had a policy of retaining two squadrons in each group as reserves and No. 214 was one of those so designated in No. 3 Group. A landing ground at Methwold had recently been established as a satellite for Feltwell and No. 214 moved its

The picture was taken from the protective wall of the station small-arms firing range, looking west from near the site of the wartime T2.

aircraft there a few days before hostilities began. On the first day of the war. No. 37 Squadron attempted a raid on German naval vessels off Heligoland. It flew several daylight anti-shipping sorties in the weeks that followed, all without major incident until December 18 when six Wellingtons from Feltwell were intercepted by enemy fighters and only one returned.

In April 1940, the New Zealand-manned flight was given squadron status as No. 75 Squadron and soon expanded to give Feltwell on average two dozen Wellingtons. However, the need to bolster the RAF bomber presence in the Middle East saw No. 37 Squadron leave the airfield in the following November. Its place was taken by No. 57 Squadron, a depleted Blenheim unit from

Feltwell possessed five Type C hangars. This is the second, most southerly one pictured in 1941.

Save for the faded camouflage, the same hangar is now used by the USAF for storage.

the Battle of France destined to be re-equipped with Wellingtons. Eventually, the complement of the two squadrons at Feltwell was established as 36 aircraft, although, through operational commitment, there were sometimes more than 40 and at other times less than 30. Even so, part of the force was frequently dispersed on the satellite at Methwold during daylight hours or operating from Mildenhall.

Feltwell was not without attention from the Luftwaffe, the first recorded attack coming on October 27, 1940 when a hangar was hit. There were five more attacks during the first half of 1941 and another hangar was set on fire during a night raid in May. This could well have resulted from enemy intelligence establishing that Feltwell was one of the Bomber Command stations frequently despatching Wellingtons to attack Reich targets. On one of these raids, that of July 7, 1941 briefed for Münster, a No. 75 Squadron Wellington was set on fire and, for his action in climbing out on a wing to extinguish the flames, Sergeant James Ward was awarded the Victoria Cross.

During the first years of operation, two grass runways were established, E-W at 1,800 yards and NE-SW at 1,400 yards. By 1941, 29 pan-shape hardstandings and one square shape had been put down. They were in clusters with hard access strips; near Grange Farm and Field Farm on the south side and to the east across the B1112. At a later date a T2 hangar was erected near Field Farm and another on the eastern dispersal cluster. Some additional domestic accommodation was built allowing for a total 1,719 males and 515 females on the whole station.

With No. 3 Group converting to Stirlings and Feltwell being of insufficient size and devoid of hard runways, it was decided to transfer the airfield to No. 2 Group for use by medium and light bombers in exchange for Downham Market which was suitable for Stirlings. In August 1942 No. 75 Squadron moved out to Mildenhall to prepare for the arrival of its Stirlings and shortly after No. 57 was transferred to No. 5 Group to reform with Lancasters. During its years of Wellington operations 170 were missing or crashed flying from Feltwell.

No. 2 Group selected Feltwell for forming two squadrons to operate the Lockheed Ventura, an aircraft too slow and poorly-armed for the low and medium level operations to which it was to be committed. The squadrons were Nos. 464 and 487, the former manned by Australian crews and the latter by New Zealanders. The first raid by Feltwell Venturas was carried out successfully on December 6, 1942, against the Philips works

Always a grass-surfaced airfield, the two runways are faintly discernible in this shot taken by No. 540 Squadron in July 1946.

at Eindhoven. In April 1943, the two Ventura squadrons were moved to the up-graded satellite at Methwold leaving Feltwell hosting the Bombing Development Unit and No. 192 Squadron which was engaged in intercepting Luftwaffe radio transmissions. By the turn of the year No. 3 Group was set on trading its Stirlings for Lancasters and the station became the home of No. 3 Lancaster Finishing School which functioned for approximately a year. The Bombing Development Unit returned and Feltwell saw out the war in an experimental capacity. Unlike most Bomber Command stations, Feltwell was never given hard runways. A total of 167 Bomber Command aircraft were lost flying from Feltwell during the war: 152 Wellingtons, 13 Venturas, a Halifax and a Mosquito.

Surplus to the requirements of the fast contracting Bomber Command, Feltwell was

passed to Flying Training Command and for 12 years No. 3 Flying Training School held sway with Tiger Moths, Harvards , Prentices and, finally, Provosts. Its use by major flying organisations terminated with the closing of the school in the spring of 1958. Feltwell returned briefly to Bomber Command when No. 77 Squadron was established as operator of the Thor medium range missile in 1958. Thereafter the station served in personnel training capacities until finally closed although part was still retained as a signals station. Like so many RAF expansion scheme stations, the high standard of the buildings found ready occupants and the USAF at Mildenhall soon made use of the camp. While some barracks are employed for domestic accommodation, an intelligence-gathering unit currently operates from the station with sophisticated electronic equipment.

Looking in more or less the same direction in September 2000 — due south — the most distinctive feature today being the radar radomes of the USAF surveillance complex.

HONINGTON

Fast . . . and on the carpet! An early Mk 1 Wellington in a low-level pass over Honington prior to the outbreak of war. A view south from the far side of the bombing circle towards the hangar line.

This was an expansion scheme aerodrome built in 1935-37 on the edge of the Breckland six miles south of Thetford. The camp was situated on the south-east corner of the landing ground which was fronted by four Type C hangars with a fifth to the rear on the west side. Technical, administrative and barrack buildings were mostly in brick with flat roofs, the camp backing onto the country road to Honington village, two miles to the east. The light nature of the soil proved to be reasonably free draining.

In July 1937 Nos. 77 and 102 Squadrons arrived, the former with Wellesleys and a few Audax, and No. 102 with Heyfords. They had come from Finningley in Yorkshire and in July 1938 returned to that county changing places with Nos. 75 and 215 Squadrons at Driffield. These newcomers were flying Harrows which were to be concentrated in No. 3 Group, albeit that the squadrons commenced conversion to Wellingtons in the summer of 1939. Both were designated as No. 3 Group Pool Squadrons and No. 75 moved to Stradishall from whence No. 9 Squadron arrived to replace it at Honington. Shortly before the outbreak of war No. 215 was also moved leaving No. 9 to undertake the first RAF bombing raid of the war on September 4, 1939, an attempt to attack naval vessels off the German Baltic coast resulting in the loss of two Wellingtons to fighters. No. 9 had Honington to itself until the summer of 1940 when two of the depleted Battle squadrons which had escaped from

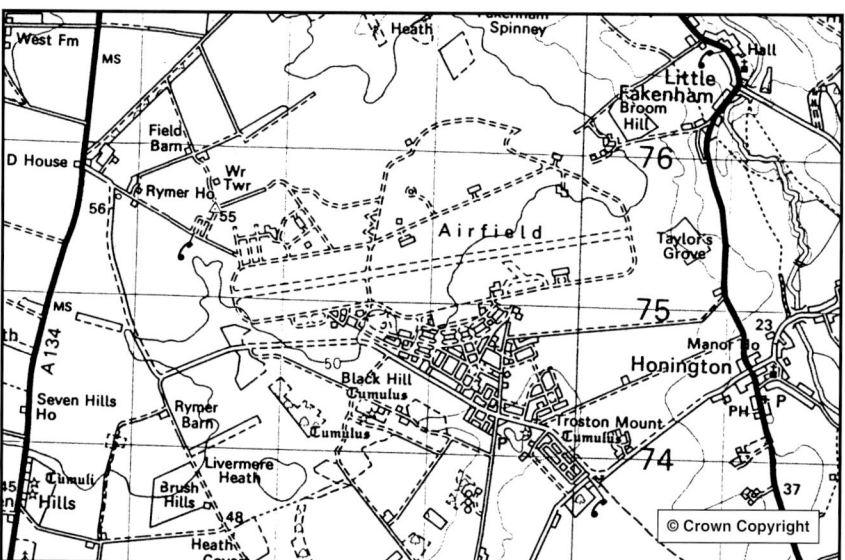

© Crown Copyright

France found shelter there for a month. In late July No. 311 Squadron was formed with Czech airmen to use Wellingtons, flying their first raid on the night of October 10/11, 1940 shortly before being moved to Honington's satellite at East Wretham. No. 9 Squadron continued as the sole resident operational unit until it was transferred to No. 5 Group in

August 1942 and left for Waddington. However, it was joined by No. 214's Wellingtons for a week in January 1942 while work was carried out on their home airfield at Stradishall. All told, 79 of No. 9's Wellingtons failed to return or were lost in operational crashes while the squadron was based at Honington.

Sixty years later, the hangar line still stands bold beyond the post-war runway.

The large USAAF service and repair installation — the 1st Strategic Air Depot — can be seen to the west of the airfield.

During 1939-41, 18 small pan hardstandings were laid down at Honington, most off exceptionally long access tracks, those to the south crossing the public road. A tarmac perimeter road was also constructed during the same period. The runways remained grass with 1,400 yard runs NE-SW and SE-NW.

Honington was then transferred to the USAAF which had been allocated the station in June 1942 for development to a Class A standard bomber base. In September, VIII Air Service Command arrived to establish an air depot which eventually became the 1st Strategic Air Depot providing major servicing, repair and modification for B-17 Fortresses of the 3rd Bomb Division.

From February 1944 the station also housed the 364th Fighter Group and its three squadrons, first flying P-38 Lightnings and later P-51 Mustangs. The fighter group departed in November 1945 but Honington continued as an air depot until February 1946 becoming the last USAAF station to be returned to the RAF.

During the American occupation a perimeter track and 68 loop and a single pan hardstandings were put down, several of these on the special depot site built on the west side of the airfield and officially named Troston. A single T2 hangar was added on this site and eight Blister type were also erected on the airfield. Concrete runways were never built but the Americans put down 2,000 yards of steel planking on the main 05-23 runway.

Post-war, Honington was used by maintenance units until the early 1950s when a 3,000-yard concrete runway was laid. When re-opened for flying in 1955, four Canberra equipped squadrons were installed. From the following year Valiants were also present and from 1959 Victors. The V-bomber squadrons were withdrawn in the mid-1960s and after four years without resident squadrons the station became host to shore-based Buccaneers. These remained until the early 1980s when Tornado squadrons took over and were present for ten years. Then in 1994 Honington became the depot station of the RAF Regiment with much upgrading of buildings. The flying field with reserve status has been maintained and improved and is used during exercises.

Active flying ceased in March 1994 when Honington became a Deployed Operating Base.

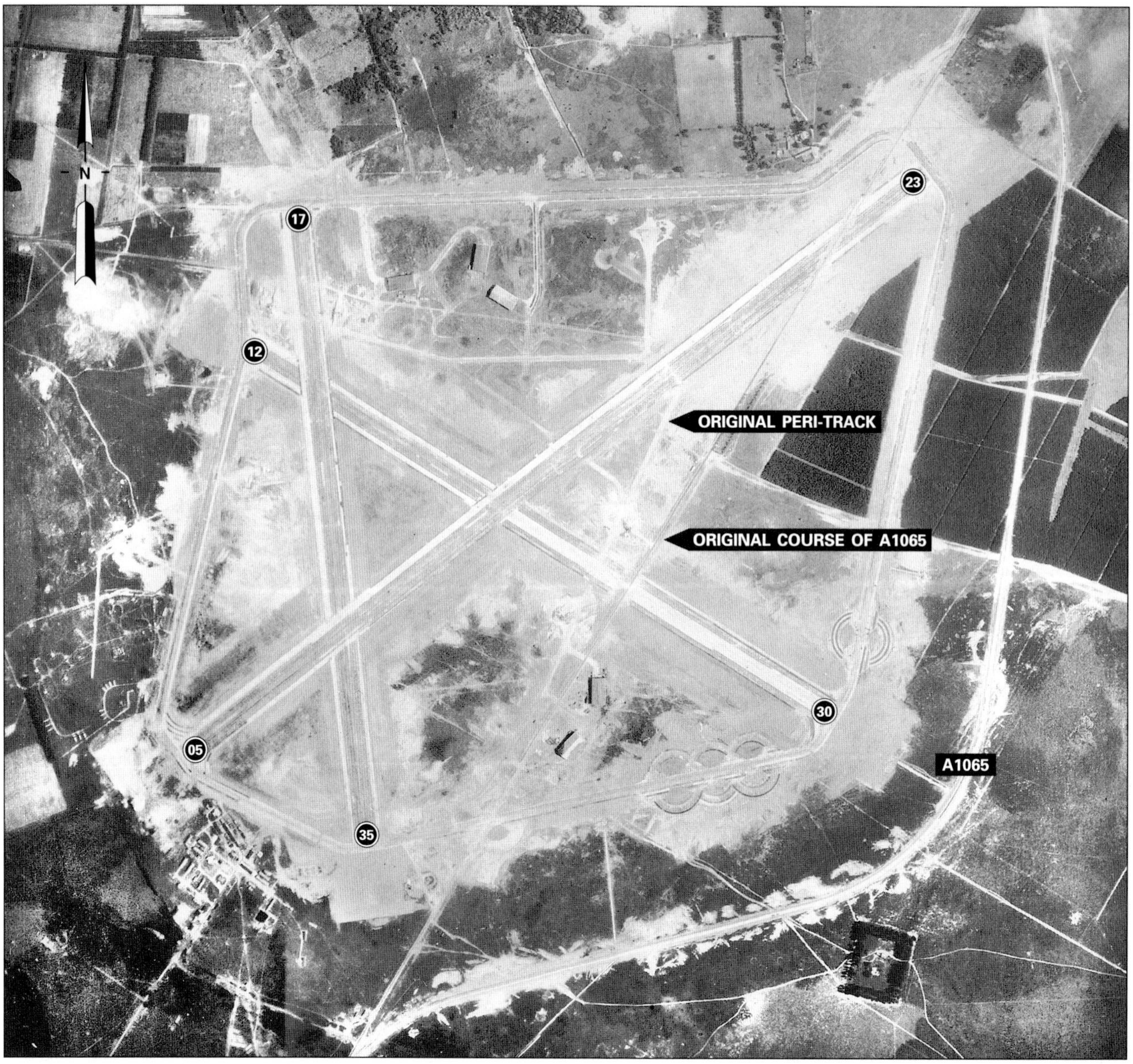

Although built only as a satellite aerodrome, with its subsequent upgrading to Very Heavy Bomber status in 1944-45 (this photo shows all the signs of its reconstruction), Lakenheath survived the post-war demolition of most of the other temporary bases and remains today a front-line airfield, occupied since 1948 by the United States Air Force.

LAKENHEATH

The sandy soil that skirts the eastern side of the Fens through much of Norfolk and Suffolk is know as the Breckland. Mostly too poor for agricultural use, it was a wild place of heather and bracken populated only by rabbits. One virtue of the soil was its good draining properties which had some bearing on the selection of several sites in the Breckland for aeroplane landing grounds. Lakenheath Warren was apparently under consideration but in the event was made into a bombing and ground-attack range for aircraft flying from elsewhere in the area. It appears to have been little used and soon given back to the rabbits when peace came in 1918.

In 1940, the Air Ministry selected Lakenheath as an alternative satellite for Mildenhall and the following year construction began east of the low hill beyond which Lakenheath village lay. Hard runways were put down by W & C French Ltd, their original lengths being extended before the airfield was completed. The main, 05-23, was 2,000 yards, and the subsidiaries, 12-30 at 1,300

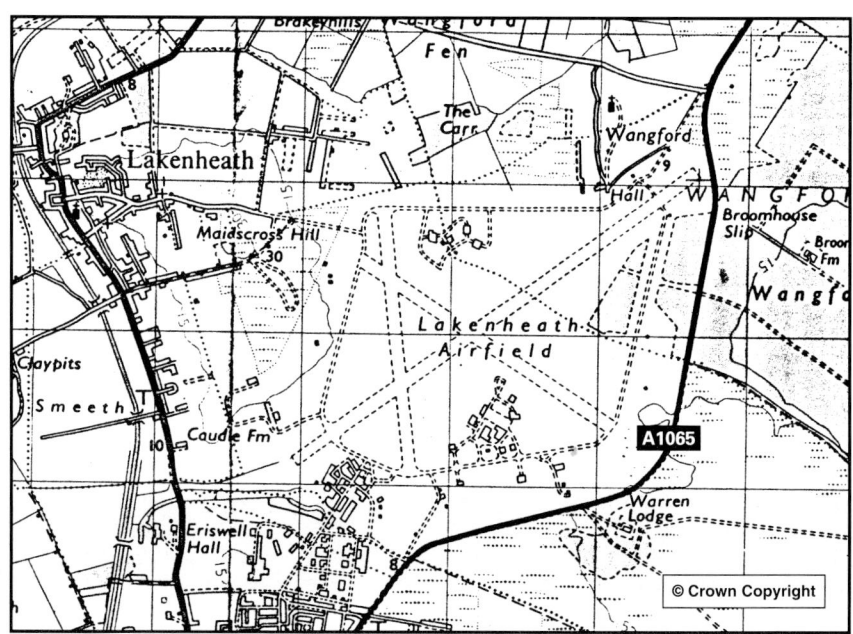

© Crown Copyright

140

Picture taken during Lakenheath's tenure by RAF Bomber Command. Sergeant Edward Brimicombe, in white overalls stands with his repair team. The Stirling is 'G'-George of No. 149 Squadron (code OJ).

Lakenheath during that year. Messrs W. Lawrence & Son Ltd and Rattee & Kett Ltd were involved in this and other construction work which gave the station accommodation for a total 1,705 male and 245 female personnel.

As part of No. 3 Group's expansion, in June 1943 No. 199 Squadron was established as a second Stirling squadron at Lakenheath. Commencing operations on July 31, it was engaged principally in mine-laying during the winter of 1943-44. At the end of April, after 68 operations, the squadron was transferred to No. 100 Group for bomber support operations moving out to North Creake in May. No. 149 Squadron ended its long association with Lakenheath the same month, taking its Stirlings to Methwold. Between them the two squadrons had lost 116 Stirlings while flying from Lakenheath.

The reason for the exodus was Lakenheath's selection for upgrading to a Very Heavy Bomber airfield, one of three RAF aerodromes being prepared to receive B-29 Superfortresses which were tentatively planned to replace some Eighth Air Force B-24 units in the spring of 1945. The work carried out by George Wimpey & Co. Ltd entailed removal of the existing runways and laying new ones comprising 12 inches of high-grade concrete. The main at 07-25 was

yards and 17-35 at 1,400 yards. At a later date, another 100 yards was added to runway 17-35. Hardstandings for 36 aircraft were built and two T2s and a B1 provided later for undercover facilities. One T2 was on the technical site and the other hangars to the east across the A1065 Mildenhall-Brandon road were reached by taxiways.

Lakenheath first came into use for flying units on detachment late in 1941. As planned, the station soon functioned as a Mildenhall satellite with Stirlings of No. 149 Squadron being dispersed from the parent airfield as soon as conditions allowed. The squadron had exchanged its Wellingtons for Stirlings late in 1941 and after becoming fully operational with its new aircraft, the squadron moved into Lakenheath the following April and remained in residence for two years. Taking part in more than 350 operations, of which more than half involved mine-laying, the unit had one of the lowest percentage loss rates of all the Stirling squadrons. One of No. 149's Stirling pilots, Flight Sergeant Rawdon Middleton, was posthumously awarded the Victoria Cross for his valour on the night of November 28/29, 1942 when he sustained serious face wounds from shell-fire during a raid on Turin. Despite great pain and loss of blood, he determinedly brought the damaged aircraft back to the coast of southern England. With fuel nearly exhausted his crew were ordered to bale out, Middleton being

The same north-western corner of the airfield where the conifer plantation is now fronted by underground stores.

killed when the Stirling, BF372 OJ-H, crashed in the Channel.

In early 1943 three T2 hangars were erected on the north side of the airfield for glider storage, some 40 Horsas being dispersed at

3,000 yards long, the subsidiaries, 01-19 and 14-32, both 2,000 yards, all three being 100 yards wide. Part of the A1065 road between Brandon and Mildenhall was closed and a new section built further to the east on the

F-15E Strike Eagles thunder where once Stirlings lumbered.

Warren. During the peak period of construction over 1,000 men were working on the site yet, instead of the 12 months planned, it actually took 18 months for the ground work alone and 2½ years before Lakenheath's transformation was considered complete. The cost was near £2 million. By this time, with hostilities over, the station was put on a care and maintenance status until the Berlin blockade crisis in 1948 required the threat of USAF nuclear bombers. In July, B-29 Superfortresses of the 2nd Bomb Group were detached to Lakenheath for a 90-day temporary duty.

A succession of bombardment groups/wings, 33 in all, rotated through Lakenheath, the B-29s giving way to the improved B-50 Superfortresses and then, in June 1954, B-47 Stratojets, the type which had previously been an itinerant visitor from another UK base. In January 1951, a detachment of the giant B-36D intercontinental bombers arrived for a few days and various tanker and transport aircraft also made periodic appear-

ances at the base. Several of the temporary detachments included in-flight refuelling tanker aircraft. Strategic Air Command's 7th Air Division control of Lakenheath was terminated at the end of 1959 following the ejection of NATO air forces from France whereupon the 48th Tactical Fighter Wing brought its three squadrons of F-100D Super Sabres over from Chaumont in France in January 1960. The Wing converted to F-4C Phantoms in January 1972 and F-111Fs in March 1977, later adding a fourth squadron. With the collapse of the Russian threat and the reduction of the USAF, the F-111s were withdrawn in 1992 and the 48th Wing re-equipped with F-15E Strike Eagles having both defensive and offensive capability. In fact, the 48th is the USAF only major strike unit with a NATO commitment remaining at a UK base at the end of the 20th Century.

Lakenheath 2000. The wartime three-runway layout is still very evident in this oblique, taken looking north.

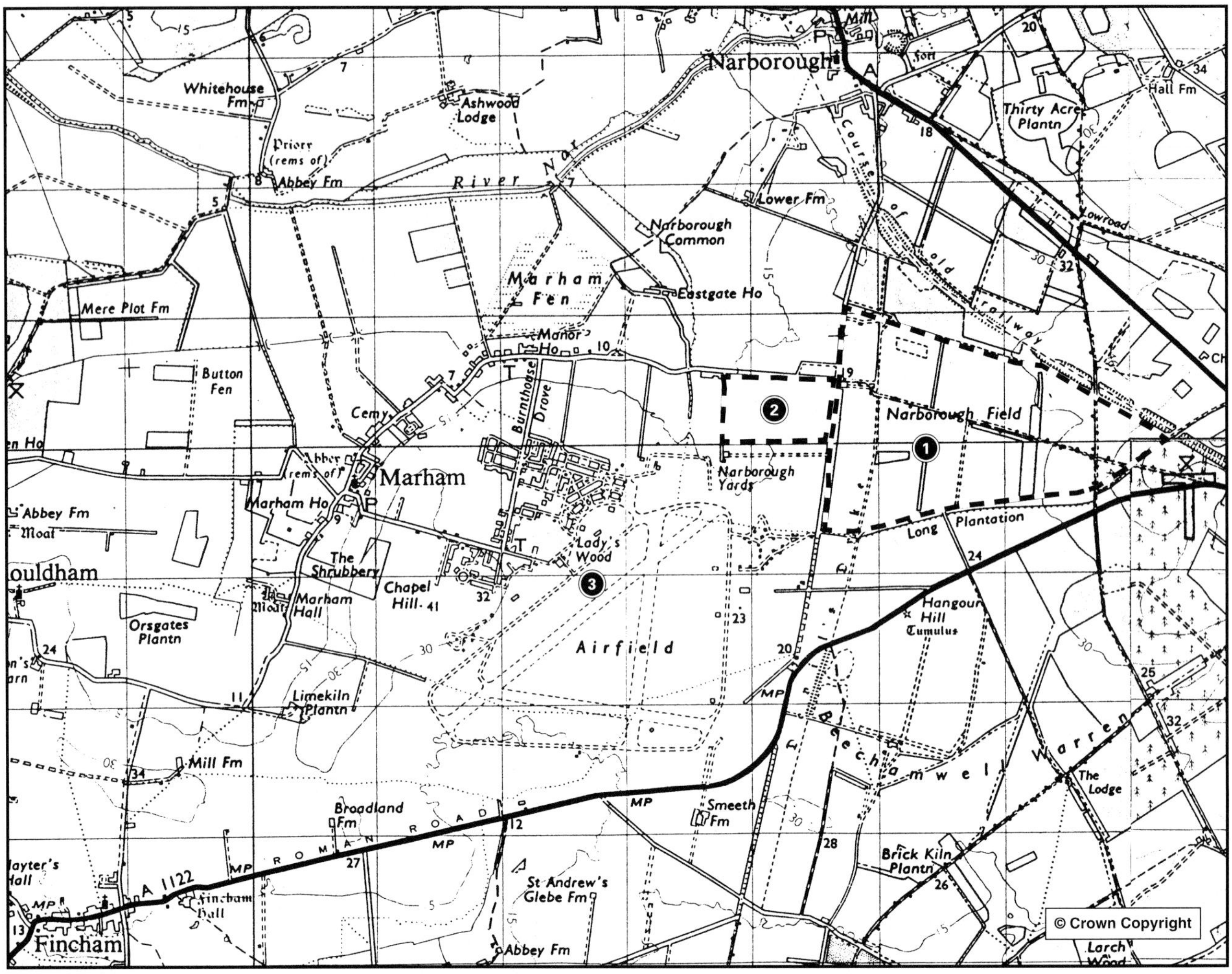

The map at top of page showing Narborough and Marham area.

There is a fascinating history of aviation in the Marham area. Back in 1915, when raids by German airships brought the air war on the Western Front to Britain itself, Narborough Field [1] — an area of common land lying just north of the old Roman Road between Fincham and Swaffam in Norfolk — was put to use as an ideal landing ground for the training airmen in the Royal Naval Air Service. Not to lose out, the Royal Flying Corps then established a training airfield [2] just to the west, and a second RFC aerodrome was opened further to the south-west near Lady's Wood, being called Marham after the nearby village.

MARHAM

The Norfolk Breckland with its free-draining heaths had attracted interest for aeroplane operations from the earliest days of aviation, and in summer 1915 a common to the south and on the west side of the road to Narborough village was prepared as an aerodrome. Its purpose was to provide a landing ground for Admiralty fighters which were operating against Zeppelin night raids. Little used for this purpose, in the following spring the Royal Flying Corps acquired a site for flying training on the opposite side of the road to the RNAS station. Another RFC site was established south-east of Lady's Wood and was known as Marham. A number of squadrons were raised at the Narborough complex and worked up before being despatched to France and a depot was also established there but demobilisation saw the sites abandoned in 1920. Over the next few years most buildings were demolished, a plaque in Narborough churchyard reminding visitors that this was the largest aerodrome in Britain during the First World War.

With the RAF expansion scheme of the mid-1930s, many First World War aerodrome sites were inspected to see if they would be suitable for the new permanent stations planned. As far as the Narborough was concerned, the proximity of a railway line and the closure of public roads were probably among the factors that made the

Apart from Narborough (left) forming the largest air station in Britain during the First World War, its other claim to fame must be that one of aviation's most prolific writers was based there in 1918. Captain W. E. Johns — the creator of every schoolboy's hero Biggles — later wrote that he was present as a training instructor at a time when there were a number of fatal crashes — he recalled 13 in as many days — which he said were attributed by the pilots to sabotage, possibly by one of the American mechanics who was of German extraction. Right: Many of their graves lie nearby in Narborough Churchyard.

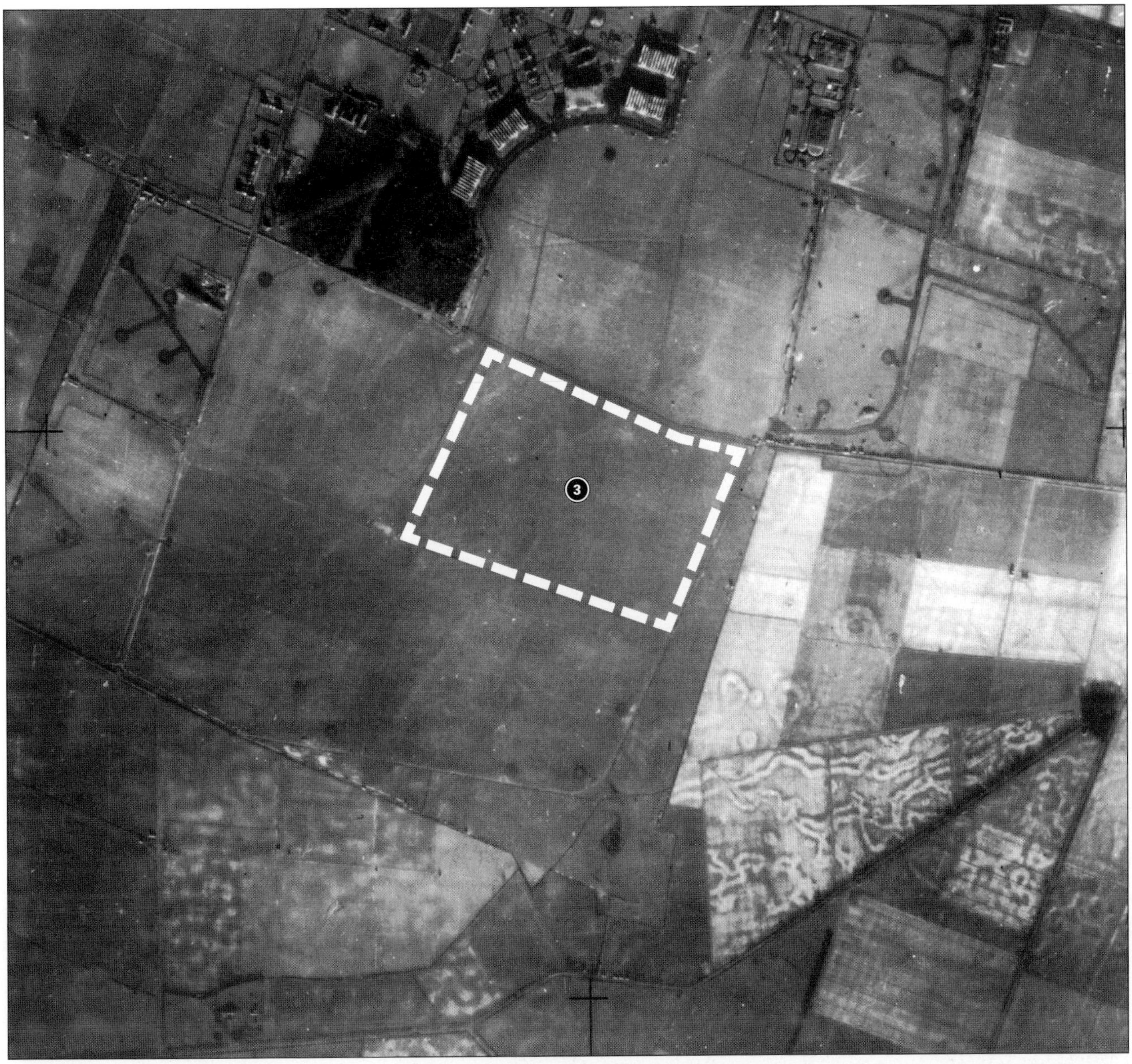

Air Ministry surveyors transfer their attention instead to a more acceptable location. This was found three quarters of a mile away to the south-west, centred on the old Royal Flying Corps aerodrome.

Work commenced in 1936 and RAF station Marham was officially opened on All Fools Day 1937 in No. 3 Group. As with other new bomber airfields constructed during the expansion period, Marham had approximately 200 acres for the flying field with four Type C hangars fronting the bombing circle in a crescent, with a fifth hangar behind the northernmost one. The hangars and the technical, administrative and barrack buildings were on the north-west side of the airfield, accessed by two roads from Marham village. The bomb stores were in the north-east corner of the site.

The first bomber squadron based at Marham, No. 38, was the only squadron to be fully equipped with the cumbersome Fairey Hendon. In pursuant of the expansion programme, six weeks after No. 38 moved in from Mildenhall it provided the nucleus for a second Marham squadron — No. 115 — which was formed from 'B' Flight which worked up to full strength with the Handley Page Harrow. Wellingtons were scheduled, No. 38 being the second squadron in No. 3 Group to receive the type. This was late in 1938 but No. 115 did not trade its Harrows for Wellingtons until the following spring.

Marham as it appeared in January 1943 still as grass-surfaced airfield. The dotted line indicates the boundary of the WW1 RFC airfield ([3] on the map opposite).

No. 115 Squadron suffered more Wellington losses than any other Bomber Command squadron but also flew the highest number of sorties with the type. X3662 KO-P was retired from operations with 36 raids to its credit.

145

The Sergeants Mess — then and now. *Left:* **Camouflaged on the outbreak of war . . . now greatly enlarged with the original block visible behind** *right.*

With the outbreak of war and the policy of, where possible, having a satellite airfield for each bomber station, Marham's Wellingtons found themselves dispersed the other side of the main road (the A1122 from Downham Market to Swaffham). This landing ground at Barton Bendish was obviously too close to home for further development and was abandoned in 1941 when a more suitable satellite became available.

North Sea patrols predominated in the early weeks of hostilities, Marham squadrons not undertaking a daylight bombing raid – against Heligoland – until December 3, 1939. As with other No. 3 Group squadrons, Marham's soon turned almost exclusively to operations during the hours of darkness. From June 1940 the Luftwaffe began to search out the station at night and though some buildings were hit by bombs the damage was never critical to the station's functioning. Commencing sometime during 1940, pan-shape asphalt hardstandings were put down, numbering at least 30 by 1942, and 12 supporting Blister hangars. A perimeter road was also laid during the early months of the war.

In November 1940 the situation in the Middle East prompted the despatch of two Wellington squadrons from No. 3 Group, No. 38 being one. The replacement at Marham was No. 218 Squadron, a one-time Fairey Battle unit temporarily re-equipped with Blenheims after being decimated during the Battle of France, re-established as an effective unit with Wellingtons in the final weeks of 1940. In January 1942, No. 218 started conversion to Stirlings, the fourth No. 3 Group squadron to fly this formidable aircraft. Although the available runway area had been extended since the airfield was laid out, Marham was still turf-surfaced and not a suitable base for bombers requiring a 900-yard take-off run when fully loaded. However, in July 1942, the Stirlings were moved to Marham's satellite Downham Market which did have hardened runways and a few weeks later No. 115's Wellingtons also changed station by going to Mildenhall.

Bomber Command had decided that it made more sense to have No. 2 Group light bombers operating from grass surfaces and the mediums and heavies from hardened runways. Thus, in late September 1942, No. 105 Squadron moved in with Mosquitos followed by No. 139 with Blenheims. The latter was to convert to Mosquito IVs but the low production of this mark delayed re-equipment and No. 139 crews often used No. 105's aircraft. During following months these two squadrons took part in a number of spectacular low-level raids. Their employment changed after May 1943 when No. 2 Group was removed from Bomber Command and Marham's Mosquitos were transferred to No. 8 Group — the Pathfinder Force. Operations were then chiefly under cover of darkness and in this work they were joined by No. 109 Squadron which arrived at Marham in July 1943.

The Mosquitos remained at Marham until the spring of 1944 when they were moved so that the site could be re-developed as a very heavy bomber base, one of first three selected for this transformation. This also marked the end of Bomber Command operations from the station which had seen 214 aircraft failing to return or destroyed in UK crashes. The total embraced 145 Wellingtons, 14 Stirlings and 55 Mosquitos.

The re-construction of Marham got underway in April. Concrete runways 100 yards wide were put down with the main, 06-24, 3,000 yards long and the subsidiaries,11-29 and 15-33, each of 2,000 yards, the airfield taking in new areas of land to the south and south-west. Part of the upgrading included moving a section of the A1122 to the southeast. Some 1,100 men were employed in this 18-month task which cost £1,740,000.

Marham is synonymous with the Mosquito which were there from September 1942 until April 1944 when work began to lay down concrete runways. These wooden wonders of No. 139 Squadron make a nice contrast with the wooden-tailed Canberra T4 (WJ874 masquerading as the prototype VN799) operated by No. 39 (1PRU) Squadron.

Narborough, now criss-crossed by woods, can be seen beyond the far end of Marham's main 06-24 runway.

Re-opened in February 1946, it became the home of the Central Bomber Establishment, engaged chiefly in experimental work using Lancasters and Lincolns. There was USAF participation in some projects with the Berlin crisis bringing in B-29 groups on temporary duty. When Bomber Command took delivery of B-29s under the Washington label, Marham held the conversion unit for the type and most of the nine squadrons that flew Washingtons were at this station at some time or other during 1950-1956. Various Valiant, Canberra and Victor equipped squadrons followed and at the end of the 20th century, Marham remains the only active Tornado strike mission station.

Some reshaping of the airfield has taken place since 1946, chiefly the construction of a new perimeter track and hardstandings in 1950 by John Mowlem & Son Ltd, at a cost of £316,445. Weapons storage sites were much modified and protected and the 1980s saw the provision of hardened aircraft shelters.

Mepel well stocked with Lancasters in the summer of 1945. Construction led to the closure of the road between Sutton and Mepal.

MEPAL

Mepal airfield was built to Class A specification as one of the two satellite stations for the Waterbeach cluster. The site on a 20-foot rise out of the Cambridgeshire fens, was confined by the New and Old Bedford Rivers to the west; the villages of Sutton to the south, Mepal to the north and Witcham due east. As the A142 between Mepal and Sutton ran

across the middle of the site it was closed off and diverted to run on the road through Witcham. Construction began in July 1942 on a £810,000 contract. The concrete runways were: main 08-26 at 2,000 yards, and 05-23 and 14-32 both at 1,400 yards. Thirty-six hard-standings were provided, all being the loop type. Hangars were a T2 and a B1 positioned on the technical site between runway heads 26 and 32, the B1 being to the north, with another T2 on the north side of the airfield between runway heads 23 and 26. The bomb

store lay to the north-west, between 08 and 14. The 11 dispersed sites were all to the east of the airfield around Witcham and consisted of two mess, one communal and eight domestic catering for 1,884 males and 346 females.

Officially opened in June 1943, its first occupants were the Stirlings of No. 75 Squadron, removed from the turf of Newmarket Heath, which conducted its first operation from Mepal on the night of July 3. Named the New Zealand Squadron and manned largely by citizens of that country, No. 75 was

With most of its concrete removed, Mepal now blends into the patchwork quilt of the South Fen.

to remain in residence for a little over two years, seeing out the war from Mepal. No other squadron was based there during this period as No. 75 maintained three flights, their complements often totalling more than 30 aircraft, particularly after Lancasters replaced the Stirlings in March 1944. The squadron lost 104 bombers in operations from Mepal, 50 being Stirlings and 52 Lancasters.

No. 75 Squadron moved out in July 1945 to make way for the assembly and training of Tiger Force, the RAF bomber contingent scheduled to move to the north-east Pacific for operations against the Japanese homeland. These were Nos. 7 and 44 Squadrons, although the latter was soon replaced by No. 49 Squadron. However, the contraction of the RAF during the first year of peace provided several stations with better accommodation than the 'tin can huts' at Mepal and the Lancasters left in July 1946. Thereafter Mepal remained empty of active units for 12 years.

In 1957, the airfield was one of the sites selected to deploy Thor medium-range missiles and three emplacements were built in the north-east corner of the original airfield. When the missiles became active, the operating unit was No. 113 Squadron. By 1963 the Thors were considered obsolete and were removed, the airfield later surrendering to commercial and agricultural use.

The road between Mepal and Sutton villages had been re-opened in the 1950s and in the 1970s the A142 from Chatteris to Ely was established on a new three mile stretch of highway built right across the airfield, bypassing all three of the local villages. Today little of the airfield remains apart from odd lengths of perimeter track used as farm roads. On the south-eastern corner of the airfield site the largest agricultural machinery sale yard in the country was opened in 1997 where monthly hundreds of farm tractors echo the thunder of long-gone heavy bombers.

'They shall beat their swords into ploughshares.' How better to illustrate the verse from Micah than with this shot showing part of Cheffins Grain & Comins — the largest agricultural sales yard in the UK.

The Mepal control tower, left, and the technical site T2, right, viewed from the far side of the airfield in September 1944. This particular Lancaster, PB421 AA-K of No. 75 Squadron, was scrapped in 1947.

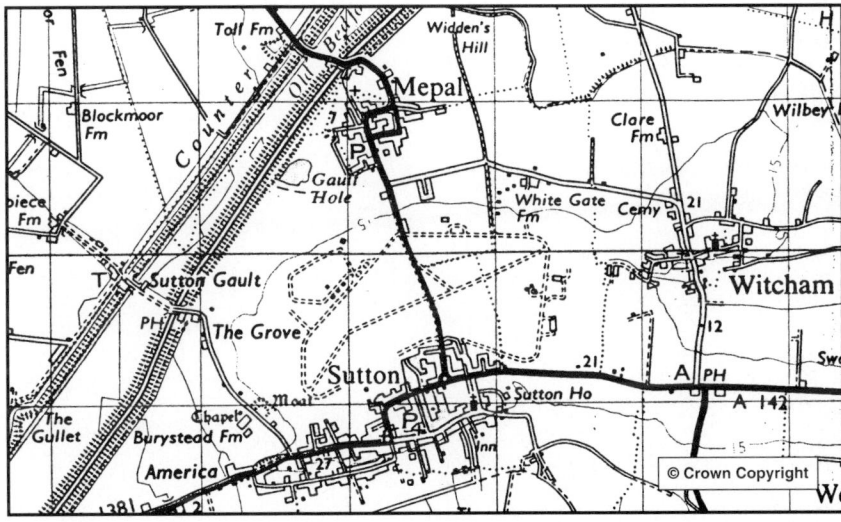

METHWOLD

When the Air Ministry sought a dispersal landing ground for Feltwell during the winter of 1938-1939, they had to look no further than a stretch of open Breckland fields, just two miles north-north-east. Directly south of the village of Methwold, bordering the B1106 Brandon to Stoke Ferry road, the site also offered camouflage cover for aircraft from a number of woods and plantations. A minor road between Methwold and Feltwell had to be closed. Feltwell's resident Nos. 37 and 214 Squadrons brought their Wellingtons here (the latter on a more permanent basis) when the Wermacht invaded Poland. No. 214 was moved from this rudimentary airfield the following February to the comparative luxury of Stradishall. Feltwell's Wellingtons continued to use Methwold as a satellite base until this grass airfield was transferred to No. 2 Group in the exchange of bases with No. 3 Group which took place in the late summer of 1942. A number of asphalt pan hardstandings were put down for aircraft during 1940-1941.

Lockheed Venturas had been assigned to No. 2 Group and Feltwell and its satellite were utilised for the three squadrons so equipped. No. 21 Squadron, based at Methwold, after working up went into action from November 3, 1942. In April 1943, when Feltwell was taken for special bomber support units, No. 21 Squadron was moved from Methwold to Oulton and the other two Ventura squadrons (Nos. 464 and 487) moved into Methwold. For his conduct leading a raid on a target in Amsterdam on May 3, 1943, Squadron Leader Leonard Trent was awarded a VC after his return from imprisonment. The Venturas stayed until August when the station was temporarily closed for flying while it was upgraded to Class A standard.

Ventura country. The three squadrons equipped with the American medium bomber were based on two grass airfields on the edge of Thetford Forest — Feltwell and its satellite Methwold. This is No. 21 Squadron just in front of the technical site.

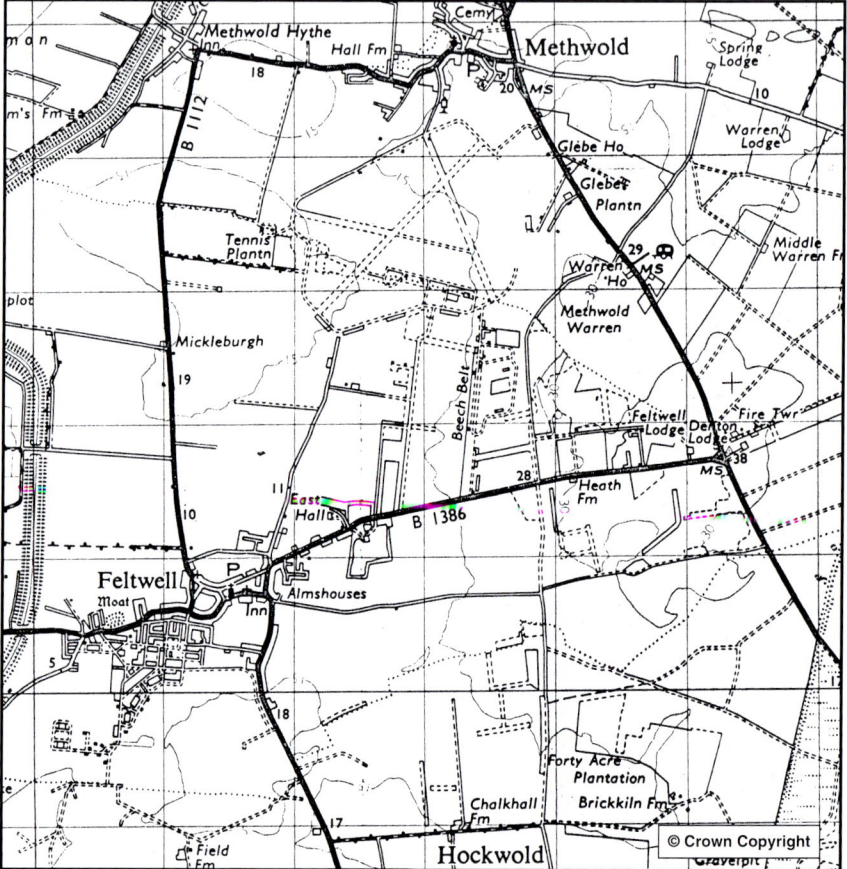

© Crown Copyright

In this shot of Venturas of No. 464 Squadron taking off in May 1943, piles of hardcore can be seen in the background, dumped in preparation for the construction of the concrete runways. (The third Ventura squadron was No. 487 — see page 137.)

Three concrete runways were laid, the main aligned on 06-24 at 2000 yards, 11-29 at 1,600 yards and 17-35 at 1,500 yards. Runway 11-29 terminated at the 06-24 runway. The 36 hardstandings were 35 of the loop type and a single pan. The surviving asphalt pans were not included. A T2 hangar had been erected earlier on the technical site which was located on the south side of the airfield between runway heads 06 and 35. Later a B1 repair hangar was put up in the north-east corner beside the B1106. During 1943, three T2 hangars were built south of the B1 for Horsa glider storage. The bomb stores were south of the airfield, just west of runway 35. The camp had developed in two areas and with additional dispersed sites accommodation provided for a total 1,810 males and 332 females. The WAAF, communal and two domestic sites were located south of the technical site towards East Hall and on the side along the B1106 were three domestic, a communal and sick quarters. F. H. Higgs Ltd was involved in the 1943 construction.

As the satellite was now of a far higher standard than its parent base only two miles away, the remodelled Methwold was assigned to No. 3 Group again and made a sub-station of Mildenhall's No. 32 Base. With the closure of Lakenheath, No. 149 Squadron found a new home at Methwold in May 1944 and was joined by another Stirling squadron, No. 218, in August. Both squadrons started conversion to Lancasters at this time. No. 218 was moved to Chedburgh in December as there were insufficient hardstandings for both squadrons which were building up to a strength of more than 30 aircraft each. In total, 43 aircraft failed to return or were destroyed in crashes flying in operations from Methwold; 25 being Venturas, six Stirlings and 12 Lancasters.

No. 149 had been joined by No. 207 Squadron in the autumn of 1945, at times both units rarely having more than a dozen Lancasters on strength during the following winter. In April 1946, Methwold said goodbye to Bomber Command and the airfield was subsequently put on care and maintenance status and for some 12 years its run-

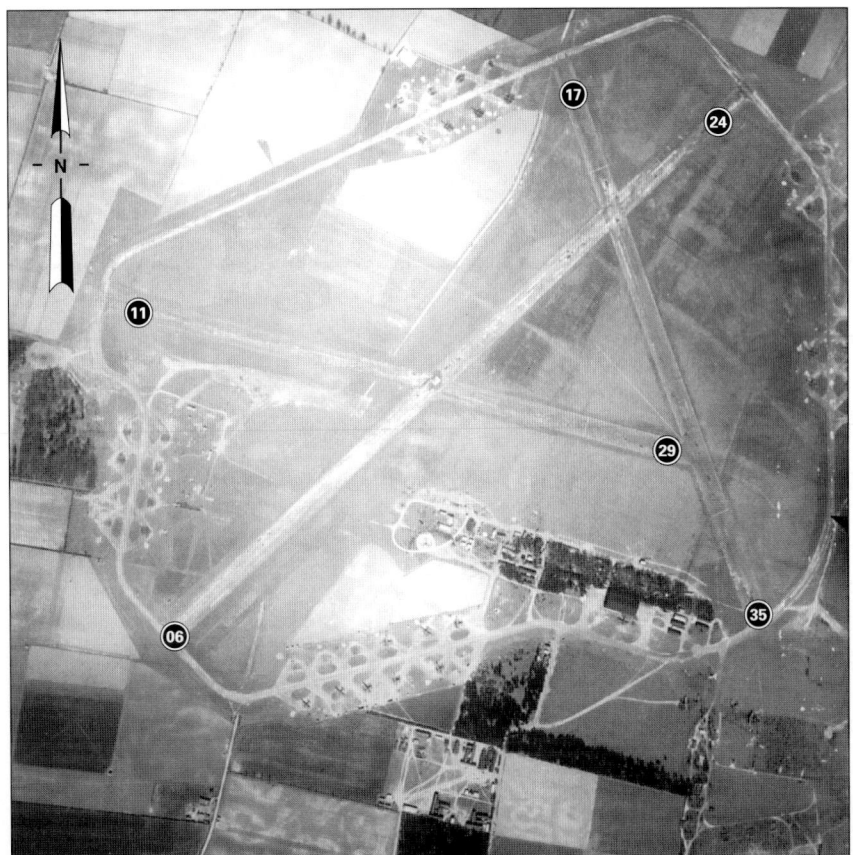

Contractors moved into Methwold in August 1943 but when the airfield opened for business again the following year as a Class A station, it was switched from No. 2 to No. 3 Group.

ways were maintainted for use by the trainers of its old companion Feltwell. Released for agricultural use in the 1960s much of the runway concrete was broken up although part of one is still used for poultry housing.

However much of the the NW-SE runway survives. Two hangars have been used for bulk grain storage for a number of years, and two others are utilised for salad preparation and packing for supermarkets.

Horticulture has now taken over, the old main runway, surrounded by high fencing, now covered with thousands of potted plants.

MILDENHALL

The west end of the hangar line with the original Mildenhall-Littleport road in the foreground photographed on July 9, 1942. The hangar nearest the road is Type A and beyond a Type C.

Arguably the most prominent airfield in East Anglia, Mildenhall airfield made headlines from its earliest days. The first of the new bomber aerodromes in the region that the RAF was allowed during the tight fiscal policies of the early 1930s, Mildenhall was also the first of several built on the edge of the Breckland close to the Fens. The original site was located two miles north-west of the small town by which name it is known. Constructed during 1933-34 with Messrs W & C French as the main contractors, it was opened on October 16, 1934, and used as the starting base for the famous MacRobertson Air Race to Australia. Two Type A hangars were erected on the technical site adjoining the main camp at Beck Row.

No. 99 Squadron arrived the following month with Handley Page Heyfords and remained until the outbreak of war in September 1939. Mention of expansion scheme aerodromes in the few remaining years of peace was not permitted in the press but Mildenhall suffered no such restrictions, and in July 1935 it played host to the assembly of some 350 military aircraft that took part in the Silver Jubilee Review inspected by King George V.

To build up strength, in September 1935 No. 99's 'B' Flight became No. 38 Squadron. A new 'B' Flight was established in No. 99 only to have a repeat of an amoeba-like act when in April 1937 this was taken to form No. 149 Squadron. To make room for the new formation No. 38 Squadron was moved to Marham. A light bomber squadron, No. 211, was also raised at Mildenhall during the same summer and equipped with Hawker Audax biplanes before moving out to Grantham. In January 1937, No. 3 Group Headquarters was established at Mildenhall to administer and control the new bomber airfields being built or scheduled for the area that would eventually support the Wellington force.

The first of the new medium bombers for squadron service arrived at Mildenhall for No. 99 in October 1938. Five years earlier No. 99 had been the first squadron to receive the Heyford, then rendered obsolete by a monoplane with a top speed 100 mph faster

Long since closed with the expansion of the airfield, the old Littleport road is now a street within the Mildenhall complex.

152

While aircrew look skywards, three Wellingtons of No. 149 Squadron make a low pass over the technical site. The hangars in the foreground are Type Cs and that in the background a Type A.

than the ungainly twin-engine biplane it replaced. Three months later Mildenhall's second squadron, No. 149, also converted to Wellingtons.

During the late 1930s three Type C hangars were added adjacent to the technical site area, one east of the Type As and the others to their west side. With the threat of war, Newmarket Heath was secured as Mildenhall's satellite and No. 99 moved there at the beginning of September 1939. Only a few hours after Britain's declaration of war, an abortive attempt was made by No. 149's Wellingtons to locate and attack German naval vessels. Succeeding operational activity was mostly directed at enemy shipping and naval installations until Bomber Command ceased Wellington daylight activity. No. 149 was not joined at Mildenhall by another Bomber Command squadron until after converting to Stirlings in the winter of

1941. In December that year an RCAF unit, No. 419 Squadron, was formed to fly Wellingtons and joined No. 149 on night raids until the Stirlings were moved to Mildenhall's new satellite at Lakenheath in April 1942. No. 419's stay at Mildenhall only lasted four more months, the squadron moving north in August following the decision to establish an all-Canadian group in Yorkshire. Its place was taken by No. 75 Squadron's Wellingtons later the same month and in September more Wellingtons arrived when No. 115 Squadron was dislodged from Marham, that airfield having

been transferred to No. 2 Group. However, both Nos. 75 and 115's tenure at Mildenhall was short and in November both were moved elsewhere for work to begin on the long-awaited hard runways.

The construction work took five months and resulted in a Class A specification with the usual three intersecting concrete runways, the main 11-29 at 2,000 yards and the others, 04-22 and 16-34, both 1,400 yards in length. A hard-surfaced perimeter track and aircraft dispersal points had been constructed piecemeal during the early war years and further additions brought the total of the

Sixty years on the same hangars are still in use under the auspices of the US Third Air Force. A new office block fronts the right-hand C.

Runways were laid during the winter of 1942-43 with the bomb dump, very unusually, being sited within the perimeter.

From December 1943 . . . to the summer of 1944. The reconstructed airfield with over 40 aircraft dispersed around the perimeter.

latter to 36. The bomb stores were left within the southern run of the perimeter track. Two T2 hangars were put up for glider storage during 1943, and much of the work carried out that year was handled by McAlpine. By 1944, Mildenhall accommodation provision being put at 2,685 male and 344 female.

On completion of the runways, No. 15 Squadron moved in from Bourn which was wanted for the expanding Pathfinder organisation, No. 8 Group. No. 15's Stirlings arrived in April 1943 and in August provided its 'C' Flight for the nucleus of No. 622 Squadron. By now, the days of the Stirling for main force bombing were numbered and at the end of the year the two squadrons converted to Lancasters. Both remained at Mildenhall until after the end of hostilities when the contraction of Bomber Command saw No. 622 Squadron disbanded in August 1945 and No. 44 Squadron taking its place. These resident squadrons moved to Wyton a year later when Mildenhall was again subject to enlargement. During hostilities 260 bombers were lost in the course of operations from Mildenhall: 108 Wellingtons, 56 Stirlings and 96 Lancasters.

Runway extension than took place with a view to meeting the needs of very heavy bombers, the work being completed in 1948.

Bombing up Stirlings OJ-N and OJ-T of No. 149 Squadron parked on the end of the south-east runway close to the Mildenhall-Thistley Green road on the south side of the airfield. (IWM) This is a part of the airfield in which photography is now not permitted — hence no comparisons of the spot today.

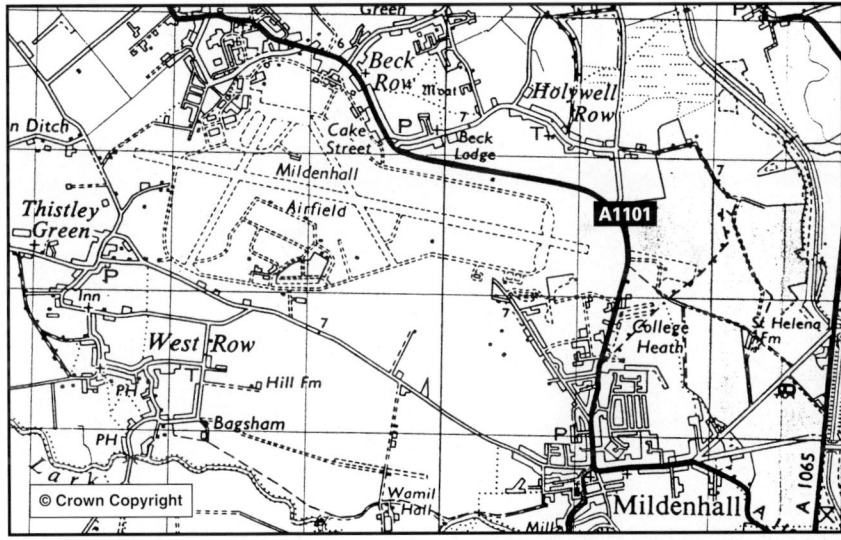

Following the closure of several other wartime US airbases in Britain in recent years like Bentwaters, Greenham Common and Alconbury, Mildenhall remains the jewel in the crown.

Left: **The station is the trans-Atlantic depot for the USAF — here a C-141 Starlifter and a giant C-5 Galaxy on the apron.** *Right:* **Special duties helicopters near one of the Type C hangars.**

Early the next year, four reduced Lancaster squadrons took up station, Nos. 35, 115, 149 and 207. The Lancasters were largely replaced by Lincolns before all these units were disbanded early the following year. The West's deteriorating relations with the USSR brought a USAF requirement for airfields suitable for the Superfortresses and in the summer of 1950 the B-50Ds of the 93rd Bomb Wing arrived for temporary duty (TDY). Strategic Air Command TDY was to continue for eight years with a dozen different bomb wings involved. Strategic Air Command tenure gave way to air transport as Mildenhall became the main UK terminal for Military Airlift Command.

In 1962 the headquarters of the Third Air Force, the USAF NATO component in the UK, moved to Mildenhall from Ruislip, and in the following years a tactical airlift wing was established to act as a host unit for C-130 Hercules squadrons on temporary duty rotation from the USA. An airborne command post unit and a temporary duty headquarters

for TDY Strategic Air Command tankers were also established leading to a permanently based KC-135 unit, eventually distinguished as the 100th Wing. Mildenhall also became the location of a US Navy facility.

In line with the post-Second World War requirement for only one major runway, the main was eventually extended to a length of 3,090 yards. Substantial building works took place over the last four decades of the century as Mildenhall, the premier American military air base in Britain, expanded to cover more than 1,200 acres with some 3,000 personnel. The station continues to serve as a major staging post for US military air transport.

Mildenhall pictured in September 2000, looking eastwards. The post-war extension of the main runway to the east necessitated the diversion of the A1101 (see map page 155). The village of Beck Row lies behind the technical area on the left with Mildenhall in the distance on the right.

NEWMARKET

The turf acres of Newmarket Heath offered a ready made landing ground for aircraft and was first so used during the 1914-1918 War. The adjacent racecourse was undoubtedly an attraction and during the inter-war years many private owners landed on the heath to attend race meetings. In 1938 the Air Ministry took an interest in the site as a satellite base for Mildenhall and on September 1, 1939 began transferring over No. 99 Squadron's Wellingtons, apparently without notifying the Clerk of the Course! This was approximately 300 acres north of the Beacon Course and Cambridge Hill providing one of the longest grass landing and take-off runs available at the time — 2,500 yards in an east-west direction. Accommodation for air and ground crews was in the racecourse administration buildings, the grandstand and requisitioned local housing until new huts were erected.

No. 99 conducted operations from Newmarket until March 1941 when it moved to the new airfield at Waterbeach. During the winter of 1940-41 and the following spring, Newmarket was often used as an alternative airfield by Stirlings from Oakington, Newmarket's freer-draining heath offering better

Newmarket Heath must be the most unusual of all Bomber Command's bases, occupying as it did the heathland north of the famous racecourse. In this picture taken in the winter of 1939-40, a Wellington belonging to No. 99 Squadron stands by the tree avenue at Cambridge Hill.

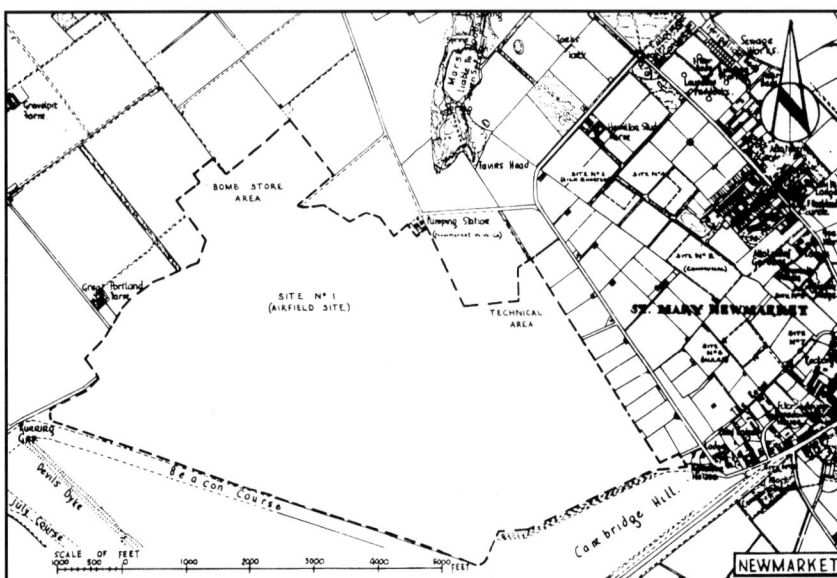

at Mepal offered a better environment for the heavy Stirlings. With several new airfields with hardened runways coming into use, Newmarket was relegated to a support role. The Bombing Development Unit was the major unit until early in 1945 with a target-towing-flight for gunnery training also present during this period. From the beginning of hostilities and throughout the following five years the heath had also served for communication flights to the nearby No. 3 Group headquarters at Exning.

During the war 76 bombers are known to have been lost in the course of flying operations from Newmarket. Wellingtons accounting for 33 of these while 43 were Stirlings.

By the early spring of 1945, as Newmarket was no longer required as an airfield, its two B1 hangars, erected in 1942, were taken over by No. 54 Maintenance Unit. Its tenure was brief and within a few weeks following VE-Day the station was closed and the heath returned to the racing fraternity. A small area was preserved for civilian flying use, principally those well-to-do race-goers who flew to meetings. All hangars except the two B1s on the north-west side were removed.

conditions. Whitley's appeared but these were used with a number of Lysanders for 'special operations' over occupied countries, delivering agents and equipment to aid resistance forces. No. 1419 Flight carried out this mission becoming No. 138 Squadron in August 1941 before moving to Graveley in December. With an increasing demand for this service, No. 3 Group formed a second squadron, No. 161, at Newmarket in the following February but it moved within weeks to Stradishall.

During 1941-42, a hard taxiway was put down along the northern perimeter to link a total of 24 loop-type aircraft standings. Three T2 hangars were erected on the technical site, on the north-east side, and a B1 to the east of the operational buildings site on the south side at the eastern end of Beacon Course. Two B1 hangars were also erected, possibly at a later date, on the north-west side of the airfield near Portland Farm and to the west of the bomb store. Additional domestic sites were dispersed to the north-east on the outskirts of the town.

In November 1942, No. 75 Squadron arrived while runways were laid at Mildenhall and operated from Newmarket Heath until June 1943 when the new Class A station

Today the trees have matured . . . only the ghost of the Wellington lingers on.

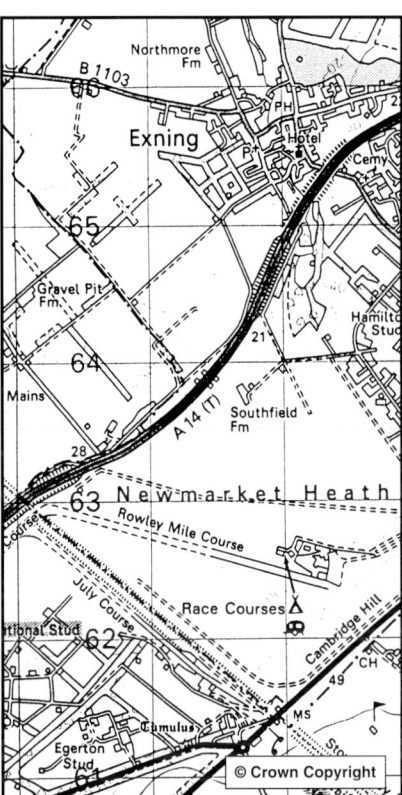

© Crown Copyright

A perimeter track and hardstandings, together with five hangars and a bomb store, were laid down on the northern side in 1941-42 but the landing ground was left as grass because of the free-draining soil. The present-day Ordnance Survey map shows the introduction of the A45 bypass and also the proximity of No. 3 Group's headquarters at Exning (see page 123).

In the 1970s' development of the A45 highway to carry the increasing traffic to and from the burgeoning container port at Felixstowe necessitated a completely new section to bypass Newmarket town. The two and three-lane carriageway skirted the north-west side of the heath passing just to the south of the two B1 hangars. These came into use for commercial storage of waste paper in post-war years, one being destroyed in 1997 by arsonists. The A45 was redesignated the A14 in 1990.

The area to the north of the course is still in use as an un-licensed airfield called the Rowley Mile Landing Area. Also a 1,000-yard grass runway, on a bearing of 14-32 called the July Strip is marked out to the south of the course but, because of its restricted manoeuvring area, all landings must be made from the west and take-offs in the opposite direction.

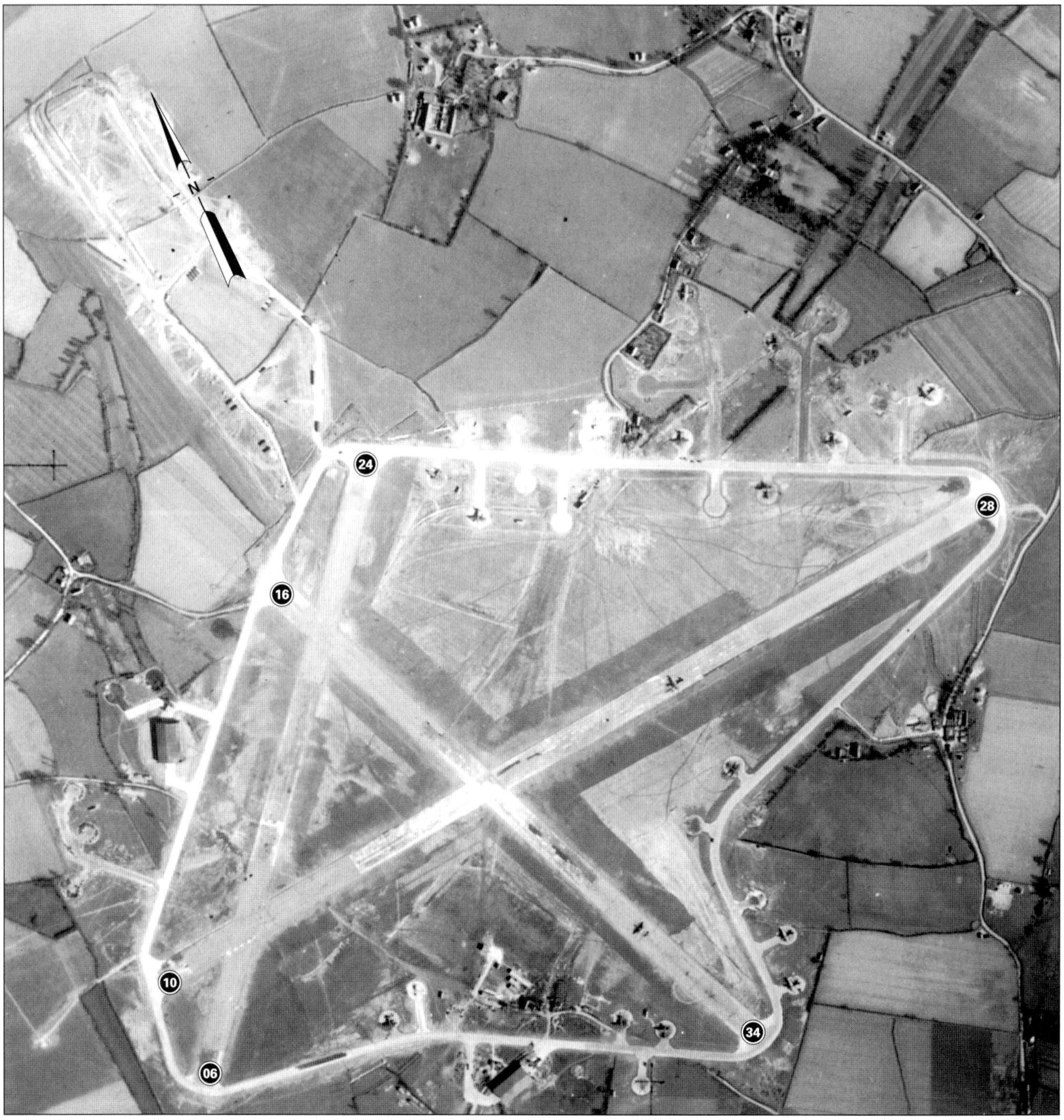

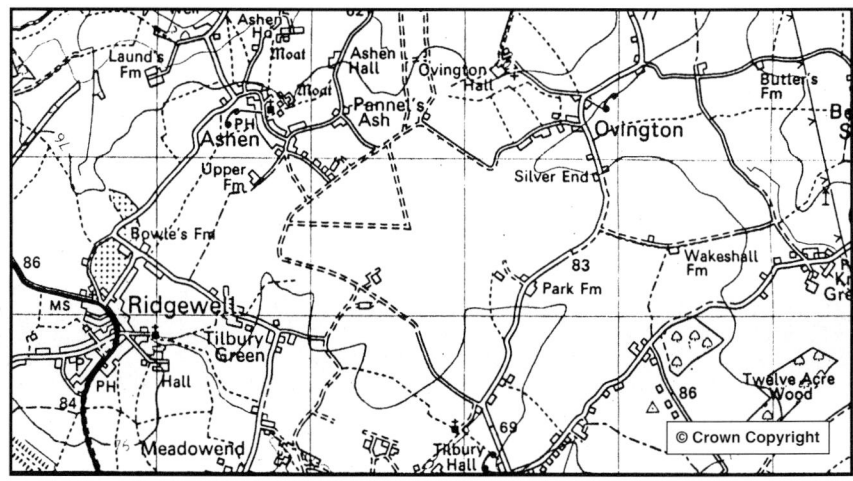

RIDGEWELL

Careful inspection of this vertical taken on March 7, 1943 reveals 18 Stirlings at Ridgewell. One machine is using runway 16-34 while another appears to have suffered an undercarriage failure on 10-28.

Ridgewell was a wartime construction to Class A standard located 7½ miles north-west of Halstead close to the A604 and west of the village of that name situated on the edge of the Stour valley. Runways were laid down in 1942, the main 10-28 at 2,000 yards and the subsidiaries 06-24 and 16-34 both 1,400 yards long. During the early months of 1943, the hardstandings were increased from 36 pans to 45, plus five loops, by Constable Hart & Co. Ltd. Two T2 hangars were provided, one on the technical site between runway heads 06 and 34, the other between runway heads 10 and 16. Bomb stores were off the north side of the airfield between runway heads 16 and 24. Accommodation provided for 2,894 personnel in nine dispersed domestic sites to the south of the airfield towards the A604, with two communal sites and sick quarters also in this area. Two country roads across the airfield site were closed prior to construction.

the night of January 8. The squadron's Stirlings continued to operate from Ridgewell until late May when No. 3 Group's new airfield at West Wickham (later renamed Wratting Common) was available. Losses were high during No. 90's stay, 24 Stirlings failing to return or crashing in the UK during the course of raids and another three lost in non-operational accidents.

Ridgewell was then handed over to the US Eighth Air Force which installed the 381st Bombardment Group and its four B-17s squadrons early in June. The 381st remained at Ridgewell for two years during which time it flew 296 missions and lost 131 B-17s in action. After the 381st Bomb Group returned to the United States in June, the USAAF handed the station back to the RAF the following months. It remained under the care of No. 94 Maintenance Unit until March 1957, the runways having been used at one time to store surplus wartime bombs.

A view looking south-east along the north-east perimeter track on May 12, 1943. No. 90 Squadron was soon to depart with its Stirlings. The closest aircraft, BK661 WP-O, piloted by Pilot Officer Joseph Gedak of the Royal Canadian Air Force, was lost that very evening on a raid to Duisburg. None of the crew were ever found. All the other Stirlings in the picture had also been shot down within a month.

Although the station was scheduled for the USAAF it was temporarily assigned to No. 3 Group which needed an operational base for a new Stirling squadron formed at Bottesford. This was a rejuvenated No. 90 Squadron which arrived at the end of December 1942 before the airfield had been fully completed. Despite limited facilities, the first operation from Ridgewell was despatched on

Part of the peri-track near this point has been incorporated into the road from Ashen to Ovington. It turns sharp left beyond the hedgerows.

With its runways lifted, little of Ridgewell survives today save for the encircling taxiway.

STRADISHALL

This vertical taken in April 1946 shows the development of Stradishall: from the pre-war 'Bombing Circle' days through the early 1,000-yard hard runways to their ultimate wartime extensions. The hardstandings on the east side of the airfield sport a score of Lancasters, the remainder exhibiting oil stained surfaces from the war days.

The site selected for the expansion scheme bomber airfield at Stradishall was located mainly in the parish of Hundon, south of the A143 road, some 11 miles from Bury St Edmunds. It lay on Suffolk clay — excellent for heavy crops of wheat but not for heavy aeroplanes. Despite the extensive under draining carried out during construction the glue-like mud that appeared after heavy rain quickly led to RAF Stradishall becoming the first airfield in Bomber Command scheduled for hardened runways.

Five Type C hangars, administrative, technical and barrack buildings were built between the bombing circle and the A143

during 1937-38 and Stradishall officially opened on February 3, 1938, although still far from complete. Sir Lindsay Parkinson & Co. Ltd carried out the £500,000 contract. Nos. 9 and 148 Squadrons moved in from Scampton the following month where the latter had recently formed from a flight of the former. No. 9 had Heyfords and No. 148 Wellesleys, although it received Heyfords when all Wellesleys were withdrawn and sent to the Middle East and East Africa. There was not long to wait for Wellingtons with which Bomber Command intended to re-equip all No. 3 Group squadrons, both units

receiving this modern type in February and March 1939. In July No. 9 moved to Honington, changing places with the No. 3 Group pool squadron, No. 75, but a few days after the outbreak of war Stradishall's Wellingtons were sent to Harwell while the airfield was closed for laying the runways.

The runways were 04-22, 07-25 and 14-32, all approximately 1,000 yards long . A total of 24, later increased to 36, hardstandings were placed round the encircling perimeter track, except on the north side. While this work was in hand, two Blenheim fighter squadrons were formed utilising the accom-

Today the airfield is virtually unrecognisable midst the green fields of summer, only a faint trace indicating the runways.

In the distance, occupying the technical site is Highpoint Prison — a high-security jail where all photography is banned.

modation and a small area of the airfield. The station re-opened in January 1940 when No. 214 Squadron's Wellingtons moved in from stark Methwold. The Luftwaffe visited Stradishall on a number of occasions, the first being on August 21, 1940, but the most damaging attack occured on November 3 that year when a hangar was hit.

No. 214 Squadron converted to Stirlings in the spring of 1941, Stradishall remaining its home for the next 2¾ years. No other operational squadrons were based at Stradishall until November 1941 when No. 138, the special duties unit, arrived from Newmarket to continue flights in support of resistance activities in occupied Europe. When this squadron moved to Tempsford in March 1942, its place was taken by another special duties unit, No. 109 Squadron, employing Wellingtons , and later a few Mosquitos, for radio and wireless detection in enemy airspace and also testing new radar aids.

In August, No. 109 moved to Wyton to join the Pathfinder Force. No. 3 Group had to surrender a number of its stations west of Cambridge to the new force and No. 101 Squadron brought it Wellingtons from Bourn to Stradishall soon after No. 109 had left. However, No. 101 spent only seven weeks at Stradishall before it was moved between groups for the second time, heading north to No. 1 Group in south Yorkshire.

The runways were extended during 1941, 07-25 at the 25 end to 2,000 yards, 14-32 at the 32 end to 1,400 and 04-22 at the 04 end to 1,500 yards. The original hard runways and perimeter track lay within the two public roads running from the A143 to Scotch Corner, but the extensions caused these to be closed. Several pan hardstandings were lost during the restructuring leaving 26 intact. To make up the numbers, 13 loops were added. Three additional hangars were provided for gliders, all T2s, one placed near the end of runway 04 on the 07 side. The other two were in the south-east corner, east of 32. Bomb stores were constructed on farmland to the west of the airfield. Total station accommodation at that time, including a few dispersed sites, was for 2,773 males and 335 females.

Stradishall then became No. 3 Group's operational training centre with the formation of No. 1657 Conversion Unit at the beginning of October 1942 to use the formi-

dable Stirling. In 1943 both Stradishall's satellite airfields, Chedburgh and Wratting Common, also carried out Stirling conversion training. The demise of the type as a bomber was followed by a period in which Stradishall finished training crews for transport squadrons. No. 3 Group Lancasters did not reach Stradishall until December 1944 when the recently reformed No. 186 Squadron was moved in from Tuddenham, remaining until disbanded the following July. During hosilities 104 aircraft were lost flying operations from Stradishall. This total was composed of 67 Wellingtons, 25 Stirlings, nine Lancasters, two Whitleys, a Halifax and a Lysander.

Stradishall passed to Transport Command in August 1945 and once again Stirlings were in residence; these being the Stirling V transports of Nos. 51 and 158 Squadrons. The latter disbanded early in 1946 when transport requirements were reduced and No. 51 moved out in August, No. 3 Group reclaiming the station for Lancasters. Nos. 35 and 115 Squadrons were the new tenants being joined late the following year by Nos. 149 and 207. All were in a diminished state and the number of Lancasters at Stradishall gradually reduced until February 1949 when all four units were transferred to Mildenhall.

From February to July 1949, the station was on care and maintenance thereafter being used for flying training, mainly conversion courses on Meteor jets. The organisation was first designated as No. 203 Advanced Flying School and later as No. 226 Operational Conversion Unit when roles were exchanged with Driffield units. New hardstandings were built by Mowlem in 1954 and blast walls for jets the following year. In 1955 the training units were withdrawn and Stradishall became a night fighter station with Meteors and Venoms. In October 1957 Javelins appeared and in 1960 Hunters. At the end of 1961 the station again reverted to a training establishment as No. 1 Air Navigation School which used a variety of aircraft but chiefly Dominies and Varsities for much of the time.

In August 1970, with a further contraction of the RAF, the training organisation was moved to Finningley and once again Stradishall was relegated to care and maintenance status. The accommodation was used to house displaced African nationals in the early 1970s following which the station was selected as the site of a high security jail. Renamed Highpoint Prison, the former administration and technical area surrounded by security fencing opened in July 1977.

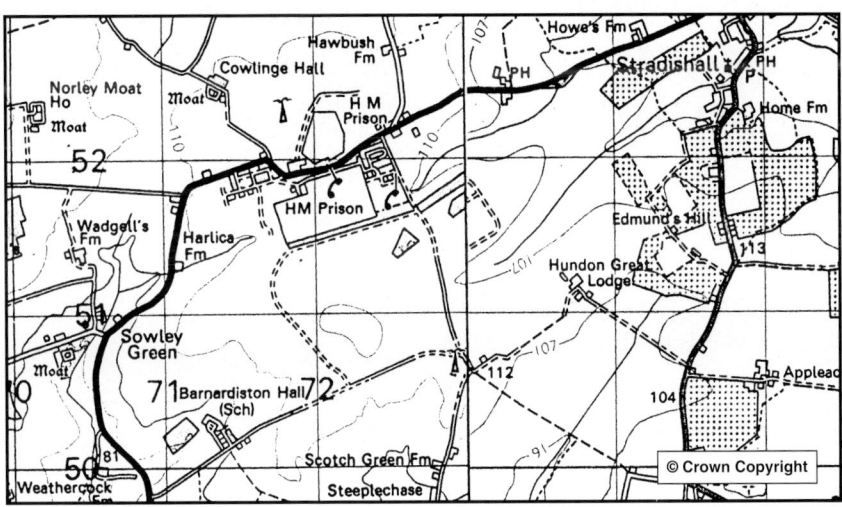

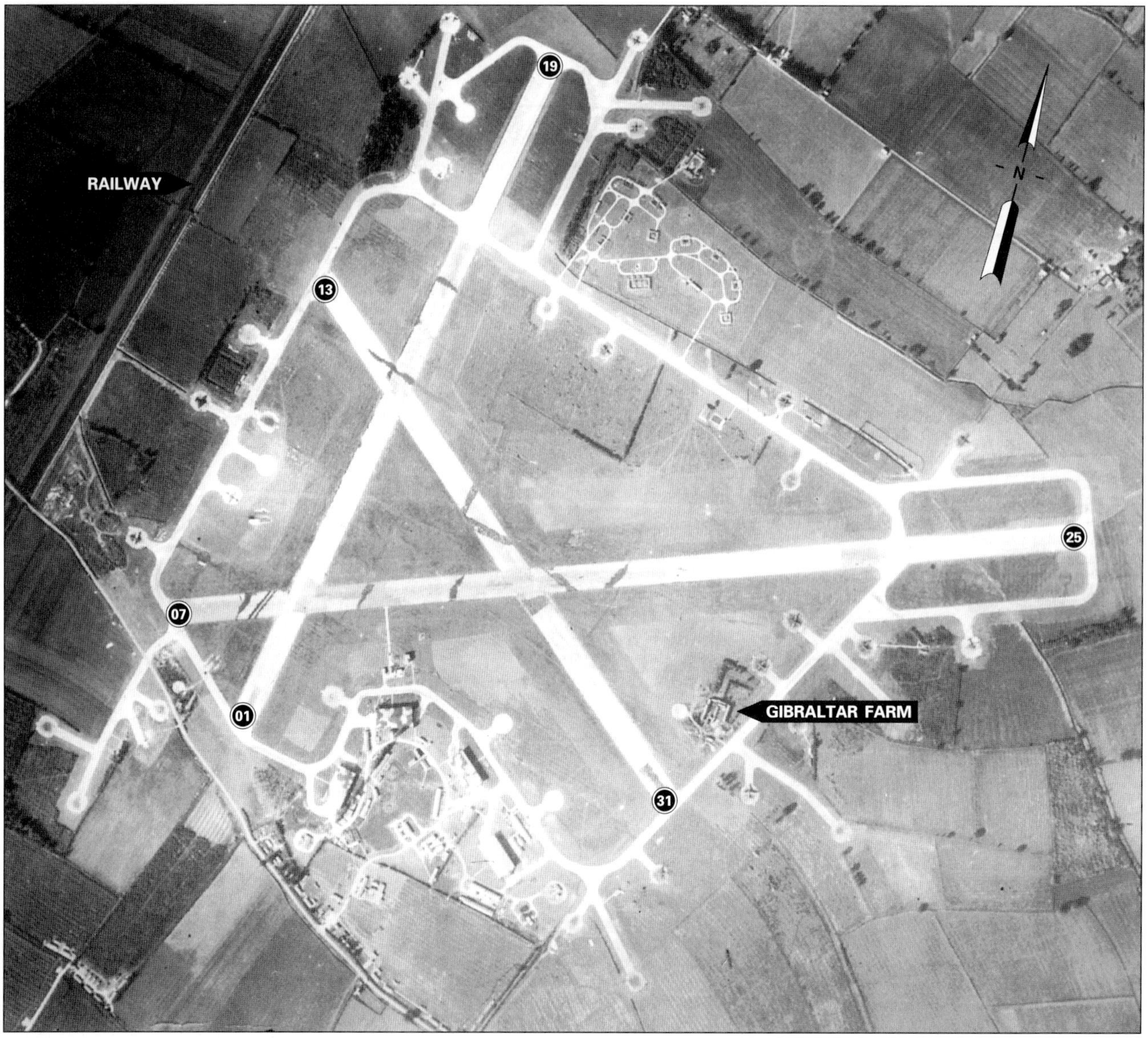

Labels on aerial photograph:
- 19
- RAILWAY
- 13
- 25
- 07
- 01
- GIBRALTAR FARM
- 31
- N (compass)

TEMPSFORD

In a shallow valley straddling the Hertfordshire/Bedfordshire county border, RAF Tempsford was located largely in the parish of Everton. Some 500 acres 4½ miles due south of St Neots and a mile from the A1 trunk road and Tempsford village, was taken over in late 1940 for airfield construction. Built to Class A standard as a satellite for Bassingbourn, the three concrete runways were 01-19 at 1,200 yards long, 07-25 at 1,580 yards and 13-31 at 1,333 yards. The usual 36 pan hardstandings were put down round the perimeter track. The technical site lay to the south between runway heads 01 and 31 and the bomb stores on the north side between runway heads 19 and 25 and close to Woodbury Logde Farm and Woodbury Low Farm.

Although the station was far from complete, in December 1941 Wellingtons from No. 11 OTU at Bassingbourn commenced using the runways while work was in progress on those at the home station. But Tempsford had been selected as a base for the special duty units which mostly operated under No. 3 Group. In January 1942, No. 109 Squadron arrived with Wellingtons engaged in experiments with new radio equipment. They were soon joined by the Wellingtons of No. 1418 Flight also engaged in radio developments although both units were soon to move to other airfields.

Bassingbourn's satellite at Tempsford lay just east of the main LNER railway line from London to Peterborough. It began life as an Operational Training Unit, this picture being taken by No. 8 OTU on October 2, 1942 when the extensions to the north-west and north-eastern ends of the runways had just been completed. Crude efforts at camouflage have been added but the bright new concrete stands out like a sore thumb.

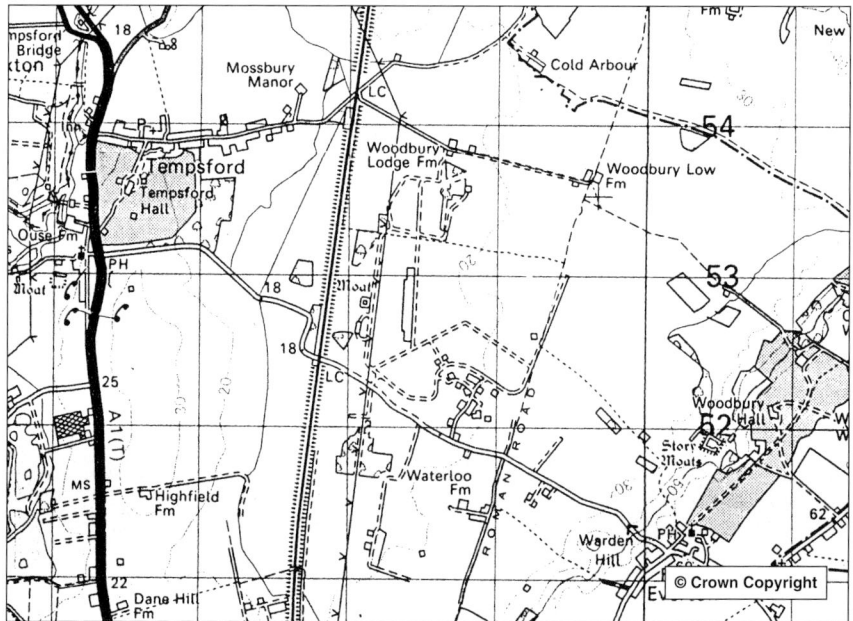

© Crown Copyright

Tempsford's role within No. 3 Group was unique in that it specialised in dropping secret agents — not bombs — and Nos. 138 and 161 Squadrons served the Special Operations Executive (SOE) for over three years. *Above:* Sir Archibald Sinclair, the Air Minister, visited the aerodrome on April 4, 1943. The Lysander of No. 161 Squadron is parked on the entrance track to a hangar, as is the lorry at the far end, the hangar being out of the picture to the left. *Below left:* In the last year of the century only a section of the perimeter track remains at the south-west corner of the former technical site. The buildings in the picture have all been removed but several others remain in good condition elsewhere on the airfield.

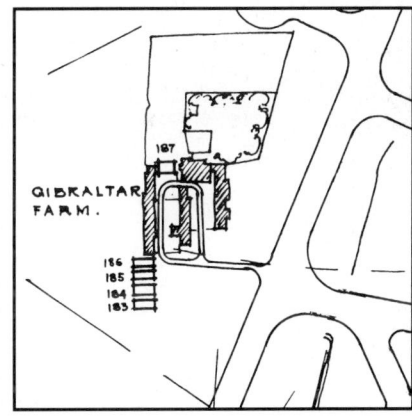

Left: Almost as famous as the airfield is Gibraltar Farm where agents were held before despatch. *Above right:* The plan shows its position within the peri-track on the eastern side, buildings 183 to 186 being designated 'Special purpose huts' and 187 'Dining room and kitchen'. *Right:* All have been demolished save only for this barn.

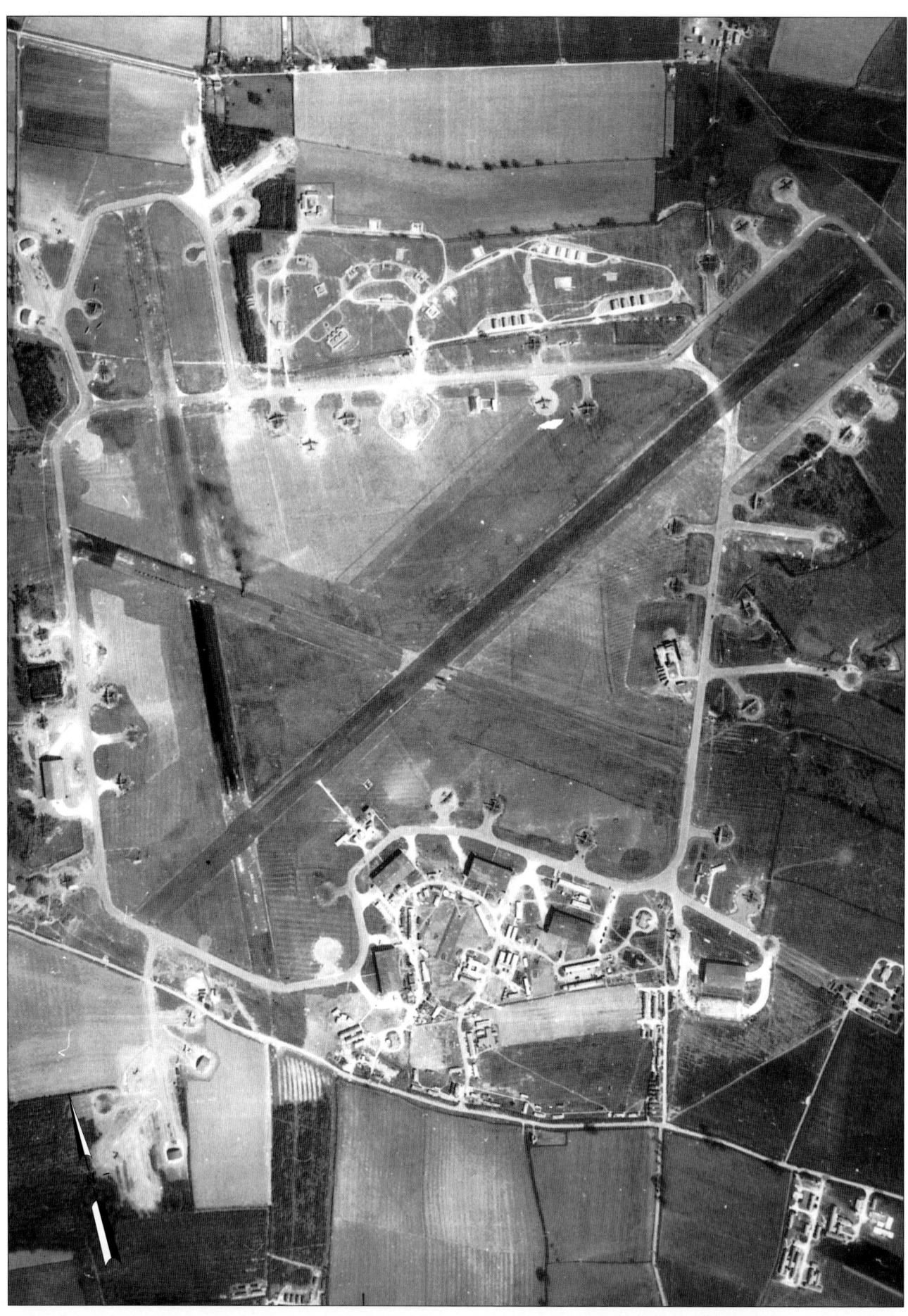

By April 1944, Tempsford had blended more with the landscape. In this fascinating shot at least 40 aircraft are visible dispersed around the airfield, 24 of which are Halifaxes. There are six Lysanders in the north-west dispersal area by the railway line, four Hudsons on south-west hardstandings and two Stirlings near the south-east corner.

GIBRALTAR FARM

In March 1942, No. 138 Squadron arrived flying Whitleys, Halifaxes and Lysanders, joined the following month by No. 161 Squadron with Whitleys and Lysanders, both units tasked with the air support of the Special Operations Executive. Tempsford had now become the main centre for this most secret of activities: the despatch of agents and material aid to resistance forces in occupied countries.

To meet the expanding requirements of SOE, Tempsford was further developed. In 1942 runways 01-19 and 07-25 were extended on their northern ends to comprise overall lengths of 1,610 and 2,000 yards respectively. Perimeter track extensions were added to the ends of the runway extensions and the number of pan hardstandings raised to 50. Hangar building now involved four Type T2s on the technical site while a B1 was erected near Biggingwood Spinney, not far from the Everton crossing gates on the LNER main line, which paralleled the west side of the airfield. The following year two more T2s were added on the east side of the technical site, south of runway head 31. Three pan standings were lost to this and other work, three loop standings being constructed elsewhere on the airfield as replacements. In addition to the large hangars Blister types were put up on four of the pan standings to provide shelter for Lysanders. The seven domestic, two communal and sick quarters site were dispersed in fields mostly on the south side of the Tempsford-Everton road, while the combined WAAF communal and domestic site was sited in Everton village. Total camp accommodation was put at 1,722 male and 240 female.

Whitleys were gradually withdrawn from the Tempsford squadrons and replaced with Halifaxes although several other types, principally Stirlings, Albermarles, Liberators, Hudsons and Havocs, were employed during the 39 months the station supported SOE activities. Operations with Lysanders were mostly flown from forward airfields to reduce the range. During the winter of 1943-44, over 40 aircraft were often present at Tempsford but by the following year activity

Tempsford in September 2000. What tales it could tell . . . of unknown deeds of bravery . . . aircraft touching down in darkened fields by torchlight . . . supplies unloaded . . . agents disappearing into the night . . . some never to return.

had dropped off to a point where the work could be handled by one squadron. Early in March 1945, No. 138 Squadron was transferred to Tuddenham for bombing operations, being rebuilt with Lancaster crews and aircraft. At this time, No. 3 Group relinquished control of No. 161 to No. 38 Group of Transport Command. During SOE and other operations flown directly from Tempsford, a total of 126 aircraft failed to return or were lost in crashes. This total was made up of 16 Whitleys, 80 Halifaxes, 18 Stirlings, 4 Hudsons, 5 Lysanders, 2 Lancasters and a Liberator.

No. 161 Squadron was disbanded in early June 1945, Tempsford then becaming a base and modification centre for Liberators employed by Transport Command. This last-

ed for a year after which the airfield passed to Maintenance Command. The RAF had withdrawn by 1950s and early in the following decade the hangars and land were sold. The majority of airfield concrete was removed for hard core apart from strips used as farm access roads. All the T2 hangars were removed but the solitary B1 still survives.

When the airfield was constructed, the buildings of Gibraltar Farm on the eastern side of the site came to be isolated within the perimeter track but were not demolished and the farm barn was used as the holding point for SOE agents before they were taken to the aircraft that was to deliver them. This building has been preserved and carries an appropriate plaque acknowledging its historic past.

Tempsford's secrets may never be known but its place in history is assured.

TUDDENHAM

Lancasters of No. 138 Squadron on north-east corner dispersals at Tuddenham in the spring of 1945. The David Brown tractor became the standard for towing purposes on Bomber Command stations.

One of the new bomber airfields to Class A standard, work commenced on Tuddenham late in 1942 on a land east of the village of that name, partly on Cavenham Heath close to the Q-site dummy airfield that had been established in the early days of the war. The main contractor was M. J. Gleeson Ltd. Layout followed the normal pattern of three intersecting runways; the main 12-30 at 2,000 yards, the others, 01-19 and 07-25, both 1,400 yards long. A total of 38 hardstandings of the loop type were constructed along the perimeter track and the standard two T2 hangars provided. One T2 was on the technical site between runway heads 01 and 07, the other just north of runway head 12. At a later date a B1 repair hangar was erected on the north-west side, not far from the T2. The airfield had FIDO fog clearance burners installed along the 12-30 runway, the first use of the equipment being in August 1944. Twelve dispersed sites among woods and farmland south of the Cavenham-Tuddenham road included domestic accommodation for 1,845 males and 250 females.

Completed during autumn of 1943, in October No. 90 Squadron's Stirlings vacated Wratting Common to settle in at Tuddenham. Like the other operational Stirling-equipped units, No. 90 engaged chiefly on minelaying until converting to Lancasters in May 1944. The squadron remained at Tuddenham for two years, until the station was closed for flying in November 1946.

As frequently happened when a new squadron was to be formed, the 'C' Flight of an active squadron was taken as the nucleus. Such was the case with re-born No. 186 Squadron, taken from No. 90 in October 1944. Two months later, when this unit had worked up to full strength, it transferred to Stradishall which was vacant and offered more pleasant accommodation. Further expansion of Bomber Command's main effort brought No.

138 Squadron from Tempsford where 'special duties' over the remaining occupied territories no longer required two squadrons. Re-equipped, the Lancasters of No. 138 joined No. 90 in bombing operations on March 29, 1945, and remained alongside at Tuddenham until the station was scheduled for closure. A total of 53 bombers were lost while on operations from Tuddenham; 17 Stirlings and 36 Lancasters.

In April 1946, two other reduced Lancaster squadrons, Nos. 149 and 207, came to Tuddenham when their wartime stations were prepared for closure. Like so many of the airfields constructed during the war, Tuddenham was soon deserted in preference for the comfort of the pre-war expansion scheme airfields with their centrally-heated barracks and spacious messes. At first the buildings were used to meet housing shortages and the

land between runways returned to agriculture. However, the Cold War saw the airfield reserved for possible use if the situation deteriorated and in 1957 its location in a rural site of low population saw Tuddenham selected as a site for a Thor medium range missile unit. In July 1959, No. 107 Squadron was re-formed to operate the three missiles deployed in the special launch area constructed in the centre of the airfield.

The Thors were withdrawn in 1963 and the site closed in July that year. This was to be the last military use of the airfield. The site was sold, buildings demolished and practically all concrete broken and removed as hardcore for new highways. The sandy soil was soon exploited and a large gravel working consumed much of the south-east corner so that by the end of the century there is little evidence remaining of Tuddenham.

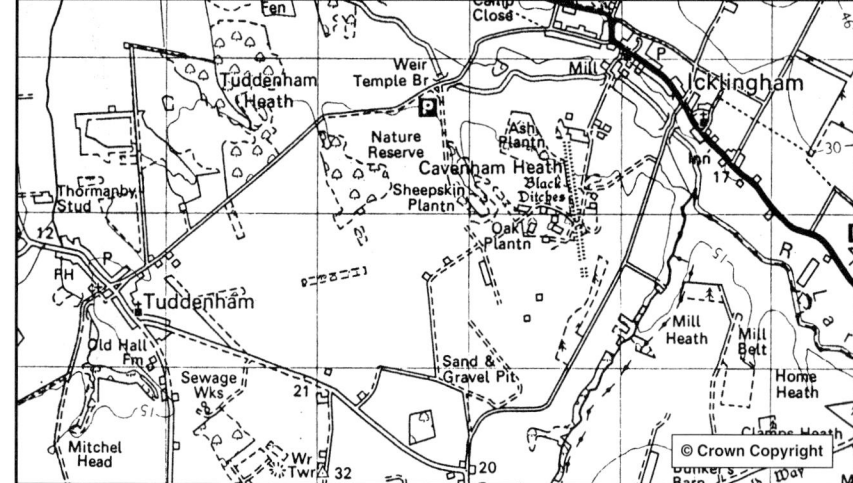

From hardstandings to agricultural 'tramlines' yet the tree-line survives, highlighted by the oak behind the Lanc's starboard wing.

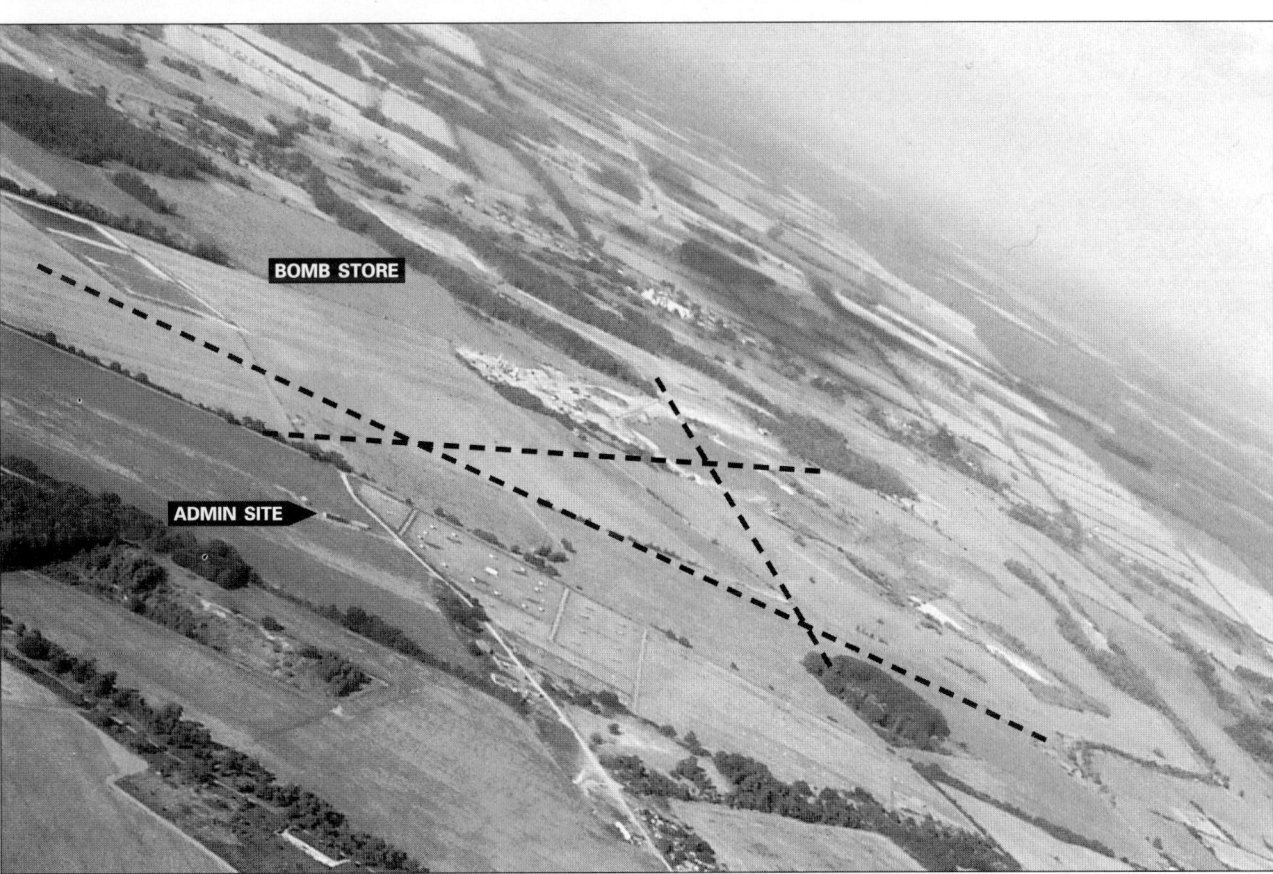

Tuddenham photographed in October 1945 with Lancasters still in residence. The lines of FIDO burners are clearly visible along the main runway as are those forming the threshold box to the south-east approach.

19

25

ANTI-GLIDER DITCHES c1940

12

07

30

01

ADMIN SITE

BOMB STORE

ADMIN SITE

Where is Tuddenham? Banking low over the area, Karel Margry found that there is now very little left to mark the existence of one of Bomber Command's Class A aerodromes. Picture taken in September 2000 looking slightly east of north.

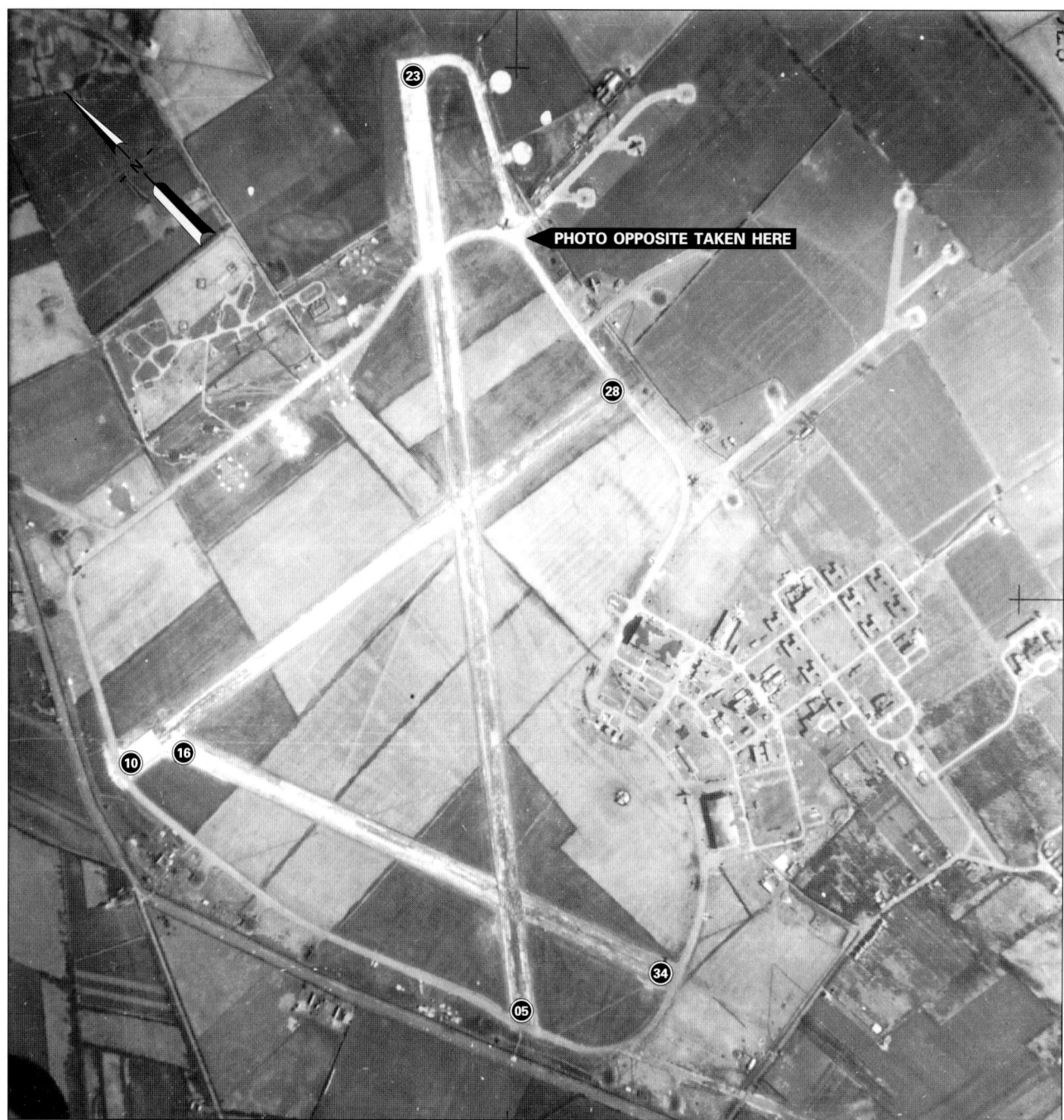

PHOTO OPPOSITE TAKEN HERE

Waterbeach photographed by No. 1 PRU on March 13, 1942. The H-block barracks and two J-type hangars show up clearly.

WATERBEACH

A late expansion scheme airfield, RAF Station Waterbeach was built on farmland at Windfold, north of Waterbeach village and adjacent to the A10 trunk road five miles outside Cambridge. Permanent buildings and the usual crescent of hangars facing the bombing circle were planned but the outbreak of war brought some modifications with only two Type J hangars erected on the technical site which lay on the south-east side. Apart from the main camp area, a few domestic sites were dispersed in former orchards around the village of Waterbeach. The low-lying location in the Fens necessitated concrete runways, a perimeter taxiway and hardstandings, although this work was not complete when the station was deemed ready to receive its first squadron in March 1941. This was No. 99 which brought its Wellingtons in from Newmarket.

The runways were 05-23 at 1,600 yards, 10-28 at 1,300 yards and 16-34 at 1,420 yards. Twenty-four pan type hardstands were eventually increased by another 12. The bomb stores lay beyond the north side of the airfield. Late in 1941 work started on lengthening runways 05-23 and 10-28 to 2,023 and 1,380 yards respectively, and during that winter and the following year a B1 hangar and three T2s were erected, all adjacent to the technical site. One of the T2s was tucked in behind the southernmost J hangar. The other T2s were on the north side with the B1 was just east of these two. The northern T2s, used for glider storage, caused the loss of a hardstanding and runway extensions cut out two other pans, resulting in three loops being put down as replacements.

No. 99 remained until March 1942 when it was ordered overseas. At this time the station was being shared with the first organisation equipped with the Short Stirling to prepare crews for handling this four-engined type in No. 3 Group squadrons. No. 1651

Conversion Unit was established in January 1941 and remained the main tutor for Stirling crews for near three years until moved to Wratting Common in November/December 1943. During this period there were a large number of accidents involving Stirlings based at this station, most occuring during take-off and landing resulting in the collapse of the type's ungainly undercarriage. By late 1943, No. 3 Group was turning to Lancasters and No. 1678 Heavy Conversion Flight appeared at Waterbeach to administer to No. 514 Squadron, one of the few equipped with Lancaster IIs, the radial-engined version.

No. 514 Squadron formed to fly the Mk II at Foulsham joined Bomber Command's mounting campaign in November 1943. These Hercules-powered Lancasters endured until the following summer by which time the Merlin-engined marks were more favoured and No. 1678 Flight was disbanded. No. 514's Lancaster IIs were finally withdrawn at the end of September 1944. The squadron remained at Waterbeach until the

A well-known publicity shot taken in April 1942 at Waterbeach. Stirling N6101/E of No. 1651 Heavy Conversion Unit has been drawn up for a press photo-call on the north-east corner of the perimeter track.

The curve of the perimeter track is still plain to see, the motor car standing in for the gound crew's lorry.

end of hostilities, for much of the time with three flights and a complement of over 30 aircraft. Operational losses from Waterbeach amounted to 122 bombers, 33 Wellingtons, eight Stirlings and 81 Lancasters.

No. 3 Group's tenure of Waterbeach came to an end in August 1945 when No. 514 Squadron disbanded. No. 47 Group of Transport Command took over the station a few weeks later and Nos. 220 and 59 Squadrons,

late of Coastal Command with Liberators, were impressed for long-range flights to the Middle and Far East. These squadrons endured until the following spring and by the time both were disbanded in May and June respectively few Liberators remained at Waterbeach. However, the station was retained by Transport Command which moved in the Yorks of No. 51 Squadron in August 1946 which stayed until July 1948.

Four Dakota squadrons were stationed at Waterbeach late in 1947, the last which disbanded early in 1950 leaving No. 24 Squadron and its mixed bag of aircraft which had moved in the previous year. It left in March 1950, the same year that runway re-structuring was carried out by Mowlem. Transport Command then surrendered the station to Fighter Command which moved in two Meteor squadrons, Nos. 56 and 63. The former was selected to

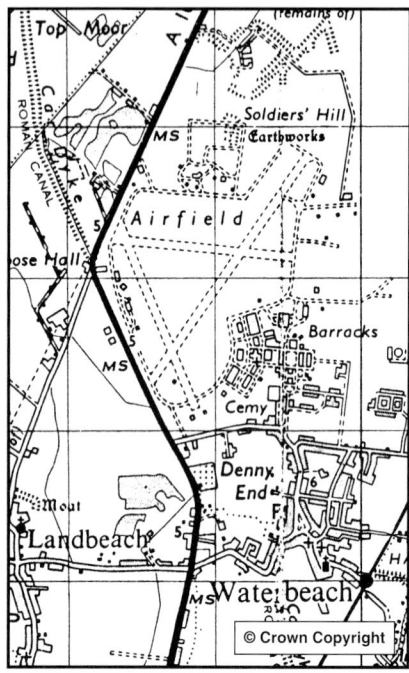

The changing face of Waterbeach. In 1974 the aerodrome was intact, retained for the Royal Air Force as a reserve airfield on a care and maintenance basis. . .

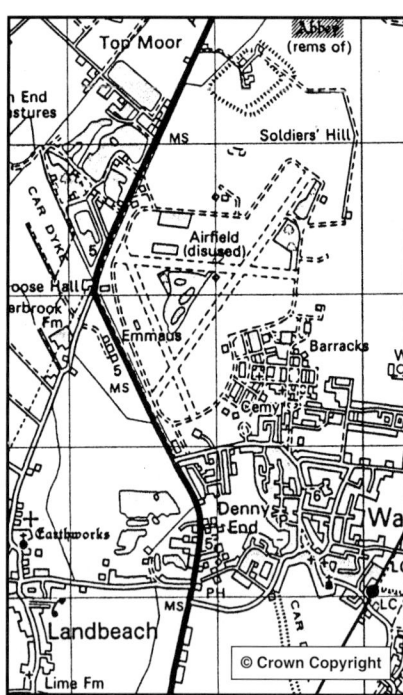

. . . but by the 1990s an additional water feature had been dug as one of the training aids for the new residents — the Royal Engineers. And the use of Waterbeach by the Army was very appropriate bearing in mind the name of the geographical feature off the northern end of the main runway!

introduce the Supermarine Swift into service but this troublesome type was withdrawn after a year and eventually both squadrons converted to Hunters. Venom night fighters were present from the spring of 1955 for two years and Javelins from July 1959 for three years. Between 1955 and 1964, Nos. 1, 25, 46, 54, 60, 153 and 253 Squadrons were at Waterbeach at sometime or another, the final fighter occupants being two Hunter squadrons.

The two decades following the Second World War saw a number of changes to the airfield. Runway 10-28 was taken out of use, two concrete aprons for aircraft parking were constructed in front of the technical site and a number of concrete blast walls were erected at selected dispersal points combining blast damage protection with engine noise barrier. Thereafter the airfield was on care and maintenance although occasionally used for manoeuvres and by training aircraft for touch and go. In the 1980s the station was transferred to the Army who viewed the domestic and administrative sites as far superior to the Victorian barracks at some of its more traditional establishments. The Royal Engineers have been in residence for several and use the airfield for training enterprises. The main runway has been maintained for visiting aircraft use.

Witchford, spring 1944. A No. 115 Squadron crew pose on the hardstanding cluster north of the east end of the main runway, the photographer looking approximately east-south-east.

Witchford, spring 2000. The scene has been reclaimed by agriculture but the distant house by the A10 highway establishes the location.

WITCHFORD

Located south-south-west of Ely near the junction of the A10 and A142 highways, Witchford was built on a ten-foot rise of stable soil, part of the outcrop in the Fens known as the Isle of Ely. Construction began in 1942 and it was officially opened as a No. 3 Group station to Class A standard in June 1943. The three intersecting runways had lengths of 2,010 yards for 10-28, 1,408 yards for 16-34 and 1,418 yards for 04 22. All 36 hardstandings were of loop type. A B1 and a T2 hangar were erected on the technical site on the north-west side of the airfield between runway heads 10 and 16, close to Witchford village. A second T2 lay between runways heads 04 and 34, close to the bomb stores near Bedwell Hey Lane. A total of 14 dispersed sites, north-west of the airfield and Witchford village catered for a maximum 1,502 males and 230 females.

Wellingtons of No. 196 Squadron posted in from No. 4 Group in July 1943 converted to Stirlings and took them into battle the following month. However, the increasing vulnerability of the type to the enemy's night defences reinforced No. 3 Group's plan to re-equip with Lancasters. In November 1943, No. 196 took its Stirlings to Leicester East for troop transport duties leaving Witchford for the Lancasters of No. 115 Squadron which had been operating from Little Snoring. No. 115 remained in residence for the rest of hostilities, flying its last raid from the station on April 25, 1945. The squadron left in August 1945 for Graveley. A total of 99 bombers despatched on operations from Witchford were lost, 8 being Stirlings and 91 Lancasters.

The airfield, not used again for flying, closed in the spring of 1946. Runways were broken up during the 1960-70s and the south hangar removed. The technical site hangars were retained for some years for military storage and currently one T2 remains on the former technical site which now forms Lancaster Way Business Park. The modern offices of Grovemere Holdings house a foyer museum display in honour of the wartime occupants. Prominent is a Hercules engine recovered from a No. 115 Squadron Lancaster shot down by an intruder on the night of April 19, 1944. Apart from an area of the runways used for poultry units, the landing ground area had been reclaimed for arable farming.

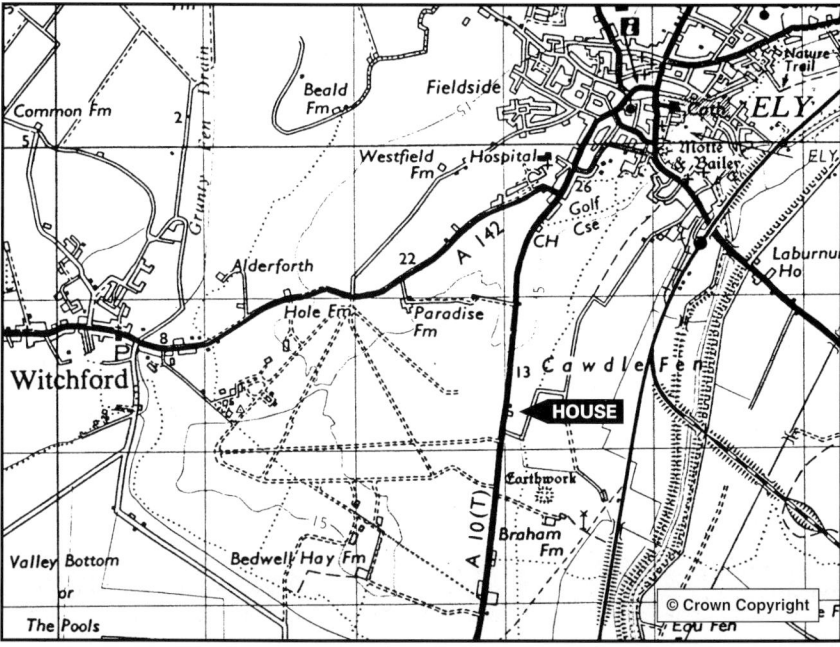

Just four miles east of Mepal (see page 148), Witchford lies just south-west of Ely. The house in the photos above is marked.

Although this shot gives only partial coverage of Witchford, our preference for the selection of the vertical coverage was to choose those wartime pictures where aircraft are present, in this case Lancasters on April 10, 1944. Vertical aerial photographs should always be reproduced with the shadows towards the reader but this can be confusing if north is not at the top of the print — so conforming with the map extracts — so in most cases, we have erred for the latter option.

On the other hand, when taking the present-day obliques, Karel Margry had to take account of lighting conditions so usually tried to shoot with the sun to his rear. In the case of Witchford we are looking north-west with the old technical site on the far side. The A10 runs in the foreground with 'the house' on the right.

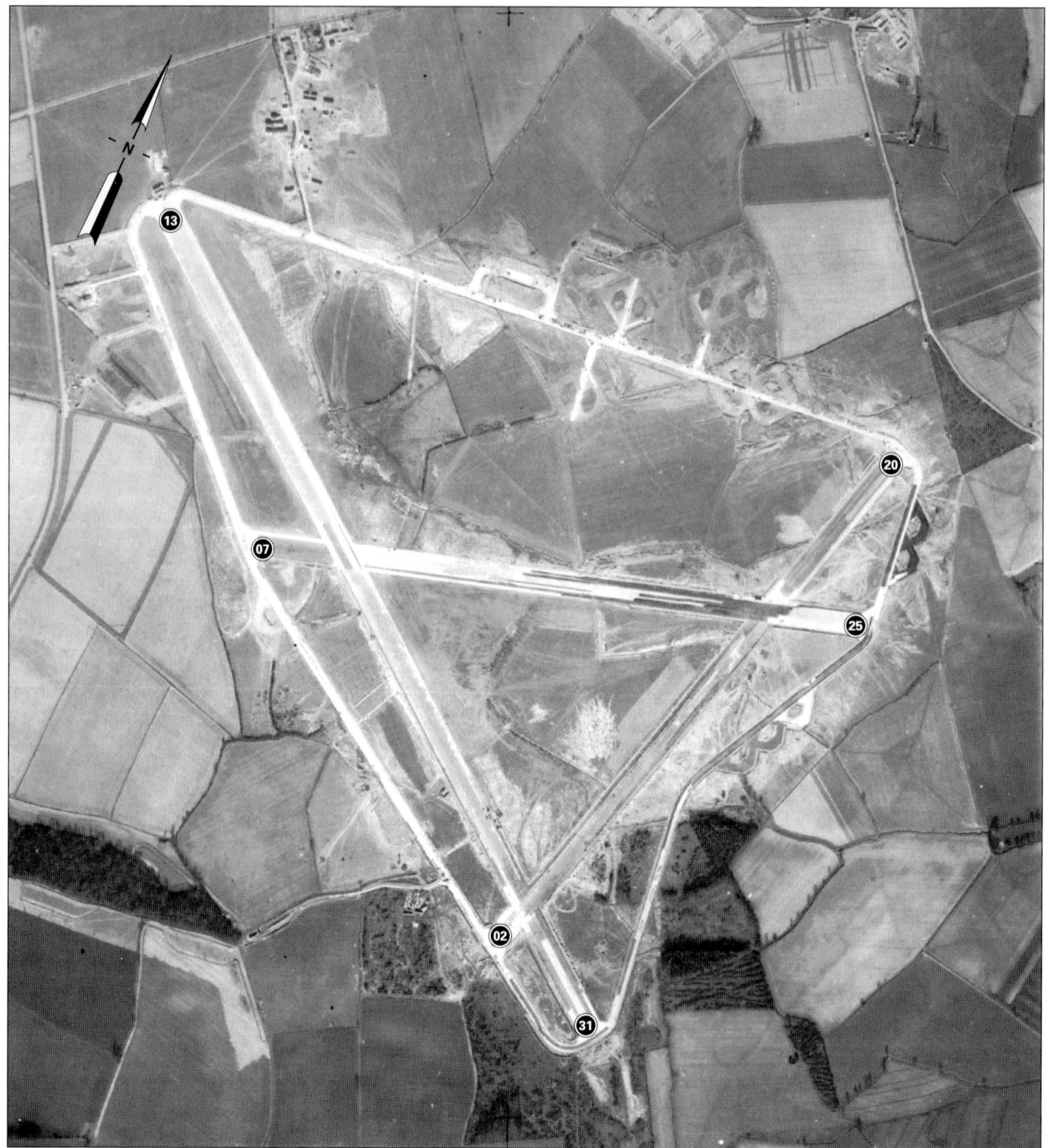

WRATTING COMMON

West Wickham under construction on March 7, 1943. At this stage, several of the loop hardstandings and most of the airfield buildings still had to be built. The reason for the name change to Wratting Common is obscure.

The bomber airfield built to Class A standard located on the Cambridgeshire side of the boundary with Suffolk in the parishes of West Wickham and Little Thurlow, three miles north-west of Haverhill, was officially named West Wickham. Built in 1942-43, the three intersecting concrete runways were 13-31 at 2,000 yards and 02-20 and 07-25 both at 1,400 yards long. All 36 hardstandings were loop types. A T2 and a B1 hangar were erected at the main technical site between runway heads 13 and 07, and another three T2s for gliders on the north side of the airfield between 13 and 20. The technical site was on Western Woods Farm and the ten dispersed domestic and mess sites, catering for 2,507 males and 486 females, were in fields towards Weston Green. Bomb stores were to the east at Skipper's Hall Farm.

The first operational unit arriving, No. 90 Squadron, came from Ridgewell where a US Eighth Air Force B-17 unit was expected. West Wickham was far from complete at this time — late May 1943 — but had sufficient facilities to enable No. 90's Stirlings to return to Bomber Command's campaign four nights after arrival. In August that year notice was received that on the 21st of the month the official name of the station would change from West Wickham to Wratting Common. Only one other such change for an operational bomber station is known, and that due to the possibility of confusion with another airfield of the same name. In West Wickham's case there was no other airfield with the same or similar name although a possiblity is confusion with High Wycombe (Bomber Command HQ), it being common practice in vocal communication to omit the 'West' or 'High'.

In October 1943, No. 90 Squadron was moved to Tuddenham when No. 3 Group decided to concentrate Stirling conversion units in the Stradishall clutch, No. 31 Base, of which Wratting Common was a satellite or sub-base. No. 1651 Heavy Conversion Unit was moved in from Waterbeach in November and remained for a year. By this date few Stirling squadrons remained in No. 3 Group and No. 1651 HCU was shifted to Woolfox Lodge where crews were trained for transport squadrons.

No. 31 Base was destined to hold operational squadrons once more and the Lancasters of No. 195 Squadron arrived from Witchford where it had been re-formed from 'C' Flight of No. 115 a few weeks earlier. No. 195

It was vitally important that place names — particularly when used on VHF — were not confused and atlthough the airfield, which straddled the Cambridgeshire-Suffolk border, lay close to West Wickham, the name was duplicated by the better known town in Kent. Shortened to 'Wickham' it could have been mistaken for the similar sounding 'Wycombe' in Buckinghamshire . . . hence the name change to Wratting Common.

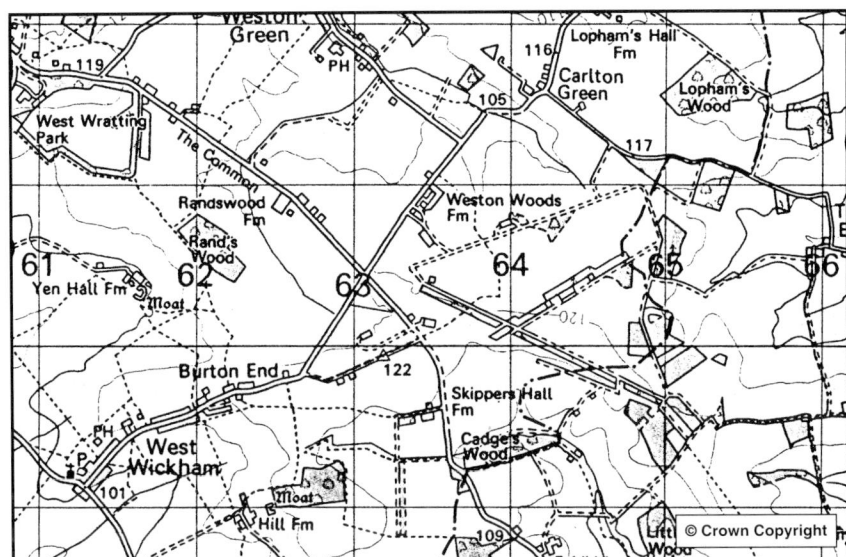

grew to three full flights with 30 Lancasters, remaining at Wratting Common to see out the war. In 79 raids from the station its losses were 9 Lancasters. The squadron ceased to exist on August 14, 1945 and following its disbandment no further flying units were based at the station. During the war bomber losses in operations flown from Wratting Common totalled 43 of which 34 were Stirlings.

Today the airfield barely shows up as such, the concrete runways having been replaced with long stands of woodland.

The surplus of wartime-built airfields that then existed found the reduced Bomber Command force moving back to the more comfortable, pre-war establishments with their permanent buildings. Wratting Common was soon reclaimed for agriculture with much of the concrete taken for hard core. The hangars survived as did many of the larger Nissen huts, serving as cover for commercial enterprises. Most of the site is part of Thurlow Estates owned by the Vesty family.

We must not lose sight of the fact that each aerodrome had a population of around 2,500 personnel — something difficult to depict pictorially or adequately describe in words. Fortunately at the majority of the airfields, altruistic-minded individuals have erected memorials to those fighting men — both ground and aircrews — of RAF Bomber Command who served on more than 100 airfields. This fine monument was unveiled beside the old main entrance at Weston Woods Farm by Air Marshal Sir Ivor Broom on May 28, 1989.

Leonard Cheshire
VARIOUS AIRFIELDS

Guy Gibson
SCAMPTON

John Hannah
SCAMPTON

Roderick Learoyd
SCAMPTON

VCs AWARDED TO PERSONNEL FLYING FROM RAF BOMBER COMMAND AIRFIELDS IN THE UK

Name	Initials	Rank	Squadron	Airfield	Date	Place
				No. 1 Group		
Cheshire	G.L.	Wing Commander	617	Various	1940-1944	Flying Operations
Gibson	Guy	Wing Commander	617	Scampton	May 17, 1943	Möhne/Eder Dams
Hannah	J.	Sergeant	83	Scampton	September 15, 1940	Antwerp
Learoyd	R.A.B.	Flight Lieutenant	49	Scampton	August 12, 1940	Dortmund-Ems Canal
				No. 2 Group		
Edwards	H.	Wing Commander	105	Swanton Morley	July 4, 1941	Bremen
				No. 3 Group		
Aaron	A.L.	Flight Sergeant	218	Downham Market	August 12/13, 1943	Turin
Bazalgette	I.W.	Squadron Leader	635	Downham Market	August 4, 1944	Trossy-St-Maxim
Middleton	R.H.	Flight Sergeant	149	Lakenheath	November 28/29, 1942	Turin
Trent	L.H.	Squadron Leader	487 (NZ)	Methwold	May 3, 1943	Amsterdam
Ward	J.A.	Sergeant	75 (NZ)	Feltwell	July 7, 1941	Over Zuider Zee
				No. 4 Group		
Barton	C.J.	Pilot Officer	578	Burn	March 30/31, 1944	Nuremberg
				No. 5 Group		
Jackson	N.C.	Sergeant	106	Metheringham	April 26/27, 1944	Schweinfurt
Manser	L.T.	Flying Officer	50	Skellingthorpe	May 30/31, 1942	Cologne
Nettleton	J.D.	Squadron Leader	44	Waddington	April 17, 1942	Augsburg
Reid	W.	Flight Lieutenant	61	Syerston	November 3/4, 1943	Düsseldorf
Thompson	G.	Flight Sergeant	9	Bardney	January 1, 1945	Dortmund-Ems Canal
				No. 6 Group		
Mynarski	A.C.	Pilot Officer	419(RCAF)	Middleton St George	June 12/13, 1944	Cambrai
				No. 8 Group		
Palmer	R.A.M.	Squadron Leader	109	Little Staughton	December 23, 1944	Cologne
Swales	E.	Captain	582	Little Staughton	February 23/24, 1945	Pforzheim

The airfield groupings in the table above conform to the period chosen for this book but, as has already been explained, aerodromes passed from one group to another during the course of the war. For example, although Scampton was in Nos 1 and 3 Groups, its VCs were awarded when it was part of No. 5 Group. And Wing Commander Cheshire was awarded his VC for outstanding service in both No. 4 and 5 Groups over a prolonged period. Airmen are listed alphabetically within each group.

Hughie Edwards
SWANTON MORLEY

Arthur Aaron
DOWNHAM MARKET

Ian Bazalgette
DOWNHAM MARKET

Rawdon Middleton
LAKENHEATH

Leonard Trent
METHWOLD

Cyril Barton
BURN

Norman Jackson
METHERINGHAM

Leslie Manser
SKELLINGTHORPE

James Ward
FELTWELL

CITATION: 'On the night of 7th July, 1941, Sergeant Ward was second pilot of a Wellington returning from an attack on Munster. When flying over the Zuider Zee at 13,000 feet, the aircraft was attacked from beneath by a Messerschmitt 110, which secured hits with cannon shell and incendiary bullets. The rear gunner was wounded in the foot but delivered a burst of fire which sent the enemy fighter down, apparently out of control. Fire then broke out near the starboard engine, and, fed by petrol from a split pipe, quickly gained an alarming hold and threatened to spread to the entire wing. The crew forced a hole in the fuselage and made strenuous efforts to reduce the fire with extinguishers and even the coffee in their vacuum flasks, but without success. They were then warned to be ready to abandon the aircraft. . . As a last resort, Sergeant Ward volunteered to make an attempt to smother the fire with an engine cover which happened to be in use as a cushion. At first he proposed to discard his parachute, to reduce wind resistance, but was finally persuaded to take it. A rope from the dinghy was tied to him, though this was of little help and might have become a danger had he been blown of the aircraft. With the help of the navigator, he then climbed through the narrow astro-hatch and put on his parachute. The bomber was flying at a reduced speed, but the wind pressure must have been sufficient to render the operation one of extreme difficulty. Breaking the fabric to make hand and foot holds where necessary, and also taking advantage of existing holes in the fabric, Sergeant Ward succeeded in descending three feet to the wing and proceeding another three feet to a position behind the engine, despite the slipstream from the airscrew, which nearly blew him off the wing. Lying in this precarious position, he smothered the fire in the wing fabric and tried to push the cover into the hold in the wing and on to the leaking pipe from which the fire came. As soon as he moved his hand, however, the terrific wind blew the cover out and when he tried again it was lost. Tired as he was, he was able with the navigator's assistance to make successfully the perilous journey back onto the aircraft. There was now no danger of the fire spreading from the petrol pipe, as there was no fabric left nearby, and in due course it burnt itself out. When the aircraft was nearly home some petrol which had collected in the wing blazed up furiously but died down quite suddenly. A safe landing was then made despite the damage sustained by the aircraft. The flight home had been made possible by the gallant action of Sergeant Ward in extinguishing the fire on the wing in circumstances of the greatest difficulty and at the risk of his life.'

John Nettleton
WADDINGTON

William Reid
SYERSTON

George Thompson
BARDNEY

Andrew Mynarski
MIDDLETON ST GEORGE

Robert Palmer
LITTLE STAUGHTON

Edwin Swales
LITTLE STAUGHTON

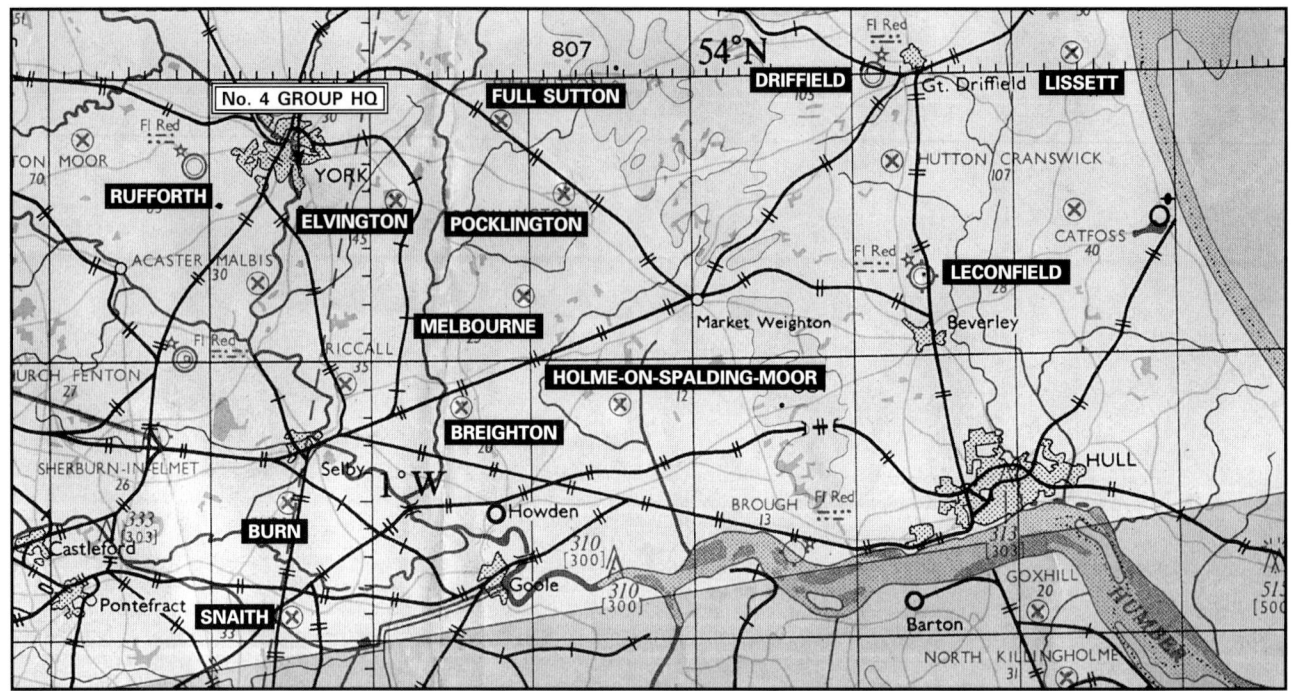

No. 4 GROUP HQ

From June 1937 when No. 4 Group came into being at Mildenhall (see page 152), the group was assigned a clutch of airfields in Yorkshire, initially with an HQ at Linton-on-Ouse (although for the purposes of this book, Linton falls within No. 6 Group).

Formed on April 1, 1937 at Mildenhall with a nucleus from No. 3 Group staff, No. 4 Group HQ took over the bomber airfields in north-east England when it moved to Linton-on-Ouse, Yorkshire, in June that year. As with other group headquarters, after the commencement of hostilities No. 4 was moved from an airfield station to a requisitioned stately home, from April 1940 the new location for the group being Heslington Hall near York. The group was to operate the Whitley, then considered a heavy bomber, and by September 1939 there were some 70 in six squadrons at three airfields. A few new Wellington-equipped squadrons served with the group during the next three years but No. 4 had been chosen to become an all-Halifax group. The first of these four-engined heavies was received in November 1940 but the last Whitley was not replaced until early 1943. Eventually there were 11 squadrons with some 340 Halifaxes at nine airfields in the York area. During the war No. 4 Group aircraft flew a total of some 61,500 sorties dropping approximately 200,000 tons of bombs and 7,000 sea mines.

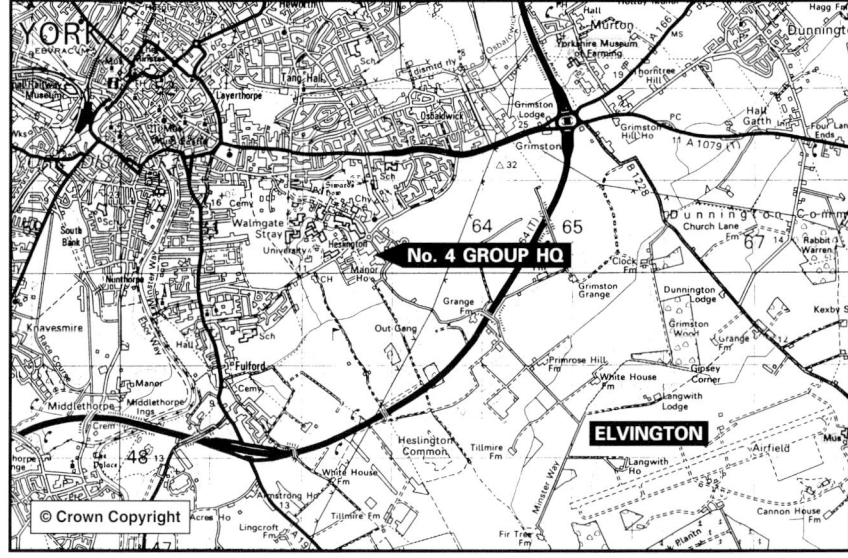

© Crown Copyright

With an expanding command, larger premises were required so in April 1940 the Elizabethan mansion at Heslington, for many years associated with Lord Deramore, was taken over. Post-war the hall became part of the University of York.

BREIGHTON

Aircrews near the briefing hut on the technical site awaiting transport to their Halifaxes on the afternoon of August 31, 1943 for a night operation to Berlin. No. 78 Squadron lost two aircraft that night: 'G'-George and 'O'-Orange.

Located six miles north-east of Selby between Breighton village and the B1228 from Howden to York, work on this bomber station started late in 1940 and took just over a year to complete. Hard runways were laid, the main 09-27 being 1,600 yards and the two subsidiaries, 04-22 and 17-35, both 1,100 yards. Unique for a Bomber Command station was their common intersection, occasioned by the restricted area of the airfield due to the land falling away to the River Derwent on the west side and to a stream on the south. Twenty-four hardstandings were positioned round the perimeter track and were all of the large pan type. Two of these were lost when hangars were erected, one on the lead in to a T2 and B1 north of runway head 09 (the B1 northernmost) near Gunby village, and the other to a T2 on the south side of the airfield west of runway head 35. The technical site was to the south-west between runway heads 04 and 09. Bomb stores were off the south-east side north of runway head 35. The camp was south-west around Breighton village and in fields to the east. Two communal, a sick quarters and nine domestic sites provided for a maximum 1,223 males and 191 females.

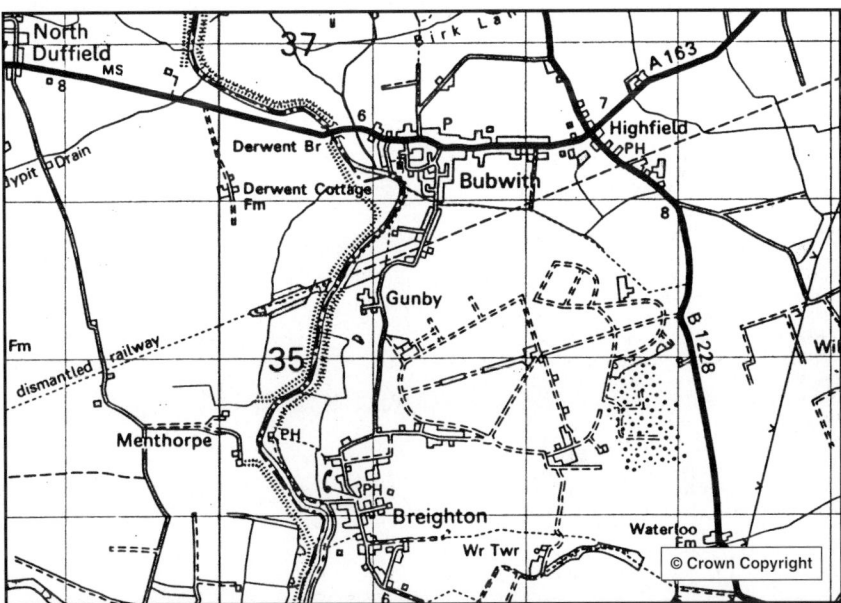

© Crown Copyright

The cheerful smiles belie the inner truth because during the previous week the squadron had lost ten aircraft . . . each with seven or eight men aboard . . . men who now lay dead in the wreckage of their machines scattered across the Continent. Mannheim . . . Berlin . . . Nuremberg . . . München-Gladbach . . . and back to Berlin again. So the Battle of Germany went on but few of these young warriors would see it through. Sixty years later Breighton basks in the bright summer sunshine, and aero engines still echo across the new mown grass as a new generation of airmen take to the skies.

The original configuration of Breighton, photographed on December 7, 1941, shows the unusual layout with all three runways intersecting at the same location. As a satellite, no hangars were initially provided and only 24 aircraft hardstandings.

Opened in No. 1 Group as a satellite station for Holme-on-Spalding-Moor, the RAAF-designated No. 460 Squadron arrived in January 1942 with Wellingtons from Molesworth where it had formed a few weeks earlier. The squadron first operated on the night of March 12, 1942, when five aircraft were despatched to Emden. In the course of the next six months, the squadron participated in 61 operations losing 29 Wellingtons, which was the highest percentage loss of all Bomber Command Wellington squadrons. Work was then underway to extend all three runways; the main to 1,950 yards and 1,400 yards for both of the others. In extending the perimeter track to the runway ends, several hardstandings were destroyed and although more pans were built the airfield total was only 34.

No. 460 Squadron was originally going to convert to Halifaxes but plans were changed to make No. 1 Group an all-Lancaster formation. The squadron returned to operations in November 1942 until mid-May the following year when it was moved to Binbrook as a result of a re-arrangement of group areas. Breighton then came under No. 4 Group with the veteran No. 78 Squadron moving its Halifaxes in from Linton-on-Ouse. No. 78 remained at the station until September 1945 having been given a transport role from the day before hostilities in Europe ended and converting to Dakotas two months later. After the squadron left to fly out to the Middle East, Breighton was put on care and maintenance. The station was then taken over by a maintenance unit which collected and stored bombs on the runways. During its use by Bomber Command 169 aircraft despatched on operations from Breighton failed to return or crashed in the UK. In addition to the 29 Wellingtons, No. 460

Squadron lost 15 Lancasters while No. 78 Squadron lost 125 Halifaxes.

The RAF withdrew from the station in 1947 and after some years of neglect the airfield was selected as a Thor missile site. Launch pads were constructed on the south side of the airfield operated by No. 240 Squadron from July 1959 until the beginning of 1963. In addition, in 1960-64 a Bloodhound ground-to-air missile site was also positioned on the airfield under No. 112 Squadron. The RAF finally withdrew in 1965 and the airfield was later sold. The technical site was taken over for light industry as were two T2 hangars. Flying recommenced in the early 1980s, using a section of the perimeter track, and the Real Aeroplane Company now operates a flying club from new hangars and offices near the old technical site. Agricultural buildings have since been erected on parts of the runways.

The 1942 extension to the main and north-east runways can be seen in the foreground of this picture taken in September 2000.

Club aircraft now use the grass strip along the original perimeter in the south-western corner (top left). This close up shows the overgrown launch pads for the Bloodhound anti-aircraft missile site which was located on the airfield in the 1960s as forward protection against an attack by the Soviet Union on Bomber Command's northern bases. The remains of the launch pads for the Thor missiles of the early 1960s can be seen in the centre of the airfield.

BURN

Flight Lieutenant 'Maxi' Baer beats up Burn in LK-W on completion of his tour of ops. (Note the car on top of the building on the left in the wartime photo. It had been 'high-jacked' from the squadron adjutant along with a large barrel of beer!)

Located 2½ miles south of Selby and sand-wiched between the A19 Doncaster to York road and the LNER rail line, construction of Burn began during the winter of 1941-42. Built to Class A standard, the main runway 02-20 was 1,990 yards long, 08-26 at 1,550 yards and 16-34 at 1,400 yards. The total of 36 hardstandings were pan-types but two were lost to hangar construction and two loop standings were added to replace them. Hangars consisted of a T2 and B1 on the south-west side of the technical site which lay between runway heads 02 and 08. A second T2 stood on the western side, between run-way heads 08 and 16 near Burn village. The bomb stores were positioned towards the Selby Canal on the north side. Nine domestic sites for 1,805 males and 276 females were dispersed north-west beyond Burn Lane and Brick Kiln Lane as were the two communal and sick quarters sites. However, while it was common at most new stations for the planned camp not to be completed until many weeks after the airfield came into use, delays and shortages saw this work continue at Burn into the summer of 1943.

The control tower and buildings have gone but the water tower still stands and can just be seen beyond the scrub silhouetted against a cooling tower of Eggborough Power Station. The airfield's lasting claim to fame must be that the only Halifax airman to be awarded the Victoria Cross took off from Burn (see page 178).

Flight Lieutenant John Bluring's LK-O *Sweet Sue* stands on a pan dispersal on the north-eastern corner of the airfield.

The aircraft was standing close to the A19 through Burn village, the houses in the left background confirming the position.

Assigned to No. 4 Group on November 11, 1942, No. 431 Squadron was formed as an RCAF unit at Burn. Initially equipped with Wellingtons, it commenced operations on the night of March 2, 1943 and resided until July when it moved to Tholthorpe in No. 6 (RCAF) Group. In some 330 sorties from Burn, No. 431 lost 20 Wellingtons. Before leaving, the squadron ceased operations ready to convert to Halifaxes.

No further bomber units were stationed at Burn until January 1944 when No. 578 Squadron was formed there from 'C' Flight of No. 51 Squadron at Snaith. During the same month an accident in the bomb stores resulted in detonations causing some loss of life.

Halifax-equipped No. 578 Squadron had 40 aircraft missing in action during 155 raids mounted from Burn. Its last operation on March 13, 1945, took place just 33 days before its disbandment. All told, 55 Halifaxes failed to return or were lost in UK crashes during operations from Burn.

No. 578's claim to fame was that one of its pilots, Pilot Officer C. J. Barton, was the only Halifax crew member of Bomber Command to be awarded — posthumously — the

Halifax LK-R of No. 578 Squadron lifts off runway 16 for a raid on Essen in November 1944. Flying Officer Eric Fox at the controls for the last operation of his tour.

The squadron at work . . . and play! Beyond the threshold of the main runway, these crewmen appear to be collecting firewood.

A prominent feature is Brayton Braff, the distant rise which was a hazard for night landings and take-offs.

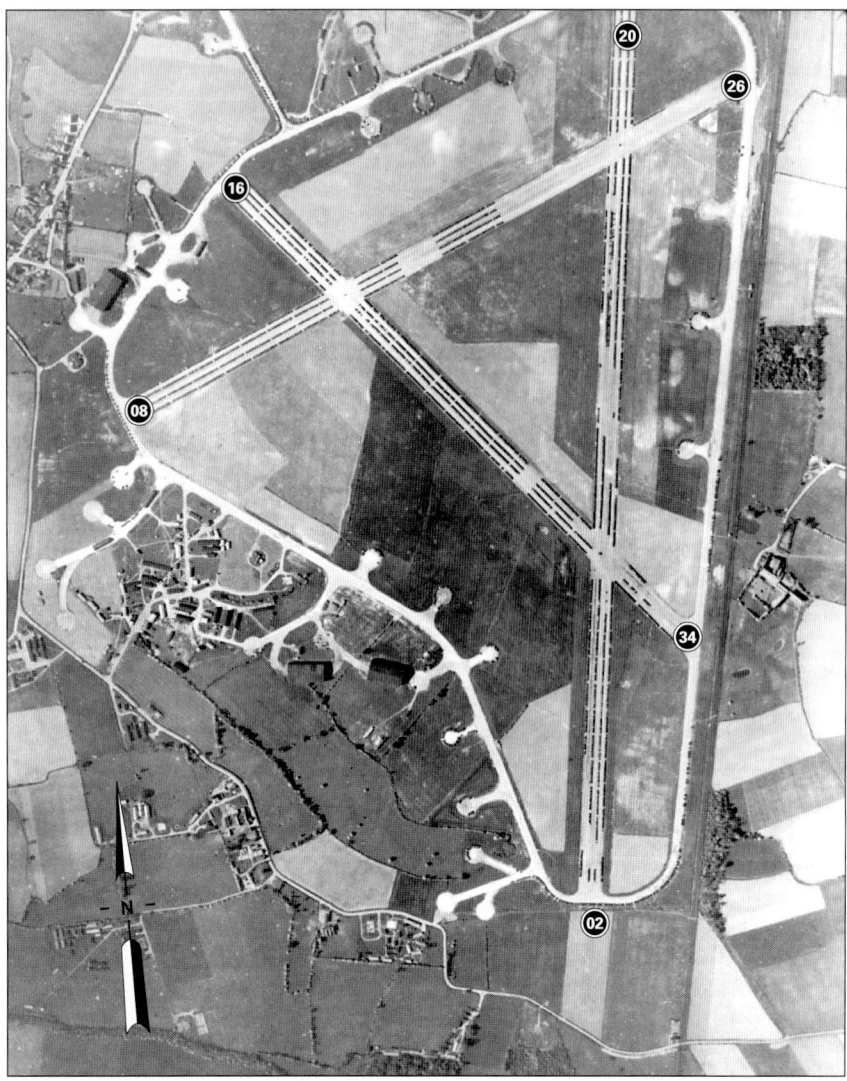

From 1945 to 1958 Burn airfield was used as an Army storage park, hundreds of unwanted armoured fighting vehicles parked in rows on the runways.

Victoria Cross. The action bringing this award occurred during the infamous raid on Nuremberg on the night of March 30/31, 1944 when Bomber Command sustained its highest losses of the war, 96 aircraft failing to return. Cyril Barton's Halifax sustained severe damage from night fighters on the way in which knocked out the intercom system; therefore the crew had to use Morse Code to communicate with each other. Owing to a misunderstood signal, the navigator, wireless operator and bomb aimer baled out but the captain continued to the target and nursed the crippled aircraft back to England, only to lose his life as the result of a crash-landing 90 miles north of Burn, at Ryhope Colliery, County Durham.

Another claim to fame, apart from 578's VC, 143 Distinguished Flying Crosses and 82 Distinguished Flying Medals over its 14-month life, was its consistent bombing accuracy, resulting in the granting of a squadron crest by His Majesty King George VI in February 1945 with the motto 'Accuracy'. Yet further accolade was earned by the squadron's ground crews, whose outstanding servicing of the Bristol Hercules XVI engines resulted in

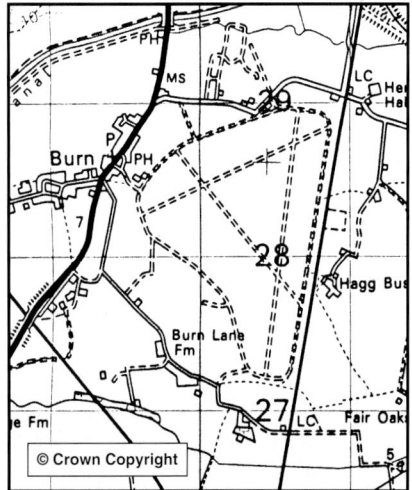

Although the secondary at Burn was designated 16-34, as explained on page 94, a change in the magnetic variation **subsequently triggered a switch to 33. The resident flying club upgraded part of the runway in 2000.**

Above: **Burn, with its intact runways and taxiways remains one of Bomber Command's best preserved disused airfields. This shot looks east towards the main railway line to Selby.**

the award by the Bristol Aeroplane Company of a shield, now on display at the Yorkshire Air Museum at Elvington near York.

Two of the squadron's Halifaxes passed the century mark on operations, flying 104 and 105 operations respectively, both aircraft surviving the war only to be scrapped.

Burn was closed for flying in July 1945. The Royal Army Service Corps moved in shortly aftetrwards and in the immediate post-war years the RASC used the station to store surplus military vehicles on its runways. During the next three decades the airfield buildings and the flying area was reclaimed for farming. Nevertheless, at the end of the century Burn remains one of the few airfields vacated by the RAF in 1945 on which all runways and most of the hardstandings still survive.

Right: **A poignant reminder of days long gone. Aircrew lockers pictured by Kerry Hutchinson in 1991 still intact in the Sergeants Mess in Holmes Farm. Since then the building has been demolished but fortunately the lockers were saved and re-erected in a new barn to store agricultural spare parts. Locker 214 bears the inscription: 'Call at Mess office for rations. F/Sgt Johnson'.**

DRIFFIELD

Whitley Vs of No. 102 Squadron outside Driffield's northern hangar, early March 1940. N1421 DY-C was brought down over Norway on April 29/30 and N1382 DY-A was lost during a raid on Augsburg on August 16/17, 1940.

In 1916, open meadowland two miles south-west of Great Driffield, on the northern side of the road running between that small town and Market Weighton, was requisitioned for use as a landing ground. The purpose was to establish a base for FE2b aircraft where they might have an opportunity of intercepting Zeppelin raids as they crossed the coast. A flight of No. 33 Squadron used the landing ground, known as Eastburn, the hamlet to the west, but was never able to attack one of the raiders. The following year Eastburn was selected for development as a military aerodrome with No. 3 and 27 Training Squadrons that later formed No. 21 Training Depot Station. Several wooden buildings including a number of small hangars were erected to house these units and their equipment. With peace the aerodrome was closed in February 1920 and most of the wartime structures were eventually demolished.

As with many other abandoned Great War aerodromes and landing grounds, when the RAF expanded during the 1930s these were the first sites reviewed for the construction of permanent stations. Eastburn/Driffield was found highly suitable and in 1934 the land was re-acquired and work commenced on what was officially to be known as RAF Station Driffield. The camp, on the Great Driffield side of the landing ground, was made up of closely grouped administrative,

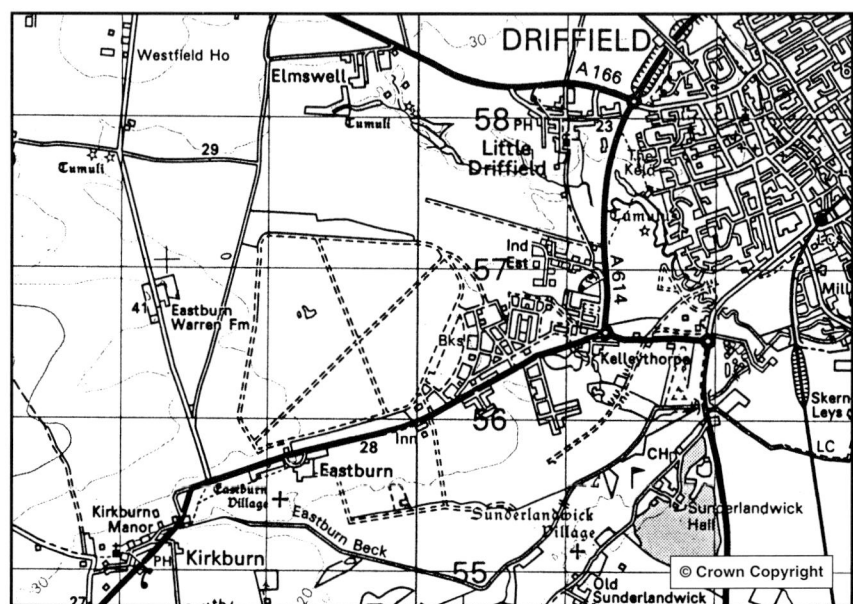

© Crown Copyright

technical and barrack buildings, constructed in brick, flat-roofed with many centrally-heated. The hallmark of the expansion period — an arc of Type C hangars fronting the bombing circle — comprised four hangars with a fifth tucked in behind that on the extreme right. Bomb stores were in the north-west corner of the holding.

The Type C hangar is now masked by trees that were planted soon after the building was erected.

Workmen prepare to fill in a bomb crater near the station armoury after the Luftwaffe raid hit the airfield the early afternoon on August 15, 1940. There were 14 fatalities including 19 year old Aircraftwoman Marguerite Hudson who was the first WAAF to be killed by enemy action in the Second World War.

Officially opened at the end of July 1936, construction was far enough advanced by September for the first squadrons selected for residence to move in. These were Nos. 58 and 215 both equipped with Virginias, both from Upper Heyford. At this time the station was under No. 3 Group but plans were afoot to form two more groups in the burgeoning Bomber Command. No. 4 Group, formed in April 1937, took over Driffield in June. At that time Nos. 75 and 215 were resident, the former having been formed from No. 215's 'B' Flight in March that year. No. 58 Squadron had moved to Boscombe Down in March a few days after its 'B' Flight became No. 51 Squadron, the move made as Driffield could

not house the complement of four squadrons. In August and September the same year, Driffield's resident squadrons converted to the Handley Page Harrow and in July 1938 they were both transferred to Honington and No. 3 Group where this bomber type was concentrated. This was an exchange between groups, the two squadrons displaced at Honington coming to Driffield, No. 77 flying Wellesleys and No. 102 Heyfords but before the year was out both had converted to Whitley IIIs.

No. 102 Squadron opened Driffield's war on the night of September 4/5, 1939, with three leaflet-dropping sorties to the Ruhr; more lethal cargoes were not to be carried until 1940. While there were numerous attacks on Bomber Command airfields by single enemy aircraft, Driffield was one of the few subjected to concentrated formation bombing. This occurred on August 15, 1940, when a large formation of Ju 88s of KG30 raided the airfield scoring 171 direct hits causing 14 deaths and the destroying of 12 Whitleys, with damage to others and several

The belt of camouflage trees have become a grove, a gap in the line indicating where the bomb exploded. The hangars are now used for machinery and storage for intervention grain for the Ministry of Fisheries and Food.

No.	NAME	DATE	WEIGHT OF BOMBS kg	No.O E.A
	AIRFIELDS			
1	CATFOSS	JAN. 3-4	550	1
		JULY 25-26	5,710	5
2	NEW ROMNEY	JAN. 22-23	940	2
3	SHOREHAM	FEB. 13-14	720	1
4	RAYDON	MAR. 3-4	1,240	1
		SEPT. 6-7	50	1
5	BRADWELL ON SEA	MAR. 3-4	1,000	2
		APR. 14-15	800	1
6	DONNA NOOK	MAR. 15-16	300	1
7	DUNSFOLD	APR. 16-17	500	1
8	OAKLEY	APR. 16-17	800	1
9	NORTHOLT	APR. 16-17	500	1
10	FINMERE	APR. 16-7	500	1
11	DEBACH	MAY. 13-14	1,808	2
12	LAVENHAM	MAY. 17-18	500	1
13	CASTLE CAMPS	JUNE 14-15	500	1
		SEPT. 6-7	250	1
		OCT. 2-3	380	1
14	STRADISHALL	JUNE 14-15	500	1
15	MILDENHALL	OCT. 2-3	400	1
16	WOMBLETON	JULY 25-26	2,540	4
17	BOREHAM	JULY 28-29	1,000	1
		DEC. 10-11	2,200	1
18	FELTWELL	AUG. 10-11	380	1
19	HOLMESLEY. SOUTH	AUG. 11-12	500	1
20	FUNTINGTON	AUG. 15-16	4,310	4
21	THORNEY ISLAND	AUG. 15-16		
22	BOXTED	AUG. 17-18	750	1
		AUG. 22-23	140	1
23	BIRCH	AUG. 17-18	250	1
		DEC. 10-11	1,500	1
24	WOODHALL SPA	AUG. 17-18	1,360	2
		SEPT. 27-28	380	1
25	FRAMLINGHAM	AUG. 22-23	90	1
26	METFIELD	AUG. 22-23	50	1
		OCT. 3-4	330	1
		FEB. 9	1,000	1
27	COLTISHALL	AUG. 22-23	50	1
		AUG. 23-24	150	1
		SEPT. 27-28	330	

No.	NAME	DATE	WEIGHT	No.O E.A
28	WATERBEACH	SEPT.	330	1
		AUG. 22-23	800	1
		OCT. 3-4	200	1
29	DOWNHAM MARKET	AUG. 23-24	560	1
		SEPT. 6-7	250	1
30	SHIPDHAM	AUG. 23-24	380	1
31	MANBY	AUG.31./1.	100	1
32	WETHERSFIELD	SEPT. 7-8	500	1
		DEC. 10-11	2,400	1
33	SNAILWELL	SEPT. 8-5	250	1
34	HEPWORTH	SEPT. 8-9	m/g	1
35	FORD	SEPT. 15-16	380	1
		OCT. 2-3	380	1
36	LYDD	SEPT.15-16	3,850	3
37	BECCLES	SEPT. 21-22	250	1
38	CHEDBURGH	SEPT. 22-23	380	1
		DEC. 10-11	2,200	1
39	HOLME	SEPT. 22-23	380	1
40	SKELLINGTHORPE	SEPT. 27-28	m/g	1
41	EAST KIRBY	SEPT. 27-28	m/g	1
42	LUDFORD MAGNA	SEPT.27-28	330	1
43	IPSWICH	SEPT.27-28	480	1
44	HALESWORTH	OCT. 2-3	1,250	1
45	TUDDENHAM	OCT. 2-3	550	1
46	OAKINGTON	OCT. 2-3	50	1
47	GRANSDEN LODGE	OCT. 2-3	380	1
		OCT. 3-4	290	1
48	WARBOYS	OCT. 3-4	320	1
49	CROYDON	OCT. 2-3	380	1
50	BARDNEY	OCT. 3-4	290	1
51	KNETTISHALL	OCT. 3-4	450	1
52	GRAVELY	OCT. 3-4	190	1
53	WYTON	OCT. 3-4	300	1
54	COLEBY GRANGE	OCT. 4-5	380	1
55	GOSFIELD	OCT.15-16	850	1
		DEC.10-11	15,300	11
56	HUTTON CRANSWICK	OCT. 20-21	1,000	1
57	LECONFIELD	OCT.20-21	140	1
58	LUDHAM	OCT.24-25	800	1
59	TANGMERE	NOV. 18-19	500	1
60	RIVENHALL	DEC.10-11	2,000	1
61	EARLS COLNE	DEC.10-11	2,200	1
62	SEETHING	JAN. 11	1,000	1
63	TARRANT RUSHTON	JAN. 31	1,000	1
64	HARROWBEER	MAR.30	1,000	2

No.	NAME	DATE	WEIGHT	No.O E.A
	DUMMY AIRFIELDS			
65	KILHAM	JAN. 22-23	1550	1
		OCT. 20-21	200	1
66	BERWICK HILL	MAR.12-13	50	1
67	LUDBOROUGH	MAR.15-16	300	1
68	SUFFIELD	MAY. 4-5	2000	1
69	BEEFORD	JULY.25-26	3000	2
70	SIBSEY	OCT. 3-4	380	1
71	LITTLEPORT	OCT. 3-4	340	1
72	LIDGATE	OCT. 4-5	540	1
73	IXWORTH	OCT. 6-7	900	1
74	POSLINGTON	NOV. 4-5	1000	1
75	LENHAM	NOV.25-26	1000	1
	R.A.F. STATIONS			
76	EASTCLIFF-WESTCLIFF	MAR-9-10	300	1
77	MARSKE	MAR.22-23	1,800	2
78	TRIMMINGHAM	MAY. 4-5	200	1
79	MUNDESLEY	MAY. 4-5	600	1
80	BARDHILL	MAY. 4-5	1000	1
81	ELSING	AUG.31/1	384	1
82	PEVENSEY	SEPT.6-7	330	1
		NOV. 6-7	250	1
83	LEISTON	SEPT.6-7	250	1
84	FELIXSTOWE	SEPT.6-7	250	1
85	WINTERTON	SEPT.6-7	650	1
86	WIX	OCT.15-16	1500	1
87	GRAVESEND	OCT.20-21	50	1
88	ELHAM	OCT.23-24	1000	1
89	LEYSDOWN	NOV.6-7	500	1
90	HAMBLE	FEB.9	m/g	1
91	BEACHY HEAD	MAR.7	500	1
92	COLETON	MAR.18	750	3
93	BLACKGANG	JUNE 1	500	1
94	BAWDSEY	JUNE 2	1000	1

Although one might expect German attacks on British airfields to have peaked in 1940, nevertheless raids continued as this official table for 1943 shows. Several are bases of Bomber Command in northern England.

buildings. Moreover, the airfield was put out of action for several days before No. 77 Squadron moved its remaining Whitleys to Linton-on-Ouse and No. 102 took theirs to Leeming. For the next four months there was no operational activity at Driffield and it appears from the placing of dummy Whitleys and vehicles around the aerodrome that there was an attempt to keep enemy attention here and hopefully away from other stations. However, Driffield was not attacked again in force.

With defence the prime concern at this stage of the war, when Driffield was returned to operational status in January 1941 it was for use as a fighter station. Hurricanes of No. 213 Squadron and later No. 1 (RCAF) were followed by No. 485 (RNZAF) Squadron with Spitfires before No. 4 Group reclaimed the station in April. The same month, No. 104 Squadron was reformed here to fly Wellingtons, undertaking its first sorties on the night of May 8/9.

A second Wellington-equipped squadron, No. 405 manned largely by RCAF personnel and the first Canadian squadron in Bomber Command, was also formed at Driffield in April 1941 and joined the fray on the night of June 12/13 with a bombing raid on the Ruhr. Six days later it was moved out to Pocklington.

The crisis situation in the Mediterranean called for air reinforcements and during October 1941 all but a few of No. 104's Wellingtons with air and ground crews were despatched to Malta. The residue at Driffield soldiered on but the main body of the air echelon did not return and the Driffield element became the re-born No. 158 Squadron on St Valentine's Day 1942. In June, the squadron was moved out to East Moor to convert to Halifaxes. Not until the autumn were other bomber squadrons present. No. 466 was formed as an Australian unit in October and No. 196 the following month although neither became operational before being moved to Leconfield in December 1943 to enable hard runways to be laid.

The programme entailed extending the station boundaries to the west. Runways were main 06-24, 2,000 yards long, and the subsidiaries, 10-28 at 1,450 yards and 16-34 at 1,350 yards. It appears that 36 hardstandings had been built in 1940 and of these, 29 pans and one odd shape survived to be linked to the encompassing perimeter track. Ten loop-type were added to make the total aircraft standings 40. A new bomb store was built off the north side near the LNER line. Additional camp sites raised the maximum accommodation to 1,884 males and 422 females.

The airfield was re-opened for flying in June 1944 when No. 466 (RAAF) Squadron returned from Leconfield and its Halifaxes remained throughout the rest of hostilities. In August, it provided the nucleus for a reformed No. 462 (RAAF) Squadron partnering No. 466 in main force operations from Driffield until late December 1944. No. 462 was then transferred to No. 100 Group for bomber support operations, moving out to Foulsham before the end of the year. No. 466 Squadron flew its last bombing raid on April 25, 1945 — the last raid from Driffield. All told, a total of 87 Bomber Command aircraft failed to return or crashed in the UK in the course of operations from the station: 22 Whitleys, 33 Wellingtons and 28 Halifaxes.

As with many other Halifax squadrons, on May 7 No. 466 was transferred to transport duties under Transport Command. It was joined later in the month by No. 426 (RCAF) Squadron which began to shed its Lancasters for cargo-configurated Liberators before moving on to Tempsford after only a month at Driffield. No. 466 Squadron, supplemented by crews from No. 10 Squadron, RAAF, moved out to Bassingbourn in September for transport duties.

Care and maintenance descended on Driffield until the autumn of 1946 when Flying Training Command took over and installed a navigation school. The station supported various training units until September 1955 when it came under the auspices of Fighter Command. Venoms were based there until the summer of 1957 and the Fighter Weapons School until the following March. The next lease of life was as a Thor missile formation headquarters which lasted from October 1958 to June 1963. A caretaker party held sway for a few months but this was basically the end of the RAF's occupation and, apart for some test flying of Buccaneers when Hawker-Siddeley's normal facilities were not available, flying ceased.

As at several other redundant RAF airfields, the permanent buildings were attractive to the Army seeking escape from spartan Victorian barracks and in January 1977 the station became Alamein Barracks for the Royal Corps of Transport. The RAF ensign was lowered for the last time at a parade on June 28, 1996.

Driffield, August 1945. The pans in the north-west corner became isolated when the concrete runways were laid.

Above: **September 2000 looking south-west more or less along the line of the old main runway and** *below* **along the 16-34 subsidiary. The tracks and mounds of earth are for army driver training for the Defence Driving School. Driffield was initially offered for sale by the Ministry of Defence in 1977 but more recently has been taken off the market.**

ELVINGTON

Crews of No. 77 Squadron about to be driven out to their Halifaxes but how many of these young faces would survive a 30-sortie operational tour? The control tower can be seen on the left.

Five miles south-east of the centre of York, this airfield lies south of the B1228 on the approach to Elvington village. Originally scheduled as a satellite landing ground, the flat extent of largely rough grazing land encroached by birch woods was requisitioned in 1940. After clearing the site and laying a gravel and cinder perimeter taxiway, upgrading took place and hard runways were put down as well as several hardstandings, ultimately 38 in number. These were 02-20 and 14-32 at 1,400 yards and the main 08-26

Elvington 2000. Surely one of the most striking comparisons taken at any of the former Bomber Command airfields?

192

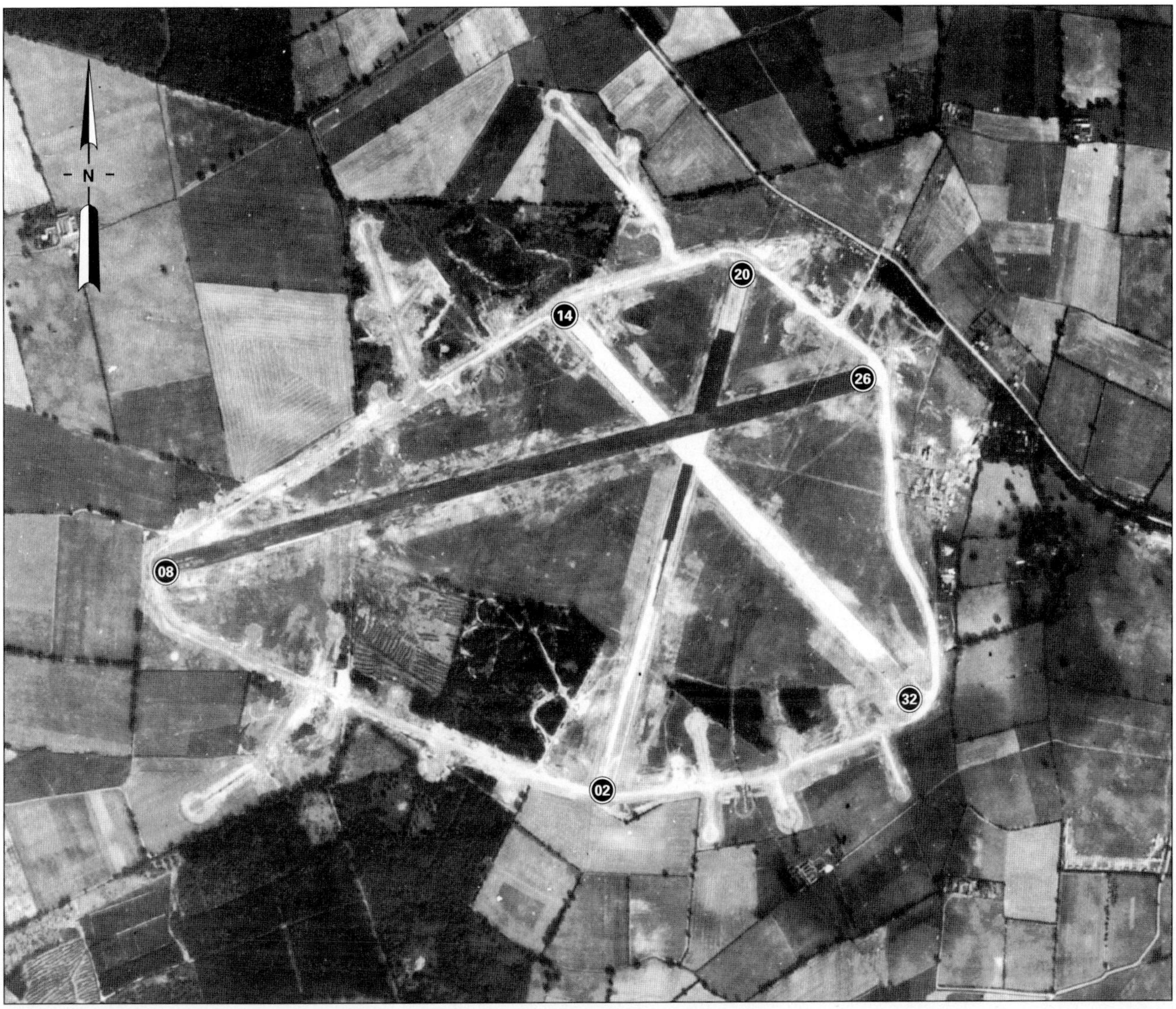

Hard runway and perimeter track construction underway at Elvington in 1942.

at 2,000 yards. A T2 hangar was erected on the technical site near the B1228 and two more T2s further to the south-east between the heads of runways 02 and 34 at a later date which eliminated one hardstanding. A B1 hangar was added early in 1943. The bomb stores were located off the south-east side of the airfield and the camp sites dispersed either side of the B1228 into Elvington village.

The station was first occupied by Whitleys of No. 77 Squadron which arrived in October 1942. A veteran No. 4 Group squadron, No. 77 had been based at Leeming prior to being loaned to Coastal Command in May 1942 when it operated from Chivenor. Following its return to Bomber Command, after a brief period of retraining and converting to Halifaxes, the squadron joined Main Force operations in December and continued to fly from Elvington until May 1944. In that month No. 77 was moved to Full Sutton as Elvington had been selected as the base for two new heavy bomber squadrons manned by Free French personnel flying Halifaxes in No. 4 Group. These were Nos. 346 and 347 Squadrons, formed at Elvington in May and June 1944 respectively, both becoming operational in the latter month.

On December 28, 1944, a loaded Halifax caught fire on dispersal, the ensuing explosions causing 18 casualties of which 13 were fatal. During some 120 operations, the last from Elvington taking place on April 25, 1945, the French had 30 Halifaxes missing in

action. A major Luftwaffe intruder operation on the night of March 3/4, 1945 resulted in a Halifax returning to Elvington being shot down. One of the Ju 88s involved struck trees and crashed while attempting to strafe the airfield. Operational losses from Elvington totaled 128 Halifaxes, including crashes, 45 of which were from the French squadrons.

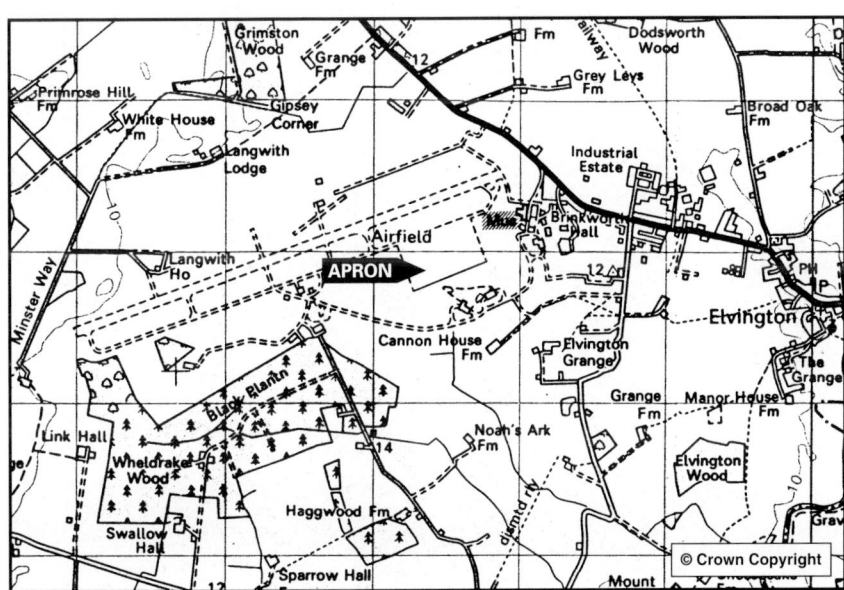

After the war the main runway was lengthened to 10,000 feet for the US Strategic Air Command although it was never used. The massive parking apron at the south-eastern end covers an area of almost 50 acres.

The RAF left Elvington in April 1992 but before they quit the base, the idea had been raised of establishing a museum on the technical site where many of the buildings were still original. The control tower was the first to be restored by the Yorkshire Air Museum which has the declared purpose to 'preserve part of a typical wartime airfield as a memorial to the Allied air and ground crews who served in World War II'.

Centrepiece of the museum's aircraft collection is the rebuilt Halifax (one of only three of the type now existing of the 6,200 built) from salvaged parts and refabrication by apprentices of British Aerospace at Brough.

Other aircraft on display include a Lightning, Canberra and this Mosquito, being rebuilt.

In the weeks following VE-Day, the French-manned Halifaxes were employed in transporting military personnel and material accross liberated Europe and in October they were officially turned over to the French Air Force, taking the aircraft with them. After their departure, Elvington was used by No. 14 Maintenance Unit to store bombs and eventually was reduced to having only a caretaker party in residence. In 1953 Elvington was one of several redundant airfields passed to the USAF for updating as reserve bases and in 1954 US engineer organisations extended and strengthened the main runway to 3,265 yards, built a 'parking ramp' and new taxiways while breaking up the other old runways and much other wartime concrete for use as hardcore. However, with lessened East-West tension and a change in strategy, the USAF withdrew its personnel although the airfield remained in reserve status. Thereafter Elvington became a relief landing ground for RAF training establishments, the long runway providing a useful safety margin for student pilots. In 1968 this runway was also used for Hovercraft trials.

In the 1970s, Elvington's technical and administrative sites were acquired by an enthusiast group who formed the Yorkshire Air Museum. This thriving organisation has developed into one of the UK's premier air museums, noted particularly for its splendid effort in re-fabricating the only externally complete example of a Halifax in existence.

To give much needed protection for the exhibits, a T2 hangar (removed from Kemble) was erected on the museum site in 1995. Being in a designated green belt area for York, no development is allowed of the airfield site, the runway remaining intact.

The eastern end of the airfield is now dominated by the huge concrete apron visible, we are told, by astronauts from space! Almost nothing remains to be seen of the two subsidiary runways.

Having one of the longest runways in Britain, Elvington has been useful in other ways . . . like attempts at breaking records. Here Richard 'Rocketman' Brown sets a new British motor cycle record of 216.55mph in his jet-powered Gillette Mach 3 in October 1998 . . . a record which stood until July 2001 when Jarrod 'Jack' Frost raised it to 222.19 mph at Woodbridge. Colin Fallows broke the British land speed record for jet-propelled cars at Elvington on July 5, 2000 reaching 303.3 mph.

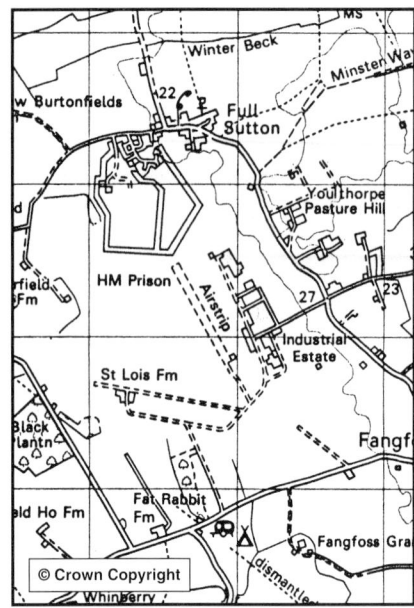

FULL SUTTON

Full Sutton . . . then and now. Fortunately the control tower still stands although the flight control room on the first floor has since been sub-divided by a partition wall making for poor comparisons.

Full Sutton was a Class A standard airfield built in the parishes of Full Sutton and Fangfoss, largely on Growthorpe Common north of the old York to Pocklington rail line located nine miles east-north-east from the city centre, work on Full Sutton commenced in 1943. Hadsphaltic Ltd constructed the flying field on a £329,000 contract and J. Gerrard & Sons Ltd the buildings for £322,000. The three concrete runways were the main 16-34 at 1,980 yards and the subsidiaries, 05-23 at 1,480 and 11-29 at 1,300 yards. The encircling perimeter track had 36 loop type hardstandings. Two T2 hangars were located on the technical site on the east side, between runway heads 23 and 34, and a B1 in the southwest dispersal area between runways 11 and

16. Bomb stores were off the north-west corner. A dozen domestic sites with utility buildings were dispersed in the parishes of Full Sutton and Growthorpe and allowed for a maximum of 1,443 males and 367 females.

The station opened in May 1944 to receive No. 77 Squadron which had been moved from Elvington to make way for an all-French establishment. No. 77's Halifaxes operated from Full Sutton from May 15, 1944 to April 25, 1945. Ninety-five Halifaxes failed to return or were lost in crashes during wartime operations flown from the airfield. At the end of hostilities No. 77 Squadron was placed under Transport Command and in July traded its Halifaxes for Dakotas. Having thus converted, the squadron was transferred south to Broadwell at the end of August.

Unlike many other wartime stations in the area which were soon placed under care and maintenance after VE-Day, Full Sutton was retained for flying, No. 231 Squadron being

This Halifax (MZ335 KN-A) on dispersal at Full Sutton was written off in a take-off crash due to engine failure on January 2, 1945. There were no fatalities.

PRISON

Out on the airfield proper, though, much has changed. The former technical site is now industrialised and a high-security prison has been established at the northen end — hence no vertical photography will be released by the authorities.

While the 16-34 runway survives in part, a grass strip (04-22) now replaces the wartime 05-23 runway. Of the 11-29 subsidiary nothing survives. A screen of trees now hides the prison from the airfield. View looking south-east.

formed in November 1945 to train on Lancastrian transports. This unit was in residence until the following April and thereafter Full Sutton's activities subsided with care and maintenance status being reintroduced in the spring of 1947.

The station was given a new lease of life in the 1950s when used as a flying school, while at the same time it was earmarked for USAF occupation if the Cold War had become hot. The next development was a Thor missile installation under the charge of No. 102 Squadron from April 1959 for four years after which it went the way of all Thor units and was disbanded. This marked the end of the RAF's association with Full Sutton. A period of commercial development of the technical site followed and during the past decade part of runway 11-29 came into use for private flying. In 1986 the north end of the airfield was selected as a site for a prison which was opened in April 1988.

Concrete and clay. Agriculture has returned again although crops do not grow well where subsoil has been mixed with top soil.

197

HOLME-ON-SPALDING-MOOR

More often simplified to just Holme, this vertical, believed taken in January 1942, shows Wellingtons on the dispersals and work underway to lengthen the main runway.

Six miles south-west of Market Weighton and a mile south of the village for which it was named, on the east side of the A614, this airfield was one of the early wartime bomber stations with hard runways. Construction began in the winter of 1940-41 with three concrete runways, a perimeter track and 36 hardstandings laid by the following summer. The runways were extended from the original planned lengths before completion of the airfield, the main 12-30 ending up at 1,800 yards, 04-22 at 1,200 yards and 08-26 at 1,100 yards. A single Type J hangar was erected by the technical site, situated on the north-east side beside the public road, with two Type T2 added alongside in the later stages of construction. Bomb stores were off the north-west corner of the airfield. The dispersed camp sites to the north-east of the airfield catered for up to 1,941 males and 381 females.

Holme-on-Spalding-Moor, more frequently referred to as plain Holme, even in official documents, was first occupied by flying units in August 1941 with the arrival of No. 458 (RAAF) Squadron which was being built up

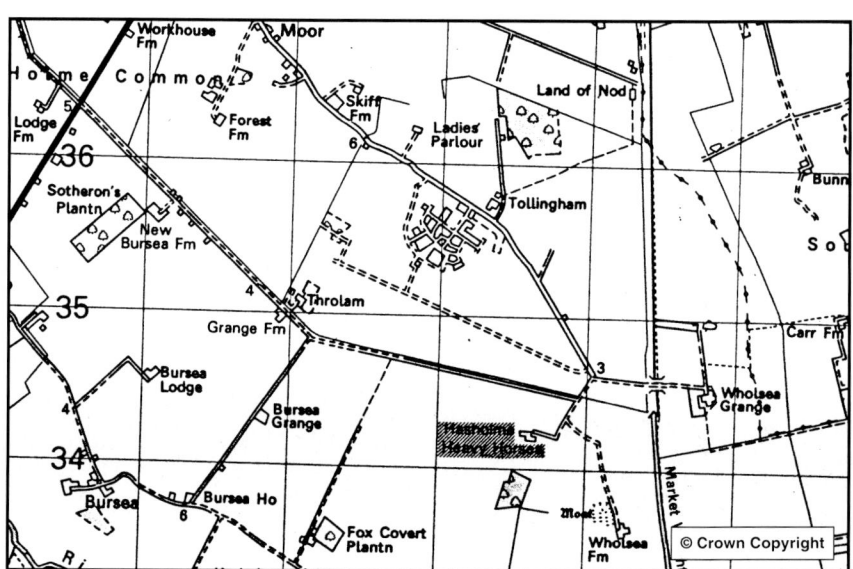

WAAFs enjoy a game of hockey near their billet as a No. 1663 HCU Halifax makes its approach to the 04-22 runway from the north.

to fly Wellingtons in No. 1 Group. The first offensive operations from Holme took place on the night of October 20/21 with ten Wellingtons attacking Antwerp. One aircraft was lost Sergeant Philip Crittenden being the first Australian serving in Bomber Command to be killed from a RAAF Squadron. Another Australian squadron, No. 460, established at Holme, began training at its satellite, Breighton, in November. Tentative plans to convert both units to the Halifax were never brought to fruition, No. 1 Group taking to the Lancaster instead, No. 458 Squadron's operational career in Bomber Command being terminated at the end of January 1942. After a few weeks spent re-equipping, No. 458 was sent out to the

Mediterranean theatre to meet an urgent requirement for anti-shipping operations. During its time at Holme, the squadron flew 65 sorties losing three aircraft.

During the winter of 1941-42 and the following spring, the runways were extended to 2,000 yards for the main (12-30); 1,400 yards for 04-22 and 1,500 yards for 08-26. The 12-30 runway was extended at the south-eastern end and the others at their southern ends. This work completed, in August No. 460 Squadron's Halifax Conversion Flight arrived for a few weeks and then departed to Breighton from whence it came. In September, No. 1 Group's expansion was accelerated by the transfer of No. 101 Squadron from No. 3 Group to No. 1 Group, the squadron

moving from Stradishall to Holme-on-Spalding-Moor. No. 101 was re-built as a Lancaster unit, the first in No. 1 Group, and took the type into action for the first time on the night of November 20/21, 1942.

No. 101 flew from Holme until June 1943 when a re-assignment of bomber stations in the Yorkshire and Lincolnshire region saw Holme-on-Spalding-Moor transferred from No. 1 to No. 4 Group. No. 101 Squadron moved to Ludford Magna and its place was taken by No. 76 Squadron from Linton-on-Ouse. This veteran Halifax squadron remained the sole operational unit throughout the remainder of hostilities, its last raid taking place on April 25, 1945 to attack a gun position at Wangerooge during which

The field at the appropriately-named Ladies' Parlour Farm now hosts cereal crops, the farmhouse still nestling behind the trees.

Safe landings! A Halifax of the Heavy Conversion Unit approaches runway 22.

two machines were lost in a mid-air collision. Bomber command losses on raids flown from Holme amounted to 151 of which six were Wellingtons, 35 Lancasters and 110 Halifaxes.

In common with several other No. 4 Group units and stations, on the penultimate day of hostilities in Europe the airfield and its resident squadron were transferred to Transport Command. In the following weeks, No. 76 changed its Halifaxes for Dakotas which it flew to the Far East on leaving Holme in July 1945. Dakotas of No. 512 Squadron arrived at Holme the same month and stayed until October when they too departed overseas. The station was then put on care and maintenance with a small caretaker unit until its runways were used for two years by a maintenance unit to store redundant bombs.

In 1951, Holme was prepared for a new lease of life, re-opening the following year to operate an advanced flying school; then early in 1954, the station became another of those

The runway has come and gone yet the house in the background has seen it all!

turned over to the USAF for upgrading in case East-West relations deteriorated. American engineers arrived to strengthen and lengthen the main runway and refurbish some installations, leaving Holme as a reserve station in 1957. In the same year, Blackburn's acquired use of this rejuvenated airfield as a flight test centre and satellite for their main airfield at Brough, an arrangement perpetuated by British Aerospace until December 1983. Buccaneers were taken by road from the Brough factory for flight testing at Holme during this period. The site was then sold. Fisher Thompson Group of seed and grain merchants acquired the hangars and Rotherham Stonemasons the technical site buildings. Most of the runway and perimeter track concrete has now been removed for hardcore and little evidence of the airfield remains.

Holme-on-Spalding-Moor in March 1958. A Bucaneer testing the arrester gear at the Hawker Siddeley Aviation Company's test facility after Blackburn Aircraft Ltd took over the airfield in 1957 for the development and test flying of the aircraft.

When British Aerospace finally relinquished their use of Holme it was very soon returned to agriculture.

LECONFIELD

Warrant Officer T. E. Mellor and his crew pose near the hangar line with their Wellington after finishing a successful tour of operations with No. 196 Squadron on July 28/29, 1943.

An early expansion scheme aerodrome in the East Riding, Leconfield was laid out on an area of level meadowland, between the LNER line from Beverley to Great Driffield in the east and the A614 road to the same locations in the west. Construction began in 1935 to the common design of the period, the permanent barrack, administrative and technical buildings being located in close proximity on the west side of the flying field adjacent to Leconfield village. Four Type C hangars fronted the bombing circle with a fifth to the rear at the southern end.

The station was ready for occupation in December 1936 and received its first resident unit, No. 166 Squadron, early the following month. A second squadron, No. 97, arrived in February, both having previously been located at Boscombe Down equipped with Heyfords. The station was under the control of No. 3 Group until No. 4 Group was established in the area on June 29, Leconfield becoming one of its five original stations. In June 1938, both squadrons were relegated from first-line status for use as an air observers school. When this work was taken over elsewhere by a training unit, Nos. 97 and 166 became the so-called Pool Squadrons of No. 4 Group. As such they had a low priority for re-equipment and, though some Whitleys were received in the summer of 1939, there were still several of the lumbering Heyford biplanes on hand when war was declared.

Both pool squadrons were moved to Abingdon in September when Leconfield was taken over by Fighter Command's No. 13 Group which required an airfield where good defensive cover could be provided for the Humber area. Two Spitfire squadrons arrived in October and during the next two months 18 different fighter squadrons were rotated at Leconfield for varying periods, the station often being used as a rest base for units exhausted by operations in the south.

Six decades later Leconfield is still a busy base . . . but now with new tenants and a new name: Normandy Barracks. Major Andrew Cooper stands in for the Wellington crew between the two northernmost hangars at what is now the Defence School of Transport. Note the arm of the lamp is still fixed to the sliding door frame.

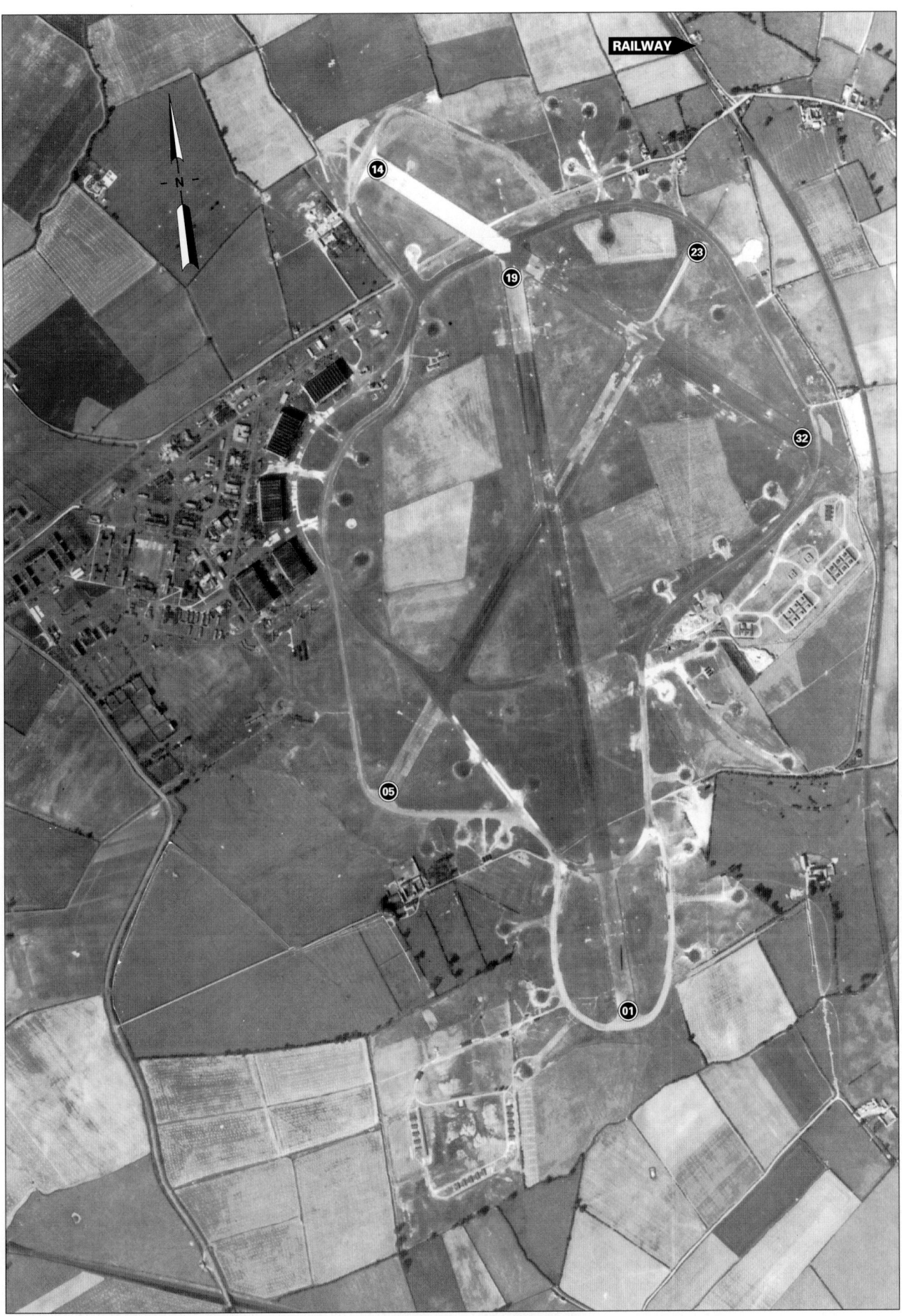

RAILWAY

Leconfield photographed in August 1945 by No. 541 Squadron. When the main runway was further extended to the north, a new public road had to be built linking Leconfield village with Arram (see Ordnance Survey map overleaf).

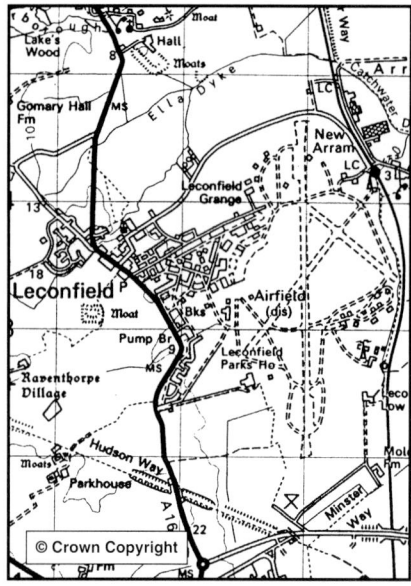

© Crown Copyright

To establish a second Halifax squadron at Leconfield, early in January 1944 No. 640 Squadron was formed at the station, its operational nucleus being the 'C' Flight of No. 158 Squadron at Lissett. The new squadron's first raid was to Berlin on the night January 20/21, this and one more raid being flown from Lissett before the flight echelon transferred to Leconfield. In early June No. 466 Squadron was transferred to Driffield (which had just been re-opened after rebuilding) where it was proposed to use No. 466 in forming an additional Australian-manned Halifax squadron.

With Snaith about to close as a bomber station, No. 51 Squadron was moved to Leconfield on April 20, 1945, and it flew its last operation of the war five days later, as did No. 640 Squadron. No. 51 Squadron then became a transport squadron, Leconfield

The airfield was returned to Bomber Command at the end of 1941, preparation work to lay concrete runways having been put in hand during the spring of that year. In October and December 1941, two Halifax conversion flights were formed at Leconfield, both moving to Marston Moor at the end of the year so that runway construction was not impeded. The runways laid were the main 01-19 at 1,300 yards, apparently later extended to 1,520 yards, and the subsidiaries 05-23 and 14-32 both at 1,300 yards. Thirty-six pan-type hardstandings, many on long access tracks into surrounding fields, were dotted all around the perimeter track. However, no sooner was this work complete than the runways were further extended for heavy bomber operation. The main ended up at 2,000 yards, and both secondaries 1,400 yards having been extended at the southern ends. Runway 05-23 had to be terminated at the 14-32 runway and not the perimeter track in order that sufficient height could be gained to clear the elevated Hull to Scarborough railway line. The perimeter track was extended to meet the ends of the runways, and a new bomb store established in fields to the south-west.

In common with many other existing RAF stations which had to be closed to flying while runways were laid, Leconfield's camp was still occupied. During this period it was used as school premises for No. 15 (Pilot) Advanced Flying Unit and to assemble and house personnel of the new Canadian No. 6 Group that was being established in north Yorkshire. At peak, the camp could provide accommodation for 2,270 males and 290 females.

The station re-opened for flying in December 1942, No. 4 Group re-asserting control and moving in Nos. 196 and 466 Squadrons from Driffield. Both were Wellington-equipped and had been recently formed. No. 466, an Australian-manned unit, undertook its first operation from Leconfield on January 13, 1942 when six aircraft were despatched to lay mines off the Frisian Islands, and No. 196 on the night of February 4/5 when eight Wellingtons bombed Lorient. No. 4 Group was gradually re-equipping as an all-Halifax formation and to this end the Wellingtons were phased out. In July 1943, No. 196 Squadron ceased operations and was moved south to Witchford in No. 3 Group to be rebuilt as a Stirling unit. During operations from Leconfield, it had undertaken 86 operations, 41 being to lay mines, and lost 13 Wellingtons in the process. No. 466 Squadron converted to Halifaxes in the late summer of 1943 having lost 25 Wellingtons in 89 raids.

being transferred to Transport Command on May 7, 1945 with No. 640 Squadron disbanding on the same date. Total Bomber Command aircraft losses from Leconfield during the war were 143, 57 being Wellingtons and 83 Halifaxes. The Halifaxes had soon departed, No. 51 Squadron re-equipping with Stirling transports which possessed more cavernous interiors. In August the squadron was moved south to Stradishall.

After the war, Leconfield first took on a training role with the Central Gunnery School established there late in 1945 and remained until the autumn of 1957 having been renamed the Fighter Weapons School. The main runway was then extended to 3,000 yards and from June 1959 for the next six years Leconfield became a fighter station hosting Hunters, Javelins and Lightnings. In January 1977 the station passed to the Army

being renamed Normandy Barracks. The Army School of Mechanical Transport, later Defence School of Transport, was the principal occupant. The RAF still have a presence on the airfield with 'E' Flight of No. 202 Squadron — an air-sea rescue helicopter unit with Sea Kings.

Normandy Barracks pictured from the south-west in September 2000.

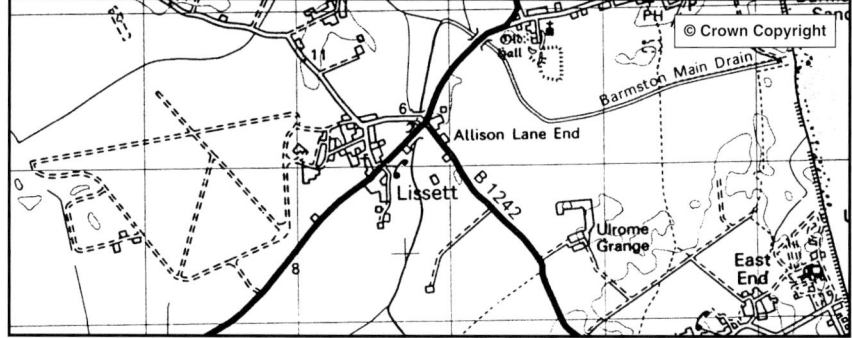

LISSETT

Built in 1942 to Class A standard, Lissett was No. 4 Group's nearest operational airfield to the coast, being only two miles from the North Sea. Located six miles due east of Great Driffield town, on the east side of Grassmore Drain and the west side of the A165 Bridlington to Hull road, the site was formerly mostly meadowland. The runways were main 09-27 at 1,900 yards, 03-21 at 1,430 yards and 15-33 at 1,400 yards long. All 36 hardstandings were pan types. One of the two Type T2 hangars was positioned on the technical site which lay on the north-east side of the airfield adjacent to Lissett village. The other T2 was located between runway heads 03 and 33 on the south-east maintenance

Above: **Lissett photographed on August 16, 1942 while still under construction. At this date no hardstandings and few buildings were to be seen.** *Bottom:* **Today the aerodrome has virtually disappeared beneath the Yorkshire landscape.**

© Crown Copyright

High drama over Cologne! Collision and being struck by bombs from higher aircraft was always a risk in mass night raids. The crew of Halifax HR837 were very fortunate on the night of June 28/29, 1943 when a bomb passed right through the fuselage of 'F' for Freddie without detonating. This night attack was Bomber Command's most damaging raid on the city.

area near the A165. As was standard practice, the bomb stores were as far removed as possible from the main technical site on the opposite side of the airfield between runway heads 09 and 03. Seven domestic sites for a maximum 1,442 males and 351 females were dispersed in farmland to the east of the A165. William Townson & Sons Ltd were involved in part of the construction work.

First occupied by a No. 4 Group operational squadron in February 1943 when No. 158 and its Halifaxes arrived from Rufforth which was to host an Operational Training Unit, it is believed that Lissett near the coast was considered preferable for an operational unit as opposed to the York area which was heavily congested. No. 158 participated in most main force operations during 1943 and in December its 'C' Flight was taken to form the nucleus of a new squadron, No. 640, which was to be based at Leconfield. No. 158, continued in occupation right up to the end of the war, flying some 250 raids from Lissett with 144 Halifaxes failing to return or destroyed in operational crashes. One of its aircraft, LV907, NP-F, named *Friday the 13th*, completed 128 operation sorties in 13 months, a record unsurpassed by any other Bomber Command Halifax. The final operation from Lissett was flown on April 25, 1945.

As with several other No. 4 Group squadrons, No. 158 was transferred to Transport Command on May 7, 1945 when it prepared to convert to Stirling Vs. Once ready for its new role, the squadron was moved south to Stradishall and Lissett was relegated to care and maintenance status with a small caretak-er detachment. This was withdrawn by the end of the year and eventually the whole airfield was abandoned. By the 1970s most of the concrete had been removed with the for-mer technical site buildings used by small industrial firms and for farm storage, and at the end of the century little remains to indi-cate there ever was an airfield at Lissett.

The far hedgerow remains and the distant wood, to the left of the airman sitting on the top of the Halifax in the wartime picture, still flourishes. Comparison photo taken looking north-west across runway 03-21 which now serves as a storage area for round straw bales.

MELBOURNE

Above: **A Halifax approaching the south-east runway with the village of Seaton Ross and its distinctive windmill silhouetted in the failing light.** *Bottom:* **Storm clouds brewing over Melbourne in July 2000. Sadly the windmill has lost its sails.**

East Common in Melbourne parish, some six miles west of Market Weighton, offered a good site for a satellite landing ground when these were anxiously being sought during 1940 as very little preparation was required to convert the flat area of meadowland east of Foss Dike into an aerodrome. Possibly Melbourne was first considered as a satellite for the new bomber station at Pocklington, just 4½ miles away, but construction of Pocklington was delayed and Melbourne first came into use for Whitleys from other No. 4 Group stations.

In the autumn of 1941 the airfield was scheduled for enlargement and the laying of hard runways. There was apparently some delay in commencing this work which was not completed until the following spring. The main runway 06-24 was originally 1,600 yards, the 01-19 1,350 yards and 15-33 1,100 yards, but the 06-24 was increased to 1,900 yards and the 15-33 to 1,400 yards, possibly before the airfield was re-opened. The technical site lay on the north side between runway heads 15 and 24, near Melbourne Lodges. There were two T2 hangars, one on the technical site and another between runway heads 33 and 24. Later, a B1 was erected near the latter, just north of runway head 33. Of the 35 pan hardstandings, one was later used to hold FIDO operating equipment when this facility was installed in late 1943. The dispersed camp sites to the north were able to accommodate 1,901 males and 382 females.

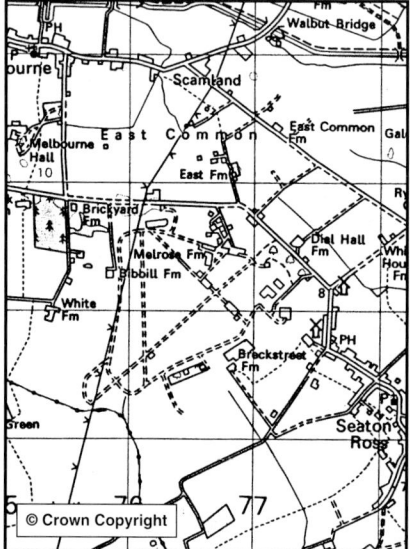

© Crown Copyright

In August 1942, No. 10 Squadron (RAAF) was transferred to Melbourne from Leeming which was about to be turned over to the new Canadian group, albeit that the airfield still lacked some facilities which were not completed until well into the winter of 1942-43. No. 10 was the only bomber squadron to be based at Melbourne and while it was in residence, the squadron lost over 100 Halifaxes in 300 raids. Its last bombing sorties were flown on April 25, 1945.

Many other bombers landed at Melbourne during periods of poor visibility, particularly during the winter of 1944-45 as the FIDO fog dispersal installation was operating from January 1944 along the main runway, Melbourne being the only bomber station in No. 4 Group to be so equipped. Total operational losses from Melbourne amounted to 128 Halifaxes, all from No. 10 Squadron.

On May 7, 1945, No. 10 Squadron was one of those transferred to Transport Command, shedding its Halifaxes during the next two months for Dakotas. In August 1945, No. 10 changed places with No. 575 Squadron at Broadwell but their Dakotas were only present for just over three months before moving south. By the spring of 1946, Melbourne was on care and maintenance and thereafter came under No. 91 Maintenance Unit for storage until the early 1950s. Surplus to requirements, the airfield was then disposed of, its technical site being utilised for local farming activities with most of the buildings being dismantled over the next two decades. Among the surviving structures at the close of the century is the B1 hangar used for several years as a grain processing plant and store. Private flying takes place from a part of the airfield and the control tower is being restored possibly to become a museum. A memorial to No. 10 Squadron has been placed near the wartime entrance.

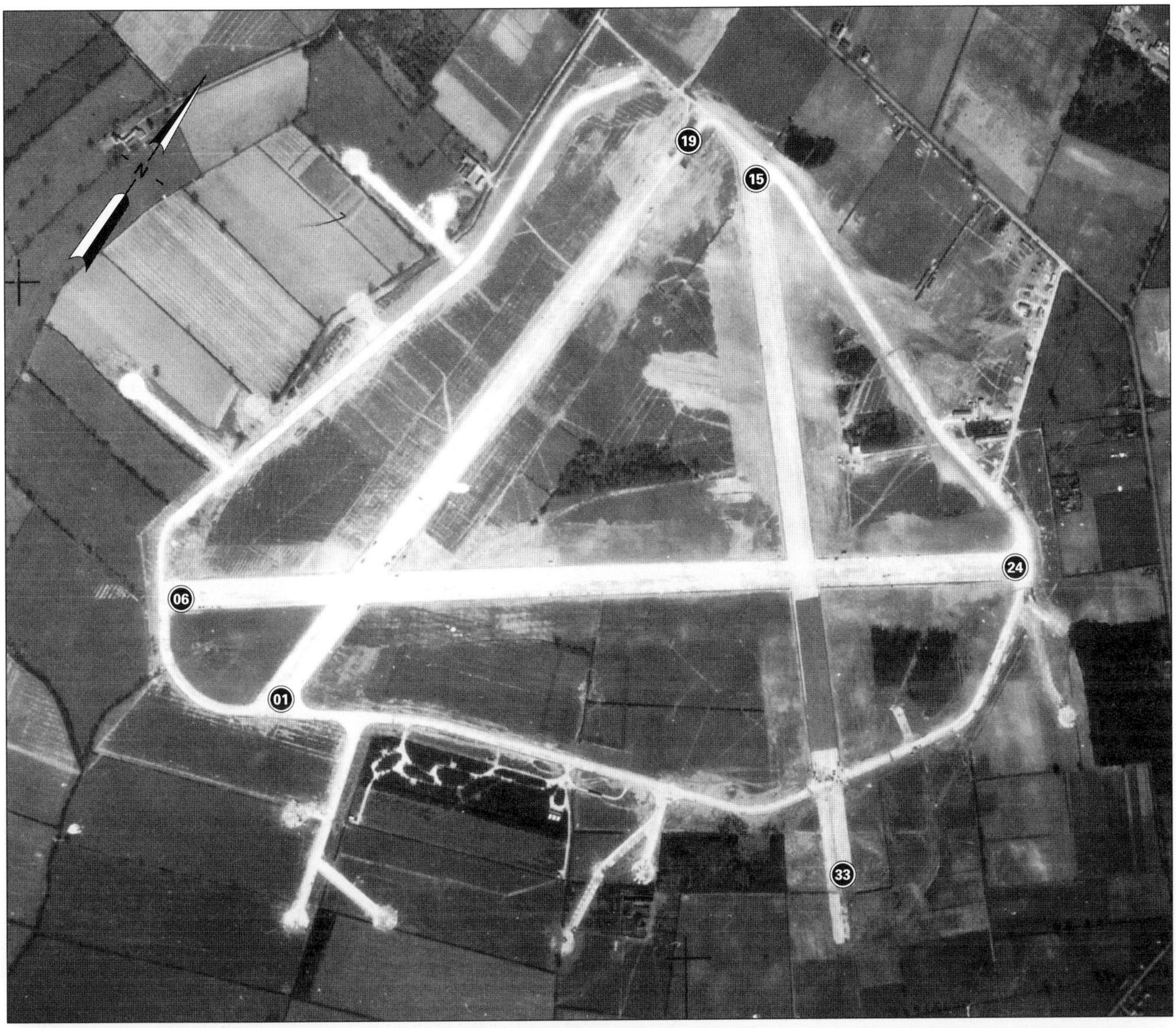

Construction was well advanced by April 27, 1942 when this picture was taken but the work was not completed until the summer.

The old main runway remains serviceable and in use although Melbourne is not an officially licensed airfield.

POCKLINGTON

This airfield lies directly south-west of Pocklington town between the angle formed by the A1079 and B1246 roads where they meet at Barmby on the Moor. There had been an RFC landing ground in Barmby parish during the First World War but this was located a mile to the west of the Second World War bomber airfield. Pocklington was first proposed as an expansion scheme airfield but work did not start until August 1940 when plans were revised to meet the strictures of wartime construction.

The original design featured a grass surface with hangars, technical site and administrative building closely grouped and work on this was underway when it was decided to install concrete runways. These were 11-29 at 1,400 yards and 01-19 and 07-25 both at 1,300 yards. However, when in an advanced state of construction, it was realised that 11-29 was aligned directly towards Pocklington town threatening a considerable hazard. This runway was thereafter abandoned and a fourth runway, 14-32, constructed 1,600 yards long. A 50-yard bulge was added to the combined ends of 25 and 19 at a later stage. Hardstandings were 35 pans and two loops. Bomb stores and one aircraft dispersal point lay on the other side of the B1246 road to Pocklington village. The technical site was situated on the south-west side of the airfield between runway heads 01 and 14. The camp, bordering the A1079, provided for a maximum 1,969 males and 428 females. Hangars were a single Type J and two T2s in close proximity on the technical site. Later two more T2s were erected in the south-west, reached by a taxiway across the A1079, as was a B1 more to the south. These served the base technical area. The main contractor involved was George Wimpey & Co. Ltd.

The first operational unit to occupy Pocklington was No. 405 Squadron with Wellingtons. This, the first Canadian squadron in Bomber Command, recently formed, had undertaken its first operation from Driffield before moving in to the new airfield. In carrying out 84 raids during the following eleven months, 20 of the squadron's Wellingtons failed to return to Pocklington. In April 1942 conversion to the Halifax commenced with which aircraft No. 405 flew another 20 raids until exchanging bases with No. 102 Squadron at Topcliffe when that station was ear-

How many will return? Waved off for good luck, Halifax DT742 piloted by Sergeant T. H. Dargavel begins its take-off run for a night raid on the Schneider armaments plant at Le Creusot on June 19/20, 1943.

On this particular attack, all 23 aircraft involved from No. 102 Squadron, including DY-O, returned safely. In the distance the silhouetted steeple of Barmby Moor church.

From night to day . . . from golden sky to golden grain . . . from the summer of 1942 to the summer of 2000. Pocklington — then and now.

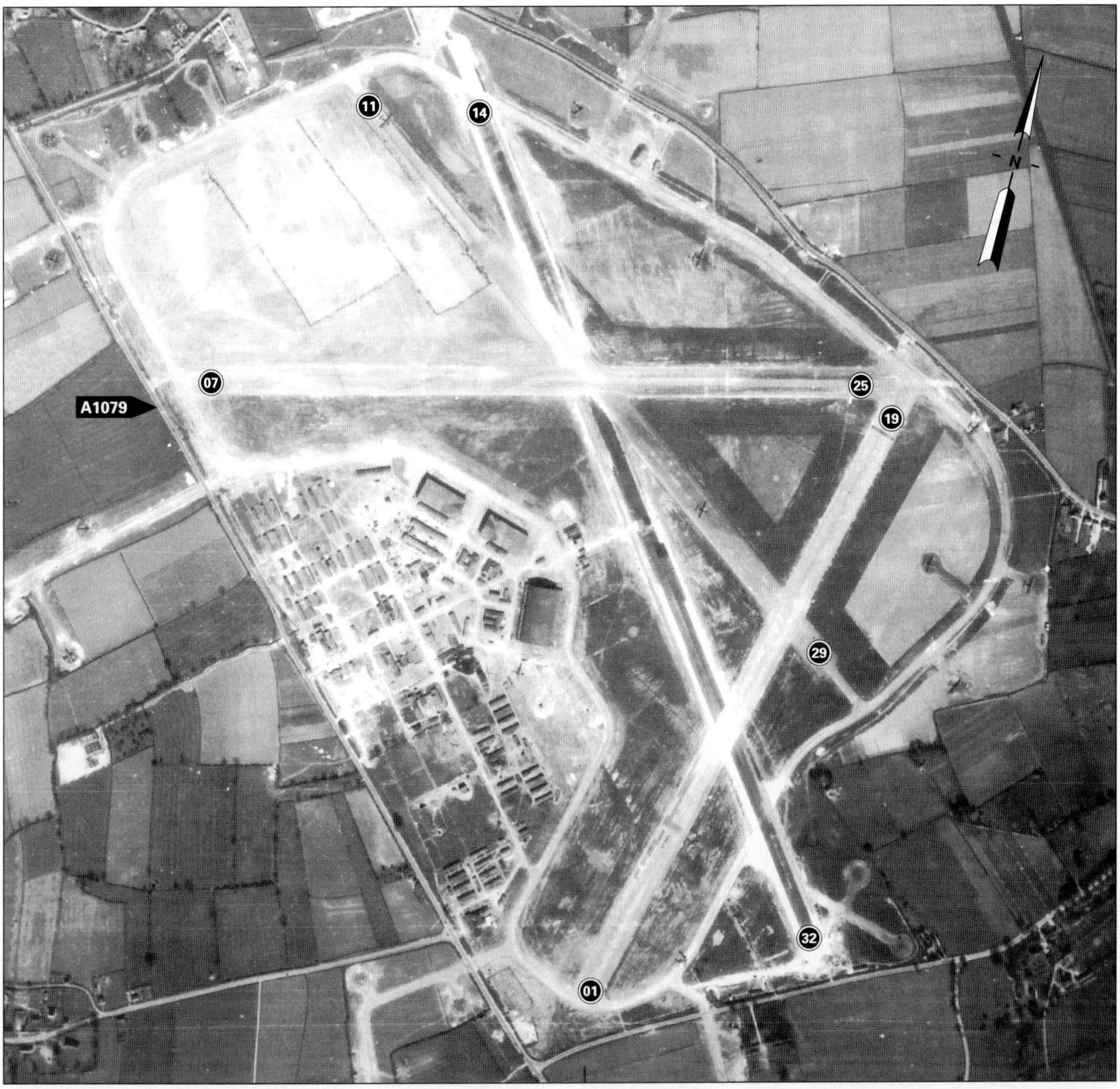

Someone slipped up badly with the planning for Pocklington aerodrome. First, the main runway was mis-aligned and had to be abandoned half finished when it was realised that aircraft using it would fly directly over Barmby Moor and Pocklington villages. Then, no sooner had the replacement runway been completed, than it became apparent that the control tower was now too close for comfort . . . and it had to be demolished! Two bombers can be seen parked on the abandoned 11-29 runway.

marked for the all-Canadian No. 6 Group. No. 102 Squadron had been in action since the second night of the war and this was its seventh move of station; it was also its last during hostilities. It remained the sole occupant of Pocklington and last squadron to be based there before closure. A total of 206 bombers despatched from this station on operations were missing or lost in UK crashes; 27 Wellingtons and 179 Halifaxes.

As with other No. 4 Group squadrons, the day before the official end of the war in Europe it was transferred to Transport Command, soon to exchange its Halifaxes for Liberators before moving to Bassingbourn in September. A holding unit for RAF personnel took over but in September 1946 the airfield was closed, eventually reverting to agricultural use and the hangars becoming grain stores. At the end of the century, two T2 and the J hangar still stand and a large industrial estate, also utilising modernised hangars, has developed on and around the technical site near the A1079. However although much of the runway concrete has gone, a thriving gliding club operates from the airfield.

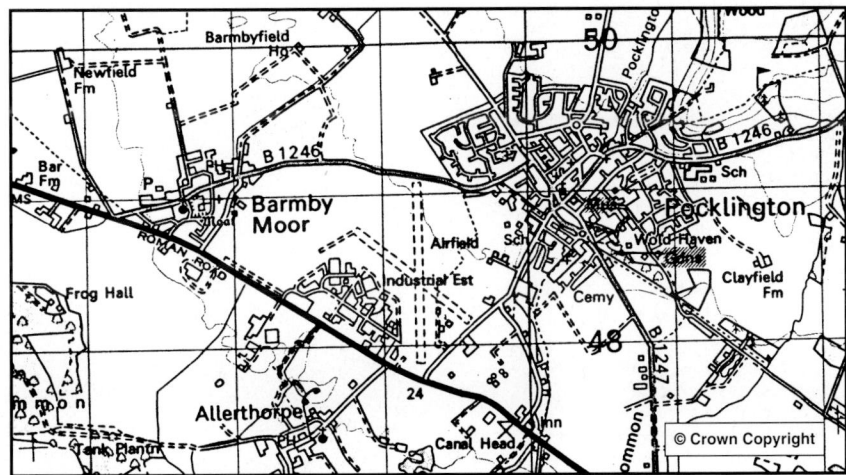

Two of the wartime runways remain in use by the Wolds Gliding Club although the magnetic bearing of the main 11-32 is now 13-31 and the subsidiary 01-19 changed to 18-36.

211

The old control tower stands below the port wing of Halifax W7710 of No. 405 Squadron. LQ-R was lost on October 1/2, 1942.

To save starting up T-Tommy, this Halifax (JD206) of No. 102 Squadron is about to be towed by a David Brown tractor.

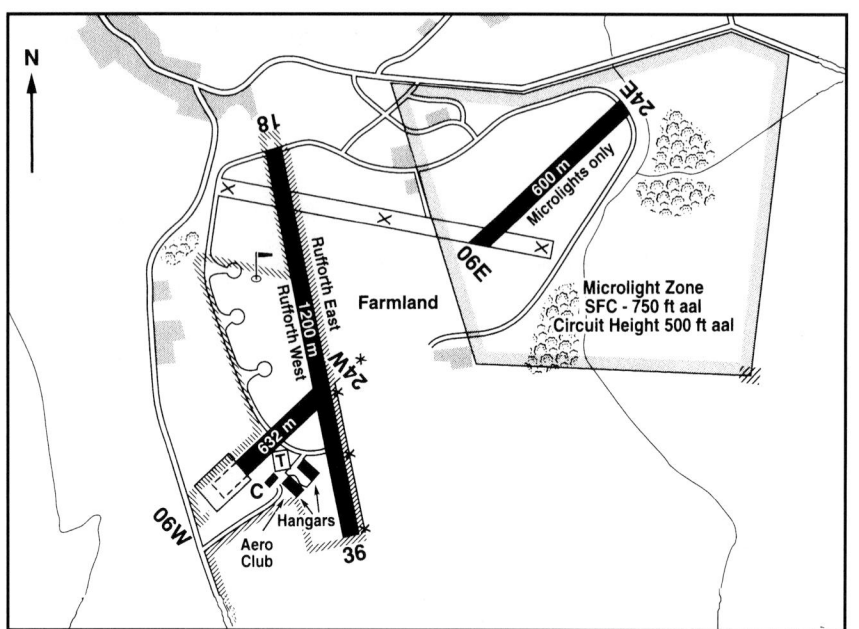

RUFFORTH

Still in use today, Rufforth now has a rather complicated set-up as this plan from *Pooleys Flight Guide* shows.

A bomber airfield built to Class A specification, Rufforth was constructed during 1941 on farmland south of the B1224 adjacent to the village of Rufforth, the main contractor being John Laing & Son Ltd. The site, bordered by Foss Dyke on its eastern perimeter, was only four miles west of the centre of York. The original plan called for a main runway of 1,600 yards and the subsidiaries to be 1,100 yards but these lengths were increased before the station was opened, the main runway 06-24 ending up 1,980 yards, the 11-29 at 1,350 yards and 18-36 at 1,400 yards. These and the encircling perimeter track and 36 hardstandings were all of concrete construction. The hangars were two T2s, one on the main technical site near the York-Wetherby road and the other on the west side of the airfield. A type B1 hangar was added at a later date. Domestic accommodation for a maximum 1,531 males and 251 females was in dispersed sites, mainly Nissen type huts.

Once the runways were ready during the summer of 1942, the airfield was opened to flying but only for use by Operational Training Units based elsewhere. The first operational squadron to arrive, No. 158, had to vacate East Moor which was to be used by Canadian units of No. 6 Group. No. 158's Halifaxes operated from Rufforth (apart from detachments throughout the winter of 1942-43), being moved to Lissett at the end of February so that Rufforth could be used for the main Halifax Operational Training Unit serving No. 4 Group. Meanwhile, a considerable amount of repair work had to be carried out on the runways and perimeter track due to the concrete cracking.

No. 1663 Heavy Conversion Unit was formed at Rufforth in March 1943 and tutored Halifax crews until disbanded in late May 1945. However, on November 1, 1944, most Bomber Command OTU's were transferred to No. 7 Group, Training Command, although the stations and functions continued much as before. Eighteen Halifaxes were lost flying operations from Rufforth, one being from No. 1663 Heavy Conversion Unit.

In the early post-war years, Rufforth was retained by the RAF for use as a gliding school and by other minor units. It then came under the umbrella of No. 60 Maintenance Unit which used it largely for storage before the RAF finally departed in November 1974 and the airfield was sold in July 1981. Thereafter the land was reclaimed for farming and the runways, 18-36 and 11-29, retained for use by the Ouse, later York Gliding Centre and private aircraft. The control tower survives having been used in the TV drama series *Airline* during the 1970s.

Sleet, snow, ice and bitter cold. Servicing the Halifaxes of No. 1663 Heavy Conversion Unit must have been a miserable task in the winter of 1943-44. (Due to the presence of a large bull in the same field, Tim prudently took the comparison *below* from outside the fence!)

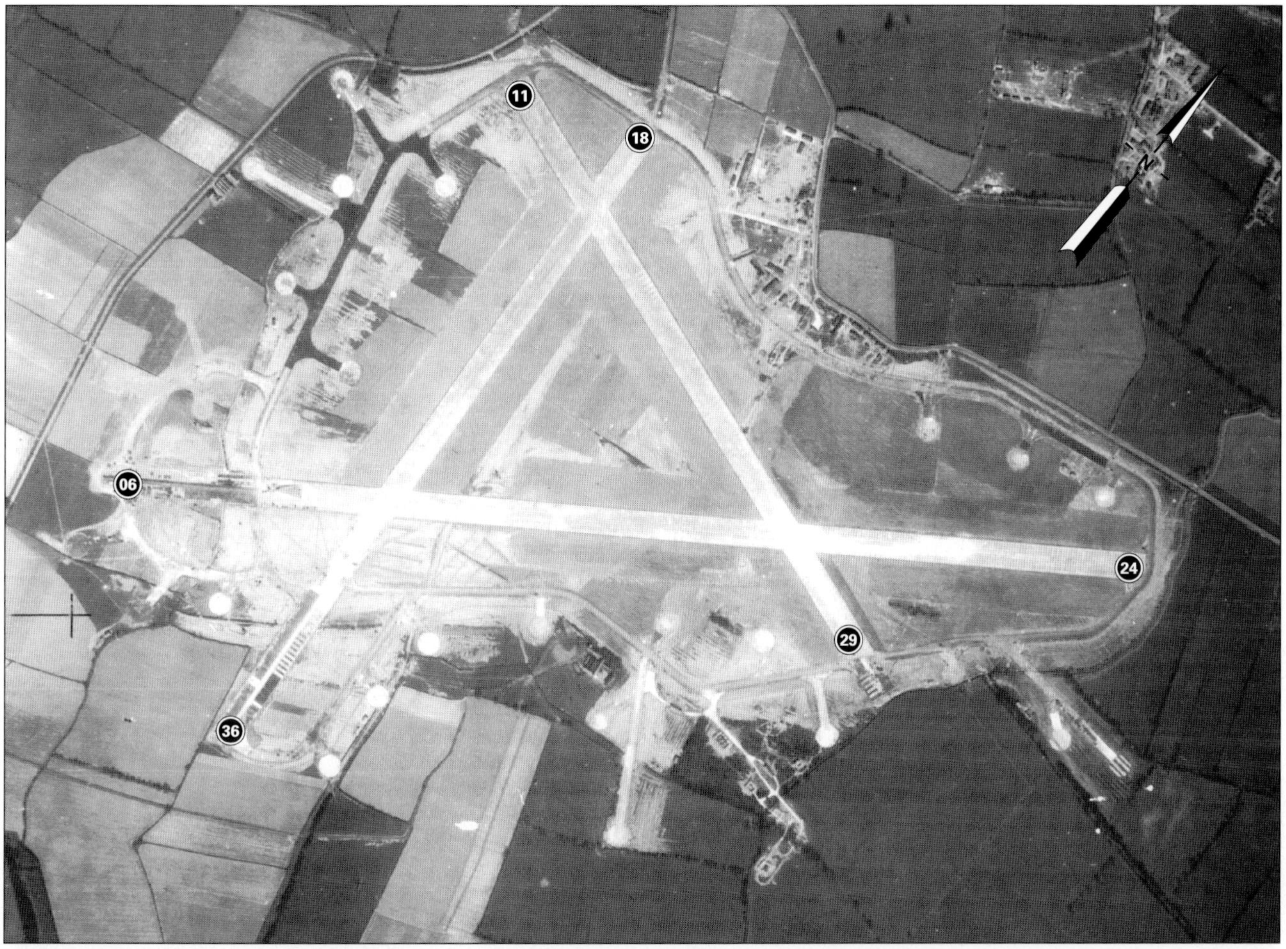

Photographed from 8,000 feet on April 27, 1942 when work was in progress to lengthen the runways.

Today Rufforth is remarkably intact save for the missing section of the old main runway.

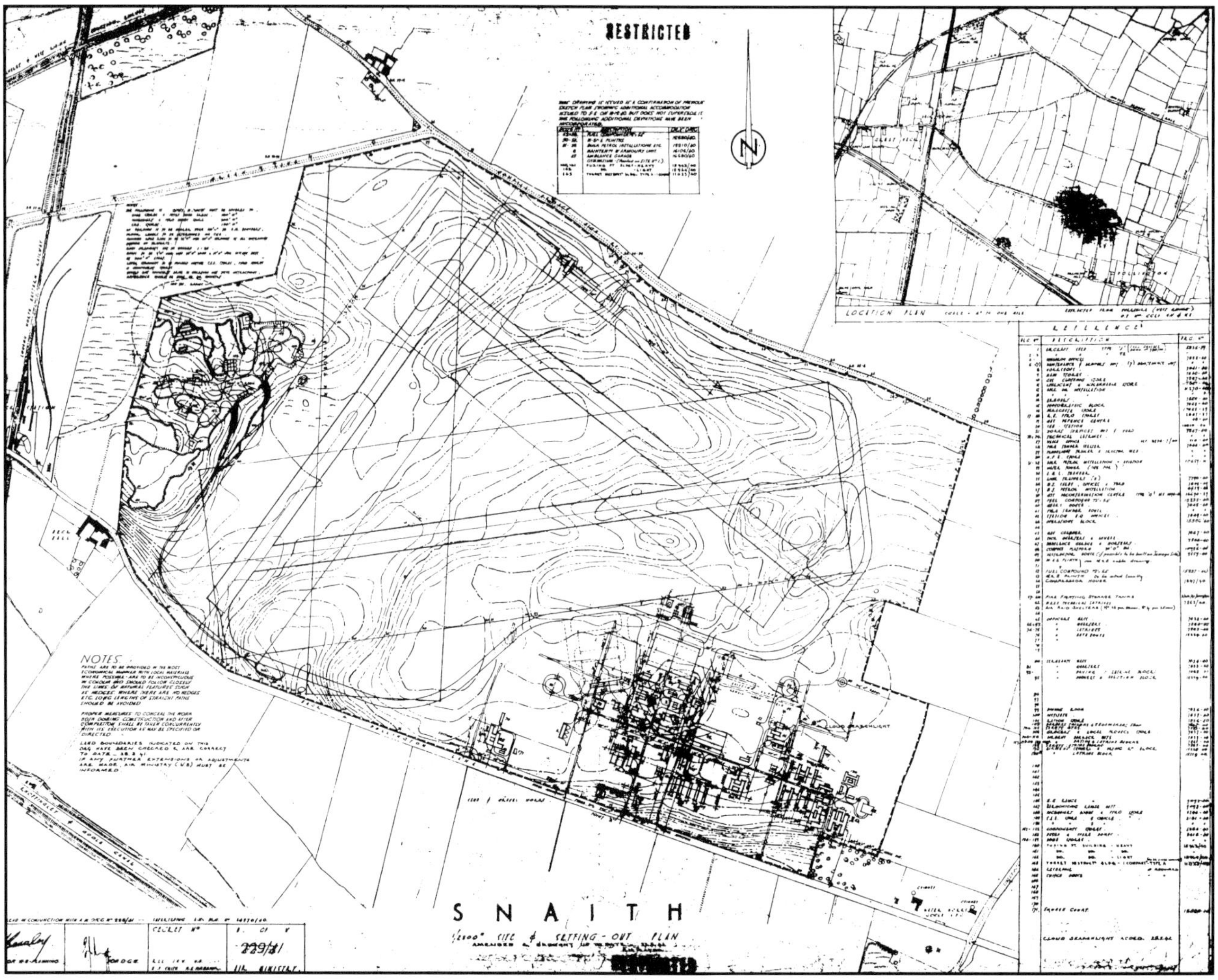

SNAITH

The birth of an aerodrome. Early Air Ministry setting-out plan for Snaith shows ground contours and runways as originally envisaged. Compare with the vertical cover below taken on July 27, 1941 with No. 150 Squadron's Wellingtons much in evidence,

Lying largely in the parish of Pollington, seven miles south-west of Goole, RAF station Snaith was designed in March 1940 with construction commencing later that year. The northern boundary was formed by the A545 and the southern side by the Great Heok to Pollington Lane. The three intersecting concrete runways measured 1,400 yards for the main and 1,100 yards each for the subsideries although these were extended in the summer of 1941: the main 14-32 to 2,000 yards, 07-23 to 1,400 yards and 09-27 to 1,100 yards. A Type J and two Type T2 hangars were erected on the technical site. The usual 36 pan-type hardstandings were accessible from the encircling perimeter track. The camp, south-east of the flying field, provided for a maximum of 2,016 males and 394 females. The bomb stores, a series of blast mound protected revetments, lay in fields to the west on the opposite side of the airfield from the main technical site and it was here that a disasterous explosion took place on June 19, 1943.

The airfield was first assigned to No. 1 Group and received No. 150 Squadron and its Wellingtons from Newton in July 1941. The squadron participated in Bomber Command main force operations from Snaith until October 1942 when the station was turned over to No. 4 Group and No. 150 Squadron moved out to Kirmington. No. 51 Squadron, having been on loan to Coastal

There were several cases of bombs detonating accidentally on Bomber Command airfields but none worse than that which occurred at Snaith on Saturday, June 19, 1943. Wing Commander John Rowlands *(left)* hurried to the scene where he was briefed by Squadron Leader H. H. Apted, the OC of No. 5131 Bomb Disposal Squadron based at the airfield. A reconnaissance of the bomb-dump where the explosion had occurred showed dead bodies and bombs scattered about, the latter already fuzed. Incendiaries had also caught fire and were burning furiously, the intense heat leading Wing Commander Rowlands to decide to do nothing for a few days to let the site cool down. By June 29, assisted by Squadron Leader Apted and Flight Lieutenant Wilson, employing a combination of remote-control fuze extraction and deliberate detonation of damaged bombs, the site was declared safe. For this operation, and conspicuous courage in bomb disposal over two years, Wing Commander Rowlands was awarded the George Cross.

Nothing now to mark the spot where 18 men lost their lives.

Left: Waiting anxiously for the return of the Halifaxes on the night of March 30/31, 1944, when Bomber Command suffered its heaviest loss of the war, 96 bombers failing to return from Nuremberg. Six of the losses were Snaith aircraft with the 35 dead and seven made prisoner. *Right:* Barley waving in the wind now covers the spot where the control tower once stood.

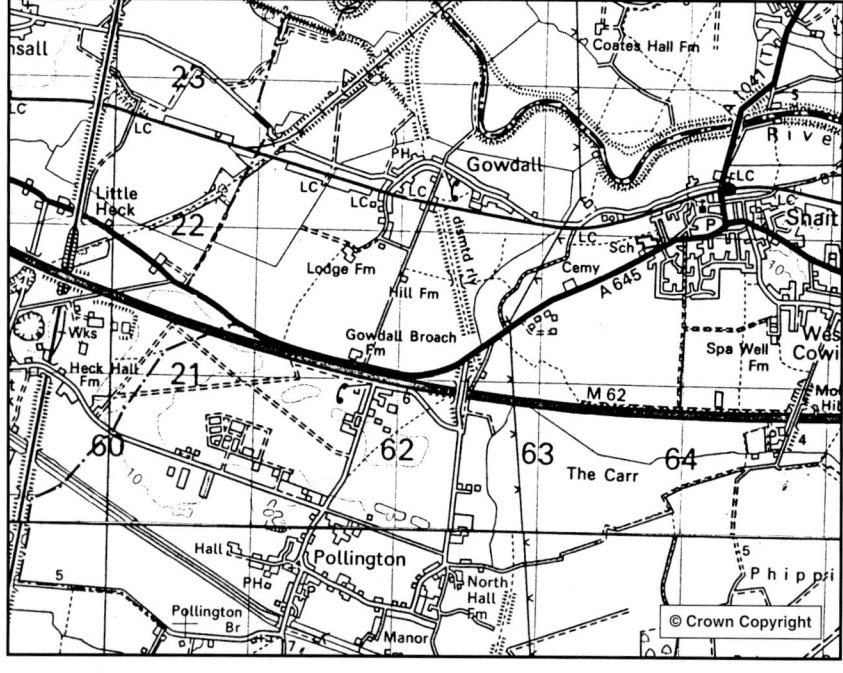

Command at Chivenor, retrained on Halifaxes which it operated from Snaith right up until the end of the war flying 264 raids and losing 148 aircraft. In January 1944, its 'C' Flight was used to form No. 578 Squadron which, as was usual procedure, moved into a vacant airfield, Burn, after its first few operations. No. 51 Squadron was transferred to the permanent station at Leconfield a few days after the last No. 4 Group bombing opera-

tion took place on April 25, 1945. A total of 205 bombers were lost from Snaith, 57 being Wellingtons of No. 150 Squadron.

In the following weeks little flying took place from Snaith until a Beam Approach Flight arrived with Oxfords in September. By the following spring, the RAF presence was no more than a care and maintenance party and this, in time, was withdrawn. Like many wartime airfields, Snaith languished unused

with a little demolition during 1950s but thereafter a more rapid reduction occurred. In the 1970s, the M62 motorway link between the Midlands and the Humber bridge sliced through the northern part of the flying field south of Snaith itself. Nevertheless, at the end of the 20th century much still remains including the MT sheds and the Sergeants' Mess still complete with its brick fireplace.

The construction of the M62, seen on the left the photograph (*above*) taken looking east in September 2000, has led to the A645, which originally formed the northern boundary to the airfield, being slightly realigned northwards. *Right:* Memorial at the main gate to days long gone. The T2 hangars are now in commercial use.

How Candidates are Selected for Flying and Air Fighting

Flying personnel are provided by enlistment in the RAF Volunteer Reserve. Vacancies in the General Duties (commissioned) branch are filled by promotion from the ranks.

Candidates for air crew duties must be men who desire to fly and fight in the air, with a reasonable standard of intelligence and good standard of alertness and character. They must be up to the necessary standard of physical fitness. No prescribed educational standards are laid down except for elementary mathematics.

Air crew applicants will undergo a preliminary medical examination at the Recruiting Centre at which they applied for enlistment. They will then proceed for interview by the Aviation Candidates Selection Board, which will decide whether the applicants are suitable for air crew training and the category in which they should be trained. Applicants may however, indicate their order of preference for training as Pilot, Observer, Observer (radio) and Wireless Operator (air gunner). If passed by the Aviation Candidates Selection board, candidates will have a further medical examination to determine fitness for flying training.

The ages for enlistment are: Pilot must be 17¼ and not yet 31, Observer and Wireless Operator (air gunner) must be 17¼ and not yet 33. Observer (radio) may in exceptional cases be accepted up to 41st birthday and need not have so high a visual standard as the other categories of air crew.

Men enlisted for air crew will not be called up for flying training until they attain the age of 18¼, and will not be called up for ground duties until they attain the age of 18.

Air Crew Training, Remustering and Promotion

Pilots and Air Observers undergo ground training at an Initial Training Wing, being mustered as Aircrafthands, Group V, on completion, and re-classified as Leading Aircraftmen, Group II, with flying instructional pay during actual flying training at Flying Training School or at Air Observer Navigation School.

Wireless Operators (air gunners) are mustered as Aircrafthands, Group V, until their training is complete as Wireless Operators, and then remustered to Wireless Operator, Group II, during actual flying training at Bombing and Gunnery School, and re-classified as Leading Aircraftmen with flying instructional pay.

On successful completion of training course Airmen are remustered to the aircrew category for which they have qualified and promoted Sergeant. Promotion of air crew, to Warrant Officer, N. or Flight Sergeant, is by selection (six months' service in an air crew category).

ABC OF THE RAF, 1943.

Halifax III LV937 (MH-E), named *Expensive Babe*, completed its 100th mission on March 25, 1945 . . . but aircraft could be replaced . . . crewmen could not. Early on, it was appreciated that a limit would have to be made for bomber crews which gave a 50-50 chance of survival. Initially, this was set at 200 hours of operational flying but in August 1942 a full operational tour was set at 30 sorties, missions accomplished being considered a fairer limit rather than hours flown. Crews would then serve nine months with an Operational Training Unit before beginning another tour. However, because of the increasing losses of experienced crews towards the end of their second operational tour, in February 1943 this was limited to 20 sorties. In the picture Flight Lieutenant R. Kemp and his crew of No. 51 Squadron have just returned to Snaith from Germany in an operation to support the Battle of the Rhine.

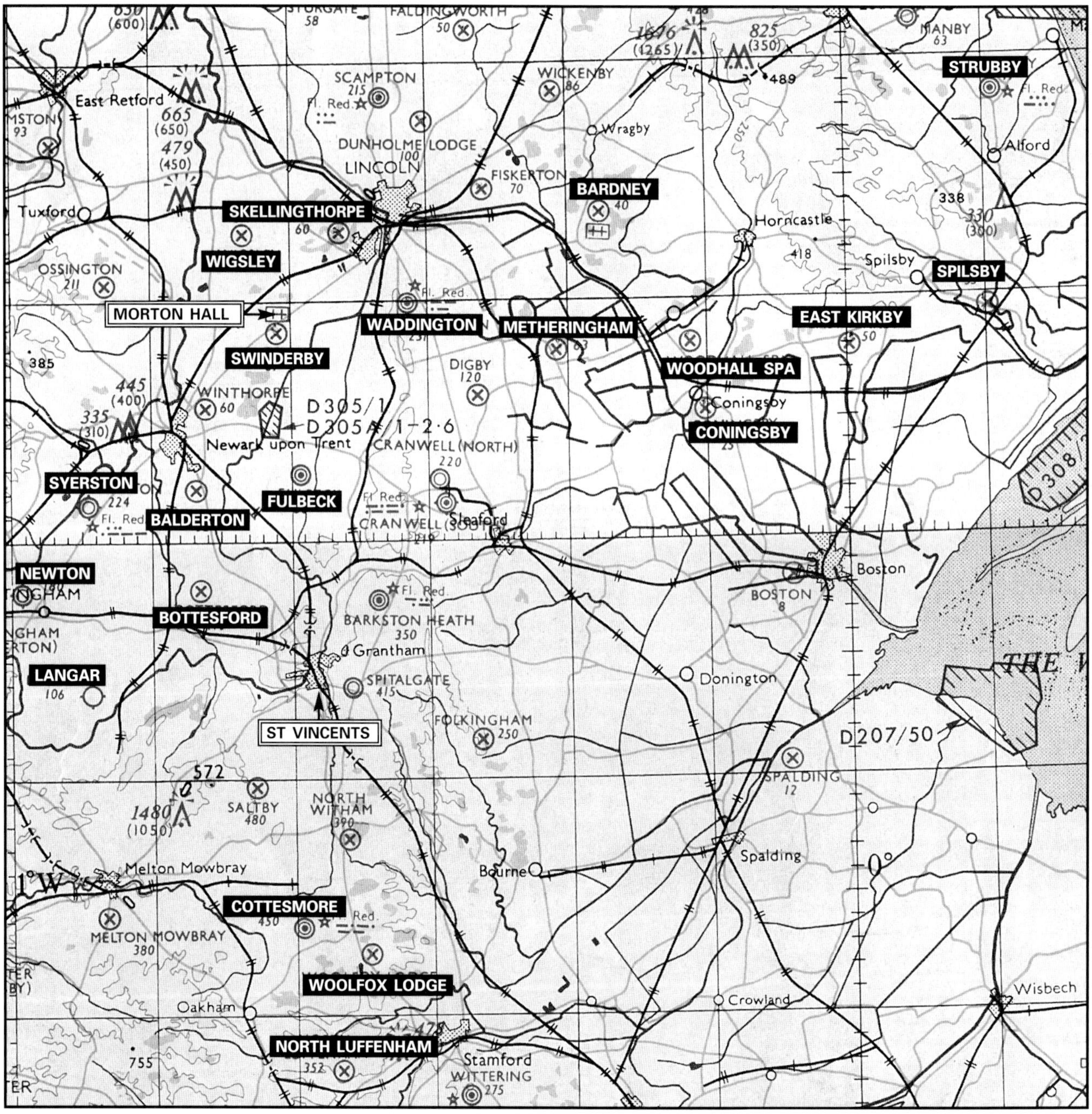

No. 5 GROUP HQ

No. 5 Group was another offspring of No. 3 Group HQ at Mildenhall, officially formed on September 1, 1937 and taking up residence at St Vincents, Grantham, a few weeks later. Allotted airfields in the Lincolnshire area the first squadrons assigned had a mixture of types, mainly Blenheims, Ansons, and Hinds, but the group was soon to receive the new Hampden medium bomber on which its units would standardise. By the outbreak of war it had eight Hampden squadrons and five assigned airfields. The Manchester was to replace the Hampden and although seven No. 5 Group squadrons received the type during 1941 and 1942, these were withdrawn in favour of the Lancaster. By spring 1943, No. 5 had become the first all-Lancaster group with ten squadrons with 180 aircraft at eight airfields. The group's squadrons carried out several special operations, including the famous raid on the German dams. In November 1943

No. 5 Group's first HQ at Grantham lay in the centre of its zone of operations.

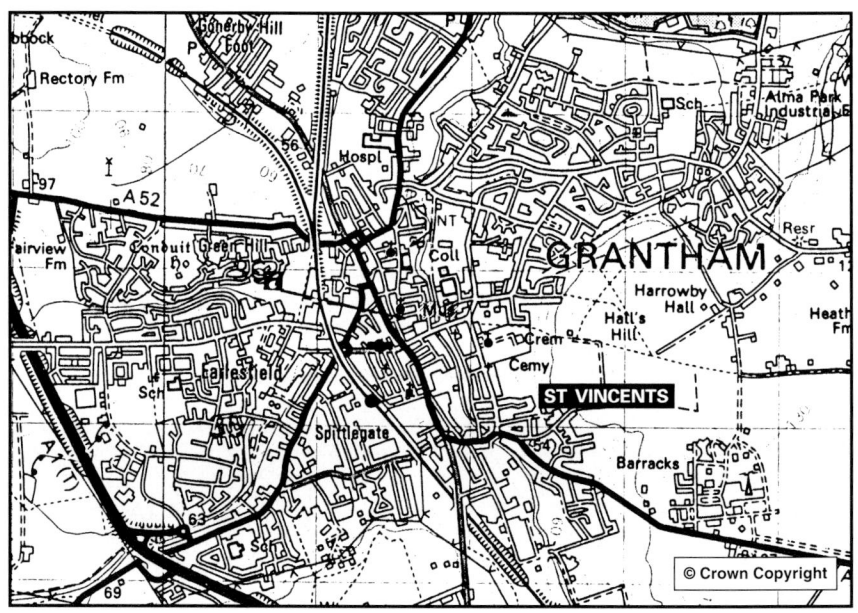

© Crown Copyright

220

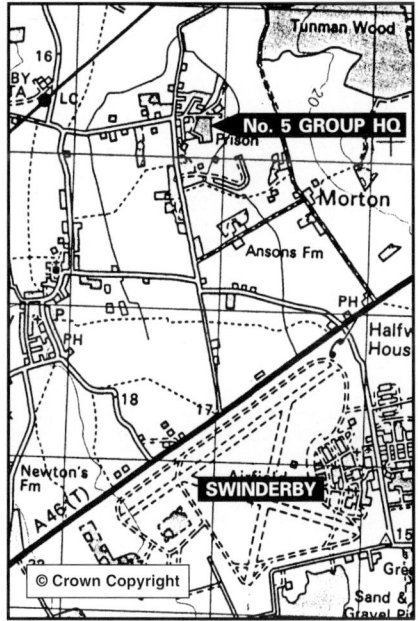

the group headquarters moved to more spacious accommodation at Morton Hall, Swinderby, remaining in residence until disbanded in December 1945. In May 1945 there were more than 300 Lancasters on strength in 15 squadrons at eleven airfields.

St Vincents *(above)*, **a country mansion on the outskirts of Grantham built around 1867, was used by the group from October 1937 until November 1943. This picture was taken when South Kesteven District Council occupied the building which had been purchased in 1979 for office accommodation. By that time, the wartime Operations Block in the grounds had been demolished. Today it is privately owned. The headquarters subsequently moved to Morton Hall near Swinderby.**

Morton Hall itself burned down in the 1980s, the site now being used for a prison.

Hampdens of No. 408 Squadron of the Royal Canadian Air Force drawn up in front of the technical site which was situated near the A1 trunk road. The spire of Balderton village church is in the far distance in this view looking north-west. The squadron was actively engaged in Gardening operations, the cover name for mining sea lanes.

BALDERTON

The airfield at Balderton was at first a simple satellite aerodrome where large fields of stiff clay south of the village were seeded with grass in 1940. It initially came into use in the summer of 1941 for use by Hampdens of No. 25 Operational Training Unit from Finningley, while work continued on a bomb store and other facilities. In December the same year, the airfield was transferred to No. 5 Group as a satellite field for Syerston from whence the Hampdens of No. 408 Squadron arrived during the first week of that month. No. 408 was the second Canadian-manned squadron raised in Bomber Command.

The condition of Balderton's four grass runways deteriorated badly during the first few weeks of No. 408's usage, so that in January the squadron used North Luffenham for operations until Balderton dried out in late March. The squadron stayed on the airfield until September when, in preparation for joining the all-Canadian No. 6 Group, it moved north to Leeming. During this period, a hard perimeter track was put down as well as 24 concrete pan hardstandings. Numerous buildings were also erected on the eastern side bordering the A1 and two T2 hangars near the south-east corner.

With the departure of No. 408 Squadron, the airfield was closed for improving to Class A standard. Additional land was requisitioned on the western side closing a small lane and extending the airfield boundary up to Grange Lane in the west and Cross Lane in the north. W & C French & Co. Ltd were the prime contractors involved in the laying of the three intersecting concrete runways. The main 08-26 was 2,000 yards long with the

03-21 and 15-33 both 1,400 yards. An additional 17 loop-type hardstandings were added around the strengthened perimeter track as only 19 pans remained. Additional accommodation was provided on the east side of the A1 in dispersed sites with mostly Nissen huts. A B1 and two further T2 hangars were erected during the first half of 1943, the latter to house the 32 Horsa gliders dispersed on the airfield from spring that year. The B1 was westernmost of two hangars between runway head 33 and Cowtham House.

By the late summer of 1943 the station was ready to re-open and in August No. 1668 Heavy Conversion Unit was formed at Balderton to provide tuition on Halifaxes and Lancasters. However, plans called for the USAAF IXth Troop Carrier Command to be based in the area and in November the conversion unit moved out. Work was put in hand by W & C French to increase the number of loop hardstandings to 31 and raise the total available accommodation to take 2,413 persons. The USAAF units moved in early in the New Year and the 64 C-47s of the 437th Troop Carrier Group arrived at the end of the month, fresh from the USA. The 437th TCG, was moved south after only a few days and its place taken by the 439th TCG also fresh from the States. The 439th departed in late April for a base in Devon. Although Balderton was retained by IX Troop Carrier Command, it was available to the RAF for training activities until September when the 439th TCG returned to participate in Operation 'Market', the airborne landings in Holland. The Americans departed in late September whereupon IX TCC returned the airfield to the RAF.

No. 5 Group had raised a new squadron — a re-formed No. 227 — initially drawing on personnel at Bardney and Strubby and bring-

ing the unit together as a whole in mid-October 1944 at Balderton. The squadron carried out its first operation from its new home on the night of October 28/29, and flew another 57 missions before moving to Strubby in the first week of April 1945. The move was reputedly due to deterioration of the runways. Thereafter no further flying units were based at the station. Total RAF bomber losses on operations from Balderton amounted to 26: seven Hampdens and 19 Lancasters.

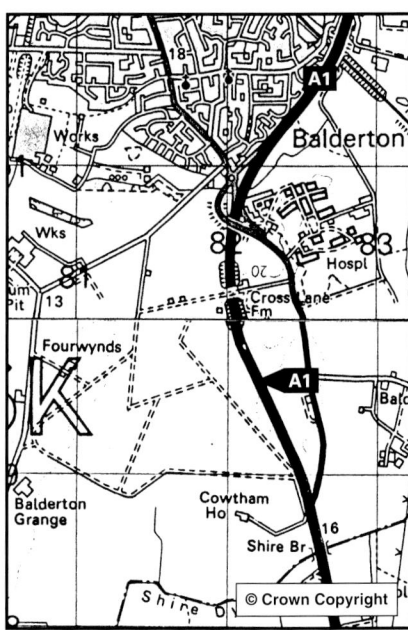

The runways soon came into use for bomb storage under No. 254 Maintenance Unit. After the munitions were eventually removed for disposal, a small holding party remained until 1954. Thereafter the airfield was returned to local farmers for agricultural use, the hangars and practically all buildings being dismantled or demolished over the next decade. The runways were broken for rubble which was mostly used as foundation material for A1 improvements during the 1960s. The new carriageway was laid down to the west of the original A1, cutting across the eastern perimeter track and the end of runway 26.

Some parts of the runway perimeter track have been retained as farm roads but very few traces of airfield structures remain. The north-west area of the site is open-cast mined for gypsum to supply the nearby British Gypsum Works. Farm crops flourish on the remaining acres.

Dominating the scene at Balderton today is the large gypsum works seen on the left of the photograph. The hedge lines remain as during wartime.

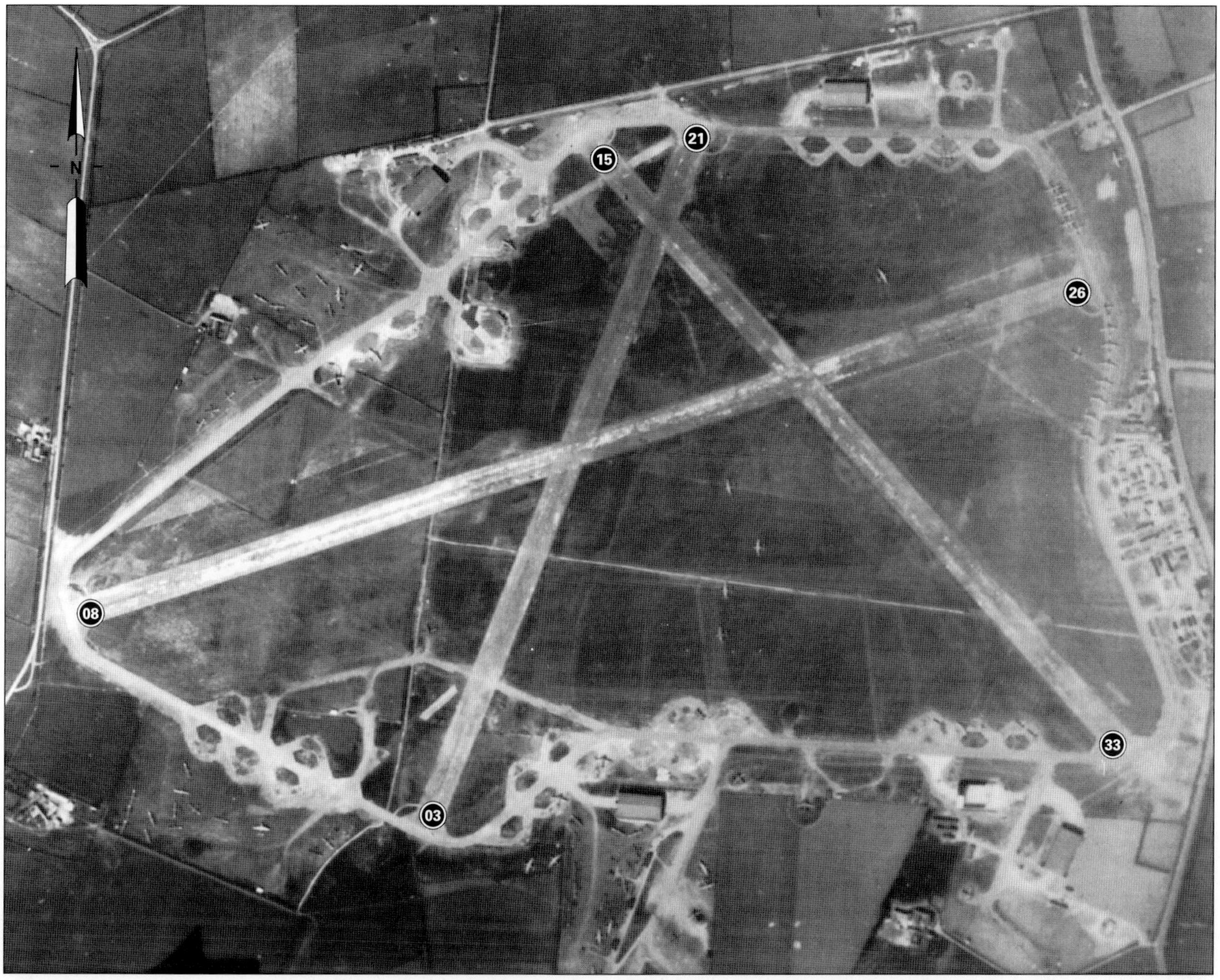

Balderton was well stocked with C-47s and Waco and Horsa gliders on April 18, 1944 when the US Ninth Air Force was in occupation.

Gypsum mining is now slowly eroding the surface of the airfield between runways 08 and 21.

BARDNEY

Bardney airfield was situated four miles south of Wragby to the east of the B1202 road and to the north-east of Bardney village beyond Scotgrove Wood. Construction began in 1942 on a Class A design. The runways were the main 07-25 at 2,000 yards and subsidiaries, 02-20 and 12-30, at 1,400 yards. The hardstandings were 36 pan-type although one was lost due to the erection of a B1 hangar just south of runway head 30. Further west on the technical site between runways 02 and 30 was a T2 hangar, and another T2 was positioned on the west side of the airfield between runway heads 07 and 12. The bomb stores were off the north-east side between runway heads 20 and 25. Seven domestic, two WAAF, two communal and a sick quarters site made up the dispersed camp to the south between New Park Wood and Birt Hill. Total accommodation was stated as 1,947 males and 401 females.

Bardney opened as a satellite to Waddington in April 1943 and it received No. 9 Squadron with its Lancasters on the 13th and 14th of the month from that station, this veteran unit remaining at Bardney for the duration of hostilities. In late September 1944,

Barely had the film been developed than this crew from No. 9 Squadron were dead at the bottom of the Rhine. On June 20, 1943, Flight Lieutenant John Wakeford and his crew of Lancaster WS-K were on their 50th mission (which ought to have been their last having completed two tours of duty — see page 219) but they flew again to Cologne two weeks later . . . an operation from which they never returned.

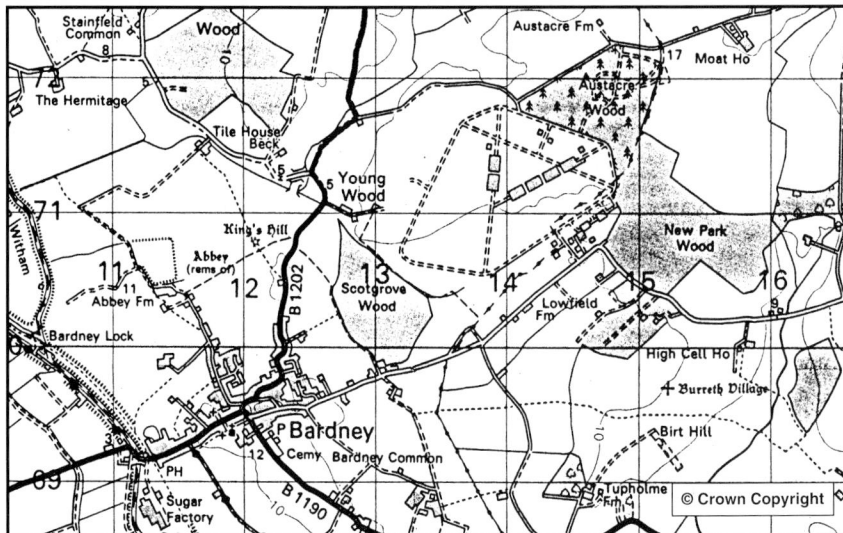

© Crown Copyright

The hardstanding on which the wartime photograph was taken has also now passed away. Beyond are grazing sheep backed by the same hedge that was there in 1943. The delapidated camp site, minus the water tower, is now partly obscured with scrub.

the USAAF transferred a number of airfields in the Grantham/Newark areas back to the RAF and Bomber Command took the opportunity to expand its strength.

In early October, No. 9 Squadron provided personnel for a flight of the re-formed No. 227 Squadron which was soon moved to Balderton. No. 9 then went on to provide for the newly-established No. 189 Squadron which flew its first raid the night of November 1/2, being moved to the vacant airfield at Fulbeck the next day. At this time the main body of No. 9 Squadron had become a specialist unit using the 12,000lb Tallboy bombs for precision daylight attacks, one of only two squadrons to do so. During one of these raids, when the Dortmund-Ems canal was the target, the aircraft in which Flight Sergeant George Thompson was acting wireless operator was crippled by anti-aircraft fire. In going to the aid of two unconscious and disabled crew members, Thompson was badly burned and he died in hospital three weeks later. His action brought the posthumous award of a Victoria Cross.

Bardney, March 1943. The flight office in the Nissen hut is flanked by the technical site latrine. On the right can be seen the crew rooms with the static water tank in front.

Apart from its intended use, the water tank was useful in other ways. Here Sergeant Jim McCubbin and his crew practice dinghy drill.

In April 1945, No. 189 Squadron returned to Bardney to carry out its final sorties. No. 9 Squadron, which lost 85 Lancasters during operations from the airfield, moved back to permanent accommodation at Waddington in July 1945, while No. 189 was transferred to Metheringham in October. Bardney was then on care and maintenance until later in the year when it was handed over to the Army. During the following decade, its runways could be seen lined with almost every conceivable type of military vehicle, many of which were disposed of at auction. In 1959, a Thor missile site was built on the airfield, the operating unit being No. 106 Squadron, but, as with other Thor sites, it was disbanded four years later. Thereafter the airfield was disposed of but all three hangars were retained as well as several of the larger buildings on the technical site. The former flying area is now solely taken up with agriculture. A memorial dedicated in 1980 to No. 9 Squadron is located in Bardney village.

The static water tank has given way to the demands of intensive agriculture with piles of roll bales and half-ton fertiliser bags. Only the skyline woodland stands much the same.

Bardney photographed from 16,600 feet in October 1948 when hundreds of surplus military vehicles lined the runways.

Lancaster WS-V rolls out at Bardney. The location is the perimeter track east of runway 07, looking south-east towards an aircraft arms equipment store and general purpose buildings.

An early casualty in the Battle of Berlin, ED656 crashed near Louth on its return from the German capital on November 23, 1943, killing six of the crew and injuring two.

The airfield in September 2000 looking slightly north of west — approximately the same perspective of the vertical shot opposite.

Time marches on and today a Volvo saloon stands in for the lost Lancaster.

BOTTESFORD

Six miles north-west of Grantham, on the eastern side of the Bottesford to Long Bennington road, Bottesford was located partly in the parishes of Normanton and Long Bennington, straddling the Lincolnshire-Leicestershire border. As Normanton was the nearest village, the airfield became known locally by that name, although the official name was Bottesford after the larger village 1½ miles to the south.

Built by George Wimpey & Co. Ltd from November 1940, it had concrete runways from the outset, one of the first in the area to do so. The main 01-19 was 1,700 yards long, the 08-26 1,200 yards and the 14-32 1,300 yards. However, the main runway was extended to 1,933 yards, the 08-26 to 1,460 yards and the 14-32 to 1,510 yards before the airfield was completed. Thirty-six pan hardstandings were provided, one grouping being located on the other side of the Bottesford-Bennington road. Five of the dispersals were lost when the hangars were erected. The main technical site was situated on the north-east side and dispersed domestic sites in fields towards the A1 trunk road. A Type T2 hangar was located on the technical site and another on the south-west corner of the airfield. Later a B1 for Ministry of Aircraft Production engineers was erected on the west side of the Bottesford-Bennington road with an access strip to the perimeter track. Bomb stores and armoury were on the east side in Noss Plantation near Big Grange. The dispersed camp sites, 11 domestic, two communal and a sick quarters providing for a maximum complement of 2,373 males and 462 females was to the north of the airfield.

The airfield became operational in November 1941 with the arrival of No. 207 Squadron from Waddington. This squadron, the first to be equipped with the troublesome Manchester, was relieved to start exchanging them for Lancasters in March 1942. No. 207

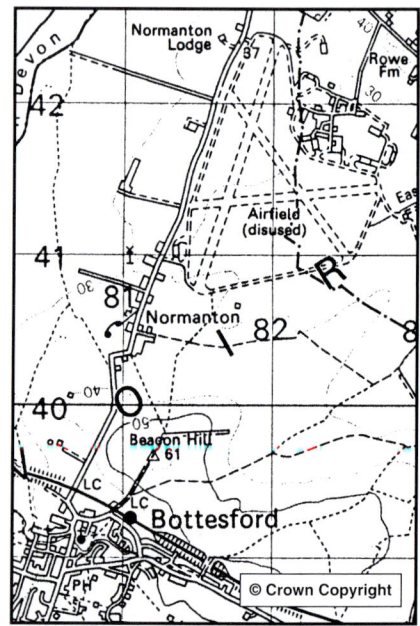

© Crown Copyright

Above: **On May 18, 1945, this Lancaster (HK739 J9-H of No. 1668 Heavy Conversion Unit) came to grief off the end of runway 08-26 at Bottesford.** *Below:* **This is the road north from Bottesford village which borders the aerodrome on its western perimeter — then and now.**

moved to Langar in September 1942, presumably to escape further construction work which included the erection of two more T2 hangars. In November 1942, No. 90 Squadron was re-formed at Bottesford to fly Stirlings in No. 3 Group and departed for Ridgewell the following month before becoming operational. A new Australian-manned squadron, No. 467, arrived in November 1942 commencing operations on the night of January 2/3, 1943.

Two more T2 hangars were erected near the technical site in 1943 specifically to protect Horsa gliders from inclement weather as Bottesford was the recipient of over 50 of these wood and canvas craft in preparation for the cross-Channel invasion. In November 1943, No. 467 Squadron was moved out to Waddington as Bottesford had been allocated to the USAAF's IX Troop Carrier Command for the forthcoming operation. Work started immediately on providing

more hardstandings, 21 loops being added in two clusters on the west side of the Bottesford-Bennington road. In the course of this work, five of the pans were destroyed. The 56 C-47s of the 436th Troop Carrier Group arrived in January 1944 and moved on in March to be replaced by the 440th TCG fresh from the USA. This group also moved south during the following month and Bottesford was then used for glider repair and modification.

Bottesford pictured on April 18, 1944 when the US IX Troop Carrier Command was in residence. Many Horsa and Waco gliders are to be seen and a C-47 towing a glider is in the process of taking off from runway 01-19.

The USAAF relinquished Bottesford to No. 5 Group Bomber Command in July 1944. No. 1668 Heavy Conversion Unit with Lancasters arrived and later some specialist flights were also based at the station with a variety of aircraft types. In November, No. 1668 HCU was re-assigned to No. 7 Training Group. Bottesford remained a Lancaster training station until the late summer of 1945, No. 1668 HCU moving to more comfortable accommodation at Cottesmore in September. Thereafter little flying took place although the hangars were used for storage by the Air Ministry. A holding party remained for a few years but the airfield was

in agricultural use by 1948 and a civilian warehousing operation was established in the hangars by John Rose, whose company was formed in 1954, and who purchased most of the airfield in 1962. The Roseland Group Ltd continues to operate from the site and uses the restored control tower as the company's office.

RAF Bomber Command operational losses sustained by the units based at Bottesford amounted to three Manchesters and 55 Lancasters, a total of 58.

Bottesford, September 2000, with the outline of the bomb store in the foreground.

CONINGSBY

A Hampden I of Coningsby's No. 106 Squadron parked near the fire tender shed by the control tower. This particular aircraft, P1228, missing on the Hamburg raid of November 30/December 1, 1941, was one of 57 Hampdens lost from this station.

This airfield was first scheduled in a 1937 expansion scheme plan but slow progress in the compulsory purchase of the land and associated problems delayed the work for two years. It was originally planned as a permanent station with Type C hangars but these were switched for two of the more utilitarian Type J. Much of the camp, with access to the A153 road, had been constructed before war began. Located immediately south of the small town of Coningsby, eleven miles north-east of Sleaford, the airfield was grass-surfaced when it was opened late in 1940.

The first Bomber Command squadron to be based at the station was No. 106 which arrived from Finningley with Hampdens in February 1941 and was involved chiefly in minelaying operations for the first few weeks. In March, No. 97 Squadron arrived with Manchesters from Waddington making its first raid with the type on the night of April 8/9, 1941. No. 97 had a difficult time with its aircraft, engine problems severely restricting operations, and in July and August 1941 the Manchester was grounded and the crews borrowed No. 106 Squadron's Hampdens for operations. However, when No. 106 converted to the troublesome machine in the summer of 1942, it faired no better. In January 1942, No. 97 started to

receive Lancasters but as the heavier aircraft tended to rut the airfield surface the squadron moved out to Waddington in March. No. 106 began to get its Lancasters in May 1942 but it remained at Coningsby throughout the summer months before moving to the hard surfaces at Syerston in September that year. During Manchester operations from Coningsby, 17 aircraft were lost.

Coningsby was then closed for the building of concrete runways on a £200,000 contract. These were aligned 08-26, for the main of 2,000 yards; 04-22 at 1,400 yards and 13-31 at 1,550 yards. Some 36 pan hardstandings had been put down round the airfield during the first year of the war but there was no perimeter track and two clusters, reached by asphalt tracks, were to the east across the Stub Hill road. In the course of the construction of the new perimeter track, a few pans were destroyed and seven loops added as replacements. A B1 hangar was erected for the Ministry of Aircraft Production on the west side of the technical site and later three Type T2s were put up behind the westernmost J hangar for No. 54 Base Maintenance. Additional accommodation at three dispersed sites, one WAAF, east of Coningsby village, raised the station maximum to 2,196 males and 384 females.

Coningsby re-opened in August 1943 with the Lancasters of the famous No. 617 Squadron moving in from Scampton. Involved in specialist operations, No. 617's activities while at Coningsby were somewhat limited. The most notable operation was the disastrous low-level raid on the Dortmund-Ems canal when five out of the eight Lancasters despatched failed to return. Because the squadron required more dispersals, in January 1944 it exchanged stations with No. 619 at Woodhall Spa.

In February 1944, the airfield became a two-squadron base with the arrival of No. 61 Squadron from Skellingthorpe while repairs were being carried out at that station. No. 61 moved back to Skellingthorpe in April and No. 619 was moved to Dunholme Lodge.

Coningsby had been selected as the base for two squadrons specialising in target marking for precision night attacks which No. 5 Group was to pursue. To this end, two of its Lancaster squadrons that had been transferred to No. 8 Pathfinder Group many months earlier, having acquired the necessary skills, were to be returned. These were Nos. 83 and 97 Squadrons, the latter having been previously based at Coningsby, to where both units moved in April 1944. They remained on the airfield for the remainder of

As at most of the wartime aerodromes which have been retained by the Royal Air Force as front-line bases, facilities have been vastly modernised and control centres modernised. Thus the tower at Coningsby has taken on a completely new appear-

ance . . . making the comparison almost meaningless . . . but this shortcoming is more than made up by the 1942-vintage Dakota parked nearby — operated by the Battle of Britain Memorial Flight which has been based on the airfield since 1976.

Coningsby has been so expanded from its original configuration that it is quite difficult to orient the features in this picture taken in April 1942 with the present layout shown in the Ordnance Survey plan.

the war when, by VE-Day, a total of 175 Bomber Command aircraft had been lost in operations flown from the airfield. Seventeen of these were Manchesters, 57 Hampdens and 101 Lancasters.

Nos. 83 and 97 Squadrons continued in residence right up until November 1946 having re-equipped with Lincolns during the summer. They were replaced by Nos. 109 and 139 Squadrons with Mosquitos until these moved out to Hemswell in 1950, the station where the Lincolns had gone. At the end of the year Coningsby received Washingtons, a complement of eight in each of four squadrons, but after three years the Washingtons gave place to Canberras. The following year these departed so that the main runway, 08-26, could be rebuilt and lengthened to 2,740 yards. When the station re-opened two years later it again hosted Canberras until the first V-bomber units arrived in 1961. The Vulcan squadrons left late in 1964 and thereafter Coningsby had no resident flying units for two years until the base was selected for a Phantom Operational Conversion Unit and, later, actual Phantom squadrons.

During the early 1980s, Coningsby was the first RAF station to have hardened aircraft shelters erected. In 1985, a Tornado OCU was set up as a training base for Tornado F3 fighters. The Battle of Britain Memorial Flight, which possesses the only airworthy Lancaster in Europe (the other is in Canada), has been based at this station using the B1 hangar since 1976.

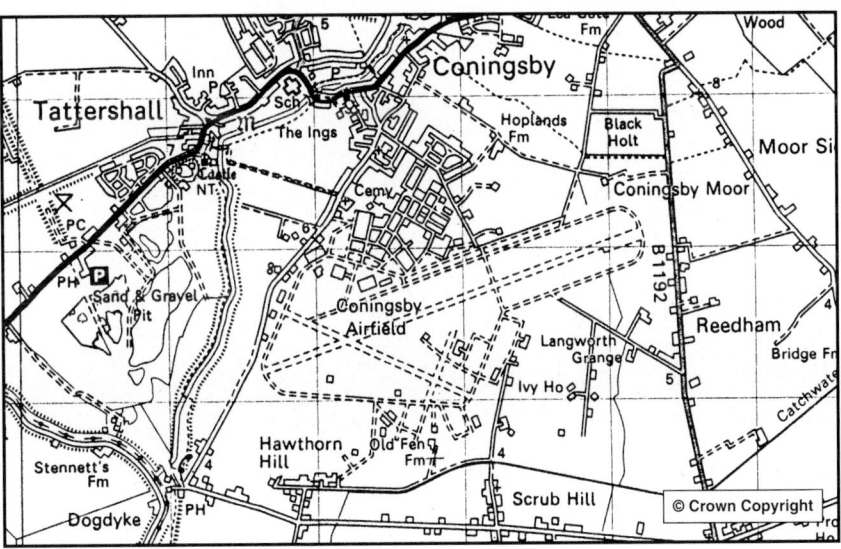

233

During the early 1980s, Coningsby was the first RAF station to have hardened aircraft shelters erected seen on the right of this photo taken looking east. In 1985, an Operational Conversion Unit was set up for training pilots on the Tornado F3.

234

Fortunately when Karel Margry took this photograph in September 2000, Europe's only airworthy Lancaster was sitting outside its B1 hangar. Although PA474 never saw action, at one time it bore the markings of Waddington's VC (see page 178).

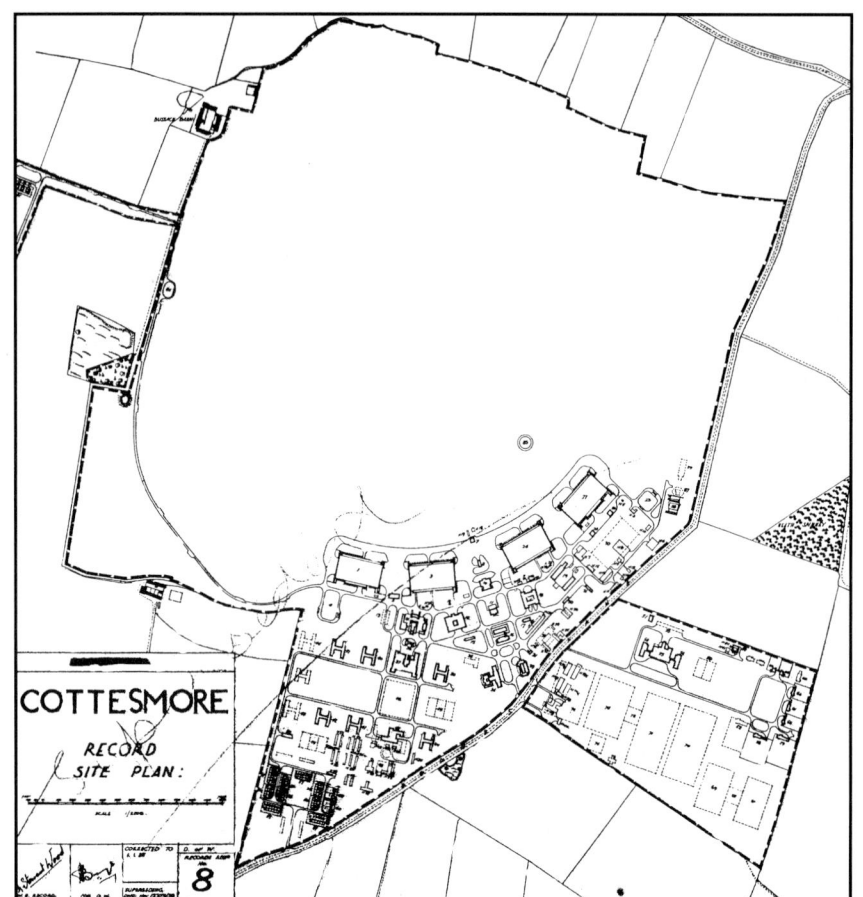

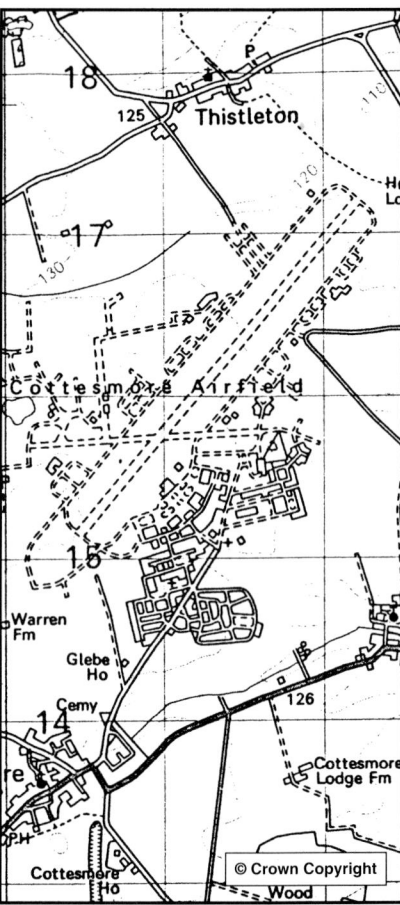

© Crown Copyright

COTTESMORE

Contemporary aerial cover of Cottesmore is withheld due to security restrictions but this plan *(left)* shows the original layout which follows the basic formula for the 1930's 'expansion period' airfield. *Right:* The Cottesmore of the 1990s.

Cottesmore was an expansion scheme air-field built in 1936-38 on 200 acres north of the village of that name which lies some 9½ miles north-west of Stamford within sight of the A1. The grass flying field, on free-draining soil, permitted for 1,100 yard take-off and landing runs. The camp to the south, adjacent to the road to Cottesmore village, was composed of administrative, technical, barrack and mess buildings built in brick and concrete, the majority being flat-roofed. In common with other new air stations of the period, the whole camp was compact with the standard Type C hangars, four in all, facing the airfield in an arc.

Initially allocated to No. 2 Group, the first occupants were Nos. 35 and 207 Squadrons, which arrived from Worthy Down with their Vickers Wellesleys in late April 1938. The Wellesleys were soon replaced by Battles and in 1939 both squadrons were moved to Cranfield, Cottesmore being passed to No. 5 Group. Shortly before the outbreak of war No. 185 Squadron arrived from Thornaby with Hampdens and Herefords and No. 106 from the same station a few weeks later. Both squadrons had pool status in No. 5 Group for providing reserves for operational units. Early in October, No. 106 was moved to Finningley while No. 185 continued in its

reserve role at Cottesmore. However, in mid-December, the airfield was passed to No. 6 Training Group and, in the following April, No. 185 Squadron and the Station Headquarters establishment were merged to form No. 14 Operational Training Unit. No. 185 Squadron was re-formed later in the month at Cottesmore but was unsustainable and was discontinued in May.

No. 14 OTU continued to provide Hampden-trained crews for No. 5 Group squadrons but, from the night of July 25, 1940, periodically undertook leaflet-dropping sorties over the Continent. None of its Hampdens were lost during these operations. The

Fairey Battles of No. 207 Squadron neatly lined up on the grass early in 1939.

Luftwaffe raided Cottesmore on April 10/11, 1941 with an estimated 10-15 aircraft. and, although flares illuminated the area, most of the bombs dropped fell outside the airfield perameter.

When No. 14 OTU was called upon to provided a sizeable force to bomb Cologne on the first of the 'Thousand Plan' raids on the night of May 30/31, 1942, one of the 29 aircraft despatched was shot down by a night fighter and two others crashed in England, one after colliding with a Halifax. Cottesmore also participated in the second and third 'Thousand Plan' raids, losing another Hampden but the station's most costly night was participation in the attack on Düsseldorf on the night of July 31 when three Hampdens were shot down by night fighters and a fourth was so badly crippled that it crashed on its return. On the night of September 13/14, 1942, a No. 14 OTU Hampden was shot down during a raid on Bremen and another crashed on its return. These were the last Hampden losses during Bomber Command operations. All told, Cottesmore had seven aircraft failing to return from operations and four lost in operational crashes.

In the autumn of 1942, No. 14 OTU converted to Wellingtons and remained at Cottesmore until August 1943 when it was moved to Market Harborough. The move was occasioned by the laying of reinforced concrete runways and the upgrading of the airfield to Class A standard. The runways were 05-23 at 2,000 yards long, 05-23 at 1,600 yards and 10-28 at 1,500 yards. Thirty-five loop-type hardstandings were put down in concrete making a total of 52 on the airfield, only 17 of the original tarmac pan-type surviving. The reason for the high number of aircraft dispersal points was that the airfield was included in the new group area which would be allocated to the USAAF for basing a transport aircraft command prior to the cross-Channel invasion planned for the following year. Additional accommodation was built by Constable Hart & Co. Ltd on sites in the Cottesmore village area. Also, a T2 was erected in the summer of 1943 for glider storage, 32 Horsas having been delivered by air in July that year.

The first personnel from the US Ninth Air Force arrived in October 1943 to set up a Troop Carrier Wing and in February 1944 the 316th Troop Carrier Group arrived from the Mediterranean Theater with its four squadrons and 52 C-47 and C-53 transports. The 316th participated in the three major airborne assaults — Normandy, Holland and the Rhine — and was the only troop carrier group still based in the UK at the end of hostilities.

Cottesmore's main runway 05-23 is now 3,000 yards long and fitted with arrester gear some 400 yards from either end.

Harriers take their place on the extended floodlit apron early in 2001.

Cottesmore was returned to the Royal Air Force on July 1, 1945, and in September No. 1668 Heavy Conversion Unit was transferred in from Bottesford although it was gradually run down. When this formation was disbanded Cottesmore was occupied by No. 16 Operational Training Unit. Two years later No. 7 Flying Training School was installed, Cottesmore's training role continuing until 1954. Canberra squadrons were next to arrive but their presence was only for eight months as a decision had been taken to upgrade the airfield for use by V-bombers. To this end, the main runway, 05-23, was rebuilt and extended to 3,000 yards and new taxiways and aircraft dispersals built. Victor squadrons came first followed by Vulcans in 1964. The latter stayed for five years before the station passed to No. 90 (Signals) Group.

From 1980, Cottesmore was the home of the Tri-National Tornado Training Establishment with British, Germany and Italian crews, the following 20 years being Cottesmore's longest association with one unit. It disbanded in 1999. Harrier squadrons took up station at the end of the century.

EAST KIRKBY

This airfield was constructed to Class A standard and built during 1942-43 in the parishes of East Kirkby and Hagnaby, 11 miles north of Boston, directly south of the A155 Coningsby to Spilsby road. Most of the land taken was that of Hagnaby Grange Farm, the farmhouse being left standing within the airfield perimeter track. A north-south minor road on the east of the site had to be closed. The main contractor was John Laing & Son Ltd. The runways were to the ideal dimensions: main 02-20 at 2,000 yards with 08-26 and 13-31 both 1,400 yards long. The perimeter track served 27 pan and eight loop-type hardstandings and the standard hangarage was provided for this period of the war: two T2s, positioned one on the technical site between runway heads 08 and 13 and the other south of runway head 26. Later, a B1 hangar was erected between the technical site T2 and runway head 08. Still later, in the spring of 1944, four T2 hangars were added adjacent to the technical site on its north side, west of runway 20 near the A155. These served No. 55 Base Maintenance. Bomb stores were situated off the north-east side between runway heads 20 and 26. The dispersed camp north of East Kirkby village consisted of six domestic, two WAAF, two communal and a sick quarters site, providing for a maximum of 1,965 males and 486 females.

When ready to receive an operational unit,

Another Lancaster fated to be missing in action with the loss of all crew members was No. 630 Squadron's LL966 LE-P which failed to return to East Kirkby on the night of February 14/15, 1945 after an operation to Rositz oil refinery near Leipzig.

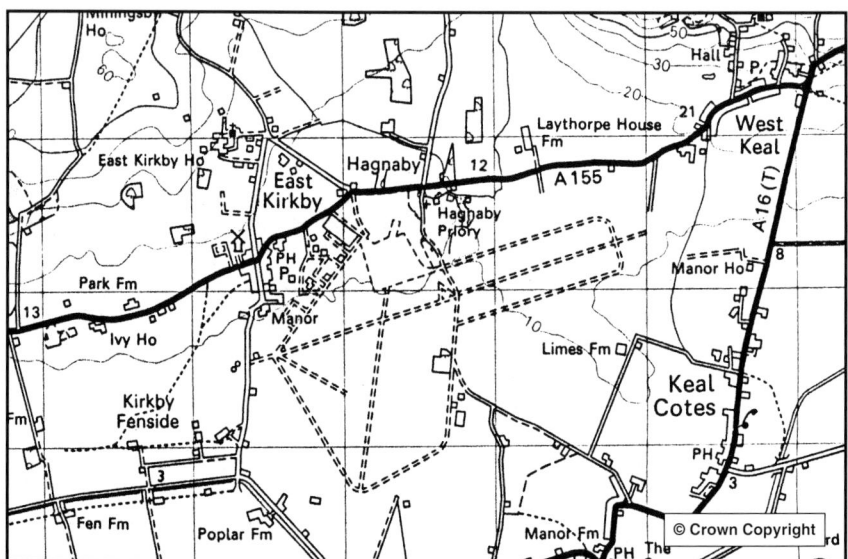

© Crown Copyright

No. 57 Squadron's Lancasters moved in from Scampton which was due to be closed for hard runways to be put down. This was in August 1943, the squadron flying its first operation from East Kirkby on the night of August 27/28 to Hamburg. In November, 'B'

Flight of No. 57 was taken to form a new squadron, No. 630. The usual practice was for the newcomer to be moved onto another airfield but, in this case, No. 630 remained with its parent at East Kirkby throughout the rest of Bomber Command's offensive.

Looking north from the same location at the south-west dispersals towards the technical site.

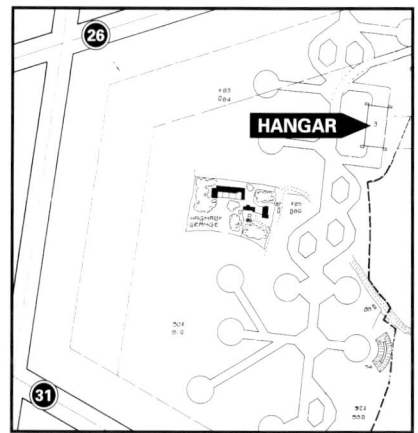

Left: **When East Kirkby was built, the property of Hagnaby Grange was left isolated between runways 31 and 26 on the eastern side of the 'drome.** *Right:* **It was used as a dispersal by No. 57 Squadron and this picture shows one of their Lancasters DX-N being refuelled outside the house.**

Shortly before the end of the war — on April 17 — a major accident occurred at East Kirkby when a 1,000lb bomb exploded during bombing-up in the darkness, setting off the remainder of the No. 57 Squadron Lancaster's load. There were 17 casualties including four killed and six Lancasters were declared Category E (beyond repair) and another 14 suffered some form of damage. The nearby hangar and Hagnaby Grange were also badly damaged.

And it was here on April 17, 1945, at 5.30 p.m., when around 30 Lancasters of Nos. 57 and 630 Squadrons were being bombed up for a night raid to marshalling yards on the German/Czech border, that a mixture of 500 and 1000lb bombs exploded in the fire. Fortunately the crews had not yet been bussed to the dispersal and 630's Lancs were far enough away to escape damage but six of the No. 57 Squadron machines were destroyed and the nearby hangar, used to store incendiary bombs, seriously damaged. Some of the bombs were set alight but due to exceptional bravery in quelling the fires, an even worse disaster was avoided. Wing Commander John McBean, who as a Flight Lieutenant was the Station Armaments Officer, comments that although a Court of Inquiry was held, the precise reason for the disaster was never fully determined but it was suspected that a spark set a fuel tank ablaze causing a chain-reaction.

Fred Panton, joint owner of the airfield, stands in front of the overgrown foundations.

Left: **The devastated No. 3 Hangar. The T2 was never fully repaired and removed post-war but the blast walls** *(right)* **remain.**

239

The last raid from East Kirkby was flown on April 25, 1945. In total, 212 operations were carried out from this airfield from which 121 Lancasters failed to return. Another 29 were lost in operational crashes or accidents.

No. 630 Squadron disbanded in July that year, its place taken by No. 460 Squadron from Binbrook. This Australian unit was to join No. 57 for transfer to the Far East as part of Tiger Force but the dropping of the atomic bombs expedited Japan's surrender. Consequently, No. 460 disbanded at East Kirkby in October and No. 57 the following month.

The airfield was then on care and maintenance although Mosquitos from Coningsby used the airfield during the autumn and winter of 1947-48 while repair work was carried out at their home station. The Cold War brought a revival for the airfield's fortunes when it was one of several enlarged and improved having been selected for possible use by the USAF. As a result, runway 08-26 was lengthened on the 26 end by 1,266 yards. The USAF remained for four years in the mid-1950s during which period Air Rescue Squadrons used the station. East Kirkby was finally sold by the government in 1964.

Apart from farming activities on the airfield, the runways were used for the isolated positioning of poultry houses holding broiler birds by Eastwoods Ltd. In 1981, the airfield was purchased by two local farmers, Fred and Harold Panton, and seven years later they acquired the rather dilapidated Lancaster gate guardian from Scampton (NX611). The aircraft was beautifully refurbished forming the nucleus of the Lincolnshire Aviation Heritage Centre set up in memory of their elder brother, Pilot Officer Christopher Panton of No. 433 Squadron, lost on the Nuremberg raid on March 30/31, 1944.

Photographed on July 28, 1948, the aftermath of the explosion can be see on the eastern side of the airfield. All that is left of Hagnaby Grange is the outline of the walls while the churned up area still shows evidence of tilling.

From opposite ends! *Above:* Looking north with the Hagnaby copse of trees in the middle distance and *(below)* a close-up of the extension which was built for the United States Air Force.

The extra length was added to the eastern end of the 08-26 subsidiary rather than extending the original main runway which was aligned more or less N-S.

FULBECK

In 1940, meadows six miles east-south-east of Newark, between the villages of Fenton and Stragglethorpe, were requisitioned for use as a relief landing ground by training aircraft from the RAF College at Cranwell. Known unofficially as Fenton, the site continued to serve Cranwell for the next 18 months, gradually collecting a number of huts through the facilities were always basic. In February 1942, Fenton was scheduled for upgrading to a full-size airfield of Class A standard when it was given the official name of Fulbeck after the village 2½ miles to the east in which parish most of the domestic sites were placed.

Built to Class A standard, the main contractor was Sir Robert McAlpine & Sons Ltd, with J. McGeoch & Son Ltd also involved. The runways were 05-23 at 2,000 yards, 12-30 and 01-19 both 1,400 yards long. Thirty-six pan-type hardstandings were dispersed round the perimeter track but two

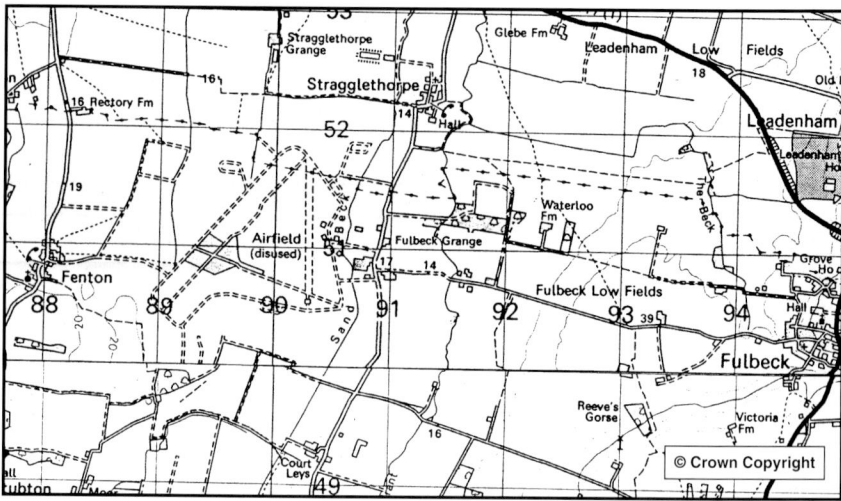

Fulbeck pictured by the US 7th Photo Group with dozens of gliders dispersed on and around the airfield on April 18, 1944.

Although the landing ground was known locally as Fenton after the nearest village, when the site was developed to **Class A standard, the official name of Fulbeck came into being after the larger community 2½ miles to the east.**

were lost by the siting of hangars. Five T2 hangars were erected; one on the south side between runway heads 01 and 05; one on the east side by the main technical site for aircraft servicing; another down a long access track more to the north-east, and two at the north-west corner near runway 19. Three of the T2s were for gliders as during the summer of 1943 upwards of 30 Horsas were brought in for storage until required. The technical and administration sites were backed up against the stream known as Sandy Beck on the east side of the airfield, and the weapons store was to the south near runway 05. Two small roads from Fenton hamlet had to be closed to construct the airfield. Seven domestic sites, two communal and the sick quarters were east of Stragglethorpe Lane in Fulbeck Low Meadows.

In May 1943, a beam approach flight used the airfield but in August Fulbeck was allocated for USAAF use and work commenced to increase accommodation and the number of hardstandings, a total of 15 loops being added. Constable Hart & Co. Ltd and F. G. Mintee Ltd were the contractors involved. In October 1943, the first of nine newly-raised troop carrier groups to reach the UK arrived at Fulbeck. The 434th TCG had 56 C-47s and started training with some detachments elsewhere until finally moving to Aldermaston in March 1944. At the end the month the 442nd TCG arrived with C-47s, moving on to Weston Zoyland in June after having taken part in the D-Day operations. During the following two months there was little activity at Fulbeck until the 440th TCG arrived in September to take part in 'Market', the air component of Operation 'Market-Garden'.

The IX Troop Carrier Command relinquished the airfield for good in late September and No. 5 Group Bomber Command moved in the distinguished No. 49 Squadron from Fiskerton, an airfield which was trans-

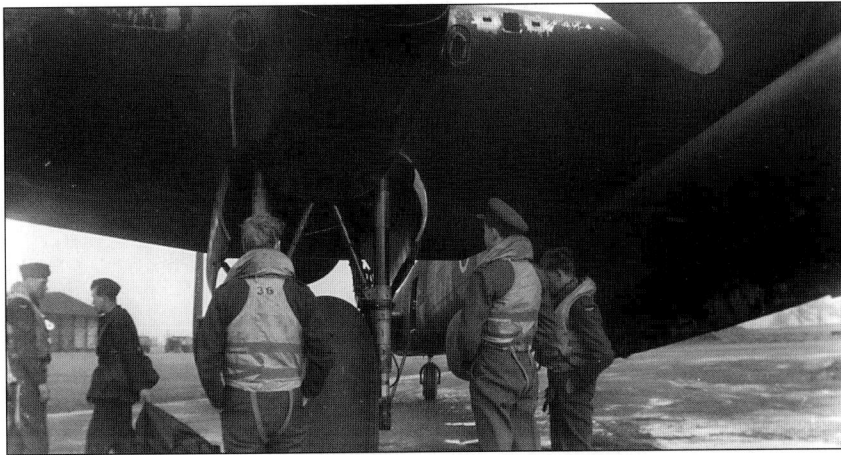

Flying Officer Reg Herbert, the skipper, and three of his crew with their No. 189 Squadron Lancaster 'C'-Charlie (PB732) on dispersal at Fulbeck in March 1945.

ferred to No. 1 Group the following month. On November 2 the recently-formed No. 189 Squadron arrived from Bardney having taken part in its first operation the previous day. Both Nos. 49 and 189 Squadron's Lancasters remained based at Fulbeck until April 1945. No. 49 flew some 60 raids from the airfield losing 15 aircraft and No. 189 took part in 40 raids with 16 aircraft lost. No. 189 moved back to Bardney on the 8th of the month and No. 49 moved to Syerston on the 22nd. On the morning of transfer, a No. 49 Squadron Lancaster making a low farewell pass across the airfield crashed into the technical area and of the resulting 24 casualties among air and ground personnel, 15 were fatal. Bomber Command operations from Fulbeck cost 38 Lancasters, either failing to return or destroyed in crashes.

With no flying unit in residence, the station came under No. 255 Maintenance Unit handling RAF surplus stores, much of the material being disposed of in auctions held during 1948. The airfield was then on a care and maintenance status for five years as a sub-station of No. 93 Maintenance Unit, and at one point the hangars housed the Air Historical Branch's static aircraft collection. Retained as a reserve airfield, Fulbeck was also used as a Ministry of Defence training area playing host to a number of military exercises. The runways, apart from narrow strips used as farm roads, were removed in the 1970s and all but three of the hardstandings but the perimeter track was kept intact. At one time Fulbeck was proposed for a nuclear waste disposal site. It is still used for military training exercises.

From the angle that the Lancaster is standing on the perimeter track, the hangar in the background is probably the most northerly of the pair which lay on the north-western corner of the airfield. As our aerial picture taken in September 2000 shows, both hangars — which lay on the loop on the right — have gone. Even the control tower which was standing within the fenced-off Ministry of Defence training area until recently, has now been demolished.

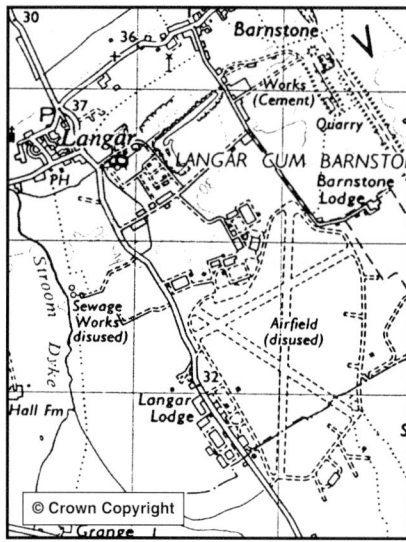
© Crown Copyright

LANGAR

Situated some 12 miles south-east from the centre of Nottingham, this aerodrome was built largely in the parish of Langar cum Barnstone during 1941-42. The flying field spanned the Nottinghamshire/ Leicestershire county border and in the early days was often referred to locally as Harby, a village to the south of the site.

Built to Class A standard, the runways were the main 01-19 at 2,000 yards, 07-25, at 1,400 yards and 13-31 also at 1,400 yards, although shorter lengths were given in the original specifications. There were 36 pan dispersals and one T2 hangar was located on the technical site between runways 01 and 07 and another between runway heads 01 and 31. Domestic sites, providing for 2,007 males and 246 females, were dispersed in farmland to the north-west around Langar village with the bomb stores located on the east side of the airfield. Additionally, a large hangar workshop complex was built on the west side of the Langar-Harby road with access tracks across the road to the airfield and an Avro unit for major repair and modification of Lancasters came into operation when the airfield opened in September 1942. A major part of the construction work was by George Wimpey & Co. Ltd.

In September 1942, the Lancasters of No. 207 Squadron moved in from Bottesford whereupon it flew raids from the airfield for just over a year. During this period, two more T2 hangars were erected for winter storage of Horsa gliders, 32 of which were placed on the airfield during the summer of 1943.

In August 1943, Langar was one of 15 airfields in the Grantham area allocated to the USAAF to receive a troop carrier division. To meet this future use, 14 loop hardstandings were added along the perimeter track and additional domestic sites constructed to provide total accommodation for 2,253 persons. Soon after No. 207 Squadron moved out in October, having lost 29 Lancasters on operations while in residence, the first US service units arrived.

Langar pictured on September 4, 1943 with the Station Headquarters and Operations Block in the foreground. No. 207 Squadron Lancasters sit on the pan hardstandings and 32 Horsa gliders are parked on the grassed areas. One of the score of Lancasters missing from a raid on Berlin the previous night was a No. 207 Squadron aircraft lost without trace. The crew included the Station Commander, Group Captain Austin McKenna.

A rather poor-quality shot — not up to the usual quality of 7th Photo Group photographs — but important as it shows Langar in April 1944 after the additional loops were added for American use.

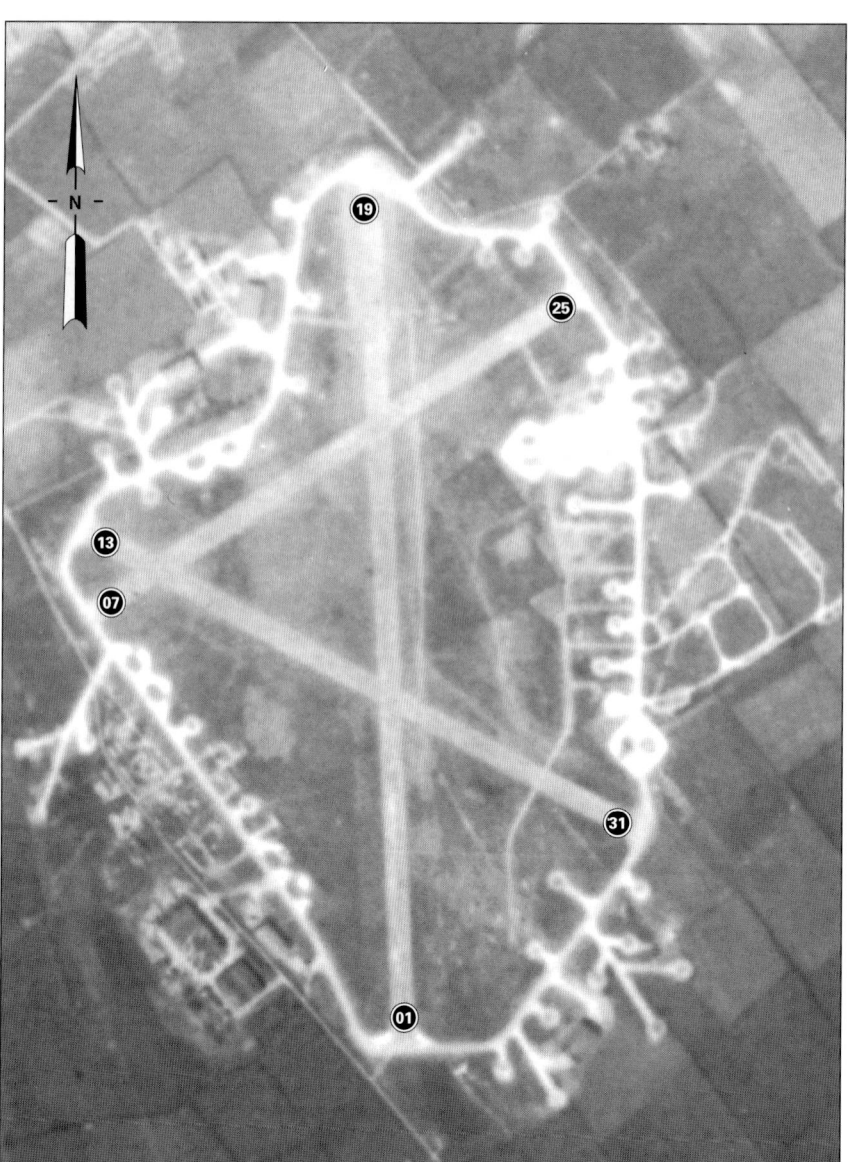

In November 1943, the 435th Troop Carrier Group flew in from the United States with C-47s and a few C-53s. It remained until late April 1944 when it moved out to Merryfield in south-east. Langar then became a glider modification station where Waco CG-4As were to be seen in large numbers. The 441st TCG arrived with 90 C-47s in September 1944 to participate in the Operation 'Market' mission to Holland after which Langar was returned to the RAF. In October, No. 1669 Heavy Conversion Unit arrived with some 30 Lancasters. This organisation remained until March 1945 when a surplus of trained crews allowed No. 7 Group to disband it. The airfield continued to be used by Avro for the reception and despatch of Lancasters to its works as had also happened during the American occupation. In fact practically all the flying activity at Langar during the rest of 1945 and until the airfield closed in December 1946 was connected with the Avro operation, and even then the company retained its workshop complex.

After five years of neglect, Langar was selected as a base for the Canadian contribution to NATO and extensive construction work took place to provided better accommodation and other facilities. The RCAF made Langar their primary supply base in Europe and their link between Canada and their fighter airfields in Britain and on the Continent. They remained at Langar for some 11 years and a variety of air transports visited during that period, including Bristol Freighters, North Stars, Expeditors and the ubiquitous Dakotas. When the Canadians departed in 1963, Avro was again using the airfield for flying before the company left in 1968. The buildings were soon acquired by various commercial outlets and the former Avro complex by the international farm machinery manufacturer John Deere. Today, the airfield remains in reasonable order and has been used by the British Parachute School for the past 23 years. Their offices are in the old control tower. Light aircraft and a gliding club also use Langar of a regular basis.

More than half a century has passed and, although the 13-31 runway is disused, Langar is still a very active airfield operated by British Parachute Schools. A photo sortie — like ours in September 2000 when we photographed all 101 Bomber Command bases — had to be specially arranged to avoid the intensive parachute training which takes place every day.

METHERINGHAM

Lancasters of No. 106 Squadron at the head of the lit main runway 02 on March 24, 1944, about to depart for Berlin. Bomber Command lost 72 aircraft on that particular night but all the squadron's aircraft returned safely.

Located nine miles south-east of Lincoln and two miles east of Metheringham village beside the B1189, this Class A standard airfield was built 1942-43. Largely in the parish of Martin it bordered the Lincolnshire fens. The runways were to the standard specification with the main 02-20 at 2,000 yards and the others, 13-31 and 07-25, at 1,400 yards length. Being to the later Class A specification, 34 of the hardstandings were loop type and only two pans. One of the standard T2 hangars was placed on the technical site, which was alongside the B1189 near Linwood Grange, between runway heads 02 and 07, and the other off the east perimeter track between runway heads 25 and 31. A B1 hangar lay north of runway head 13 near Barff Farm. The bomb store was situated around Blackthorn Holt and other woodland between runway heads 13 and 20. The camp sites were built directly south around the B1189 and consisted of one mess, one communal, one WAAF, four domestic and a sick quarters. Accommodation was given as for 1,685 males and 345 females.

Lancasters from No. 106 Squadron, moving in from the comforts of Syerston in November 1943, undertook their first raid from the new station on the 11th. The squadron was destined to remain at Metheringham until February 1946, and was the only operational unit based there during hostilities. During a raid on Schweinfurt on the night of April 26/27 1944, Sergeant Norman Jackson, flight engineer of a Lancaster, was awarded the Victoria Cross for his action when his aircraft was set on fire by an enemy fighter. Jackson volunteered to climb out on to the wing to try and extinguish the flames but, badly burned, he was swept off and landed heavily to be made prisoner.

The view to the south-west from the loop dispersals near the head of runway 20. The vertical supports for the high-level water storage tanks, on domestic site No. 4, can just be made out beyond the Lancaster in the far distance at the extreme left of the photograph.

Sugar beet now grows beside what is left of the perimeter track, but the water tower, partly masked by a tree on the left, still stands.

By the end of hostilities No. 106 Squadron had lost 65 Lancasters in operations flown from the airfield. After VE-Day, No. 467, an RAAF squadron, arrived with Lancasters to train with No. 106 for operations in the Far East but the end of the war made this plan redundant and No. 467 was disbanded at the end of September 1945. No. 189 Squadron took its place but this too was soon stood down. No. 106 Squadron endured until February 1946 when it met the same fate and Metheringham was closed to flying soon after.

Although remaining in a fairly complete state until the early 'fifties, the hangars and most domestic site buildings had been demolished by the end of the next decade. Sold in 1961-62 and returned to agriculture, some of the concrete was removed and parts of runways 07-25 and 13-31 were used to reinstate two small roads closed during the construction of the airfield. Several technical site buildings remain in use for commercial purposes and the former ration store is now a museum devoted to Bomber Command's wartime tenure.

This RAF vertical cover taken on April 16, 1947 from 16,400 feet by a Benson-based Mosquito of No. 58 Squadron, shows the deserted airfield with white cross 'out of use' markings at the ends of the runways. The tell-tale oil stains on the loop hardstandings indicate where Lancasters were once dispersed. The photograph also clearly shows where work on the perimeter track at the south-east corner was stopped and redesigned to incorporate more loop hardstandings.

Above left: **The public road from the B1189 to Lonwood Moor, closed when the airfield was made, has been reopened using part of the perimeter track and runways. This memorial to No. 106 Squadron stands just off the junction B1189.** *Above right:* **An even more interesting memorial which once stood at Metheringham is now on display in Newark Air Museum. The single stone commemorating the service of No. 106 originally marked a mock grave in which the squadron buried their colours and other souvenirs when it was disbanded in 1946. Roy Bradley, who flew Lancasters with the squadron, found the smashed stone lying beside the pillaged grave in which only a hat band and two cartridges remained which he arranged to go to the museum for preservation.**

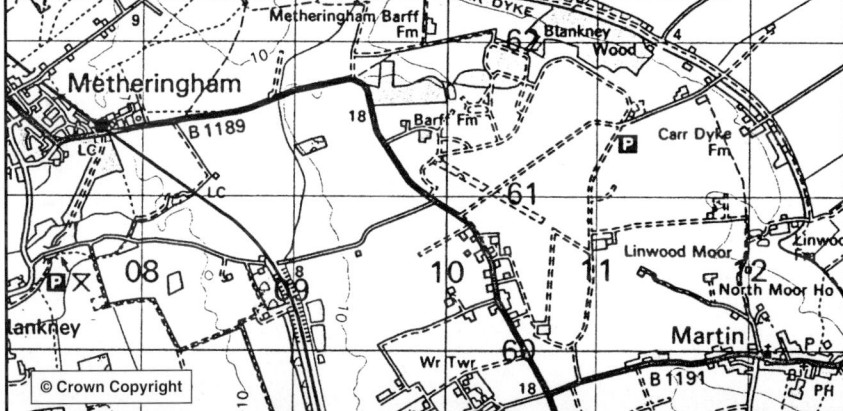

A double loop dispersal remains intact at the western end of the 13-31 subsidiary runway but the hangar has gone.

The bomb stores lay in the fields bordering the wood on the left. In the right foreground, Barff Farm.

NEWTON

Newton aerodrome lay just south of the village of that name six miles east of Nottingham between the A46 and A6097. It was an expansion scheme airfield built in 1938 to the usual pattern with four Type C hangars fronting the bombing circle with a fifth hangar tucked in behind that on the eastern side. The technical administrative and barrack buildings were of brick construction with flat roofs, most with central heating. During 1940-41, a total of 24 pan aircraft standings were put down, 18 on the south side of which all but four were connected to three taxiway tracks, and six on the north side where three were linked to a hard track. Later the number of standings was raised to 35. Grass runways were established as 07-25 at 1,230 yards, and 13-31 and 01-19 both at 770 yards.

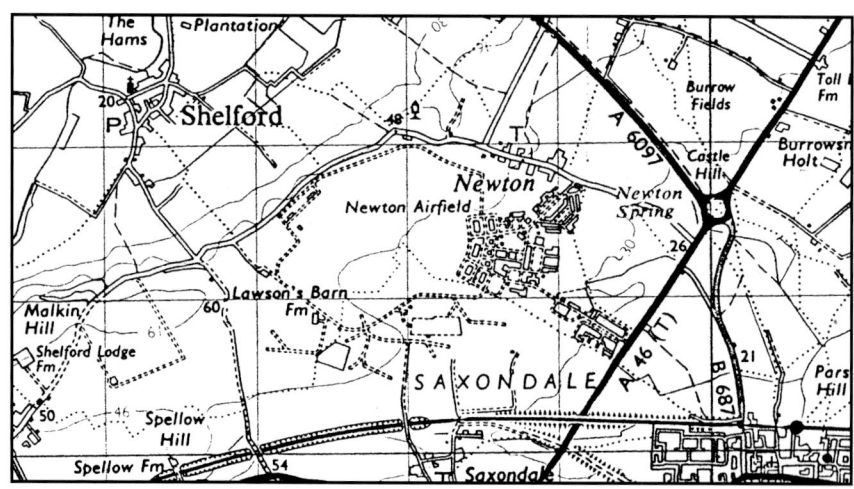

Newton was pictured by No. 540 Squadron on February 26, 1946. All told, 17 blister hangars can be seen widely dispersed.

In June 1940 Newton was one of the stations assigned to No. 1 Group when it gathered its battered Battle squadrons together after their mauling in France. Nos. 103 and 150 Squadrons arrived at the airfield in July and made the occasional night foray over occupied Holland during following weeks until re-equipped with Wellingtons in October. Thus endowed, attacks on German targets were pursued until July 1941 when No. 103 went to Elsham Wolds and No. 150 to Snaith. The move was occasioned by more suitable bomber airfields and the decision to turn Newton over to training activities. At this time Newton was able to accommodate

Then . . . and now. *Left:* **Group Captain G. T. Tyrrell and his staff outside Station headquarters when RAF Newton first opened for business in 1940.** *Right:* **Squadron Leader C. R. Rawe, Detachment Commander, with two of his staff outside the same doorway in 1999.**

1,773 males and 304 females. This marked the end of Bomber Command's operational use of the station, a year in which one Battle and 15 Wellingtons had been lost.

For the next five years No. 16 (Polish) Service Flying Training School provided basic and advanced training for the hundreds of Polish airmen serving with the RAF, the unit only being disbanded in October 1946. Although various training activities contin-

ued, the station then became the headquarters of No. 12 Group, Fighter Command, In 1958 Technical Training Command took over and several ground schools followed during the 'sixties and 'seventies. Flying continued by the East Midlands University Air Squadron with Bulldog aircraft and the civilian-operated Slingsby Fireflies on behalf of RAF Cranwell. In 1996 part of the camp was sold and the airfield closed in November 2000.

When our picture was taken in September 2000, the grass runways were still being used for training — as they were during **the war — but now under the auspices of Cranwell, some 20 miles to the east.**

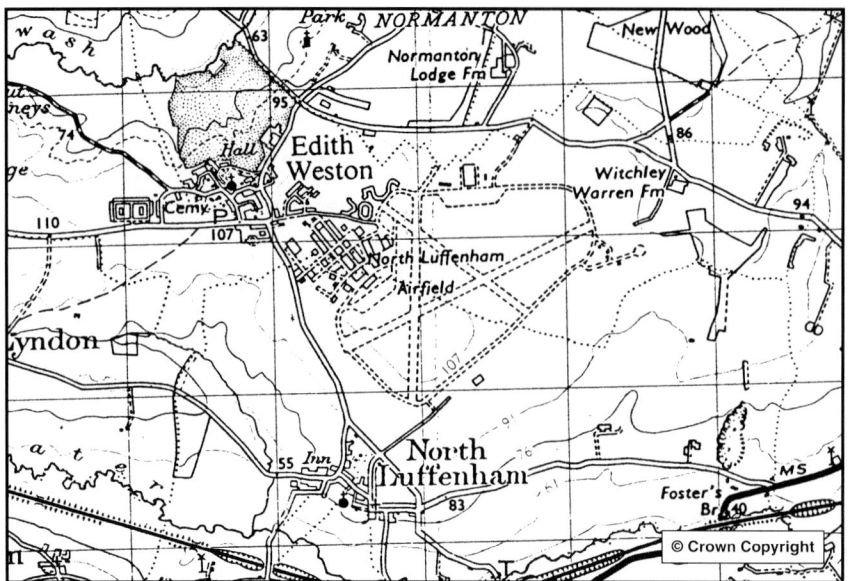

© Crown Copyright

A Manchester conversion flight for No. 61 Squadron was brought into being at North Luffenham in late March 1942 but this moved to Syerston after five weeks where the squadron was then based. With hard surfaced runways desirable for its heavy bombers, No. 5 Group relinquished North Luffenham to training command in April 1942 and No. 29 Operational Training Unit was formed to raise crews on Wellingtons remaining at the station until June 1943. During its occupation, three T2 hangars were erected on the north side of the airfield for Hamilcar glider accommodation. A Ministry of Aircraft Production B1 hangar was also erected on the technical site during 1943, presumably in connection with work on the Hamilcars.

No. 29 OTU moved to Bruntingthorpe in June 1943 so that George Wimpey & Co. Ltd could start work at North Luffenham on laying hard runways. The usual arrangement of intersecting strips featured a main 08-26, of 2,000 yards and 01-19 and 14-32 both at 1,400 yards long. The hardstandings were 36 loops. Additional buildings by Token Construction Co. Ltd brought accommodation up to 2,118 males and 311 females.

NORTH LUFFENHAM

A site on high ground between the villages of Edith Weston and North Luffenham, five miles south-west of Stamford, was found suitable for an airfield and construction commenced in 1939. The flying field was turf and the administration, technical and some accommodation were based in permanent buildings grouped near Edith Weston. Hangars, in keeping with the specification of early wartime airfields, consisted of two Type J erected adjacent to the technical site.

North Luffenham opened in December 1940 with a training mission, No. 17 Elementary Flying Training School being formed at the station in January. Tiger Moths predominated in serving the basic pilot tutelage.

By the summer of 1941 additional airfields were required for No. 5 Group and the EFTS was moved to Peterborough. In July, Nos. 61 and 144 Squadrons were brought into Luffenham from Hemswell which had been selected as a base for Polish bomber squadrons. Both squadrons flew Hampdens and were fully operational, much of their work being minelaying. No. 61 began to receive Manchesters with their attendant problems in October 1941 and was transferred to the new airfield with hard runways at Woolfox Lodge when this became available for use. No. 144 Squadron was the sole resident at North Luffenham until late April 1942 when it was transferred from Bomber to Coastal Command and torpedo work, moving north to Scotland.

The circuits of the close-packed airfields must have intermeshed like the wheels of a precision watch and collisions were an ever-present possibility with hundreds of aircraft using the same crowded airspace. Where the landscape permitted, runways of adjacent airfields were aligned so as not to interfere with each other, some even having to vary circuits from left-handed to right-handed to avoid clashing with a neighbour. This is a good illustration (taken in April 1944 by the 7th Photo Group based at Mount Farm) of the three southernmost airfields in Bomber Command's No. 5 Group. Each aerodrome had its own two-letter recognition code displayed in the signals square in front of the control tower. In the case of these three airfields, Cottesmore was CT, Woolfox Lodge WL with NL for North Luffenham. Identification in Morse Code was flashed at night to help returning bombers.

COTTESMORE

WOOLFOX LODGE

GREAT NORTH ROAD

NORTH LUFFENHAM

Miles 1 2 3

A Lanc from No. 1653 Heavy Conversion Unit with a J Type hangar in the background. The firing butts seen on the left still stand and, being on a bomber station, will have stopped many bullets from Browning .303 machine guns. This type superceded the Vickers .303, beginning life before the First World War as a .300 weapon designed by John Browning, made by the Colt Patent Firearms Co. Post-war, Armstrong Whitworth acquired the manufacturing rights and in 1926 produced six .303 examples for the Air Ministry. By 1934 Colt had made the gun more suitable for air use, and the Air Ministry had taken up the manufacturing rights. After much development work under Captain E. S. R. Adams of the Directorate of Armament Development's Gun Section, the RAF began receiving .303 Brownings in 1936. These British Brownings could fire 1,150 rounds a minute and most were manufactured at home by BSA and Vickers-Armstrong Ltd, production peaking at 2,000 a week in 1941. Apart from the unarmed Mosquito, all of Bomber Command's British-designed aircraft were armed in all or part with .303 Brownings, although towards the war's end some were replaced by the heavier .5-inch gun.

Although the Army now occupy North Luffenham, it was nice to be able to picture this retired McDonnell Phantom sitting at the eastern end of the main runway maintaining a tenuous link with the past. One of the most significant combat aircraft of the 1960s, the RAF and Royal Navy operated Rolls-Royce-powered versions (the F4-M and F4-K respectively), with guns and air-to-air missiles.

When re-opened in March 1944, the station was used by No. 21 Heavy Glider Conversion Unit with Whitleys and Horsas. This HGCU began to receive Albemarles to replace the Whitleys shortly before moving out in September that year. North Luffenham then went back to bomber crew training with the arrival of No. 1653 Heavy Conversion Unit from Chedburgh equipped largely with Stirlings but gradually took on Lancasters and other types. The HCU stayed until October 1945 and, after a period of care and maintenance, No. 21 HGCU returned equipped mainly with Dakotas and Halifax tugs and Horsa and Hamilcar gliders. However, the day of the glider was over so that early in 1948 the unit was re-organised as No. 230 Operational Conversion Unit with a mission to train crews for Transport Command. New hardstandings were built in 1950 by Mowlem. The OCU moved on in 1951 and later the same year the RCAF established three Sabre-equipped fighter squadrons at North Luffenham under a NATO directive. These eventually moved on to the Continent and in April 1954 the RAF took over the station for operational training,

Nos. 228 and 238 OCUs being the principal residents until the airfield was selected for another mission in June 1958. It became a headquarters location for one of the Thor missile wings the RAF established during the years 1959 to 1963. Also, from late 1963 for the next decade, North Luffenham was home to a succession of ground signals organisations that were nominally grouped under Support Command. The last of these units was relocated in 1997, the RAF station closing late that year. However, in 1998 the Royal Anglian Regiment moved to North Luffenham from Oakington, presumably for its superior facilities.

During the Second World War Bomber Command lost a total of 60 bombers missing or crashed in the UK on operational flights from North Luffenham. Fifty-six of these were Hampdens, three Manchesters and one a Wellington.

North Luffenham pictured since the RAF quit the base. The old Thor launch pads can be seen on the far side — somewhat incongruous stablemates with the golf course in the foreground!

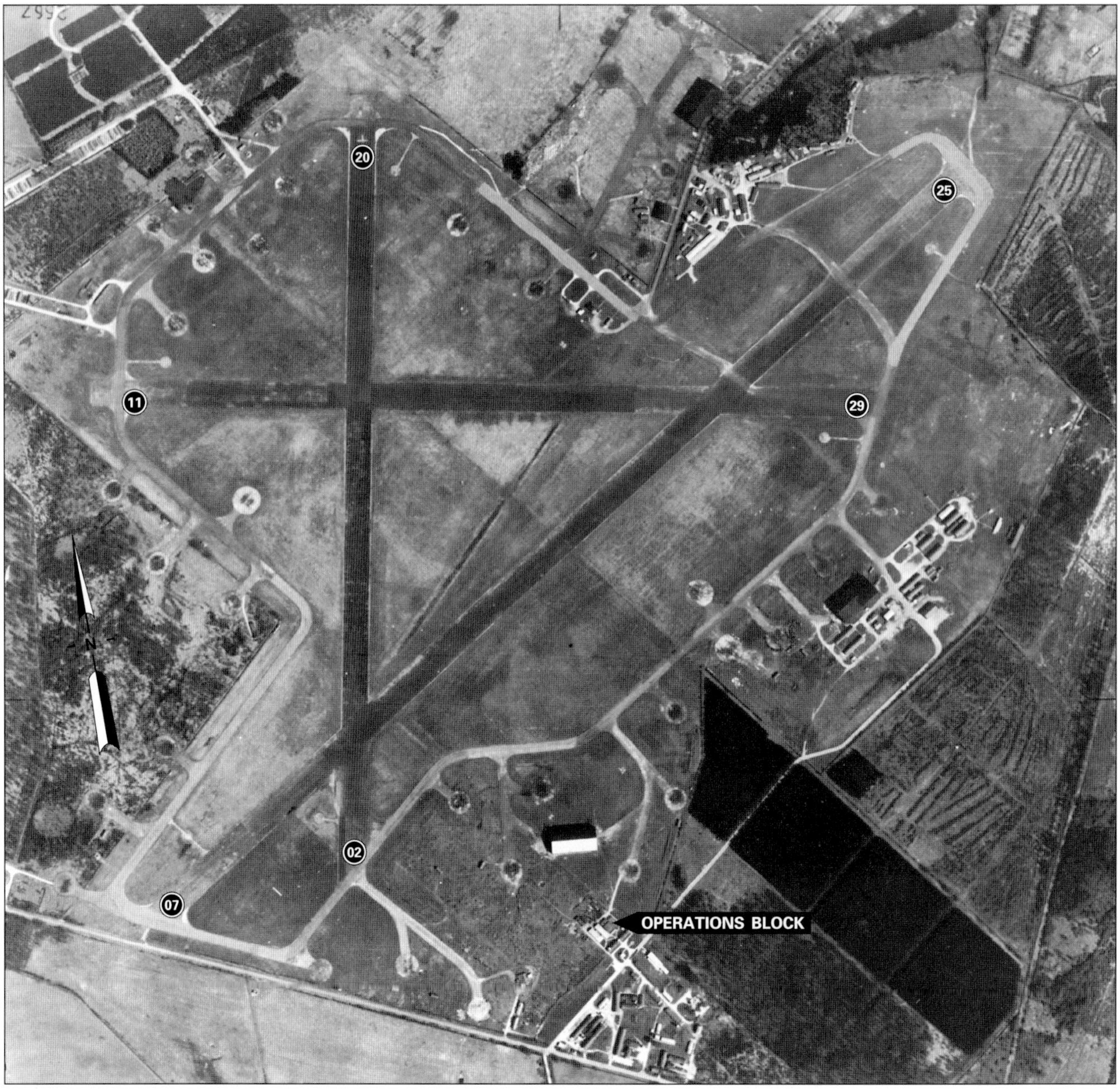

SKELLINGTHORPE

Once a vital cornerstone in Bomber Command's wartime inventory . . . now expunged from the face of the earth. Skellingthorpe has now been swallowed up by the westwood expansion of Lincoln's suburbia.

Of the many bomber airfields that ringed the city of Lincoln, the nearest was Skellingthorpe being only two miles south-west of the outskirts, its original purpose being the need to provide a satellite airfield for Waddington. The site was an area of pasture known as Black Moor, 2½ miles south of the village of Skellingthorpe amongst several large woods and bordering the B1190. Hard runways were laid during 1941, the main 07-25 at 1,650 yards long and the subsidiaries 02-20 and 11-29 both 1,400 yards. Hardstandings were all pan type and 36 in number. The main technical site with a T2 hangar was near Stone's Place fish pond on the north side of the field to the west side of runway head 25. A second T2 with a technical sub-site was south-east between runway heads 02 and 29, and later a B1 was erected further south, not far from runway head 02.

In November 1941, No. 50 Squadron's Hampdens transferred from Swinderby to 'Skelly', its popular abbreviation among RAF personnel. No. 455 RAAF Squadron also removed its Hampdens from Swinderby to Skellingthorpe so that hard runways could be put down, although most of its personnel

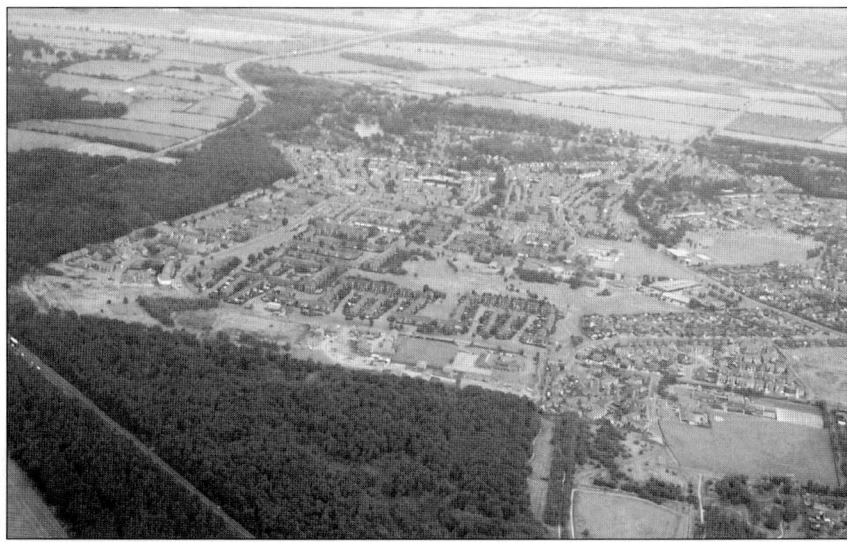

This oblique was taken looking north from the southern perimeter.

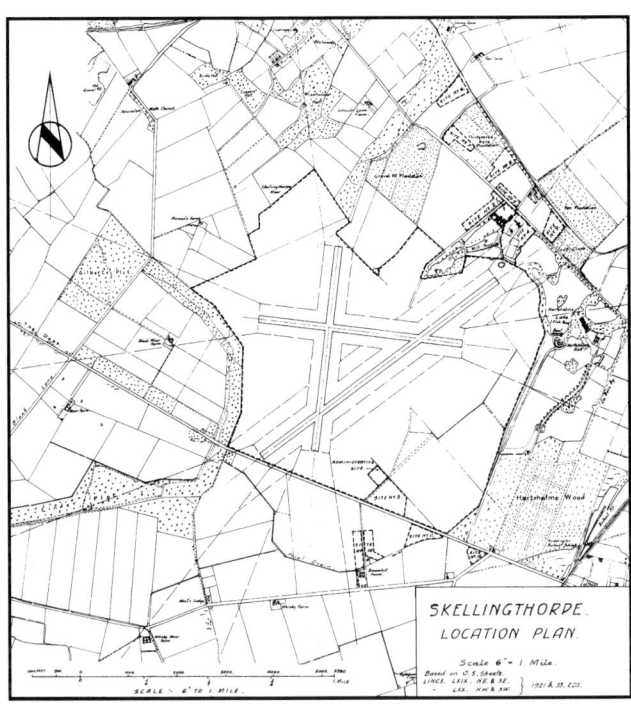

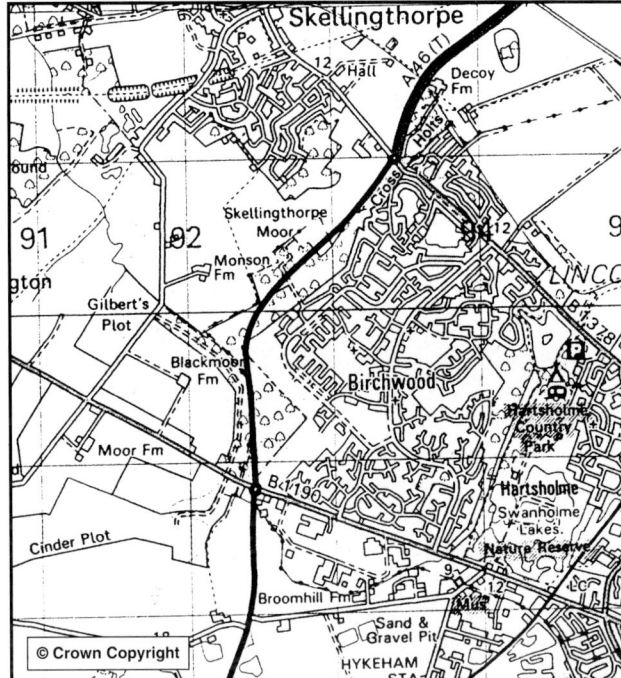

© Crown Copyright

The plans show just how the airfield has been lost beneath the encroaching development of the Birchwood estate.

remained billeted at Swinderby owing to insufficient accommodation at the new station. No. 455 moved out to Wigsley in February 1942.

In April 1942, No. 50 commenced conversion to the Manchester but then its troubles began. During two months only some 120 sorties were flown with the type and seven lost before it was replaced by Lancasters. Nevertheless, the only Victoria Cross gained by a Manchester crewman went to a No. 50 Squadron pilot flying from Skellingthorpe. On the night of May 30/31, 1942, during the famous 1,000 bomber raid on Cologne, Flying Officer Leslie Manser's aircraft was repeatedly damaged by anti-aircraft fire. Despite a critical situation, Manser was determined to bring the Manchester and crew home but having regained friendly airspace the aircraft became untenable. After having given his crew time to parachute to safety, Manser gave his life in the crash which followed.

To convert to Lancasters and allow the main runway to be extended, the squadron returned to Swinderby in June 1942. Some 350 yards were added to the north-east end of 07-25, the work being completed by September. The station was developed in two areas: two communal, two WAAF, five domestic and sick quarters along the Boultham road to the north, while on the south side along the B1190 were a communal, two domestic and a second sick quarters site dispersed in fields and woodland. Maximum accommodation was given as 1,803 males and 295 females. Bomb stores lay to the north-west, between runway heads 11 and 20, in woodland on Skellingthorpe Moor.

No. 50 Squadron returned in October 1942 and for a year was the sole operational unit at the station. With sufficient accommodation and facilities to take a second squadron, in November 1943 No. 61 arrived from Syerston which was to be used for operational training. There were then 30 to 36 Lancasters regularly based at Skellingthorpe but, as airspace in the Lincoln area was becoming heavily congested, to lessen the risk of collisions and ease control, No. 61 was moved to Coningsby at the beginning of February 1944. It returned in April when Coningsby became the headquarters of No. 5 Group's special duties operations.

Lancaster ND991 VN-P on its pan hardstanding near the north-east corner of the airfield near the 72,000-gallon fuel store. The bombs in the foreground are 500lb HE.

Comparisons today at Skelly are meaningless. Nevertheless, by carefully overlaying the plans, the exact view can be matched today on Clematis Approach looking south-east towards the Birchwood Leisure Centre.

257

One hundred up! By this date — June 30, 1944 — 'N'-Nuts had become 'N'-Nan following the phonetic code change in January 1943. This veteran Lancaster ED860 of No. 61 Squadron pictured with her crew went on to fly 130 sorties before retirement. The windowless Operations Block can be seen in the background.

On May 19, 1944, the deaths of two airmen and substantial damage to a hangar resulted from the detonation of three 1,000lb bombs dislodged from a tractor-towed bomb trolley train. A total of 208 bombers failed to return or were lost in UK crashes during the operations flown from Skellingthorpe: 15 Hampdens, six Manchesters and 187 Lancasters.

Post-war, Nos. 50 and 61 Squadrons moved to Sturgate in June 1945 and No. 619 Squadron arrived at 'Skelly' the same month only to be disbanded in July. Then came No. 463 Squadron and this too was disbanded late in September marking the end of resident flying units although the runways continued to have occasional use by aircraft from other stations, notably Swinderby.

A proposal in 1948 to convert the airfield into a civil airport came to nothing and the main occupant until the early 'fifties was No. 58 Maintenance Unit using hangars for storage. During the following decade the runways and other concrete was broken up for hard core and the land mostly used for farming. In the 1970s-80s, close proximity to Lincoln brought the site to the attention of developers resulting in the gradual encroachment of housing estates on the north-eastern side so that few visible traces of the airfield remain at the end of the century. There is a memorial to Nos. 50 and 61 Squadrons in the nearby Birchwood Community Centre.

This is the same view on Abingdon Avenue in 2001 with the Editor standing in for the long-forgotten crew. The ops block stood on the left between Abingdon and Woodvale Avenues. *Below left:* Odd remnants can still be spotted dotted midst the new housing. Hugh Leadbetter of Fen Plantation Farm points out an old concrete culvert now built into a small brook and *(centre)* a building on the WAAF dispersed site near his farm. *Below right:* Thankfully, a memorial has been erected to remind the residents of the historic past of the hallowed ground on which they live.

Labels on image: 11, 16, 23, 29, 05, 34, REINSTATED ROAD, SURVIVING LOOPS

SPILSBY

Although very little is left of Spilsby on the ground, just like the ghostly image of long forgotten First World War trenches in Belgium and France, from the air the outline of the airfield can be retraced in the ploughed fields.

Three miles east of Spilsby town, and taking in much of the parish of Monksthorpe, this was a Class A standard airfield built during 1942-43. Construction contracts issued allowed £62,000 for preparing the site, £260,000 for runways, £60,000 for aircraft dispersals and £175,000 for buildings. Several minor roads had to be closed including that between Monkthorpe and Gunby. The runways were 05-23, 11-29 and 16-34 of which the first two were 1,400 yards long and the 16-34 at 1,430 yards. The 05-23 and 11-29 were both later extended to 2,000 yards although 11-29 was, for some unrecorded reason, restricted to 1,400 yards use, one source stating that it was extended due to an Air Ministry clerical error! Hardstandings were 17 pans and 19 loops, but two of the pans were lost through later ground work. There were three T2 hangars, one on the technical site between runway heads 05 and 11, another south-west between runway heads 29 and 34 and a third east of runway head 16. The bomb store was off the north side between runway heads 16 and 23. The camp, to the south-west of the airfield around Monkthorpe village and the area known as Sand Hills, consisted of two communal, two WAAF, six domestic and a sick quarters site with maximum accommodation for 2,112 males and 222 females.

The first occupant of the station was No. 207 Squadron, removed from Langar in October 1943 to make way for USAAF occupation. The squadron had Spilsby to itself for a year when it was joined by another Lancaster squadron, No. 44, which had to vacate Dunholme Lodge when that airfield was transferred to No. 1 Group. The two squadrons were not disturbed from their base until after

Fuelling a Lancaster on one of the loop dispersals at Spilsby in February 1945. This aircraft is LM625 *Sky Floosie* of No. 44 Squadron coded KM-H. Full tanks held 2,154 Imperial gallons and, depending on the altitude flown, the mixture and boost settings and the RPM, the Lanc would burn between 125 and 500 gallons per hour.

victory in Europe. Their combined operational loss in raids flown from this station was 85 Lancasters. In July, No. 44, selected to form part of Tiger Force to be sent to the Far East, exchanging places with No. 75 Squadron at Mepal, the New Zealand-manned unit disbanding at Spilsby in October that year. The same month No. 207 was

Smile boys! Airmen Ted Peek, left, Ron White with Lloyd Hahn in the turret of a No. 207 Squadron Lancaster at Spilsby in the late summer of 1944. The hardstanding was the most northerly of the loop dispersals on the east side of the airfield.

The hedges remain as seen in the wartime photograph above but the northernmost hardstanding has been lifted. A view from the remains of the perimeter track looking south-east.

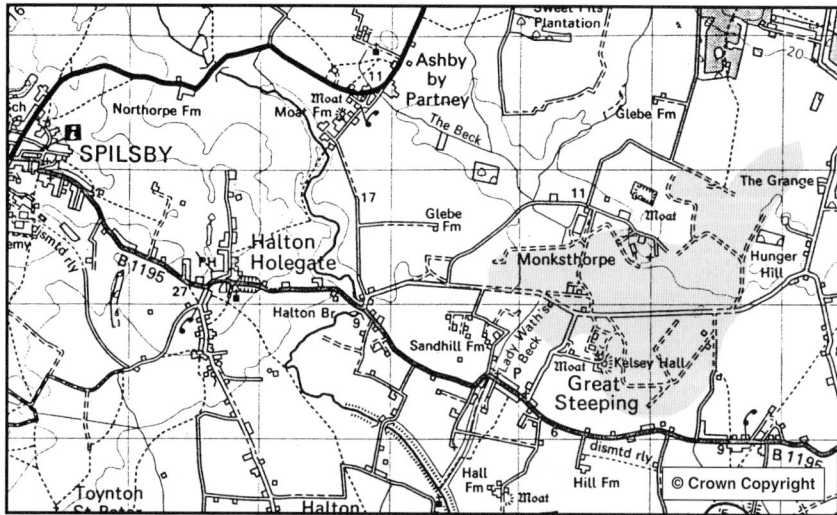

Compared with the Spilsby of May 1946 (right) very little remains on the present-day Ordnance Survey map so we have shaded in the area it once occupied.

moved to Methwold whereupon Spilsby closed for flying.

An armament practice school was installed at the station in November which remained for a year, after which the base was relegated to care and maintenance status. The caretaker party was withdrawn in 1947 and the airfield left unattended but it remained in a reasonably complete state until the early 'fifties. The Cold War had brought a considerable number of USAF personnel to the UK and Spilsby was one of the stations held ready for possible reception of flying units should the Cold War intensify. The Americans carried out some refurbishment and also modified the control tower but the USAF occupation was brief and they were gone by the end of the 'fifties. No further military use was made of the airfield and most of the concrete was removed over the following two decades apart from lengths used for reinstating minor roads. A memorial to No. 207 Squadron stands on the base of the Fire Tender shed.

STRUBBY

Strubby was a late Class A standard airfield lying some eight miles south-east of Louth directly south of the village of Strubby and within the area bounded by the A157, A1104 and B1373 roads. Three minor roads connecting Strubby to Beesby and Claythorpe were closed soon after construction started in July 1942. The main contractor was William Moss & Sons Ltd who held the contract worth £810,000. Runway lengths were 09-27 at 2,033 yards, 03-21 at 1,470 yards and 15-33 at 1,576 yards. The 36 hardstandings were all loop type and hangarage two type T2s on the technical site near Woodthorpe House, and a B1 on the east side between runway heads 27 and 33. The bomb store was beyond the north side, east of runway head 15 and west of Strubby village. Most domestic sites were dispersed in Woodthorpe parish allowing accommodation for 1,999 males and 402 females.

January 1945 was hard on ground crews, seen here working on *Dumbo* on dispersal at Strubby. Lanc PG-D (LM630) was serving with 'A' Flight of No. 619 Squadron when this photo was taken.

Although intended as a sub-station for East Kirkby in No. 5 Group, being only four miles from the coast, the airfield was first assigned to Coastal Command which brought in No. 280 Squadron and its Warwicks for air-sea rescue duties early in May 1944. They were joined two months later by two Beaufighter strike squadrons which carried out anti-shipping sorties. Coastal Command's tenure was short for in September all units moved out and the station was transferred to No. 5 Group Bomber Command.

A re-allocation of stations between Nos. 1 and 5 Groups brought No. 619 Squadron and its Lancasters to Strubby from Dunholme Lodge which had passed to No. 1 Group. A few days after its arrival, No. 619 raised a 'B' Flight for re-formed No. 227 Squadron and this soon moved to Balderton. Commencing operations from Strubby on October 8, No. 619 and was to have the station to itself

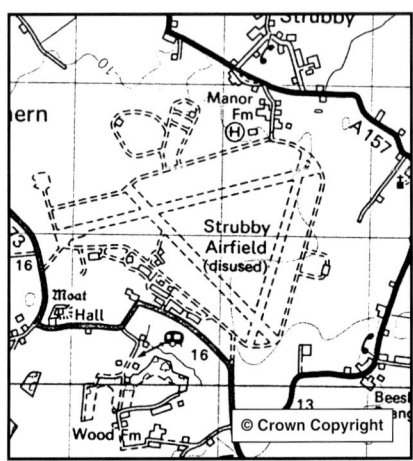

© Crown Copyright

Strubby then . . . Strubby now! The map extract dates from 1980; the aerial oblique from a pleasant day in the late summer of 2000. Time has eroded the runways leaving only a short stretch of the 03-21 intact.

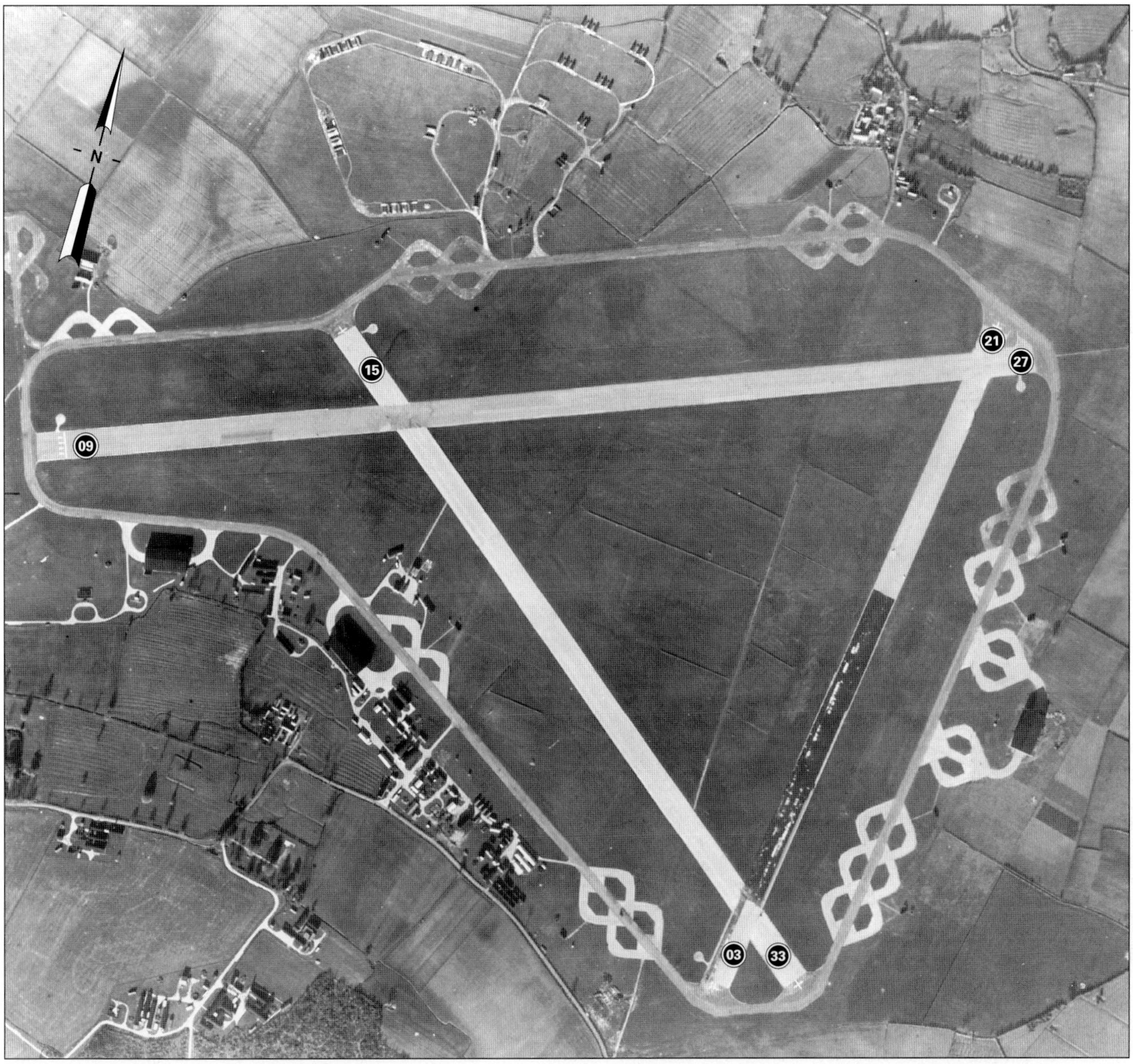

Strubby in good order but empty in November 1947, a photograph taken from 16,600 feet by a No. 82 Squadron aircraft.

for the next six months until No. 227 Squadron arrived from Balderton on April 5, 1945. The last sorties from the station took place on April 25/26, 1945 to lay mines off Norway. Sixty-five Lancasters failed to return or were destroyed in crashes during operations from Strubby, all from No. 619 Squadron.

Following VE-Day both units engaged in repatriating British POWs from the Continent. In June the Lancaster squadrons departed, No. 619 going to Skellingthorpe and No. 227 to Graveley. The station was then used for a number of ground units before being put on care and maintenance in September 1945. However, many unwanted Lancasters continued to be stored on its runways.

It was re-opened for flying in 1949 when it was designated a relief landing ground for training aircraft from Manby. In the years that followed some additional work was carried out to airfield facilities, most notably a modern 'glass house' on top of the existing wartime control tower. Strubby was finally closed for flying in 1972 and after a few years of stagnation was sold for agricultural use at auction in 1980. At the end of the 'nineties all three hangars remain but little of the runway concrete remains. A heliport for North Sea gas operations closed in 1999, the airfield now being owned by Anglian Water for a support depot.

The post-war addition to the control tower which has fallen into disrepair.

SWINDERBY

Panorama of the airfield from the top of the earth-covered battle headquarters beside Norton Lane, looking west-north-west with Lancaster R5689 VN-N on the perimeter track. A publicity photograph taken on August 28, 1942.

Eight miles from Lincoln and seven from Newark, on the east side of the A46 — the Roman Fosse Way — this was one of the last expansion plan airfields to be built. Like several other stations that were still incomplete on the outbreak of war, Swinderby received three of the economic curved-roof Type J hangars instead of the Type Cs. However, the barracks, administrative and much of the technical site buildings were built to the pre-war specification and grouped together on the A46 side of the station. A public road ran through camp on the east side. The main contractors were John Laing & Son Ltd whose first task was to clear and level the landing ground so that it could be re-seeded where necessary.

Swinderby was allocated to No. 1 Group and in late August 1940 Nos. 300 and 301 Squadrons arrived from the training station at Bramcote. These were the first Polish-manned bomber squadrons in the RAF and had only been formed a few weeks earlier. Equipped with Fairey Battles, they undertook their first operation on the night of September 14/15 when three aircraft from each squadron bombed barges in Boulogne harbour. The Battle was quite unsuited for night

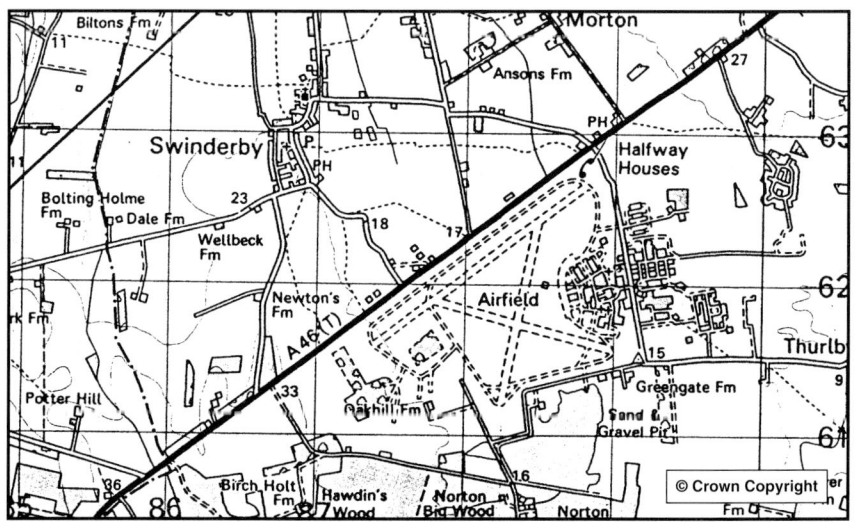

No mistaking this location at Swinderby for even after more than half a century the distinctive features of woodland, taxiways and runways are still clearly in evidence. Only the Lancasters are missing!

operations and in October No. 300 Squadron began to re-equip with Wellingtons. No. 301 followed suit the following month.

Twenty-four pan hardstandings and a concrete perimeter track were constructed during the winter of 1940-41, three spurs with three pans each being positioned on the far side of the A46. Consequently, traffic had to be halted when aircraft crossed the road to and from these dispersal points.

The two Polish squadrons continued to operate from Swinderby until July 1941 at which time the station had been passed to No. 5 Group in a general re-allocation of airfields in Bomber Command. No. 50 Squadron was moved in from Lindholme, resuming operations with its Hampdens on July 20 but personnel and equipment for No. 455 Squadron (an RAAF unit which was being re-established in the UK to fly Hampdens) were so long in arriving that its first raid — a single sortie — did not take place until August 29/30.

Swinderby had been waterlogged the previous winter and was badly rutted from taxying Wellingtons. As a result, the airfield had a priority for the installation of hard runways and in November 1941 the two resident squadrons took their Hampdens to Skellingthorpe so that construction could commence.

The main runway, 07-25, ran parallel with the A46, and was 1,450 yards long while the 11-29 and 02-20 runways were both 1,230 yards, terminating at the main to allow clearance over the A46. The runways were completed by April 1942 but then lengthened to comply with revised specifications, the main being extended to 2,000 yards across the Swinderby-Norton Disney road which was closed. There were also small extensions to 02-20 and 11-29 at the 20 and 29 ends making both 1,370 yards long, the former causing the closure of Norton Lane. At the time the runways were laid down, the number of pan hardstadings was increased to 36 and three Type T2 hangars were erected on the north side of the technical site during 1941- 42. Bomb stores were situated beyond the south side of the airfield between the heads of runways 02 and 29. Three additional domestic sites were dispersed in countryside towards Thurlby raising the total accommodation to 2,127 males and 349 females.

The airfield was ready for use by June 1942 so No. 50 Squadron returned to convert to Manchesters while runways were being put down at Skellingthorpe. This lasted until October when the squadron returned to its former base. A No. 50 Squadron Lancaster failing to return on the night of September 23/24, 1942 is

believed to be the last Bomber Command aircraft lost in operations from Swinderby, bringing the total wartime losses to 84. These were two Battles, 54 Hampdens, 12 Wellingtons, two Manchesters and seven Lancasters.

Swinderby was then selected to become an operational training station for No. 5 Group with the formation of No. 1660 Heavy Conversion Unit using Manchesters and Lancasters. However, a shortage of Lancasters in the autumn of 1943 caused most to be withdrawn from the HCU and Stirlings were employed instead until the position improved. Some form of training activity was henceforth to be Swinderby's lot. No. 1660 HCU came under the control of No. 7 Training Group in November 1944 and remained for two more years before moving to Lindholme. It was replaced at Swinderby by No. 17 OTU — initially with Wellingtons — later redesignated No. 201 Advanced Flying School being joined by No. 204 AFS using Mosquitos. In following years, further changes of unit and equipment occurred with Swinderby remaining a flying training establishment until March 1964. During the 'fifties there was ongoing construction work at the station with the addition of a new apron while improvements were made to the taxiways and several buildings including the control tower.

August 1945. Despite the rogue cloud, many Lancasters can still be seen dispersed around the airfield.

Summer 1941. A bomb-train on the perimeter track near the control tower. The Wellington belongs to No. 301 Squadron.

In 1964 Swinderby embraced a new role, that of recruit training. A flying unit was added to the ground school in 1979 for the express purpose of prospective pilot assessment. For over 30 years the station was the RAF's major establishment for recruit assessment and basic training, the airfield remaining open for flying visitors but this activity ceased in the early 'nineties. The 629 acres were put up for sale in 1995 with permission to develop the site for new homes and a business park.

The sad face of a derelict airfield. Thousands of recruits will have passed through Swinderby . . . but now it is just another of the RAF's historic airfields declared 'surplus to requirements'. The technical site is currently used for light industry and storage and the proposed housing developments are limited to the former domestic sites to the east of the airfield. However, the rest of the station is owned by RMC Butterley Aggregates which will eventually excavate the airfield for gravel.

A new section of perimeter track was built in 1942 to take taxiing aircraft further away from the technical site and hangars.

Pedal power! Airmen on the ubiquitous station mounts, cycle to their dispersal — a familiar sight on Bomber Command airfields.

SYERSTON

Syerston was an expansion scheme airfield located ten miles north-east of Nottingham between the A46 Nottingham-Newark road and the River Trent. Work commenced in 1938 but the station was not completed until late in 1940. It was to the standard specification with the camp of permanent building grouped close to the A46. Two Type J hangars provided aircraft repair and maintenance cover. At a later date three T2 and a B1 hangar were erected on the site.

Allocated to No. 1 Group, the station was first occupied in December 1940 by Nos. 304 and 305 Squadrons, manned largely by Poles, which had transferred from Bramcote where both units had been formed in August. Working up on Wellingtons, both squadrons made their first operation from Syerston on the night of April 25/26, 1941, attacking oil storage at Rotterdam. In July, Syerston was transferred to No. 5 Group and Lindholme to No. 1 Group, the Polish squadrons departing for the latter and No. 408 Squadron, an RCAF unit, arriving from the former. Like the Poles when they first arrived at Syerston, the Canadian squadron had yet to become operational. Its first raid came on August 11/12 when, also like the Poles, Rotterdam docks were again the target. In December that year, No. 408 and its Hampdens moved to Balderton so hard runways could be laid at Syerston which, despite extensive under-draining, always tended to have a high water table after prolonged rain.

The three intersecting runways laid down were the main 07-25 at 1,950 yards long and 12-30 and 16-34, both at 1,400 yards. The surrounding perimeter track provided access to 36 pan type hardstandings. At the same time, additional domestic sites were built on land to the north-east, chiefly in Flintham Park, providing accommodation for 1,782 males and 411 females. The station was ready for re-occupation by flying units in April 1942. At sometime during the following eighteen months, three more T2 hangars were erected for glider storage.

Fifty-six years later the Officers' Mess, now partly derelict and vandalised, still carries vestiges of its wartime camouflage. Our photographer, Tim Wingham, stands in for the famous airman on the same spot . . . but for how long will the historic building remain?

Nice photo of Wing Commander Guy Gibson and fellow members of No. 106 Squadron outside the Officers' Mess at Syerston on January 18, 1943.

No. 61 Squadron with Manchesters and Lancasters arrived in May from Woolfox Lodge, joined in September by No. 106 Squadron from Coningsby, both units remaining until November 1943. During their participation in Bomber Command main force operations, Syerston aircrew were awarded many decorations for their conduct. This included a VC to Flight Lieutenant William Reid who, despite wounds from two night fighter attacks, pressed on to attack the target at Düsseldorf and brought his aircraft safely home. This occurred on the night of November 3/4, 1943 shortly before No. 61 Squadron, moved to Skellingthorpe and No. 106 to Metheringham. The move gave both squadrons an airfield to themselves and allowed expansion to three full flights.

Syerston was then turned over to operational training with No. 1668 Heavy Conversion Unit providing Lancaster experience for new crews. A redesignation in January 1944 made this organisation No. 5 Group Lancaster Finishing School which existed until the end of March 1945. During this period, other

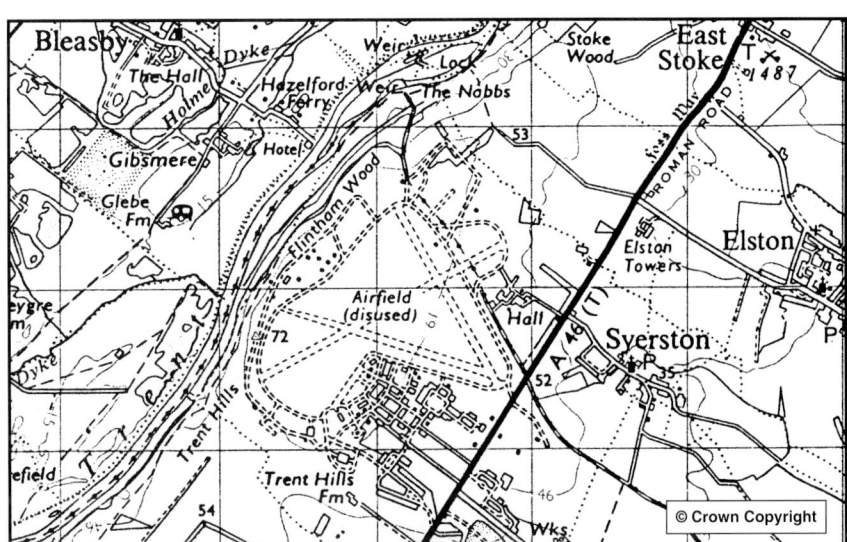

RIVER TRENT

A46

April 18, 1944 found Syerston under the lens of an American photo-reconnaissance aircraft from the 7th Photo Group — not that there was any intention of turning the airfield over to the Eighth Air Force.

269

Above and opposite: **Syerston is now the home of the Air Cadet Gliding School.**

specialist training flights took place. Then on April 22, No. 49 Squadron's Lancasters left austere Fulbeck for permanent lodgings at Syerston, flying their only and last raid of the war from the station — the attack on Hitler's retreat at Obersalzberg on April 25. Altogether, 147 aircraft failed to return or were lost in UK crashes during operations flown from Syerston: five Hampdens, four Manchesters, 14 Wellingtons and 124 Lancasters.

Post-war No. 49 Squadron's residence at Syerston was terminated in October 1945 when it was moved south to Mepal. Syerston was then turned over to Transport Command which installed a succession of training

Below: **The airfield photographed looking north-west in September 2000.**

units. However, in May 1946, No. 504 (County of Nottingham) Squadron, Auxilliary Air Force, re-formed at Syerston to fly Mosquitos and was present for eleven months. The station then passed to Flying Training Command in November 1947 which held sway until 1971 with basic instructional units. From 1971 Syerston was on care and maintenance with its accommodation and flying field used by service units, notably in connection with gliding activities. Most of the buildings were demolished in 1997 save for the control tower, two hangars and one H-Block used today by the Central Gliding School for the Air Training Corps.

WADDINGTON

Hampdens of No. 44 Squadron being armed with mines on the north-east corner of the airfield on November 18, 1941. 'O'-Orange (AE260) later served with No. 420 Squadron (RCAF) and went missing on the night of June 2/3, 1942 mining off Lorient.

One of the oldest military airfields in Lincolnshire, Waddington came into use for flying units of the Royal Flying Corps back in 1916. In that year a grazing area some five miles due south of Lincoln, and to the east of Waddington village and south of the road to Potter Hanworth, was prepared for use by training squadrons under No. 27 Training Wing which was succeeded by No. 48 Training Depot Station in July 1918. A variety of aircraft types were used until the Armistice reduced activity. There were two camp areas with a number of wooden buildings including Belfast truss aeroplane sheds, seven on the main site and three on the second site.

Closed in 1919, the station was in use again for flying from October 1926 when an RAF reserve unit, No. 503 Squadron, was formed to fly Fairey Fawn light bombers, later changing to Hyderabads. Expansion of the RAF saw extensive building with permanent barracks and substantial administrative and technical site development, including five Type C hangars. The airfield was then bounded by Ermine Street in the west, the B1178 to the south and the A15 to the east. Three of the First World War hangars still remained on the west side of the airfield but were not used for aircraft.

On completion of this work Waddington came under Bomber Command and two squadrons were re-formed there in 1937. In May Nos. 50 and 110 Squadrons were brought into existence equipped with Hinds and the following month part of No. 110's complement were used to re-form No. 88 Squadron, also to fly Hinds. That same month a fourth Hind-equipped squadron arrived from Wyton: No. 44. At the time, No. 503 Squadron was an Auxiliary Air Force unit with part-time personnel flying Harts; thus for a few weeks five squadrons occupied Waddington although Nos. 50 and 88 still had some way to go to reach full strength. No. 88, however, was moved out to Boscombe Down in July.

In December 1937 No. 44 received Blenheims and No. 110 likewise the following month. No. 503 received some of the cast-off Hinds but in October 1938 it was moved to Doncaster to be reincarnated as a fighter squadron under a different designation. No. 5 Group was destined to be an all-Hampden formation and in December 1938 No. 50 Squadron traded its Hinds for Hampdens with No. 44 giving up the Blenheims for the Handley Page 'pan handle' bomber two

months later. No. 110 Squadron was to retain its Blenheims and, when Wattisham was ready to receive it in May 1939, the squadron moved south to No. 2 Group.

Unfortunately security restrictions precluded a comparison of the Hampden shot which in any case would have been somewhat meaningless bearing in mind the developments that have occurred at what is one of the RAF's front-line stations. *Above:* We were allowed to match up this shot of the central heating plant with the dispersals of No. 61 Squadron visible beyond although today from this vantage point the airfield is masked by young trees *(below)*. It is important to remember that Bomber Command lost more aircraft operating out of Waddington than from any other airfield.

Waddington Hampdens were in action from the first day of the war, nine setting out to reconnoitre the Heligoland area for enemy naval activity, sea searches being the main occupation in the months that followed. After the fall of France, the remnants of No. 142 Squadron were given sanctuary at Waddington for a few weeks before moving to the No. 1 Group station at Binbrook in July. The same month No. 50 Squadron was moved to the recently opened Hatfield Woodhouse (later re-named Lindholme), but No. 44 Squadron's association with Waddington was to continue until May 1943 when the airfield was closed to permit the construction of runways.

Waddington — the premier No. 5 Group station — was to receive the first Avro Manchester heavy bombers and to take them into battle, No. 207 Squadron being re-formed at Waddington specially for the task in November 1940. The first operational use of the Manchester took place on the night of February 24/25, 1941 when six aircraft were detailed to attack the docks at Brest. The following day a nucleus from No. 207 Squadron became the third reformation of No. 97 Squadron. The fledgling unit took a few Manchesters to Coningsby to expand in

March 1941 while No. 207 struggled on with the type. Waddington received attention from the Luftwaffe on a number of occasions, usually with little harm, but on May 9, 1941 bombing took the lives of 11 station personnel.

In November 1941, No. 207 moved to the new station at Bottesford and in December No. 420 Squadron, an RCAF unit, was formed at Waddington to fly Hampdens. Later the same month No. 44 Squadron became the first to receive the new Lancaster, which was taken into action for the first time on March 10/11, 1942 when two No. 44 Squadron aircraft attacked Essen. In April the Lancaster made its grand entry into the bombing war when No. 44 was one of elements from two squadrons attempting to destroy the MAN diesel works at Augsburg in a rare daylight raid. Squadron Leader John Nettleton, who led the formation of six, received the Victoria Cross for his conduct that day.

The other Waddington squadron, No. 420, flying its first raid on the night of January 21/22, 1942, continued to operate Hampdens, one of the last units in Bomber Command to do so. In August the same year it was transferred to No. 4 Group at Skipton-on Swale

preparatory to joining the planned all-Canadian group. No. 420 was replaced by No. 9 Squadron from No. 3 Group at Honington, a station which was to be taken over by the USAAF. On its arrival in August, conversion to Lancasters commenced. Nos. 9 and 44 Squadrons continued to mount raids from Waddington until May 1943 when hard runways were due to be laid by George Wimpey & Co. Ltd. In April No. 9 Squadron moved to Bardney and No. 44 to Dunholme Lodge in May.

The three concrete runway lengths were main 03-21 at 2,000 yards and the subsidiaries, 07-25 and 17-35, both 1,400 yards. The main runway crossed the B1178 and was closed between Waddington and the A15 (see Ordnance Survey map overleaf). At least 33 pan hardstandings had been laid round the airfield and linked to a perimeter track during 1940-41 (one was lost during runway work) and new pans were added to bring the total to 36. An improved bomb store was located east of runway head 21. More domestic accommodation raised the total available to cater for 2,085 males and 390 females. A.T. Rowley Ltd and Public Works Construction Ltd were involved in this work which was completed in October 1943.

Waddington on April 12, 1942 with Lancasters and Hampdens, many on the dispersals on the east side of the A15.

A view from high on the hangar line showing No. 463 Squadron's snow-bound aircraft in January 1945. The perimeter track in the foreground has been cleared as has runway 03-21 visible behind the Lancasters. Another shot which security considerations prevented us from taking a comparison.

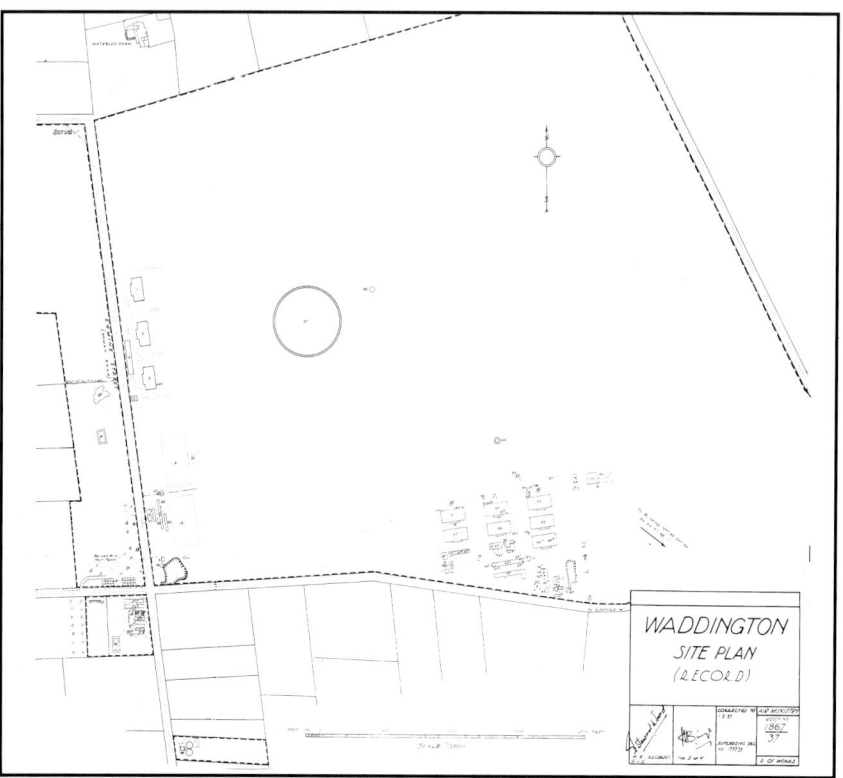

WADDINGTON
SITE PLAN
(RECORD)

Waddington then . . . Waddington now. The airfield has been expanded out of recognition from its early beginnings as a grass field. *Above:* This plan, which is a 1937 update of the original drawing of 1933, still shows the three First World War hangars on the western perimeter. *Right:* This map from 1997 shows how the three wartime runways have now been superceded by the extension of the main runway. *Above:* Due to the restrictions of two major 'A' roads on either side of the airfield, runway 03-21 was the only one which could be lengthened and an additional 1,000 yards were added at its southern end. The other two runways have now been converted into dispersals. Arrester gear is now fitted 610 metres from either end of the main runway, and pilots are warned to be mindful that a public road crosses the final approach to runway 21.

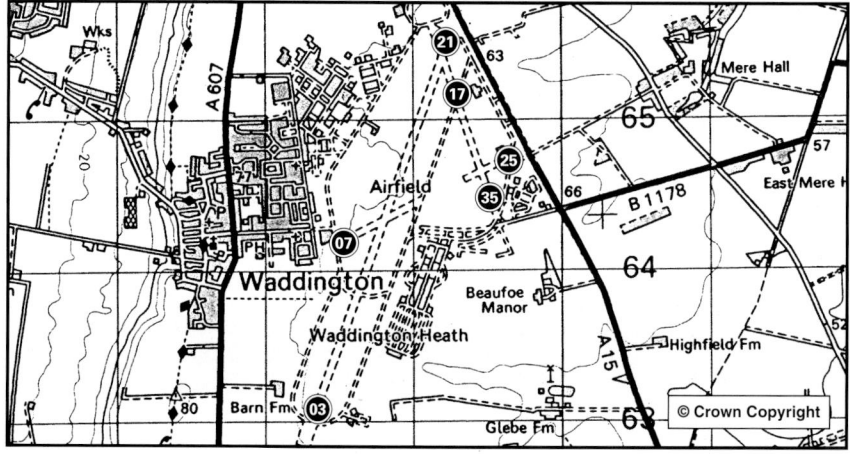

© Crown Copyright

274

ALPHA DISPERSAL

A15

BRAVO DISPERSAL

FOXTROT DISPERSAL

CHARLIE DISPERSAL

DELTA DISPERSAL

ECHO DISPERSAL

Waddington's new occupants were Australian. No. 463 brought its 30 Lancasters from Bottesford in November 1943 as that station was to be taken over by the USAAF and, soon after its arrival, the squadron's 'C' Flight was transformed into the new No. 467 Squadron. The squadron's strength of ten aircraft enabled it to become operational immediately and it participated in the raid on Berlin on November 23/24, just a few hours after it was formed. Both Nos. 463 and 467 Squadrons were based at Waddington until after VE-Day. In June 1945, No. 467 was moved to Metheringham and the following month No. 463 went to Skellingthorpe. One of the Waddington hangars was used by A. V. Roe during the last three years of the war to rebuild Lancasters with components received from their Bracebridge Heath reclamation works. Altogether, Waddington lost more bombers on operations than any other

Bomber Command station, a total of 345. Of these 103 were Hampdens, 15 were Manchesters and 227 Lancasters.

In the immediate post-war period, No. 5 Group moved its prestigious No. 617 Squadron into Waddington and, when that unit was sent out to India in January 1946, No. 61 Squadron was brought in from Sturgate to replace it. During the same year, Waddington collected Nos. 12 and 57 Squadrons, all three units eventually being equipped with Lincolns. Other squadrons with Lincolns were also based at Waddington during the next eight years, until the high summer of 1953 when all removed to Wittering. During the next two years the flying field was revamped to the standard required for very heavy aircraft. This entailed reconstructing the main runway to 3,000 by 67 yards with the additional length at the southern end. Taxiways, parking

Waddington looking north in September 2000.

apron and other standings also had to be rebuilt to specifications calling for stronger construction.

Having been brought up to the Class 1 standard required, Nos. 21 and 27 Squadrons arrived with Canberras, both to be disbanded in 1957 when Waddington became a Vulcan base. Still a premier Bomber Command base, Waddington hosted the first Vulcan squadron formed, the re-born No. 83; later another friend, a re-formed No. 44 Squadron arrived. No. 83 Squadron eventually moved elsewhere but over the next 15 years Waddington gathered three other Vulcan squadrons. In the 1980/90s, Nimrods and Sentry airborne early-warning aircraft were on station which is also used as a NATO base for the North Sea training areas.

WIGSLEY

Disused Wigsley in April 1947. Like so many bomber airfields, runway lengths had had to be increased to cope with heavier aircraft, in this case by crossing the road to the east of the technical site.

A wartime airfield to Class A standard 7½ miles from the centre of Lincoln and directly south-west of the village of the same name, Wigsley was built in 1941-42, the main contractor being Sir Robert McAlpine & Sons Ltd. Three concrete runways were 09-27, 03-21 and 14-32 which were increased in length in the later stages of construction, 09-27 and 14-32 being extended across the Wigsley-Besthorpe road which was closed. The new lengths were 09-27, 2,000 yards and 1,400 yards for both the others. There was also the usual encircling perimeter track with 36 hardstandings. Two T2 hangars were provided, one between runway heads 09 and 32 by the Spalford road and the other on the technical site which was on the south-east side of the airfield between runways 27 and 32. A B1 hangar was positioned to the north-east between runway heads 14 and 21. Bomb stores lay in the wood between and beyond runway heads 14 and 21 and the camp sites were dispersed around and beyond Wigsley village and consisted of eight domestic, two communal and sick quarters. Maximum accommodation was put at 1,450 males and 351 females.

Early in February 1942, No. 455 Squadron, an RAAF unit, arrived from Swinderby, Wigsley's parent station. Its Hampdens were soon in action and, as with most Hampden squadrons, minelaying played a big part in their operational duties. However, their tenure at Wigsley was brief for in mid-April the squadron was withdrawn from Bomber Command and sent north to become a Coastal Command torpedo-bomber unit. Seven Hampdens failed to return from operations and four others were lost in crashes

while flying from Wigsley. This also brought an end to the airfield's short history as a operational squadron station in Bomber Command, as from thereon all the units based there were involved in some form of operational training.

No. 1654 Heavy Conversion Unit with a few Lancasters and Manchesters was installed in May 1942 to finish crews for No. 5 Group. Four Lancasters were lost on operations when the unit was called upon to assist in the bombing campaign. As with other

Lancaster HCUs, a severe shortage of aircraft saw them withdrawn and replaced by Stirlings for several months. Wigsley came under No. 7 Group when most bomber OTUs and HCUs were transferred to this revived formation in November 1944 but No. 1654 HCU continued in residence until September 1945 when it was moved to Woolfox Lodge. Bomber Command operations from Wigsley had cost 17 aircraft missing or crashed in the UK, 13 being Hampdens with four Lancasters.

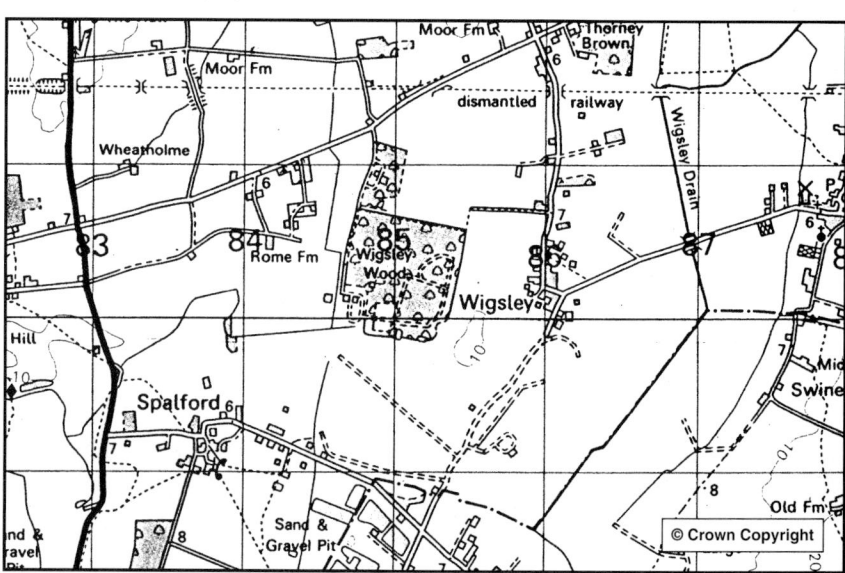

Although little remains to be seen of Wigsley on the ground, from the air the basic outline still remains. In this shot taken in September 2000 we are looking south-west along the main runway with the extension in the left foreground and Wigsley Woods on the right. The Wigsley road has been reinstated using part of the old perimeter track.

Wigsley received no further flying units although as Swinderby's satellite it was frequently used by training aircraft from that station and, with a small holding party, the airfield continued to function for 'circuits and bumps' until the summer of 1958 when the RAF finally withdrew. It was sold during the next decade and by the 1970s few buildings remained, agriculture having taken over.

Right: **Armourer Arthur Hart, of the Royal Australian Air Force, driving a Fordson tractor converted into a semi-track layer in the Wigsley bomb-dump in early 1942.**
Below: **The brickwork and revetments of the bomb-store in Wigsley Wood can still be seen but are slowly being submerged in the undergrowth.**

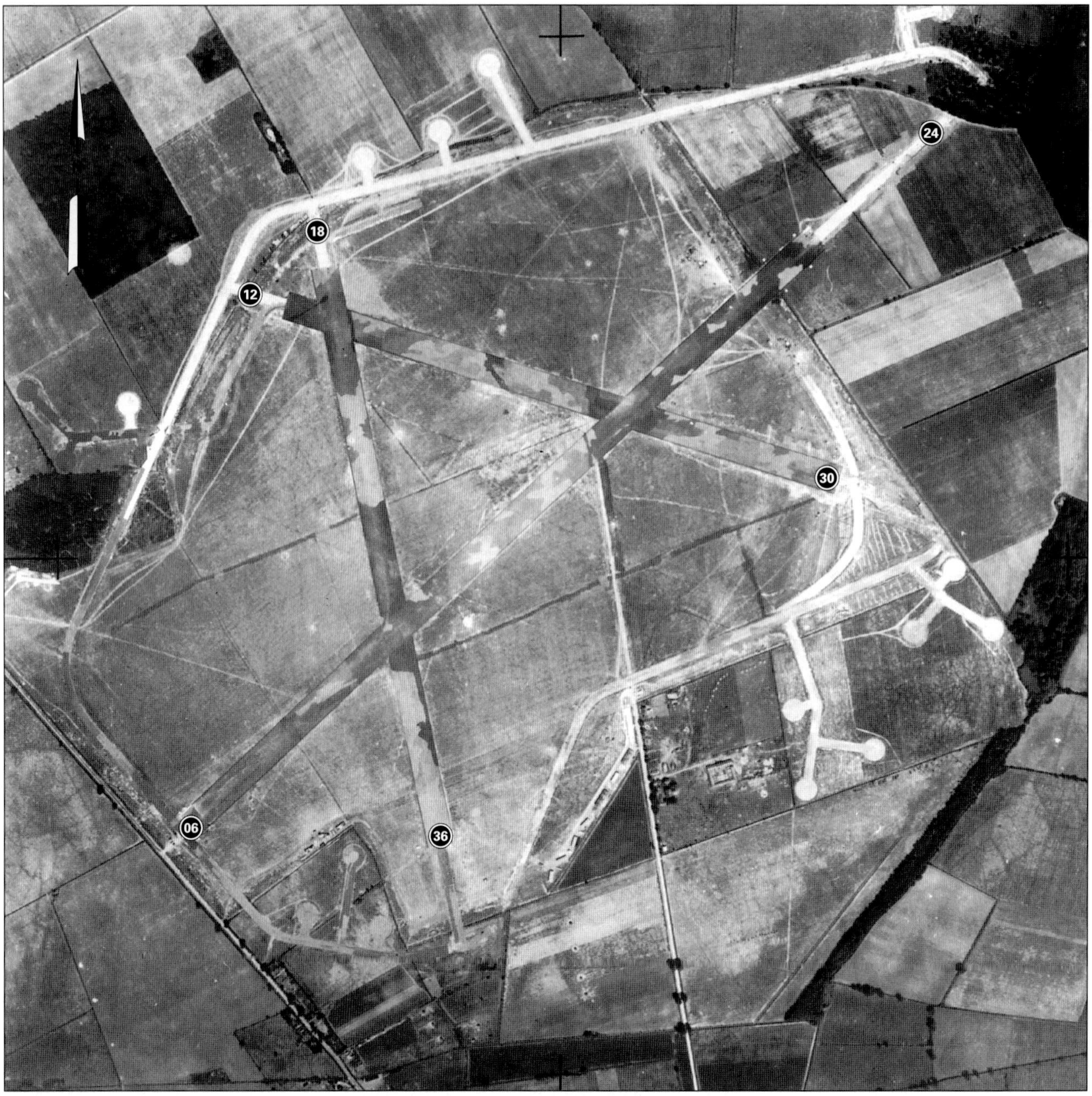

WOODHALL SPA

Woodhall Spa under construction on June 16, 1941. The runway extensions are in hand which entailed abandoning parts of the perimeter track which had already been built. So far only 19 of the pan hardstandings have been laid down.

This airfield was built to Class A standard and was located a mile south of Woodhall Spa village between the B1192 Woodhall Spa to Tattershall Thorpe road and the LNER Boston to Lincoln line. Built in 1941, the lengths of the three concrete runways were increased in the later stages of construction, the main 06-24 to 2,075 yards, the 18-36 to 1,410 yards and the 12-30 to 1,415 yards. A concrete perimeter track served the runway ends and 36 pan type hardstandings and one loop. The technical site was located towards Tattershall Thorpe between runway heads 30 and 36 with one Type T2 hangar and there was another T2 near the station main entrance on the south-west side with a B1 close by to the north. Bomb stores lay beyond the north perimeter in woodland between runway heads 18 and 24. The dispersed camp was south, mostly in Tattershall Thorpe parish, consisting of two communal, six domestic sites and sick quarters.

Woodhall Spa lies just three miles north of its parent station, Coningsby.

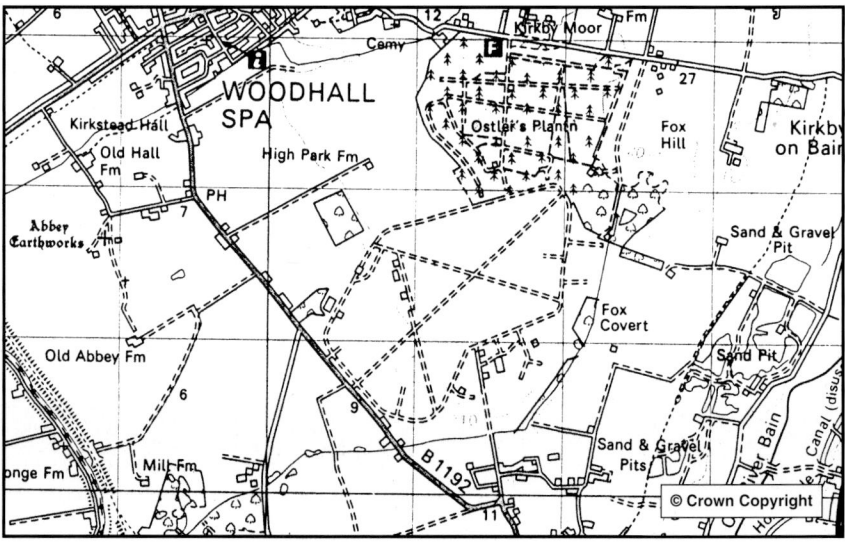

Lancaster from No. 617 Squadron on or near hardstandng 28 with a 12,000 pounder — three 4,000lb 'Cookies' bolted together — ready for loading. Another Lanc is landing on runway 36.

The eastern side of the airfield is slowly disappearing under sand and gravel extraction but fortunately this hardstanding on the south-western corner survives, albeit somewhat weedy.

Opened as a satellite station for Coningsby, Woodhall Spa was first used by No. 106 Squadron Hampdens when the parent station suffered winter waterlogging. No. 97 Squadron and its Lancasters removed from Coningsby to Woodhall Spa's paved surfaces in March 1942, the squadron having only just converted to Lancasters. It flew its maiden mission with the type from the new station on March 20/21. The squadron operated from Woodhall Spa until mid-April 1943 when it was selected to transfer to No. 8 Group and develop pathfinder techniques.

The day after departing for Bourn, a detachment from No. 97 was left behind to form No. 619 Squadron which flew its first raid on June 11/12. It stayed until January 1944 when it moved to Coningsby 3½ miles to the south. This was an exchange of stations with No. 617 Squadron which was pioneering the use of special weapons and tactics, notably the 12,000lb and 22,000lb bombs. The reason for the move is understood to be because No. 617 required more dispersals and Coningsby was only a two-squadron station.

In April 1944 another specialist squadron, No. 627 equipped with Mosquitos, arrived from Oakington and No. 8 Group to furnish No. 5 Group with its own pathfinders. It was acting as Master Bomber in one of No. 627's Mosquitos that Wing Commander Guy Gibson lost his life on the night of September 19/20, 1944 in a sortie from Woodhall Spa. Wing Commander J. B. Tait took over in July, the former commander of No. 617, Wing Commander Leonard Cheshire, the other famous Master Bomber, being awarded the Victoria Cross for his record of gallant actions and leadership.

The two élite squadrons operated from Woodhall Spa up until the end of hostilities. No. 617 was moved to Waddington in June and No. 627 was re-numbered No. 109 Squadron on October 1, 1945 and moved to Wickenby. Operational losses from Woodhall Spa amounted to 91 aircraft; 74 Lancasters and 17 Mosquitos.

Care and maintenance followed and this was soon reduced to a caretaker party as Woodhall Spa became one of several 'mothballed' airfields left to decay. However, revival came in 1960 when it was selected as a base for a Bloodhound ground-to-air missile site for the defence of the Lincolnshire's V-bomber stations. The first operating unit was No. 222 Squadron, replaced by No. 112 Squadron with a new mark of Bloodhound four years later. The missiles were removed in 1965 but the site was retained for exercises. The RAF continues to hold part of the airfield as a satellite to Coningsby, albeit for component servicing and storage. There is a No. 617 'Dambuster' Squadron memorial at Woodhall Spa.

The ultra heavy bomb store with the ultimate conventional weapon — the Grand Slam 'earthquake' bomb. Weighing 22,000lbs — 10 tons — the 26-foot-long bomb was fabricated from molybdenum steel by the English Steel Corporation at Sheffield. It needed a specially-modified Lancaster to carry it and, to minimise take-off weight, the wireless operator and mid-upper gunner were dispensed with. The Grand Slam's debut came on March 14, 1945, with an attack on the Bielefeld viaduct (see *After the Battle* No. 79). Altogether, 41 Grand Slams were dropped by No. 617, the only squadron equipped to deliver it.

Jim Shortland, Dambuster aficionado and squadron historian, inspects the same overgrown bomb-store in Ostler's Plantation on the northern perimeter.

Those who came through. VE-Day celebration outside the NAAFI on May 8, 1945, now the Tattershall Thorpe Camp Museum.

Cheers! The curator, Mike Hodgson, raises his glass . . . an original one found buried in rubbish behind the site!

WOOLFOX LODGE

This is November 1941 at Woolfox Lodge. At the time, No. 61 Squadron was trying to come to grips with the Manchester. This one (R5786 QR-D) was photographed on a pan dispersal in the south-east corner of the aerodrome.

The need for a satellite airfield for Cottesmore resulted in the selection of an area of large grazing meadows four miles away on the eastern side of the A1 trunk road five miles north of Stamford. The site lay mostly in the parish of Pickworth but due to the requisition of the nearby country mansion, Woolfox Lodge, for aircrew accommodation, this was the name by which the satellite became known.

No more than a landing ground when first used by the Hampdens of No. 14 OTU in 1940, it was soon developed into an independent airfield with the necessary fuel and bomb stores (in woodland to the north), two T2 hangars and, later, a B1 on the main technical site alongside the A1. A hard taxiway, 24 pan aircraft standings were added besides the three concrete runways. Construction was carried out by John Mowlem & Son Ltd, at a cost of £644,000 for the ground work. No. 5 Group then acquired Woolfox Lodge as a satellite for North Luffenham and brought in No. 61 Squadron from there in October 1941. The squadron had just converted to the Manchester and it spent a dis-

mal winter on the airfield endeavouring to master this beast which was to produce the highest loss per sortie ratio of any other type used by Bomber Command. While at Woolfox Lodge, No. 61 lost 12 Manchesters and another four in crashes out of some 180 sorties. Lancasters started to arrive as replacements in April 1942 but the squadron still had a dozen Manchesters when it moved to Syerston in May.

The airfield was then scheduled for extensions to the runways. While this work was being carried out, No. 1429 (Czech) Operational Training Flight with a few Wellingtons was brought in from East Wretham where it had previously served the Czech Wellington squadron. After two months the flight moved on to Church Broughton. Construction of the main runway was virtually parallel to the A1 on a bearing of 15-33, extended to 1,850 yards at the 15 end. The other runways, 04-22 and 09-27, were pushed out to 1,430 yards, with the 04 and 09 thresholds starting at the main runway. This was to allow enough distance from the A1 for aircraft on approach or departure to clear the road at a safe

height. Additional perimeter track was laid to take in the extensions. A total of 28 pan hardstandings remained after this work and eight loops were added. An additional technical site was built on the north side near runway head 15 and an extra camp area of dispersed sites constructed on the western side of the A1 among the woodland adjoining Exton Park. Maximum accommodation was then given as for 1,946 males and 192 females.

When it reopened, Woolfox Lodge was allocated to No. 3 Group which was hard-pressed for airfields in its own area. No. 1665 Heavy Conversion Unit from Waterbeach with its Stirlings arrived in June 1943 to prepare crews for the Group's squadrons. During 1943, two more T2 hangars were erected between runway heads 27 and 33 to house 32 Horsa gliders. At the end of January 1944, No. 1665 HCU moved west to Tilstock as the station was wanted for an operational squadron although there was some delay before this could be effected as the runway lighting system had to be overhauled. In March, No. 218 Squadron and its Stirlings were trans-

Although the concrete has been lifted, the drought pattern still shows the outline of the dispersal through the grass.

A frosty Woolfox Lodge in January 1947 when military vehicles were being stored on some of the hardstandings.

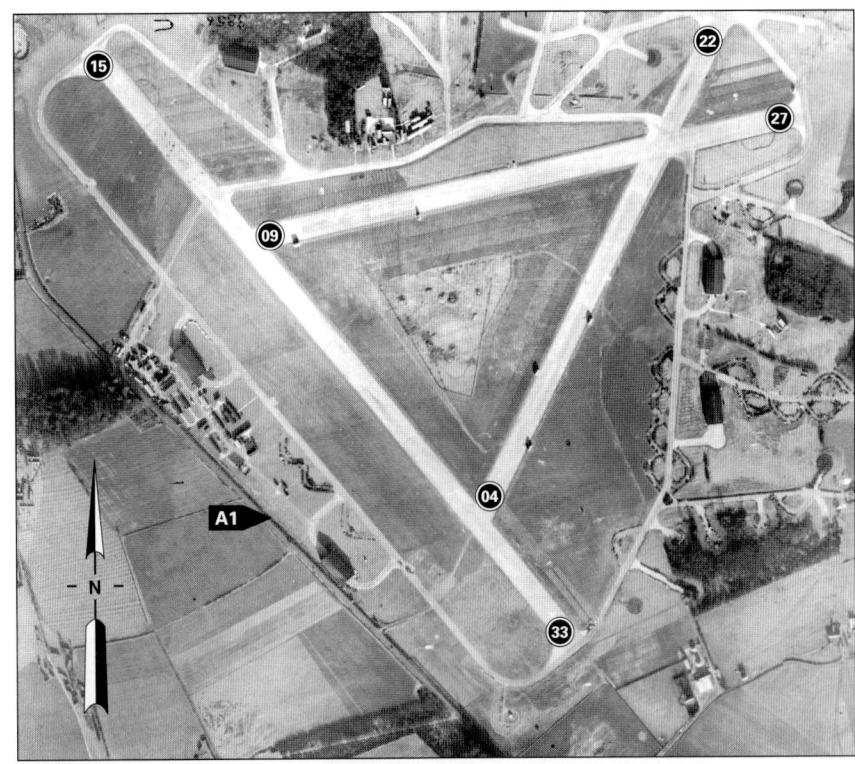

ferred in from Downham Market and conducted operations from Woolfox Lodge until soon after converting to Lancasters in late July, the squadron carrying out its last raid from the station on August 2.

After No. 218 went to Methwold, the station had no resident flying units for three months during which time 24 loop hardstandings were added. At the end of August, No. 3 Group handed over the station to the USAAF for use by a C-47 group of IX Troop Carrier Command for Operation 'Market'. However, apart from odd support units and the occasional flying visitor, the USAAF never based an operational flying group on the airfield. The Americans relinquished the station on October 20 whereupon it became a sub-station of North Luffenham, receiving No. 1651 HCU from Chedburgh during the second week of November 1944. This unit operated Stirlings but gradually shed these when Lancasters became available. Twenty Bomber Command aircraft — ten Manchesters and ten Stirlings — failed to return or crashed in the UK in the course of operations launched from Woolfox Lodge. No. 1651 HCU was disbanded in July 1945 and in the same month another Lancaster Heavy Conversion Unit, No. 1654, was brought in from Wigsley yet its days were also numbered and it was disbanded at the beginning of September.

Care and maintenance then descended under the watch of No. 259 Maintenance Unit which had the hangars for storage. In later years it was used as a relief landing ground by training aircraft, but the runways had deteriorated to such a degree by the spring of 1954 that the airfield had to be closed to flying. In 1960 a Bloodhound missile site under No. 62 Squadron was positioned in a secure area adjacent to the A1 road near the former technical site. These missiles were removed in 1964 and the RAF withdrew completely the following year. Sold in 1966, the flying area returned to agriculture with the removal of runways for A1 improvement hard-core. The technical area came into use by commercial organisations and in the last years of the century was used as a vehicle depot.

The concrete foundations for the Bloodhound launch site can still be seen to the left of the 15-33 runway.

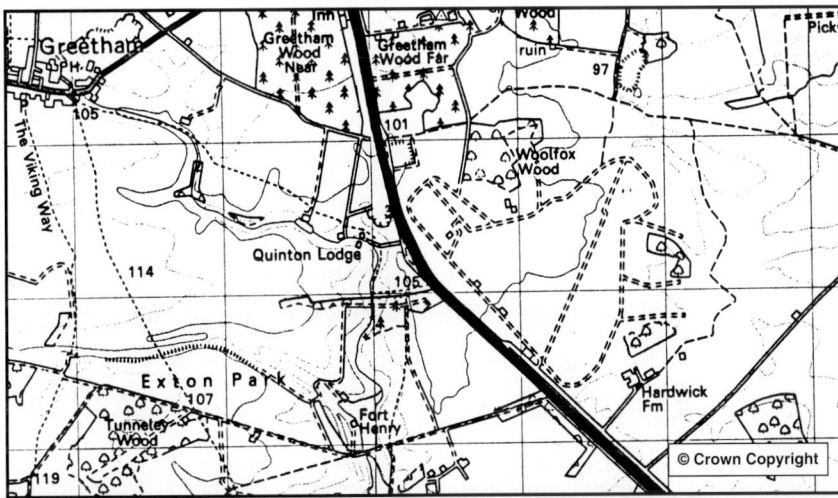

© Crown Copyright

283

| JAN | 17 | " | W | " | RICHARD DIMBLEBY F/O Russell sub/Lt. Mullins P/Lt Olims. P/O Mutchison F/O Wickers Sgt McGregor. | OPS. BERLIN. 1 X 8000 LB. A good trip and fairly successful. The residential quarters got it. / Dimbleby broadcast next day. This is my 67th Bombing trip. |

In January 1943, Bomber Command returned to Berlin for the first time in 14 months and, to get the maximum publicity for its opening shot in the battle against the city, the RAF took along the media. Richard Dimbleby represented the BBC and he flew with Wing Commander Guy Gibson from Syerston (see page 268) although the raid which would make him a legend was still four months in the future. This is Gibson's entry for the flight, the round trip taking 9 hours 15 minutes.

The Berlin raid was a big show as heavy bomber operations go: it was also quite a long raid, and the Wing Commander who took me stayed over Berlin for half an hour. The flak was hot, but it has been hotter. For me it was a pretty hair-raising experience, and I was glad when it was over, though I wouldn't have missed it for the world. But we must all remember that these men do it as a regular routine job. The various crews who were flying last night from the bomber station where I'd been staying had flown on several of the Essen raids, and that means that night after night they've been out over one of the hottest parts of Germany, returning to eat, drink and sleep before going out again. That's their life, and I can promise you it's hard, tiring and dangerous.

Four-engined Lancasters, Halifaxes and Stirlings roared out over the North-Sea. We flew among them, and turning back from the cockpit to look into the gorgeous sunset, I counted 30 or 40 Lancasters seemingly suspended in the evening sky. They were there wherever you looked — in front, behind, above and below — each a separate monster; each separately navigated, but all bound by a co-ordinated plan of approach and attack. Up above the clouds, the dusk was short. The orange and crimson of sunset died back there where the coast of England lay, and ahead of us the brilliant moon hung with the stars around her; below us, the thick clouds hid the sea. We were climbing steadily, and as it grew dark we put on our oxygen masks when the air grew too rarified for normal breathing.

As we approached the enemy coast I saw the German Ack-Ack. It was bursting away from us and much lower. I didn't see any long streams of it soaring into the air, as the pictures suggest: it burst in little yellow, winking flashes, and you couldn't hear it above the roar of the engines. Sometimes it closes in on you, and the mid- or tail-gunner will call up calmly and report its position to the Captain so that he can dodge it. We dodged it last night, particularly over Berlin: literally jumped over it and nipped round with the Wing Commander sitting up in his seat as cool as a cucumber, pushing and pulling his great bomber about as though it were a toy.

We knew well enough when we were approaching Berlin. There was a complete ring of powerful searchlights waving and crossing, though it seemed to me that most of our bombers were over the city. Many of

the lights were doused: there was also intense flak. First of all they didn't seem to be aiming at us. It was bursting away to starboard and away to port in thick, yellow clusters and dark, smokey puffs. As we turned in for our first run across the city it closed right round us. For a moment it seemed impossible that we could miss it, and one burst lifted us in the air as though a giant hand had pushed up the belly of the machine but we flew on.

Just then another Lancaster dropped a load of incendiaries, and where, a moment before, there had been a dark patch of the city, a dazzling silver pattern spread itself — a rectangle of brilliant lights — hundreds, thousands of them — winking and gleaming and lighting the outlines of the city around them. As though this unloading had been the signal, score after score of fire bombs went down, and all over the dark face of the German capital these great incandescent flower-beds spread themselves. It was a fascinating sight. As I watched and tried to photograph the flares with a cine-camera, I saw the pin-points merging, and the white glare turning to a dull, ugly red as the fires of bricks and mortar and wood spread from the chemical flares.

We flew over the city three times, for more than half an hour, while the guns

sought us out and failed to hit us. At last our bomb-aimer sighted his objective below, and for one unpleasant minute we flew steady and straight. Then he pressed the button and the biggest bomb of the evening, our 3½-tonner, fell away and down. I didn't see it burst but I know what a giant bomb does and I couldn't help wondering whether, anywhere in the area of the devastation, such a man as Hitler, Göring, Himmler or Goebbels might be cowering in a shelter. It was engrossing to realise that the Nazi leaders and their Ministries were only a few thousand feet from us, and that this shimmering mass of flares and bombs and gun-flashes was their stronghold.

We turned away from Berlin at last — it seemed we were there for an age — and we came home. We saw no night fighters, to our amazement, nor did any of the flak on the homeward journey come very near us. We came back across the North Sea, exchanged greetings of the day with a little coastwise convoy, and came in to England again, nine hours after we had flown out. There were so many machines circling impatiently round our aerodrome that we had to wait up above for an hour and twenty minutes before we could land, and it was two o'clock in the morning when the Wing Commander brought us down to the flarepath and taxied us in.

We climbed stiffly out, Johnny from the tail turret, Brian who used to be a policeman from the mid-upper, Hutch, the radio operator, Junior the navigator — by far the youngest of us all. Then the Scots co-pilot, a quiet calm sergeant, and last the short sturdy Wing-Co who has flown in every major air raid of this war and been a night fighter pilot in between times. They were the crew — six brave, cool and exceedingly skilful men.

Perhaps I am shooting a line for them but I think somebody ought to. They and their magnificent Lancasters and all the others like them are taking the war right into Germany. They have been attacking and giving their lives in attack since the first day of the war and their squadron went on that show too. 'Per ardua ad astra' is the RAF motto. Perhaps I can translate it 'Through hardship to the stars'. I understand the hardship now, and I'm proud to have seen the stars with them.

RICHARD DIMBLEBY, 7.00 and 8.00 a.m., JANUARY 18, 1943, BROADCAST ON THE BBC HOME SERVICE

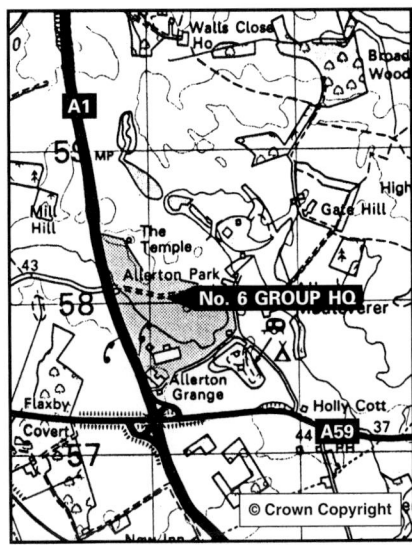

No. 6 GROUP HQ

The first No. 6 Group in Bomber Command administered the Auxiliary and later, Pool squadrons, ultimately being disbanded when the latter were replaced by operational training units. With Canada's growing contribution to Bomber Command it was decided to organise the RCAF squadrons in their own group and on 25 October 1942 a new No. 6 Group HQ came into being at Linton-on-Ouse soon to be moved to Allerton Park Castle near the Great North Road. The Group's airfields were all in North Yorkshire and the first seven came under its administration early in January 1943. At this time seven of the nine RCAF bomber squadrons were flying Wellingtons and two Halifaxes. During following months the Wellingtons gave way to more Halifaxes and Lancasters. From early 1944 Lancasters from Canadian production were received and nine of 14 squadrons were operational or converting to this type from Halifaxes by May 1945. The group had seven operational airfields at that time. No. 6 Group bombers are credited with some 40,800 sorties and delivering over 126,000 tons of ordnance.

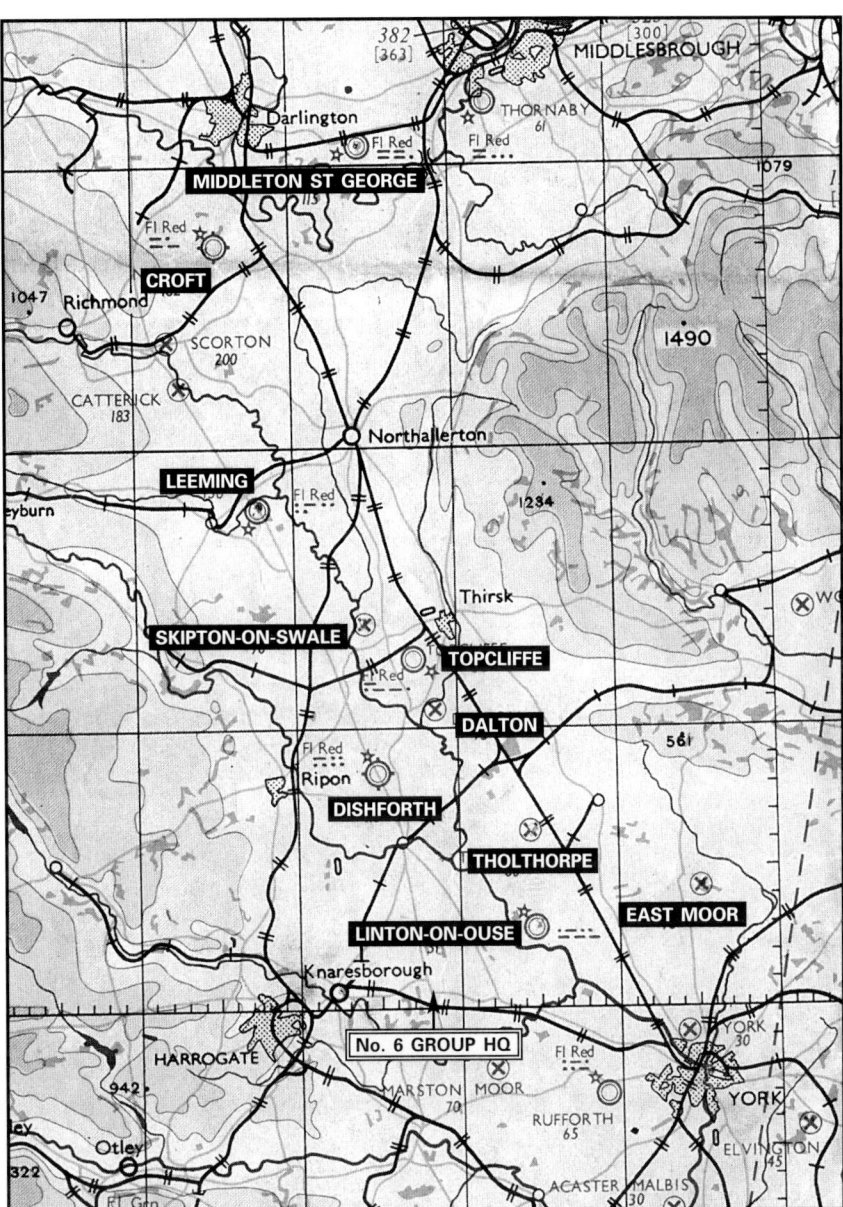

Allerton Park Castle, an ornate building standing in extensive parkland at the junction of the A59 with the A1, housed the headquarters of No. 6 Group from its inception in October 1942 until disbandment in August 1945. Although called a castle, it was actually a Victorian mansion. After the war the building fell into a state of disrepair but it has since been restored to its former glory and is now owned by the Canadian-based Gerald Arthur Rolph Foundation.

CROFT (NEASHAM)

This vertical shot of Croft was taken by No. 1 Photographic Reconnaissance unit on June 11, 1942, when the work to extend the runways was nearing completion. The main was lengthened from 1,650 to 2,000 yards and arrester gear fitted.

Six miles south of Darlington, to the west of the LNER main line, a suitable area of meadowland was requisitioned in late 1940 as a satellite landing ground for the No. 4 Group bomber station at Middleton St George. The remote location was in an area known as the Walmires with the nearest sizeable village Dalton on the A167 road. The official name for the proposed airfield was Croft, possibly because an airfield at another Dalton was already under consideration. Built during 1941 with hard runways, perimeter track and aircraft standings, the airfield was available for occupation in October 1941. The final runway lengths were to 2,000 yards for the 09-27 and 1,400 yards for the secondaries aligned 03-21 and 15-33. Hardstandings were 36 pans of which three were lost during runway extensions and replaced by three loop type. Hangars were the usual two Type T2 and a single B1. Dispersed accommodation provided for a maximum 2,460 males and 323 females.

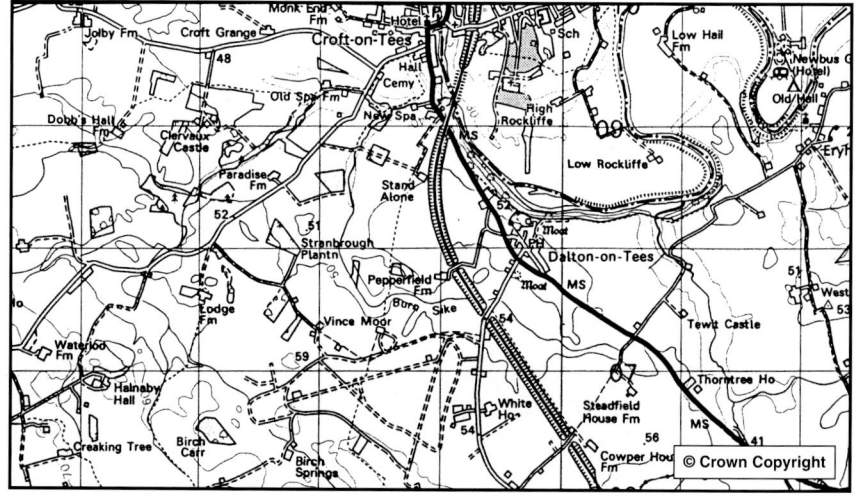

Left: **Outside the main entrance, WAAF Corporal Olga Turnbull adjusts her helmet.** *Right:* **Amazingly, the sentry's shelter still stands.**

Taking it easy. Olga, centre, with ACW Dorothy Brooks and Sergeant Flo Foster relax on WAAF Site No. 1.

Today the site is shared by Intertractor Ltd and Savage's Paddock Farm Nurseries' garden centre.

During October 1941, No. 78 Squadron was removed from Middleton St George to Croft, its Whitleys flying their first sorties from the station on October 22/23. The squadron converted to Halifaxes in March-April 1942 and returned to Middleton St George in June. The station was then upgraded to Class A standard with extensions to the runways which had deteriorated.

Croft was one of the northern airfields to be used by an all-Canadian group. Before its official formation, No. 419 Squadron with Wellingtons was moved in from Topcliffe only to be posted to Middleton St George a month later. Before it departed it provided personnel for a nucleus of a new squadron No. 427. Its first operational sorties came on the night of December 14 when it took off to

mine enemy waters. This was under No. 4 Group, the squadron transferring to No. 6 Group on New Year's Day. Wellingtons were flown until May 1943 when the squadron converted to Halifaxes and in the same month was moved to Leeming.

For undisclosed reasons, Croft was now to become a base for a Halifax conversion unit serving No. 6 Group, No. 1664 Heavy

Left: **Another snapshot from Corporal Turnbull's album taken of her (rear right) with mates at the MT Section.** *Above:* **The vehicle ramp on the old communal site still survives.**

Bomber base then . . . race track today. Runways which once saw Halifaxes lined up ready for take-off to support the Normandy landings in June 1944 now echo to the squealing tyres of high-speed motor cars.

Conversion Unit being formed at the station in May 1943 until it was transferred to Dishforth in December. Croft again became an operational station with Nos. 431 and 434 Squadrons arriving from Tholthorpe the same month. Both operated with Halifaxes until the closing months of 1944, No. 431 converting to Lancasters in October and No. 434 in December. After VE-Day the Croft Lancasters were employed in ferrying released POWs back to the UK and in June both squadrons went to Canada taking their Lancaster Xs with them. A total of 138 Bomber Command aircraft despatched from Croft failed to return or crashed in the UK. Ten were Whitleys, 20 Wellingtons, 87 Halifaxes and 21 Lancasters.

After the war, John Neasham, who owned a garage in Darlington, leased the disused airfield and joined with other local businessmen to open the Darlington and District Aero Club in August 1947. Neasham's motoring background soon led to the creation of a motor racing track on the airfield which is now an established rallycross circuit.

In the immediate post-war period Croft (renamed Neasham) continued to serve as the Middleton St George satellite and was available for 'circuits and bumps' by No. 13 OTU's Mosquitos. When the OTU left the parent station the airfield closed to flying and, after a period under a holding party, was finally abandoned by the RAF. It remained in a fairly intact state for some years followed by the inevitable agricultural and commercial intrusions.

Between 1995 and 1997 an international class motor race track was built on the site of the airfield at a reputed cost of some two million pounds, following earlier use of the runways for this sport.

John Neasham's influence was widespread, so much so that when the RAF at nearby Middleton St George designated Croft as a relief landing ground for pupils of their advance flying school, they renamed his airfield 'RAF Neasham'!

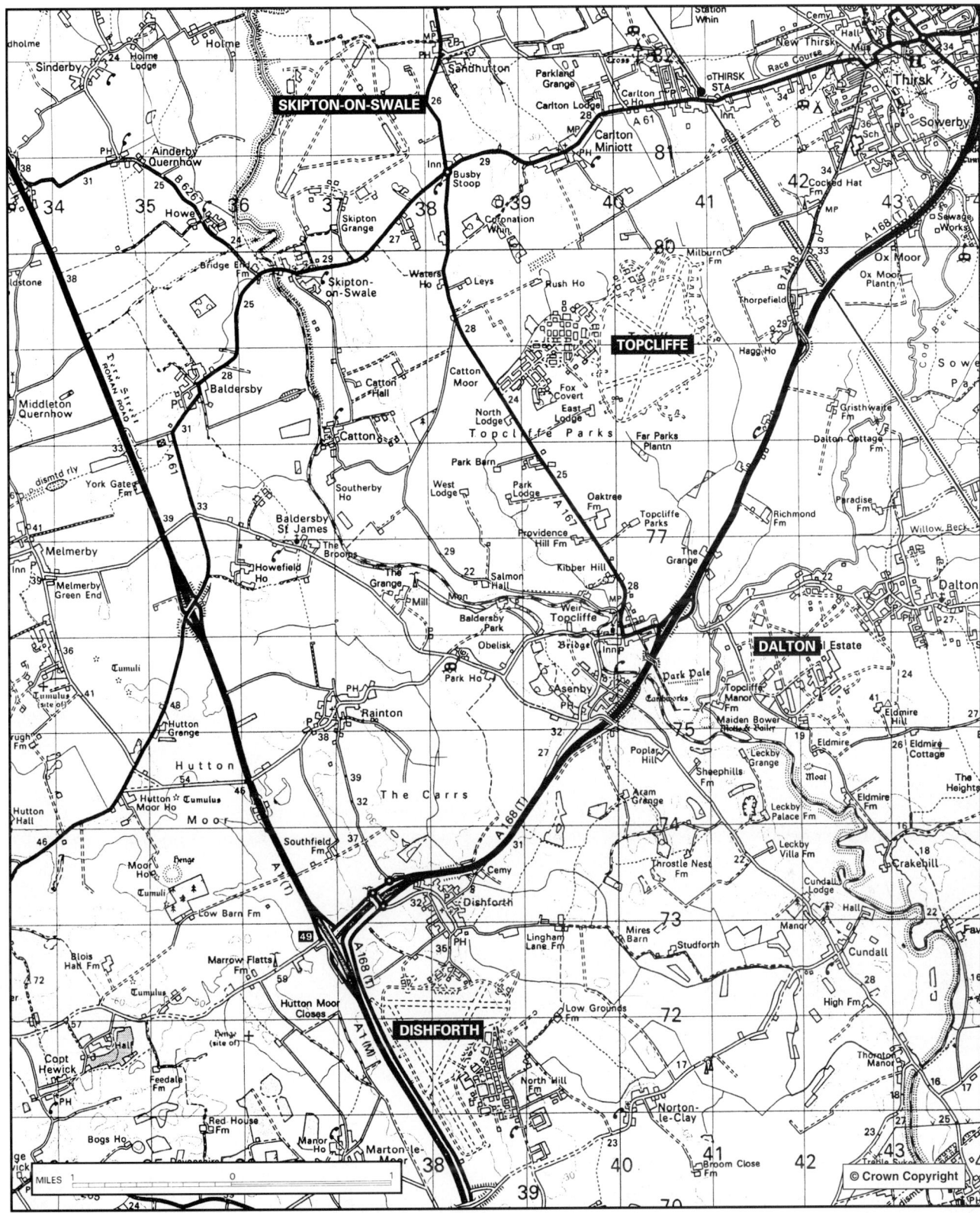

As a civilian, John Neasham is unique in having a former Bomber Command aerodrome named after him as all the other airfields were named after local towns or villages. Croft ought to have been called Dalton after the nearest village but another base with that name had already been established further south as a satellite for Topcliffe. This plan shows just how close the Group 6 airfields were in the Thirsk area, all four within a radius of three miles.

DALTON

Dalton airfield started life as meadowland hurriedly cleared to provide a satellite for Topcliffe. The site was only two miles south of the No. 4 Group parent airfield and actually nearer to the village of Topcliffe than the station so named! At first, Dalton was no more than a relief and dispersal landing ground but it was gradually improved to a point where the Whitleys of No. 102 Squadron at the parent station could make the satellite home. This was in November 1941 after concrete runways had been put down. These were 18-36, 1,100 yards long with 06-24 and 12-30 both 1,000 yards long. The usual 36 pan hardstandings and encircling perimeter track were provided and eventually three hangars, a B1 and T2 on the technical site and another T2 between runway heads 24 and 30 were built. The technical site was on the north side near the river and took in the road from Topcliffe to Dalton. The bomb stores were off to the south between runway heads 30 and 36, and the camp of a dozen dispersed sites was located to the north-east around the village of Dalton. Initially some requisitioned accommodation was used.

Work underway on runway extensions, June 11, 1942. A half dozen Halifaxes of No. 1652 HCU still occupy some of the hardstandings.

Operations were flown from Dalton until June 1942 when No. 102 returned to Topcliffe and Dalton briefly hosted No. 1652 Heavy Conversion Unit with Halifaxes. Work began on extending runways in the spring of 1942 but it became necessary to halt flying in August when much of the perimeter track on the south and east sides had to be broken up. The new runway lengths were 18-36 at 1,410 yards, 06-24 at 1,560 yards and 12-30 at 1,800 yards, all the extensions being made at the eastern ends. Six pan hardstandings were lost through this work but replaced elsewhere on the airfield. The camp in 11 dispersed sites had accommodation for 2,276 males and 238 females.

On completion, the airfield was to be allocated to the new Canadian bomber group, and to this end No. 428 Squadron formed at Dalton in November 1942 to fly Wellingtons, before the official transfer of the station from No. 4 to No. 6 Group on New Year's Day 1943. No. 428 Squadron joined the

bombing campaign on the night of January 26/27 and had the station to itself until May when No. 424 Squadron's Wellingtons arrived from Leeming although this was only to prepare for an overseas posting to meet a request for more night bombing capability in the Mediterranean. After only two weeks, No. 424's Wellingtons departed and No. 1666 Heavy Conversion Unit was formed to provide additional operational training on the Halifax. As this activity would not be compatible with an operational station the resident squadron was moved to the parent station early in June. However, in October 1943 No. 1666 HCU went to Wombleton, the remote and notorious airfield on the southern edge of the North York Moors; reputedly, the reason given was to lessen the air activity in the Thirsk area with its many operational airfields. This left Dalton with only a gunnery flight, although in November 1943 the personnel of No. 420 Squadron, one of the Wellington squadrons sent to North

Africa in the previous year, returned to prepare to re-equip with the Halifax before moving on to Tholthorpe a month later. A total of 29 bombers had been lost on operations launched from Dalton; five Whitleys, 20 Wellingtons and four Halifaxes.

The station now passed from the control of No. 6 Group to No. 7, the training group. While no other units were based at Dalton until August 1944 (when No. 6 Group Aircrew School was established), the flying field was regularly used as a relief landing ground by operational training unit aircraft. All the station's units had been disbanded or transferred by early August 1945 and a state of care and maintenance declared. Under maintenance unit control, the airfield hangars were used for surplus stores and in the early 'fifties old bombs were stockpiled on the runways prior to disposal. As with most technical sites, commercial and industrial uses took occupancy and fortunately Dalton has retained its three hangars.

While an industrial complex has now grown up on the south-eastern dispersals, from the air the airfield at Dalton still retains its wartime outline. *Above:* Looking north-west and *below* south-west along the 06-24 subsidiary. Note the old section of the extended perimeter track cutting through the field in the foreground.

DISHFORTH

Since 1936 the most conspicuous airfield along the length of the Great North Road — the A1 — has been Dishforth. Three miles north of Boroughbridge, it borders the eastern side of the road which, until recent improvements, was slightly elevated providing a panorama of the airfield that could not fail to be noticed. An expansion scheme establishment, it had the usual grass surface of some 200 acres with a crescent of Type C hangars fronting the bombing circle, five in number with the fifth tucked in behind the fourth and backed by the technical workshops and administrative offices. Behind these the communal buildings and barracks, all in brick, steel and concrete and centrally heated.

By January 1937 work was far enough advanced for No. 10 Squadron and its Heyfords to be brought up from Boscombe Down and the following month for No. 78 Squadron to arrive from the same station with the same aircraft type. In March, No. 10 Squadron became the first to convert to the Whitley, then considered a heavy bomber. No. 78 also received Whitleys but the supply was slow and it was not fully equpped until the summer.

On the outbreak of hostilities, No. 78 was a reserve squadron in No. 4 Group so it did not go to war from this station. On the other hand No. 10 despatched the first sorties from Dishforth on September 8 when that evening eight Whitleys were sent to distribute leaflets over Germany. No. 78 was moved to Linton-on-Ouse in December 1939 in an exchange with No. 51 Squadron. In July 1940, No. 10 was moved to Leeming and No. 78 returned from Linton and entered operations. No. 78 operated at Dish-

A Luftwaffe reconnaissance photograph taken in October 1940 showing the line of five Type C hangars and the camp. It appears that the German aircraft was flying over the Great North Road — a good navigational aid.

forth until the following April when it left for Middleton St George. No. 51 Squadron, a longer tenant, was not moved until May 1942 when it was loaned to Coastal Command and based at Chivenor. During the early war years a number of pan type hardstandings were put down, mostly on long access tracks, two crossing the A1.

Bomber Command was then planning to raise an all-Royal Canadian Air Force group

and in June 1942 a new squadron, No. 425, was formed at Dishforth to fly Wellingtons. It undertook its first raid on the night of October 5 and ten days later a second RCAF squadron, No. 426, was formed, also to fly Wellingtons, becoming operational on the night of January 14/15, 1943. At this time Dishforth came under No. 6 Group, the formal transfer having occurred on New Year's Day.

Lying alongside the A1, Dishforth had no resident RAF squadrons when we pictured the airfield in September 2000 although the hangars have recently undergone extensive modernisation for the helicopters of No. 9 Regiment, Army Air Corps.

Line up of Wellingtons from No. 426 Squadron in early 1943. Looking north-east from the hangar line apron.

No. 425 was one of the Wellington squadrons picked to increase bombing capability in the Mediterranean and it left Dishforth in May for North Africa. The following month its sister squadron was transferred to Linton-on-Ouse so that hard runways could be laid at Dishforth. This work, carried out by F. Haslam Ltd taking nearly six months, brought the airfield up to Class A standard. The main runway 16-34, was 1,976 yards long and the 04-22 and 10-28 at 1,500 and 1,488 yards respectively. The existing perimeter taxiway was enlarged and the pan hardstandings built during the preceding year linked to it, increasing the total to 36. Additional domestic buildings brought the maximum personnel that could be accommodated to 1,782 males and 332 females.

At the beginning of November 1943, No. 1664 Heavy Conversion Unit and its Halifaxes moved in from Croft soon to be joined by No. 425 Squadron which had returned from North Africa. Re-trained on Halifaxes, No. 425 departed for Tholthorpe and operations a month later. For the rest of the war in Europe, Dishforth was to maintain a training role. No. 1664 HCU being disbanded in early April 1945. Combined with the break-up of No. 6 Group in June, this meant the station was soon completely deserted by the Canadians. The war had seen 128 of the bombers despatched on operations from Dishforth go missing or crash in the UK: 90 Whitleys, 37 Wellingtons and a Halifax.

Later that summer Transport Command took over and installed Nos. 1659 and 1665 Heavy Transport Conversion Units which were later merged into No. 1332 Transport Conversion Unit. These formations were engaged in training crews to operate Liberators and Yorks. In 1948 another change of designation for the resident unit made it No. 241 Operational Conversion Unit which endured until 1950 when it was combined with another formation at Topcliffe and established at Dishforth as No. 242 OCU. This label proved more durable and No. 242

Dishforth on June 11, 1942. Note the group of pan hardstandings accessed by crossing Britain's premier road! Also the patching of the grass to give the impression of farm fields. (For the Ordnance Survey plan see page 289.)

OCU carried on the work of producing crews for Transport Command until the end of 1961. After the OCU had been moved, no further major flying formations were based at Dishforth. It has, however, been maintained in good order for three decades as a Relief Landing Ground for Linton-on-Ouse and those of regular squadrons during exercises. The Army Air Corps has been in residence since 1988.

A view across the airfield and runway 10-28 on which the Wellingtons were parked long ago. Dishforth village is on the skyline.

EAST MOOR

By mid-July 1942 when this picture was taken, Halifaxes of No. 158 Squadron had already arrived even though the hangarage had not yet been built. The aerodrome had officially opened the previous month, the squadron arriving from Driffield on June 6.

Seven miles due north from the centre of York in the parish of Sutton-on-the-Forest, this airfield was built to the east of the B1363 road to Helmsley, largely on the moor for which it was named. Built 1941-42, the concrete runways were main 17-35 at 1,610 yards, 04-22 at 1,540 yards and 08-26 at 1,300 yards. Before the airfield was completed runway 17-35 was extended to 1,900 yards at the 35 end and 08-26 to 1,430 yards on the end of 26. The encircling perimeter track led to 36 pan type hardstandings although none were situated on the western side where the technical site was built. A T2 hangar lay just north of runway head 04 and another on the opposite side of the airfield midway between runway heads 35 and 26. A B1 hangar was erected on the north side between runway heads 17 and 22. The camp was to the west consisting of fourteen dispersed sites for accommodating a maximum 2,094 males and 407 females.

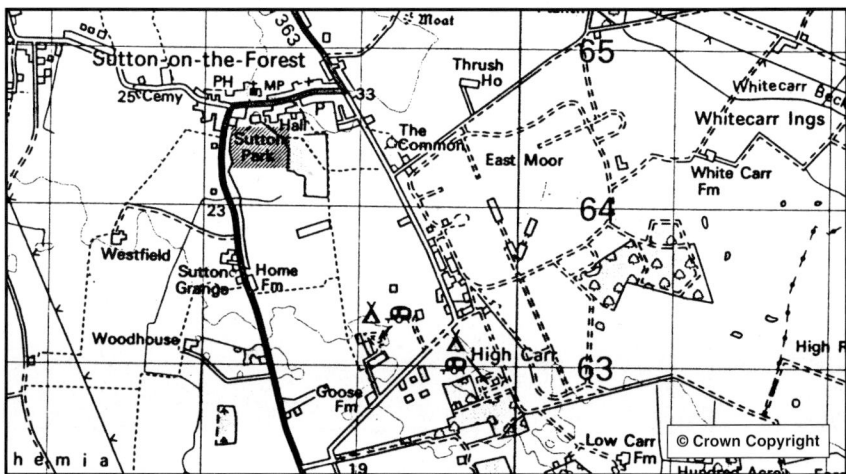

294

Bombing up! No. 432 Squadron Halifax III QO-E photographed on May 26, 1944 near the station's B1 hangar.

First opened as a No. 4 Group station, No. 158 Squadron, in the process of converting to Halifaxes, moved in from Driffield in early June 1942. The squadron flew the first raid from East Moor on the night of June 25, also its first with the Halifax. In October No. 158 left East Moor for Rufforth as part of the plan to establish an all-Canadian bomber group in the area north of York. To this end, No. 429 Squadron, RCAF, was formed at East Moor early in November, although for the time being it was under No. 4 Group. Equipped with Wellingtons, it made its first raid on the night of January 26/27, 1943 and continued operations from East Moor until early August when it transferred to Leeming. The squadron lost 30 Wellingtons on operations while at East Moor.

In May 1943, No. 1679 Heavy Conversion Unit was formed at East Moor to provide crew training on the radial-engined Lancas-ter II which was to equip three of the Canadian squadrons. No. 1679 HCU departed in December that year for Wombleton.

No. 432 Squadron had arrived in September 1943 to convert to the Mk II Lancaster, flying its first raid with this version from East Moor on November 26/27. However, the supply of Lancaster IIs was limited and in February these were exchanged for similarly-powered Halifax IIIs.

In late July 1944, No. 415 Squadron was transferred from Coastal Command to No. 6 Group and bomber operations at East Moor. Equipped with Halifaxes, it carried out its first raid from the station on July 28/29. There were no further changes of occupation during hostilities, Nos. 415 and 432 Squadrons continuing on bombing operations until April 25, 1945. No. 415 flew 104 raids from East Moor losing 20 Halifaxes and No. 432 carried out 183 missions losing 10 Lancasters

and 47 Halifaxes. Both squadrons were reduced and disbanded during May 1945. Total operational losses from East Moor, including crashes in the UK, amounted to 107 aircraft. Ten were Lancasters, 67 Halifaxes and 30 Wellingtons.

No. 54 OTU with Mosquito night fighters came to East Moor in May 1945 and remained for a year before finally moving to Leeming. East Moor was closed to flying in June 1946 and thereafter left to decay. The hangars were sold and removed in the 'sixties and most of the domestic site buildings demolished. A decade later the runways were being broken up apart from some sections retained as bases for poultry houses. Agriculture has now reclaimed practically all the airfield, the former technical site being occupied as a gypsy encampment for several years but now replaced by a caravan park and light industrial estate.

By 2000 all traces of the hangar and concrete had gone but the gappy crop of potatoes reflect the disturbed soil.

'F' for Freddie, nicknamed *Ferdinand the Bull* pictured on one of the south-east hardstandings after completing 84 ops.

Depressions in the ground and discoloured crops still mark where the concrete was removed.

Monuments to a former age. *Above:* Surviving defence position near the northern boundary. *Below:* More formal memorial in Sutton-on-the-Forest village to Nos. 415, 429 and 432 Squadrons. *Left:* On the airfield itself, livestock sheds now occupy the remaining runways.

LEEMING

In 1937 an area of open meadowland adjacent to the Newton Grange estate, south of the village of Leeming, was acquired by Yorkshire Air Services for an aerodrome for club and passenger flying. However, no sooner was it established than the site was taken over for an expansion scheme RAF station. Five miles south-west of Northallerton, and adjacent to the A1 trunk road, Leeming airfield was built during 1939-40 to the standard pre-war specification with some economies made in the final stages of construction. The landing ground was enlarged with the three of the later Type C hangars in a crescent before the bombing circle, and a fourth and fifth placed behind the first and third. The camp, behind the hangar line, consisted of the usual brick-built buildings of a permanent station.

First used by Blenheim night fighters of No. 219 Squadron in June 1940, Leeming was allocated to No. 4 Group and in July No. 10 Squadron was transferred from Dishforth. Its Whitleys flew their first raid from the station on the night of July 20. Despite there being two operational squadrons at Leeming, the station was chosen to re-form No. 7 Squadron to operate the first of the new four-engined heavy bombers, the Short Stirling.

Halifax L9621 ZA-P of No. 10 Squadron being towed from a hangar at Leeming by a Fordson in January 1942. Basically a 1918 design farm tractor but fuelled by petrol instead of vaporising oil, the Fordson needed full power to move a 15-ton Halifax.

Leeming photographed on June 22, 1942 when runway 17-35 was newly extended but the associated perimeter track had yet to be built. The picture also shows the heavy camouflage of imitation field boundaries and roads.

*Left: **Easy Does It** of No. 429 Squadron pictured on a north side dispersal on November 22, 1943. Above:* **Open dispersals have given way to reinforced concrete aircraft shelters . . . Halifax AL-E being replaced by a Hawk XX330. The wooded skyline remains the same.**

They were delivered in August so that training could be carried out in an area hopefully less troubled by the Luftwaffe. In the same month No. 102 Squadron moved in from Driffield, albeit that for much of the time its Whitleys were on detachment at Coastal Command stations. In October came relief as the Blenheim night fighters departed as did both No. 102 Squadron to Linton-on-Ouse and No. 7 Squadron to Oakington. No. 7 Squadron and its Stirlings were replaced by a

squadron re-formed to fly the second of the new four-engined bombers, the Halifax, No. 35 Squadron arriving from Boscombe Down in early November. Only present for two weeks, the few Halifaxes departed for Linton-on-Ouse in December. Thereafter No. 10 Squadron and its Whitleys had Leeming all to themselves for ten months. In September 1941, No. 77 Squadron returned from Coastal Command bringing its Whitleys, only to be loaned back to Coastal the follow-

ing May. No. 10 converted to the Halifax in November 1941 and was operational with the type from Leeming until August 1942.

The runways laid in 1940-41 were 17-35 at 1,650 yards, 02-22 at 1,200 yards and 13-31 at 1,100 yards, but by the end of 1941 work was in hand to extend the main to 1,950 yards, 02-22 to 1,650 yards and 13-31 to 1,400 yards. Several pan hardstandings were put down the previous year and after completion of the runway there were 32 and four loops.

Leeming in the 1960s when a new apron had been laid down in front of the tower and new readiness hardstandings constructed on the western perimeter track for the V-Bomber force. The main runway was extended to its present day 2,500 yards.

The Canadian squadrons at Leeming incorporated names alongside their unit numbers. These included *Goose, Leaside, Swordfish* and *Thunderbird*. To continue the theme, No. 427 adopted the Lion or rather the Lion adopted them! On May 24, 1943, the squadron was formally adopted by the Metro-Goldwyn-Mayer film company of Hollywood and took the Lion for their badge. A formal presentation by Samuel Eckman Jnr, Managing Director of MGM (UK), took place beside a Halifax named *London's Revenge* when he presented the squadron with an inscribed bronze lion and, of more interest to the airmen, a crate of whisky and free tickets to the company's theatre in London.

The last gesture was extended to all members of the squadron who were given special Lion medals which entitled them to two free seats at any cinema showing an MGM film. For obvious reasons, this proved extremely popular! A list of 17 of the film studio's stars had been selected by the squadron and their names were drawn from a hat by the 427 pilots to determine which star was going to be their 'foster mother' or 'father' and sponsor their particular aircraft. The list included some of the great names of the day: Crawford, Garson, Lamarr and Tracey and after the presentation, a sergeant pilot added the name Lana Turner alongside the bomb.

Like most original watch office/control towers still in use, Leeming's has gathered a high-vision air traffic control on the roof.

In preparation for Leeming being taken over by the RCAF group being raised in Bomber Command, No. 10 was sent to the new airfield at Melbourne. No. 419 Squadron and its Wellingtons were transferred in from No. 3 Group in August, spending four days at Leeming while awaiting transfer to Topcliffe. The following month No. 408 Squadron arrived from No. 5 Group bringing its Hampdens from Balderton and trading them for Halifaxes. In October 1942, to aid the re-equipment of RCAF squadrons with heavy bombers, No. 1659 Heavy Conversion Unit was formed at Leeming with Halifaxes. The conversion unit was moved out to Topcliffe in March 1943 and No. 405 Squadron moved into Leeming from that station. However No. 405's stay was short for a few weeks later it was selected to join No. 8 Pathfinder Group, taking its Halifaxes south to Gransden Lodge. Also in April No. 424 Squadron arrived from Topcliffe with Wellingtons only to move on to Dalton in early May. Then came No. 427 Squadron from Croft which began exchanging its Wellingtons for Halifaxes. Yet another squadron came to Leeming to convert to Halifaxes: No. 429 from East Moor. Two weeks after its arrival, No. 408 Squadron was moved to Linton-on-Ouse. From thenceforth Nos. 427 and 429 became established as the Leeming squadrons with no further changes of units to the conclusion of the war in Europe. Both were re-equipped with Lancasters in March 1945 and ceased operations in late April. By this date the maximum personnel numbers that could be housed at Leeming were 2,392 males and 317 females.

By the end of the war Leeming had lost a total of 283 bombers on operations, 72 Whitleys, 208 Halifaxes, 2 Wellingtons and a solitary Lancaster. Unlike most RCAF squadrons, those at Leeming were not quickly disbanded but continued to serve Bomber Command after No. 6 Group was wound up at the end of August 1945. Both existed, if in decreasing strength, until June 1946 when

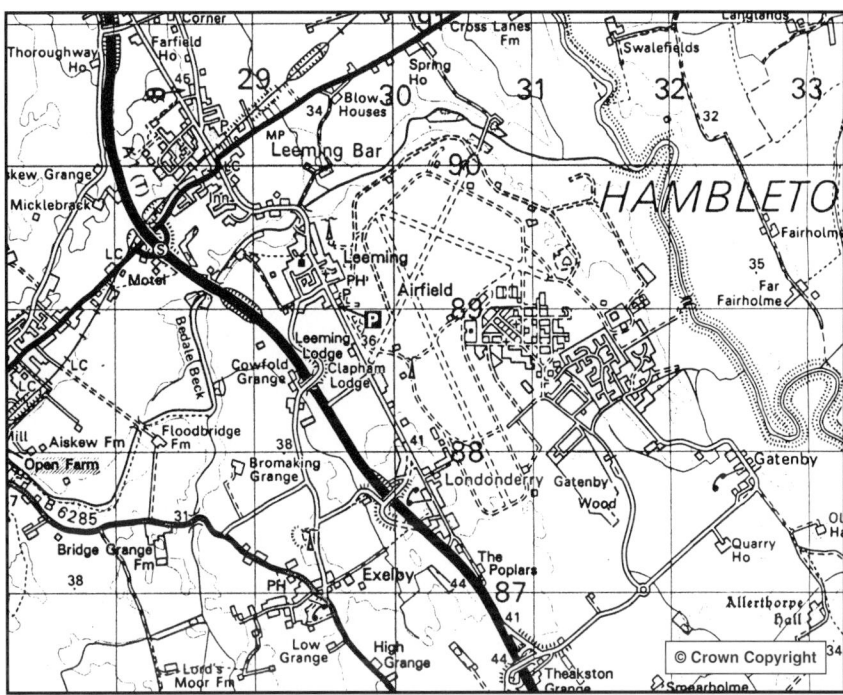

disbandment was officially proclaimed. No. 54 OTU forsook the discomforts of East Moor soon after and remained in residence at Leeming until merging with No. 13 OTU to form No. 228 Operational Conversion Unit. Mosquitos and Brigands gave way to Meteors and later Javelins before the OCU was disbanded in 1961. In 1950, Mowlems constructed aircraft servicing platforms on the airfield and during the mid-'fifties runway extensions were carried out, although the station remained active during the reconstruction With No. 228 OCU's termination, No. 3 Flying Training School was re-formed

at the station remaining until 1984 when it was moved, along with others at Leeming, as the station was to be used by fighters. This development, was delayed until 1987 when runway 16-34 (ex-17-35) was lengthened to 2,506 yards and facility rebuilding took place. Leeming then became the base for Tornado F3 fighters housing Nos. 11, 23 and 25 Squadrons. No. 23 Squadron disbanded in April 1994, since being reformed as an AWACS unit flying Sentry AEW1 from Waddington. No. 11 and 25 Squadrons were joined by No. 100 Squadron in September 1995 flying Hawks in a target facilities role.

The V-Bomber apron was lined with Tornados when we took this shot in September 2000. For many years, three Phantom FGR2s were parked nose towards the runway as airfield decoys. Ordnance storage in the right foreground. With the shift in magnetic variation, the main runway has now been changed to 16-34.

LINTON-ON-OUSE

Linton in the summer of 1940 adorned with Whitleys of No. 58 Squadron. The nearest aircraft, P5028 GE-R survived operations to serve as a trainer but the furthest aircraft, N1469 'H'-Harry flew into a Morayshire hill during bad weather in January 1943.

Located nine miles north-west of the centre of York and directly north of Linton-on-Ouse village, this airfield was built 1936-38 under an expansion scheme. The camp of brick flat-roofed permanent buildings was immediately adjacent to the village and at the south-east corner of the landing ground. Four Type C hangars formed a crescent before the landing ground with a fifth placed behind the westernmost hangar of the line.

The first squadrons, No. 51 and 58, brought their Whitleys in from Boscombe Down in April 1938 to this premier airfield of No. 4 Group that had its headquarters at the station for the next two years. Low-lying, despite extensive drainage it was soon found that in winter the landing ground was subject to waterlogging. Consequently the station became the first in northern England and the second in Bomber Command on which work was in hand (in August 1939) to lay concrete runways. These were 04-22 at 1,100 yards and 11-29 at 1,150 yards. A concrete perimeter track was also provided and 34 pan hardstandings, several accessed down long tracks.

It is interesting to see in this shot taken in 1940 from 13,000 feet that 04-22 was extended before the third runway (18-36) was started (see also pages 8, 9 and 10).

Linton, summer 2000. Tucanos in the black livery of No. 1 Flying Training School.

The crew of a No. 58 Squadron Whitley prepare for a flight. In the background is the most northerly Type C hangar. Runway 11-29 can be made out between this and the airmen.

Whitleys were despatched on operations on the first night of the war, albeit to dispense propaganda leaflets, which were loaded at Leconfield where the aircraft lodged while runway work was in progress. These squadrons were on detachment for much of the time, No. 58 returning to Boscombe Down for four months and No. 51 moving to Dishforth in December 1940. This was an exchange with No. 78 Squadron whose aircraft and crews had also been detached to serve elsewhere. The first bombing raid from Linton was made on the night of April 18/19, 1940 by three Whitleys of No. 58 Squadron. No. 78 Squadron not being fully available until the summer and did not enter the night bombing campaign until July 19/20. The squadron was no sooner operational than it was moved to Dishforth and its place taken at Linton by No. 77 Squadron. This unit, already operational, joined with No. 51 in frequent night raids until it was moved to Topcliffe in October 1940. For a month No. 102 Squadron, removed from

More greenery and a few new buildings but otherwise the view is little changed apart from the runway now being designated 10-28.

Leeming, was based at Linton although most of its force was still on detachment to Coastal Command. It moved on to Topcliffe the following month. The next arrival, No. 35 Squadron, pioneered the Halifax whose technical problems delayed entry into combat until the night of March 10/11, 1941. One of the six aircraft despatched to Le Havre docks that night was shot down by an RAF night fighter shortly after returning over the English coast.

A second Halifax-equipped squadron was formed by taking No. 35's 'C' Flight and redesignating it No. 76 Squadron on May Day 1941. Whether German intelligence knew Linton was the base of the new British bomber at this juncture is not known but the Luftwaffe had some success on the night of May 10/11, 1941 when at least three raiders dropped a number of bombs killing several airmen, including the station CO, Group Captain Frederick Garraway. In June, No. 76 Squadron left for Middleton St George leaving Nos. 35 and 58 to carry on. No. 58 still had its faithful Whitleys but instead of being converted to Halifaxes, it was turned over permanently to Coastal Command, moving out in April 1942 having made over 200 raids from Linton for the loss of 49 Whitleys.

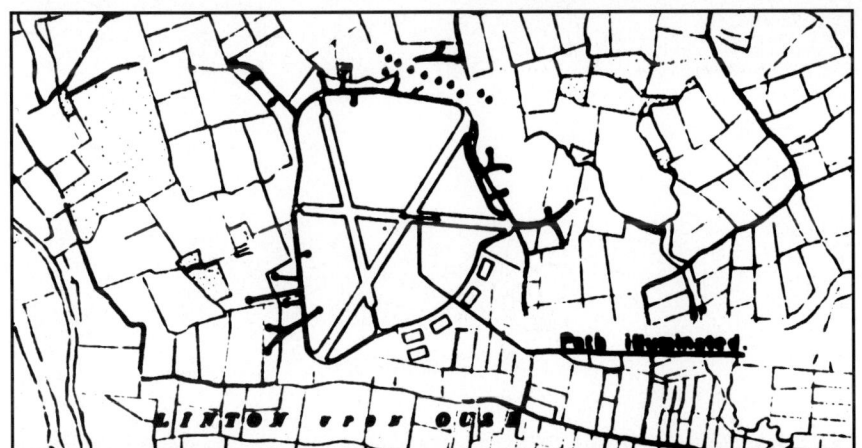

Following the raid on the night of May 10/11, 1941, the Luftwaffe returned on August 17. The official report states that 'strip lighting [was] illuminated for two minutes to assist two damaged bombers in landing. Three minutes later, intruder dropped stick of bombs'. The attack at 0311 hours was believed to have been from an altitude of 7,300 feet, the ten 50kg bombs missing the target to explode off the northern perimeter as shown on the plan attached to the report, slightly damaging one of the dispersals. There were no casualties.

Pilot Officer Leonard Cheshire: 'I was posted away from Whitleys to another squadron [No. 35], equipped with four-engined Halifaxes. The aircraft were new, and as yet not ready to operate; in consequence there followed a period of training and development. Whitleys had been homely and simple, but here was a new atmosphere altogether; new equipment, new technique of flying and everything vastly more complicated. And so, I threw myself into hibernation — to learn. Throughout the hours of this long hibernation there was time in abundance to meditate, and nothing but memories to live on. The memories were sweet and often exhilarating. The carefree, cheerful life: the trust and companionship in danger: the splendour of success: the frustration of failure. These were the qualities that made the memories sweet, but behind all this there was an inescapable note of sadness. When Napoleon considered the appointment of a new general, he invariably asked: "Is he lucky?" Time and again I have wondered at that, but now I know that Napoleon was right.' *Above:* Pilot Officer Cheshire surrounded by his Linton crew — in his biography *Bomber Pilot* he referred to them as Revs, Brown, Taffy, Hares, Gutteridge, Jacko and Weldon — pose for a picture between Nos. 2 and 3 hangars in June 1941.

The young trees have gone . . . just as the young men have faded into history, their survival, as Cheshire — the most distinguished of all Bomber Command's airmen — mused, hinging merely on luck.

No. 35 Squadron remained at Linton-on-Ouse until August 1942 when, selected to become a pathfinder unit, it was transferred to No. 8 Group and Graveley. During the summer of 1942 the length of runway 04-22 was increased to 2,040 yards, 11-29 to 1,460 yards and a third runway 18-36 constructed of 1,400 yards.

Following No. 35's departure, Linton became a two squadron base again with Nos. 76 and 78 Squadrons arriving from Middleton St George. The two Halifax squadrons took part in main force operations until the following June when the airfield was required for the expanding No. 6 Group, the headquarters of which had originally formed at the station before being set up in Allerton Park Castle. No. 76 Squadron was moved to Holme-on-Spalding Moor and No. 78 to Breighton while No. 426 Squadron, RCAF, came to Linton from Dishforth to convert to the Lancaster II. No. 426 flew its first Lancaster raid on August 17/18, 1943 losing two aircraft including the CO's. Later that month No. 408 Squadron was moved in from Leeming when it started to shed its Halifaxes and embrace the radial-engined Lancaster. It entered operations with the Lancaster on October 7/8. Further domestic building at the station raised accommodation to 1,447 males and 368 females

With the cessation of Lancaster II production, No. 426 Squadron re-equipped with Halifax IIIs in April 1944 but No. 408 continued with the Lancaster until September when it joined No. 426 in flying the radial-engined Halifaxes. Following VE-Day No. 426 Squadron was transferred to Transport Command and moved to Driffield. No. 405 Squadron returned from Gransden Lodge with Lancasters and joined No. 408 which had again converted to the Lancaster but this time the Canadian-built Lancaster Xs.

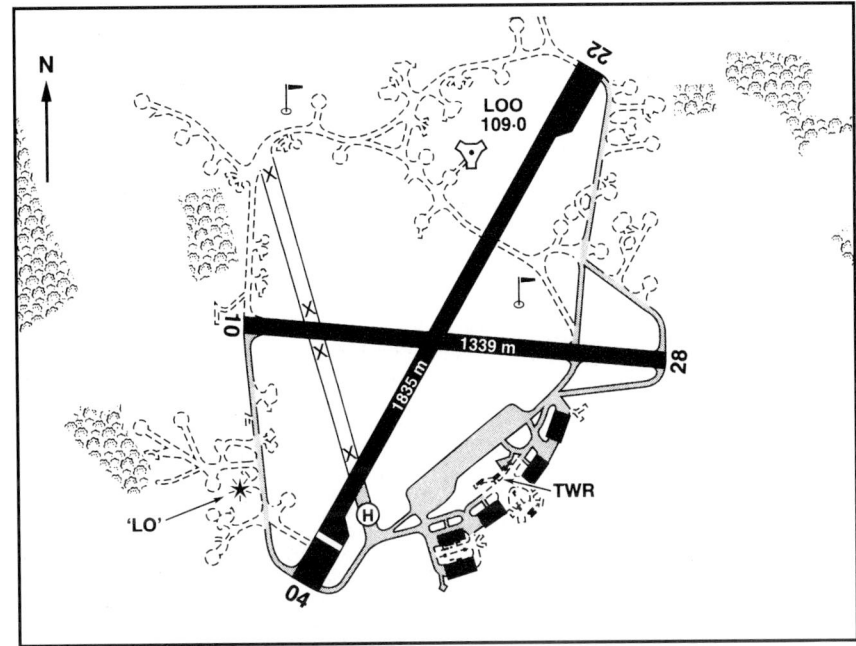

In mid-June both squadrons left Linton to fly back to Canada. All told, a total of 339 bombers had failed to return or were destroyed in crashes during operations from Linton-on-Ouse, the second highest loss for a Bomber Command airfield. Seventy-two were Whitleys, 76 Lancasters and 191 Halifaxes.

No. 4 Group, now under Transport Command, brought No. 1665 Heavy Conversion Unit to the station in November 1945 which operated Halifax transports until disbandment in July 1946. In the same month, Linton was taken over by Fighter Command and squadrons with Mosquitos, Hornets and Meteors and then Sabres and Hunters were on station for various periods up to 1957. The main runway, 04-22, was then extended to 3,010 yards. The next phase in Linton-on-Ouse's history was training activities with No. 1 Flying Training School first with mostly Vampires and then Jet Provosts and currently Tucanos. There are also Air Cadet gliding facilities.

Although the old E-W (11-29) runway has become 10-28 because of the change in magnetic north, for some reason the main N-S runway has retained its wartime description.

As the plan from _Pooleys Flight Guide_ at the top of the page shows, the third runway, 18-36, is no longer in use save for a helicopter pad at its southern end.

MIDDLETON ST GEORGE

The most northerly of all Bomber Command stations, Middleton St George was an expansion scheme development on which work started in 1939. Located five miles due east of the centre of Darlington, the airfield took its name from the Middleton St George Hall estate which provided most of the land. With the outbreak of war the specification was amended and only one of the planned Type C hangars was built together with a single Type J on the technical site, behind which the camp stretched up to the A67 Darlington to Saltburn road. Several of the planned barrack structures were cancelled and utility buildings substituted on dispersed sites. Although a grass surface had been prepared for the landing ground, an ash and hard core perimeter track was put down in the winter of 1939-40 and later in 1940 concrete runways were laid. These were 05-23 and 09-27 at 1,333 yards and 01-19 at 1,100 yards soon subject to extension. Before the work was completed, 05-23 was lengthened to 2,100 yards and 09-27 to 1,400. A total of 40 pan hardstandings were provided with two loops added later. The bomb store was

A vertical of Middleton St George taken on November 28, 1940 shows intense activity in the provision of hardsurfaces for aircraft movement. Extension to the runways is already being carried out.

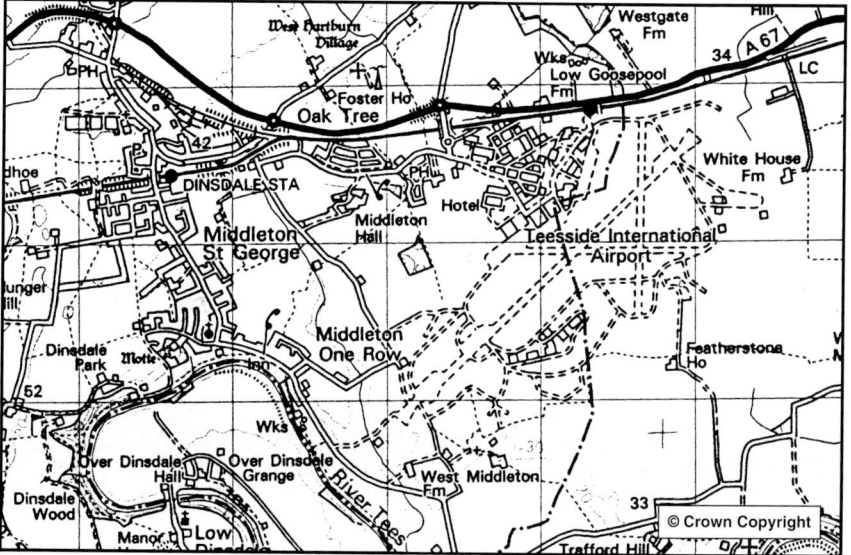

Left: **Harold 'Tobe' Geer, a radar mechanic with No. 428 Squadron, outside the radar hut.** *Right:* **A new building has replaced** the old workshop and the crew rest rooms on the left became the airport's first terminal building back in 1966.

positioned on the south east side of the airfield between runway heads 01 and 05. Later, additional hangars were also erected, a B1 and two T2s on the north side of the technical site.

Allocated to No. 4 Group, Middleton St George received its first flying unit in April 1941 when No. 78 Squadron with Whitleys arrived from Dishforth. It was joined in June that year by No. 76 Squadron with newly-acquired Halifaxes. No. 78 was transferred to the satellite airfield at Croft in October to give more space for conversion activities but it returned to the parent station in June 1942. Both squadrons were moved out to Linton-on-Ouse in September 1942 as part of the plan to base units of an all-RCAF group on airfields north of York.

The first Canadian squadron to arrive in October 1942 was No. 420 with Wellingtons, having previously been based at Skipton-on-Swale. It was joined the following month by similarly-equipped No. 419 Squadron from Croft, which re-equipped with Halifaxes. In May 1943 No. 420 Squadron was packed off to North Africa to increase the night bomber capability in the build-up to the invasion of Sicily. Then in early June No. 428 Squadron came from Dalton to take its place and at once started to shed its Wellingtons to embrace the Halifax. In April 1944, No. 419 exchanged its Halifaxes for Lancasters and No. 428 followed suit in June. It was during a raid from Middleton on the night of June 12/13, 1944 that the action of Pilot Officer Andrew Mynarski, trying to save the life of the rear gunner in a doomed No. 419 Lancaster, brought the award of a posthumous Victoria Cross.

The last raid from Middleton was flown on April 25, 1945 and in June both RCAF squadrons flew their Lancasters back to Canada. Wartime operations from the airfield had resulted in the loss of 279 bombers: 22 Whitleys, 18 Wellingtons, 169 Halifaxes and 70 Lancasters.

The Mosquitos of No. 13 OTU appeared in July 1945 and stayed until May 1947. During that year No. 608 (North Riding) Squadron of the Royal Auxiliary Air Force was established at Middleton sharing the station with No. 2 Air Navigation School and later No. 4 Flying Training School. These departed in 1956 following which there was a brief

Above: **A Canadian-built Lancaster X (KB882 NA-R) of No. 428 Squadron on a hardstanding near the firing butts, May 1945.**

Below: **Once a farmhouse, the ruined building was demolished during the early post-war years.**

Air Chief Marshal Sir Arthur Harris at a ceremony held on May 3, 1945 to mark the return of the Middleton St George squadrons to Canada. The airfield's two T2s and B1 hangars can be seen on the far side of the airfield.

spell of fighter squadron use with Meteors and Hunters. In 1950 aircraft servicing platforms were constructed by Mowlem and new hardstandings in 1953. In the autumn of 1957 the main runway was extended to 2,500 yards. The following year, when this work was completed, Hunters and Javelins appeared. In 1963 No. 226 OCU was re-formed to handle English Electric Lightnings but it departed in the spring of 1964.

Surplus to RAF requirements, Middleton St George was then acquired by the regional council for Tees-side and for conversion into a civil airport serving the area. Opened in November 1966, the airport has since been gradually developed with the addition of a new terminal building. In 1987 the airfield officially became Teesside International Airport when the main runway was lengthened to 3,330 yards. In the late 'nineties the airport was on average handling more than 150 air movements a day.

The location was the east side of the north end of runway 01-19 and still instantly recognisable 55 years later.

From wartime bomber station . . . to international airport. Teesside International Airport looking just east of north in September 2000. Unusually, the runway designations of Middleton St George have not been altered from their wartime compass bearings, the main (still 2,100 yards although now given as 2291 metres) remaining 05-23. Just 740 metres of the southerly end of 01-19 is in use today and 09-27 is disused as its western end would run too close to the terminal building.

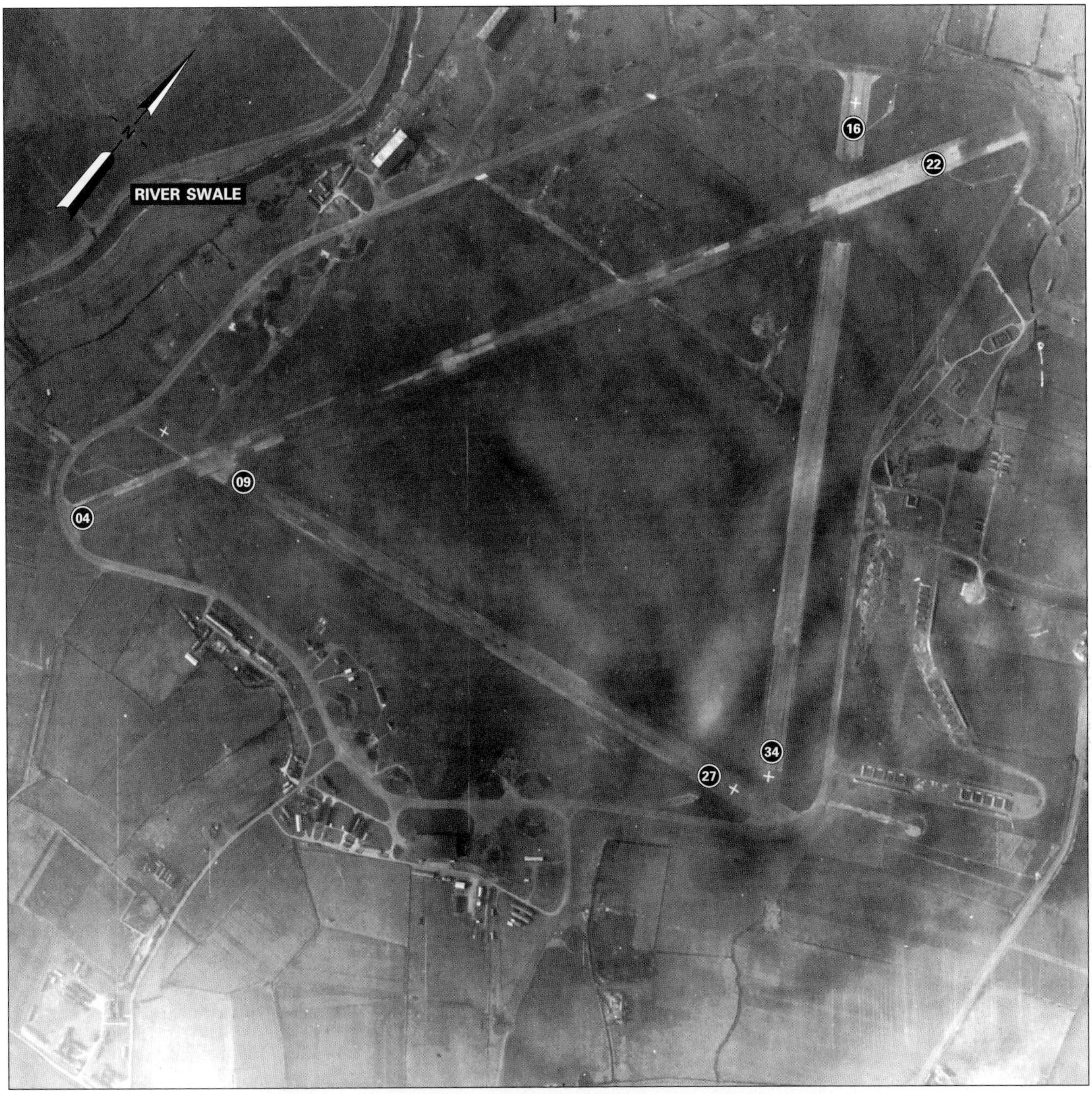

SKIPTON-ON-SWALE

Three-and-a-half miles west south-west of Thirsk, with the A61 Thirsk to Ripon road forming its south-eastern boundary, Skipton-on-Swale was one of the closely-packed bomber stations in the Vale of York. Farmland in the parishes of Skipton-on-Swale and Sand Hutton was acquired for the satellite for Leeming late in 1940. It was originally planned to have 1,400 and 1,100 yard runways but after construction of the perimeter track and 24 pan type hardstandings, much of this work was torn up so that longer runways could be installed. The main runway 04-22 then became 1,900 yards long, the 09-27 1,400 yards and 16-34 1,350 yards. The proximity of the River Swale on the west side caused a rather unusual arrangement of hardstandings and their access lanes. The technical site was on the north-east side and approached from the A167. A T2 and B1 hangar were positioned on the technical site and another T2 on the opposite side of the airfield. The dispersed domestic sites catered for 1,924 males and 166 females. Main contractor was George Wimpey & Co. Ltd.

White crosses adorn the runways of Skipton-on-Swale in March 1946 — just another disused Yorkshire bomber airfield 'surplus to requirements'. (See page 289 for the Ordnance Survey map of Skipton barely a couple of miles north-west of Topcliffe.)

One of the T2 hangars and the distant moors lay behind this Halifax II (MZ910) of No. 433 Squadron. This machine, 'Y'-Yoke, was lost March 18/19, 1945 while serving with No. 420 Squadron at Tholthorpe, one crewman being killed, the remainder being taken prisoner.

Six months earlier a disaster had befallen the little village after which the aerodrome was named. Halifax MZ828 of No. 433 Squadron, coded BM-H, was returning from an operation to attack the flying bomb depot at St-Leu-d'Esserant when an engine failed and the aircraft came down half-a-mile short of the main runway. This was a daylight raid and the crash occurred just after 3.30 on the afternoon on Saturday, August 5, 1944. Poor little Kenneth Battensby, five years old, was killed playing outside when the bomber came crashing through some trees. It careered across the road ending up with its nose against a huge elm in the centre of the village green. Flying Officer James Harrison, RCAF, and Sergeant Dennis Whitbread were both killed and the remainder of the crew — Flying Officers J. F. Kinder, E. T. Widenoja, L. E. Dufresne and Flight Sergeant R. Bourne (all Canadians) and Pilot Officer N. S. Godfrey — were all injured. *Right:* On May 19, 1984 a monument was unveiled on the very spot where the Halifax came to rest, dedicated to honour all those who served at Skipton from Nos. 420, 424, 432 and 433 Squadrons.

Today the green at Skipton-on-Swale has been extended, eliminating the slip road seen on the right in the wartime picture.

Looking back across the airfield with the 16-34 runway on the left, towards Skipton village beyond the far end of the main runway.

At first Skipton came under the auspices of No. 4 Group but, earmarked for No. 6, the station received No. 420 Squadron and its Wellingtons when these were transferred from No. 1 Group at Waddington in preparation for joining the planned RCAF group. This was in August 1942 but in mid-October the squadron was moved on to Middleton St George, reputedly because of the incomplete state of Skipton's camp. Not until the following spring was the station again occupied by a flying unit. Officially born at Skipton-on-Swale on May Day 1943, No. 432 Squadron started operations with Wellingtons on the night of the 23rd/24th of that month. In September, No. 432 was moved to East Moor and another RCAF squadron was formed to replace it.

No. 433 Squadron came into being in late September 1943 to fly Halifaxes, being joined in November by No. 424 recently returned from North Africa to re-equip with Halifaxes. No. 433 entered combat on the night of January 2/3, 1944 and No. 424 made its first raid with the Halifax to Berlin on February 15/16. These squadrons were to see out the war at Skipton, converting to Lancasters in January 1945. By the end of hostilities 98 bombers had been lost in operations flown from this station; 21 Wellingtons, 66 Halifaxes and 11 Lancasters.

Following VE-Day, both squadrons remained in Bomber Command until disbanded in mid-October 1945. Although the RAF maintained a housekeeper unit at the airfield for a few months under the auspices of a Maintenance Unit, there was no further use for the base and by the 'fifties it was returned to agriculture. Today, parts of the runways remain intact as bases for poultry houses, the greater part of the area having been devoted to poultry farming for the past three decades.

This is the runway the Halifax never made. The threshold of 04-22 is now covered with poultry sheds.

THOLTHORPE

Twelve miles north-west of the centre of York and three from Easingwold, an area of Tholthorpe Moor north of Carle Beck was requisitioned soon after war was declared for a satellite landing ground for Linton-on-Ouse. As such, it first came into use as a dispersal for the Whitleys of the parent station in the late summer of 1940. However, it was reportedly unsuitable for winter use and was not used beyond early December after which a narrow hard core perimeter track was put down. The site was then developed further, although work did not commence until late 1941 on what was eventually to end up as a bomber airfield to Class A standard. The three intersecting concrete runways were main 10-28 at 2,000 yards, 06-24 at 1,430 yards and 16-34 at 1,400 yards. The old perimeter track was abandoned when the airfield area was expanded and the road from Derring's Farm to Tholthorpe village closed. At this stage, only 21 of the original hardstandings remained so 15 loop type were

added. The technical site was on the south side of the airfield between 06 and 34 near Moor Lane. A T2 hangar lay a little to the east and a second T2 near the closed road on the north-west side between 10 and 16. A third T2 stood on the north-east side between 24 and 28. Bomb stores were between runway heads 28 and 34 behind Carle House. The 12 camp sites were mostly dispersed along the road between Tholthorpe village and Flawith with accommodation for 1,501 males and 233 females.

Allocated to No. 6 Group, in June 1943 No. 434 Squadron was formed at the station to fly Halifaxes and in July No. 431 Squadron arrived from Burn with its recently-acquired Halifaxes. No. 431 joined No. 434 on operations on the night of August 12/13 against Italian targets. In early December both squadrons were switched to Croft. That same month Nos. 420 and 425 were posted in from Dalton and Dishforth respectively but, having recently returned from service with Wellingtons in North Africa, it took some weeks for the squadrons to work up on their newly-acquired Halifaxes, their first raids from Tholthorpe not being flown until Feb-

ruary 15/16, 1944 for No. 420 and five days later by No. 425. Both squadrons remained at Tholthorpe right up to the end of the war, No. 420 flying its final raid on April 22 and No. 425 on April 25, 1945. A hasty conversion to Lancasters followed before both squadrons left for Canada in June. No. 420 Squadron undertook 160 raids from Tholthorpe losing 25 Halifaxes and No. 425 flew 162 for the loss of 28 aircraft. All told, 119 Halifaxes were either missing or crashed in the UK in ops flown from Tholthorpe.

During June 1945 Tholthorpe came under care and maintenance but little of either was seen and the RAF holding party had departed by the end of the year. For a few years the airfield remained in a fairly intact state with hangars in use for individual purposes. Private flying took place from the airfield during the 'eighties but by the 'nineties farming activities had erased most of the buildings and all of the runways save for a few odd lengths left as farm roads. Light industry now occupies the old technical site area. Both the earlier Type 13079/41 watch office and Type 343/43 control tower still stand, the latter converted into a house in 1995.

Crews being taken to their aircraft by lorry and towed trailer. The T2 hangar is at the north-west corner of the airfield.

The T2 near Webb's Plantation still stands and a strip of the perimeter track has been retained as a farm road.

An interesting series of comparisons showing Tholthorpe's development — and demise! The first, taken on April 25, 1941 from 9,000 feet, shows runways which appear to be a tar surface. The second photograph was taken on July 21 1942 when work constructing a perimeter track and pan hardstandings was nearing completion. By this time the airfield appears to have been ploughed up and false fields created to aid camouflage. On October 21, 1942, when the third picture was taken, work had begun on laying concrete runways and modifying the perimeter track to meet the ends, isolating or destroying several of the hardstandings already built. *Below:* The airfield today as seen from the east with the main extension in the foreground.

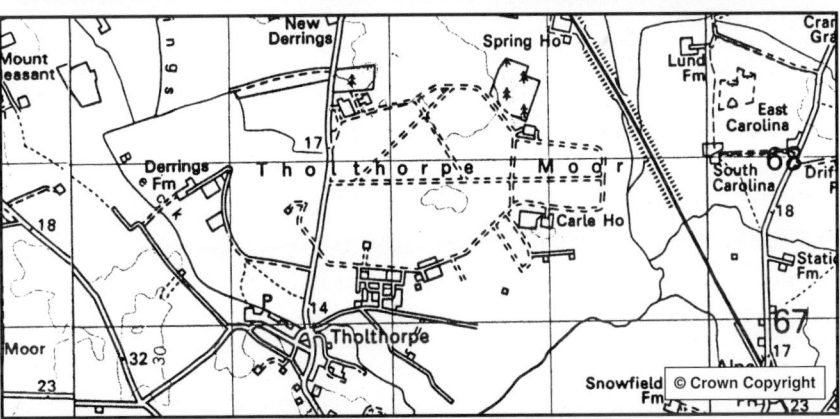

TOPCLIFFE

A late expansion scheme airfield, Topcliffe was not begun until shortly before the outbreak of war and not completed until late 1940. Some 2½ miles south-west of Thirsk and 1½ miles from Topcliffe village on the west side of the A168, the station had a bombing circle in some 200 acres of seeded grass, fronted on the west side by three of the later Type C hangars with two more behind and the permanent camp to the rear.

Topcliffe on June 22, 1942. Although the perimeter track is still not complete and many hardstandings are yet to be built, the Halifaxes of No. 102 Squadron are already in residence. (Refer to page 289 for the Ordnance Survey plan.)

In September 1940, No. 77 Squadron's Whitleys were moved in from Linton-on-Ouse with No. 102's following a few weeks later. The first operation from Topcliffe was carried out on the night of October 8/9, 1940. A year later No. 77 Squadron departed for Leeming and No. 102 Squadron moved the two miles to Dalton when Topcliffe was scheduled to receive hard runways. This work was carried out during the winter of 1941-42, the runways being the main 03-21 at 2,009 yards and both subsidiaries, 09-27 and 13-31, at 1,380 yards. (The main runway was originally shorter but lengthened before the station was re-opened.) The 37 pan-type hardstandings that existed, several on long access lanes, were linked to the perimeter track, and two loops added. Bomb stores were on the north side of the airfield, between 13 and 21. Additional domestic sites

A No. 405 Squadron Halifax undergoing engine maintenance at Topcliffe in July 1942.

The interior of all the Type C hangars are the same — this is the one currently used by the RAF for their Tucanos.

were dispersed in fields to the west and maximum accommodation was given as for 2,039 males and 420 females.

No. 102 Squadron returned in June 1943 with Halifaxes although its tenure was brief for Topcliffe was one of the airfields that No. 4 Group would bequeath to the Canadian No. 6 Group. To this end, in early August No. 405 Squadron arrived at Topcliffe from Pocklington in an exchange of stations with No. 102. To further the concentration of Canadian-manned units in the area, No. 419 Squadron brought its Wellingtons over from Leeming during the same month but was moved on to Croft six weeks later. However, a critical situation in the Battle of the Atlantic saw No. 405 Squadron take its Halifaxes south on detachment to Coastal Command in early October 1942. In its absence, No. 424 Squadron was formed at Topcliffe to fly Wellingtons in mid-October, going operational for its first raid on January 15/16, 1943.

No. 405 Squadron returned in March but was almost immediately moved on to Leeming. No. 424 Squadron's Wellingtons were to follow in April, the reason being a decision to concentrate the operational training activities in No. 6 Group on the Topcliffe clutch of stations, the first move being to transfer No. 1659 Heavy Conversion Unit from Leeming to Topcliffe after the operational squadrons had left. In November 1944, the OTU establishments passed from No. 6 Group to No. 7 (Training) Group and No. 1659 HCU began to dispose of its Halifaxes in exchange for Lancasters. A total of 123 bombers were lost while flying from Topcliffe on operations, 83 Whitleys, 9 Wellingtons and 31 Halifaxes.

With the disbandment of No. 1659 HCU in September 1945, there was a short period of care and maintenance after which No. 5 — later redesignated No. 1 Air Navigation

Long disused for the purpose for which they were built, the bomb stores are now used for more peaceful purposes — as hay storage for the Army's horses! The officer is Flight Lieutenant 'Baf' Baker.

School — was installed at Topcliffe. This formation remained until 1949 after which Transport Command held sway with Hastings aircraft. During the next two decades there was a considerable amount of new building and improvements to the flying field, the airfield being taken over by Coastal Command in 1952 with Lancasters and Neptunes. It was back to Training Command in

1957 and No. 1 Air Navigation School but this moved south in 1962. Ten years later the base as an RAF station closed when it was transferred to the Army. Re-named Alanbrooke Barracks, the whole complex is currently well maintained with little demolition and the flying field retained in serviceable condition. In 1993 the RAF returned with the Joint Elementary Flying Training School.

Nice examples of loop and pan types of dispersal on the eastern side of Topcliffe. Skipton-on-Swale, less than two miles away directly in line with the 31 runway, is lost in the misty background.

Pilot Officer Jack Wetherly with his crew of No. 214 Squadron in 1941. L-R: Sergeant Hubert Barr, Jack Wetherly, Pilot Officer Ian Lawson, Sergeant Nigel Walker and Sergeant Albert Livsey. Behind Livsey stands Flight Lieutenant Culley, the rear gunner.

Operation to Berlin

At Bomber Command airfields throughout East Anglia, Lincolnshire and Yorkshire, rumours had abounded since the ground crews had been told the bomb-load and fuel requirements of their aircraft. Tonight's was clearly a distant target but only at briefing would the aircrews know if it would be Nuremberg, Munich, Stuttgart or Berlin.

No. 76 Squadron, based at Linton-on-Ouse, had bombed each of these targets in the past month: Nuremberg on the 8th, Munich on the 9th, Stuttgart on the 11th and twice to Berlin — on the 1st and, two nights ago, on the 27th. They had been lucky. In twelve operations in March they had lost only five aircraft but two of these, including one captained by one of their flight commanders, had been lost on the first trip to Berlin. The German capital, with its long haul across Germany and its active flak and many night

fighters, was the worst target of all. Many aircrew must have prayed hard that it would not be the 'Big City' again tonight.

It was. Their new Commanding Officer, Wing Commander Don Smith, confirmed the target at briefing. Twelve of the squadron's Halifaxes would be among the first wave of the 330 aircraft detailed for the raid. Take-off would be at 1900. Each Halifax would carry 5,000 pounds of high explosives and incendiaries and the squadron would bomb between 2210 and 2231 from 18,000 feet.

The briefing room was silent as all synchronised their watches on the Bombing Leader's mark. The squadron Bombing Leader was Flight Lieutenant Bert Beck, who had often flown as bomb-aimer in the crew of the previous CO, Leonard Cheshire, who had become a good friend. Tonight, however, Cheshire was on leave awaiting posting on promotion to RAF Marston Moor and Bert Beck would take the place of the regular bomb-aimer in another crew, captained by Flight Lieutenant Jack Wetherly.

A Halifax of No. 76 Squadron departs at dusk for an operation in 1943.

Jack Wetherly was one of the squadron's most experienced captains. He had arrived seven weeks earlier after a happy two-year spell as a flying instructor in Flying Training Command, having already completed a tour of ops with No. 214 Squadron flying Wellingtons. Tonight's would be the fifteenth op of his second tour and his fourth trip to Berlin. Another five ops would complete his tour and enable him to return to instructing for good.

At 28 his maturity, experience and unflappable instructor's temperament made Jack an obvious captain to take novice pilots on their first trip. When the new CO had joined the squadron earlier in the month, after two tours of very different operations in the Middle East, Jack had taken him as 'second dickey' on his first raid over Germany. He had taken six other new pilots on ops and tonight he would take another, Sergeant Whittle. One of Cheshire's last acts as CO had been to recommend Jack for the Distinguished Flying Cross. The recommendation had reached the desk of Air Vice-Marshal Roderick Carr, the Air Officer Commanding No. 4 Group, that morning: March 29, 1943.

Take-off was postponed by nearly three hours and Jack's Halifax, 'K-King', finally took off from Linton at 2148 with its crew of eight. Only eleven of the squadron's aircraft took off. The twelfth, Sergeant Sanderson's 'Q-Queen', had technical trouble. They immediately climbed into thick cloud with violent hailstorms and much stronger winds than had been forecast by the Met reports. The persistent hail wore off the de-icing paste smeared on the leading edge of the wings, leaving them vulnerable to severe icing. Ice formed on the wings of some aircraft, making them unstable and unmanoeuvrable, and six of the eleven remaining squadron aircraft turned back. Five crews, including those of Don Smith and Jack, pressed on in a bomber stream already depleted by the loss of 76 aircraft from other squadrons whose captains had also decided to turn back. Of 65 Halifaxes despatched by No. 4 Group from its Yorkshire bases, 24 turned for home.

The 247 crews who pressed on found that the weather cleared only as they reached the western coast of Schleswig-Holstein. Until then they flew on instruments, struggling to keep control of their ice-covered aircraft, aware of the presence of other aeroplanes only when they felt the buffeting caused by hitting the slipstream of another bomber. Over the German coast the weather cleared but it had delayed them and they were late bombing their target. The patchy and scattered bombing showed that few aircraft had got through and this depletion of the bomber stream, together with the clear weather over Germany, made them more vulnerable to the German flak and night fighters.

Berlin, March 29, 1943. Soon after crossing the German coast north of Wesselburen, K-King was shot down by Leutnant August Geiger who claimed five British aircraft that night. The Halifax crashed near Gaushorn-Welmbutte, north-east of Heide, in Schleswig-Holstein. Jack Wetherly (above) and six of his crew were killed instantly and the mid-upper gunner, Sergeant Leonard Havenhand, died of his injuries in hospital.

The raid was not a success. The Pathfinders had dropped their Target Indicators too far south and many bombs fell in open country six miles south-east of Berlin. Twenty-one aircraft were lost, and a further twelve from another raid that night on Bochum.

Back at Linton, by dawn it was clear that, of the five No. 76 Squadron aircraft which had pressed on, two were missing. There would be no survivors from either crew. One was the Halifax of Sergeant Leslie Cursley, who was on the last but one op of his tour. The other was Jack Wetherly's 'K-King'.

PORTRAIT OF A BOMBER PILOT
CHRISTOPHER JARY, 1990

They were buried in Schleswig Cemetery but now lie in the Commonwealth War Graves Commission Cemetery at Kiel.

Jack's granddaughter Alex pictured beside the grave on March 29, 1993 — exactly 50 years after that fateful raid on Berlin.

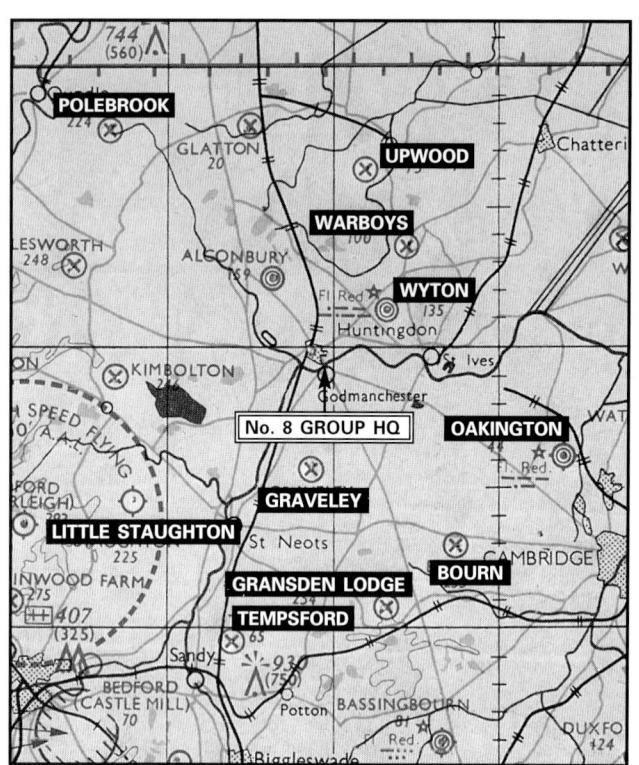

© Crown Copyright

No. 8 Group

Originally acquired by the Air Ministry in October 1939 as an headquarters for No. 2 Group, Castle Hill House was passed to No. 8 Group in June 1943. This Georgian dwelling served the group as its HQ until disbandment in December 1945.

No. 8 Group was established at Brampton Grange in September 1941. It was to control squadrons equipped with American-made heavy bombers — Fortresses and Liberators — to be based on the new airfields being built in the Northamptonshire/Huntingdonshire area. However, with the entry of the United States into hostilities in December 1941, this plan was abandoned and the headquarters disbanded in January 1942.

On August 15, 1942 the headquarters of the specialist Pathfinder Force was established at Wyton. On January 8, 1943 it was given group status as No. 8 (P.F.F.) Group with an airfield domain in the Cambridge/Huntingdon area. Two of its five squadrons flew Lancasters, one Halifaxes, one Stirlings and the other Wellingtons and Mosquitos. By the end of the war the group had become the largest in Bomber Command with approximately 440 aircraft in 19

squadrons, 11 of which were Mosquito-equipped the remainder flying Lancasters. Apart from its main roll in target location and marking, most of the Mosquito squadrons became part of the Light Night Striking Force designed to cause maximum disruption of enemy defences by nuisance raids. Group HQ moved into Huntingdon to the site that previously housed No. 2 Group HQ in June 1943, remaining there until disbandment in December 1945.

Today Castle Hill House is used by Huntingdon District Council. A blue plaque outside commemorates the wartime Pathfinder links.

BOURN

With a record-breaking 203 sorties painted on its nose, Mosquito B.IX LR503 of No. 105 Squadron was pictured parked on the first pan hardstanding north of runway 07 on the west side of the airfield.

This site was acquired in 1940 as a satellite for Oakington under No. 3 Group. Six miles west of Cambridge, it borders the south side of the old A45 to St Neots. Some four hundred acres of farmland between Bourn Grange in the south, Great Common Farm in the west and Highfield Farm in the east were eventually taken over for the airfield which was not completed until the winter of 1941-42 although it is reported to have been used by Oakington during the summer of 1941.

The runways as first laid down were 07-25 at 1,430 yards, 01-19 at 1,180 yards and 13-31 at 1,050 yards. A number of pan-type aircraft standings had been put down during 1940-41 and it is believed that these eventually totalled 36. The technical site lay on the west side near Great Common Farm with a T2 hangar south of runway head 13 and a B1 nearby to the west. A second T2 stood north of Bourn Grange. The bomb stores were off the south-east in Bucket Hill Plantation

between runway heads 01 and 31. Dispersed camp sites were situated to the west and south along Broad Way consisting of six domestic, one WAAF, two communal and a sick quarters, the last being right beside Bourn Grange. The eventual total accommodation provided was for 1,805 males and 276 females. This was provided in an assortment of huts, mainly Nissen, but some requisitioned buildings were used in the early days.

The building behind 'F' for Freddie was the motor transport washdown and workshop. It was reclad in 1996 and is the only surviving wartime building on the flying site and is used by the Cambridge Wine Warehouse.

This shot of Bourn was taken on June 26, 1942 before the full number of hardstandings were built.

In the spring of 1942 work was carried out to lengthen the main runway to 1,960 yards with the 01-19 going to 1,600 yards and the 13-31 to 1,400 yards, the main 07-25 being extended at both ends while 01-19 only at the 01 end. When this work was completed only 27 of the original pan standings remained so nine of the loop type were added.

In February 1942, No. 101 Squadron with its Wellingtons left the parent airfield and took up station at Bourn. The squadron left for Stradishall in August and No. 15 Squadron brought its Stirlings in to Bourn the same month. It had vacated Wyton as this was the headquarters airfield of the Pathfinder Force formed on August 15, the same day as No. 15's Stirlings set off on their first raid from the airfield. In April 1943, the squadron was

again moved on to the No. 3 Group station at Mildenhall to make way for Pathfinder units. The expanding No. 8 Group acquired Bourn for the Lancasters of No. 97 Squadron from Woodhall Spa in No. 5 Group. During No. 15 Squadron's tenure three T2 hangars were erected in the Grange Farm area to provide cover for Stirlings sent for repair and modification by a branch of Short Bros. Ltd.

In late March 1944, No. 105 Squadron and its Mosquitos were switched from Marham to Bourn when the former was scheduled to be upgraded to a very heavy bomber airfield. No. 97 Squadron's stay lasted a year and in mid-April 1944 it returned to No. 5 Group to practice its pathfinder arts out of Coningsby. No. 105 Squadron had Bourn all to itself until December 1944 when No. 162 Squad-

ron was re-formed with a nucleus from the established resident to expand the Mosquito force. The last Mosquito operation from Bourn was flown on the night of May 2/3, 1945. A total of 135 Bomber Command aircraft were lost in operations flown from Bourn; 19 Wellingtons, 32 Stirlings, 60 Lancasters and 24 Mosquitos.

No. 105 Squadron went to Upwood in June 1945 and No. 162 to Blackbushe in July. Thereafter, care and maintenance descended on Bourn and no further flying units were based there. The airfield was returned to agriculture during the 'fifties and in the following decade a heliport was established near the old Stirling hangars near the Cambridge road. The Highfields farm area has now been developed into an industrial estate.

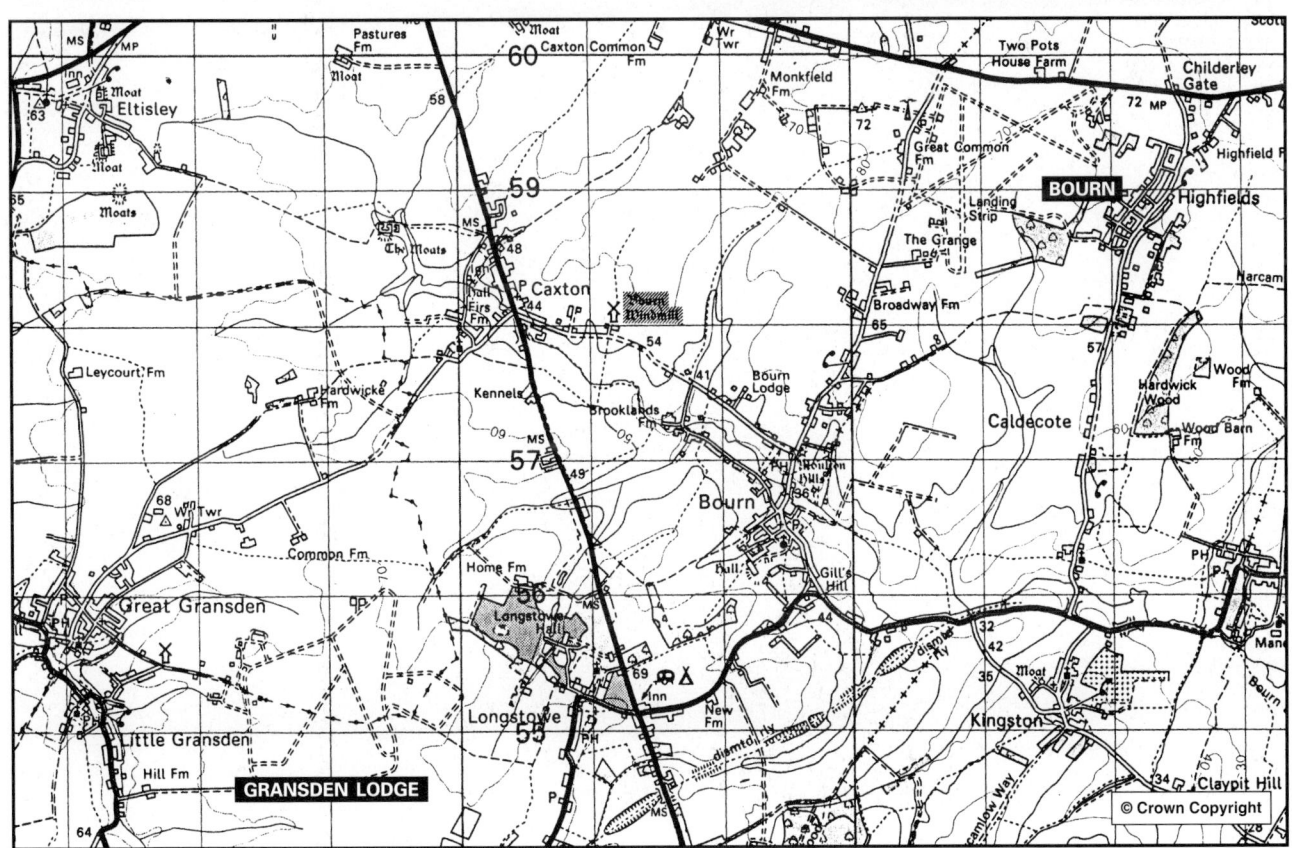

A very active flying club, the Rural Flying Corps, has been based on the southern side of the airfield (in the foreground) since 1977. Two strips are in use, one of 633 metres on the southern end of the main runway (01-19) and the other of 568 metres in the centre part of the 07-25 — now redesignated 06-24.

One nice touch that the Corps have adopted is that any exotic, interesting or unusual flying machines can land for free, providing they give a fly-by! However care has to be taken as gliding takes place at Gransden Lodge — the next airfield in No. 8 Group — which lies three miles away to the south-west.

GRANSDEN LODGE

The first Canadian-built Lancaster (KB700), named the *Ruhr Express* being bombed up on the hardstanding to the west of the northernmost T2 at Gransden Lodge. She belonged to No. 405 Squadron and was coded LQ-Q.

Gransden Lodge was an airfield built to Class A standard during 1941-42. Located seven miles south-east of St Neots, it was necessary to close the road between Great Gransden and Longstowe and another lane running from the latter to the north. Gransden Lodge, after which the airfield was named, lay on the northern boundary of the airfield.

The three concrete runways were 04-22 at 1,600 yards, 10-28 at 1,220 yards and 17-35 at 1,200 yards. However, it appears that the runways were lengthened before the airfield was brought into use, 04-22 out to 2,000 yards and the others to 1,400 yards each. Of the 36 pan hardstandings, two were lost by hangar construction being replaced by two loops. A B1 and T2 hangar lay north of the technical site between runway heads 17 and 22, near Great Gransden village. A second T2 stood on the south side of the airfield between runway heads 04 and 35 and the bomb stores were situated off the east side between runway heads 28 and 35. The dispersed camp lay in fields to the north-west around Great Gransden village and consisted of two communal, two WAAF, six domestic and sick quarters. Total accommodation allowed for 1,867 males and 252 females.

First allocated to No. 3 Group as a satellite for Tempsford, the secluded location made the station ideal for secret activities. Its first occupants were Nos. 1418 and 1474 Flights with Wellingtons which arrived in April 1942. These were engaged respectively in radio navigation checking and wireless interrogation. No. 1418 Flight was later absorbed by the Bomber Development Unit while No. 1474 became the source of No. 192 Squadron formed at the station in January 1943. Both were moved to Feltwell in April 1943 when the station was passed to No. 8 Group.

Under No. 8 Group, Gransden Lodge received No. 405 Squadron and its Halifaxes transferred to pathfinder duties from No. 6 (RCAF) Group at Leeming. This had been the first Canadian heavy bomber unit in Bomber Command and the squadron had suffered severely. It converted to Lancasters in August 1943. In October that year No. 142 Squadron was re-formed at Gransden equipped with Mosquitos to expand the highly successful Light Night Striking Force. One hundred and two Bomber Command aircraft were missing or crashed in the UK in operations flown from this station; 27 Halifaxes, 61 Lancasters and 14 Mosquitos.

After VE-Day No. 405 Squadron rejoined No. 6 Group and took its Lancasters to Linton-on-Ouse. No. 692 Squadron's Mosquitoes arrived from Graveley in June and gradually wasted until disbandment in September 1945. The station then passed to Transport Command and for a few weeks Liberators of No. 53 Squadron were in residence. Thereafter the airfield was run down, although kept in a fairly intact until the early 1950s. In subsequent years agriculture took over resulting in the removal of most of the runways. The B1 hangar and control tower remain together with a reduced width of the perimeter track as a farm road.

Looking north-north-east in 1999. The T2 and all other structures and concrete have given way to a vast expanse of emergent cereals. In the far distance glider trailers for the incumbent gliding club occupying the site of the original Gransden Lodge which was demolished.

GRANSDEN LODGE

N

22

17

35

28

10

04

Above: **Another inactive airfield photographed in May 1946. In this case the full runway bearings have been painted on the thresholds (See page 321 for the Ordnance Survey plan.)**

Below: **This oblique was taken in September 2000 looking north so can be compared directly with the vertical taken by No. 540 Squadron. Wide grass strips mimic the runways.**

GRAVELEY

This was a Class A airfield constructed 1941-42 to the west of Graveley village which itself lies 4½ miles south of Huntingdon. Most of the land used was that of Cotton Farm and the construction also involved the closure of the ancient Roman Way road. The main contractor was Messrs W & C French, the three runways being 09-27 at 1,600 yards, 15-33 at 1,320 yards and 03-21 at 1,307 yards. The usual total of 36 pan-type hardstandings were distributed round the perimeter track. There were two T2 hangars on the technical site between runway heads 15 and 21 and a B1 and T2 in the south-east corner of the airfield between runway heads 27 and 33. The bomb store was located in open country to the south-west. Dispersed camp sites lay to the north of the airfield, consisting of nine domestic, one communal and sick quarters with maximum accommodation for 2,300 males and 299 females.

The station came into use in the spring of 1942 as part of the Tempsford clutch of airfields where 'special duties' units were concentrated in No. 3 Group. No. 161 Squadron with Lysanders and Wellingtons arrived from Newmarket in March and was moved on to Tempsford the following month. Little activity occurred at the station during the next three months apart from runway lengthening, the main 09-27 being extended at the 09 end to 2,000 yards; 15-33 on the 33 end to 1,420 yards; and 03-21 at the 03 end to 1,407 yards. This improvement and associated works affected three pans, three loop standings being furnished to make up their loss.

P3 was the code of No. 692 Squadron — part of the Light Night Striking Force — which carried out the very last raid of the war on May 2/3, 1945 to Kiel though MM183 had already been wrecked in a wheels-up landing at Manston on February 1.

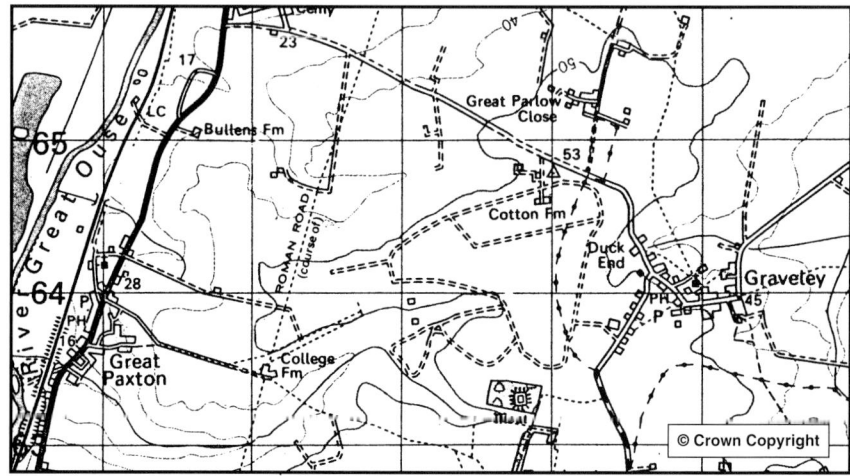

© Crown Copyright

During the course of this work, extensions of taxiways to the ends of the extended runways caused the destruction of three pan hardstandings.

At the beginning of August, Graveley was re-allocated to the Pathfinder Force which brought in No. 35 Squadron and its Halifaxes from No. 4 Group at Linton-on-Ouse. Their first operation from Graveley took place the night of August 18/19, 1942. On New Year's Day 1944, No. 692 Squadron formed at Graveley to fly Mosquitos for No. 8 Group, undertaking its first sorties exactly a month later, the squadron becoming part of what was known as the Light Night Striking Force. In March, No. 35 Squadron exchanged its Halifaxes for Lancasters which it operated until its final sorties on April 25, 1945. No. 692 Squadron Mosquitos carried out their last raid on May 2/3, 1945 with an attack on Kiel. In 310 operations from Graveley the squadron lost 17 Mosquitos and a total of 150 Bomber Command aircraft were missing or crashed in the UK in operations flown from this station: 83 Halifaxes, 32 Lancasters and 35 Mosquitos.

Most of the technical site has been cleared, replaced by agricultural buildings with a private house on the site of the control tower.

August 1947 under the watchful eyes of the reconnaissance cameras of No. 58 Squadron.

In June 1945, No. 692 Squadron was moved to Gransden Lodge and No. 227 Squadron with Lancasters joined No. 35 at Graveley to prepare for movement to the Far East as part of Tiger Force. Cancellation of this venture brought disbandment of No. 227 Squadron in September with No. 115 Squadron being moved in from Witchford to replace it. The Lancasters of Nos. 35 and 115 remained at Graveley for a year before being transferred to Stradishall with its permanent camp. During this time, No. 35 Squadron took its Lancasters on a goodwill tour to the USA.

Although Graveley was put on care and maintenance in September 1945, and no more RAF units were based there, this wartime airfield was kept as a reserve for the next 12 years. During this time the main runway was maintained in good condition and regularly used by training aircraft for 'circuits and bumps'. Graveley was closed at the end of 1968 and was eventually reclaimed by Cotton Farm. The eastern end of the main runway still survived in the late 'nineties and a reduced perimeter track is used as a farm road.

Bomber Command's war in Europe ended here . . . midst these peaceful fields on the Hunts/Cambridgeshire border.

LITTLE STAUGHTON

Above: **Bombing up No. 582 Squadron on the double loop on the eastern side with the technical site in the background.**

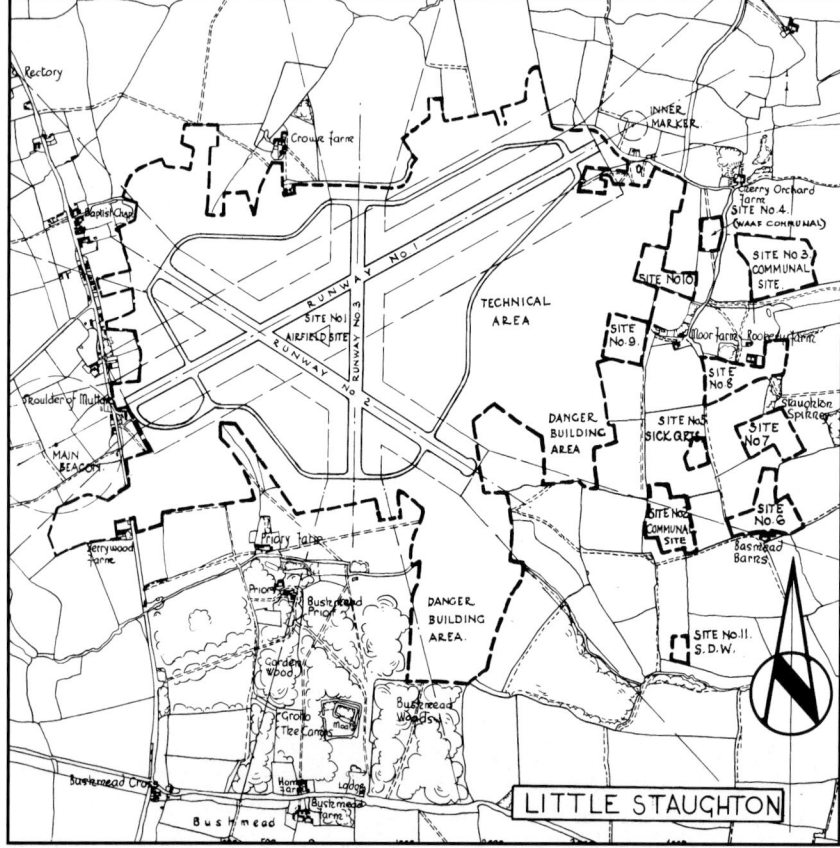

Compare the vertical shot taken by the US 7th Photographic Group on February 10, 1944 with the layout depicted on the Record Site Plan of the same year.

WAAF's pose beside a Mosquito of No. 109 Squadron outside the eastern end of the northern T2.

Four miles west of the centre of St Neots, Little Staughton airfield lies just inside the Huntingdonshire border with Bedfordshire. Built 1941-42 to Class A standard, it was necessary to close a minor road across the north of the site. The concrete runways were main 07-25 at 1,616 yards, 13-31 at 1,156 yards and 01-19 at 1,020 yards. Before completion, runways 07-25 and 13-31 were extended to 1,920 yards and 1,340 yards, respectively. Originally 37 pan hardstandings were put down but when the airfield was allocated to the USAAF in May 1942 another 17 of the loop type were added. One cluster of loops lay across the road to Little Staughton village near Berrywood Farm. A T2 hangar was positioned on the technical site between runway heads 25 and 31 near Moor Farm; a second T2 between runway heads 01 and 07, and a third between 19 and 25. Bomb stores were to the south between runway heads 01 and 31. The dispersed camp lay to the east of the airfield comprising of six domestic, two WAAF, two communal and a sick quarters site. Maximum accomodation was given as 2,496 males and 126 female.

In September 1942, the station was temporarily allocated to the USAAF as an advanced air depot and as such was first occupied by the Eighth Air Force in January 1943. Officially transferred to the USAAF on May 1, 1943, the station was in use from April that year as the 2nd Advanced Air Depot for repair of B-17s of the 1st Bomb Wing. Additional work on the eastern side of the airfield was put in hand to develop an independent depot but evidently the Americans felt the road communications to Little Staughton were poor and it was decided instead to build at Alconbury. As RAF No 8 Group required more airfields in the area, an exchange was arranged whereby Little Staughton would be returned to RAF con-

trol and the new airfield at Harrington allocated for USAAF use.

The RAF officially took over Little Staughton on March 1, 1944. On April 1, the 'C' Flights of No. 7 Squadron at Oakington and No. 156 Squadron at Upwood were transferred with their Lancasters to Little Staughton to form No. 582 Squadron. Next day, No. 109 Squadron with its Mosquitos came in from Marham. These two squadrons were to be the only occupants of the station

for the remainder of hostilities. No. 582 flew its first raid on the night of April 9/10, 1944 and its last on April 25, 1945, a total of 165 raids during which it lost 28 Lancasters.

Two Victoria Crosses were awarded posthumously to Little Staughton airmen. On December 23, 1944, Squadron Leader Robert Palmer, a No. 109 Squadron pilot flying a No. 582 Lancaster, perished after determinedly attacking the target despite crippling damage to his aircraft. Then on the

A Lancaster from No. 582 Squadron pictured prior to the launch of the daylight raid on April 25, 1945 to knock out coastal batteries on Wangerooge which defended Bremen and Wilhelmshaven. The parachute store and Romney main workshops can be seen in the background. Looking due west from the loop dispersals to the east of the technical site.

The workshops have gone but fortunately the parachute building is a survivor.

The old technical site has now been developed into a large industrial and commercial complex known as Staughton Moor.

night of February 23/24, 1945, Captain Edwin Swales of No. 582 Squadron lost his life in a gallant effort to save both his crew and aircraft.

No. 109 Squadron flew its last sorties on the night of May 2/3, 1945 and was disbanded at Little Staughton at the end of September, No. 582 Squadron having been disbanded earlier that month. A total of 57 Bomber Command aircraft were lost in offensive operations from this station; 34 Lancasters and 23 Mosquitos.

A state of care and maintenance then descended on the station and agricultural use was made of the land not covered with concrete. In the 'fifties the airfield was one of a number turned over to the USAF for upgrading and the main runway was increased to 3,000 yards and other work carried out to enable jet aircraft to use the base in an emergency. Although the USAF departed in the late 'fifties, the runway was maintained in good condition for several years and for a period the airfield was used by Brooklands Aviation as a repair depot.

The recognition letters for each airfield were displayed in the signals square laid out in front of the control tower. The characters were usually about 10ft high and Little Staughton's LX still remain cast in concrete. At night, code letters would be flashed in Morse Code in red by a mobile beacon known as a 'Pundit' but, so as not to identify any particular airfield to enemy intruders, the beacon was located away from the airfield and was moved about so crews were briefed each night as to the relationship of the Pundit to their airfield. The code was also changed regularly. Approach lighting could be switched on, each aerodrome being surrounded by a circle of lights with a diameter of 6,500 yards. 'On raid nights these airfields were like close-set necklaces of pearls', recalled Colonel Jean Calmel, 'and England gleamed with all its fires like a woman wearing her diamonds when we returned.'

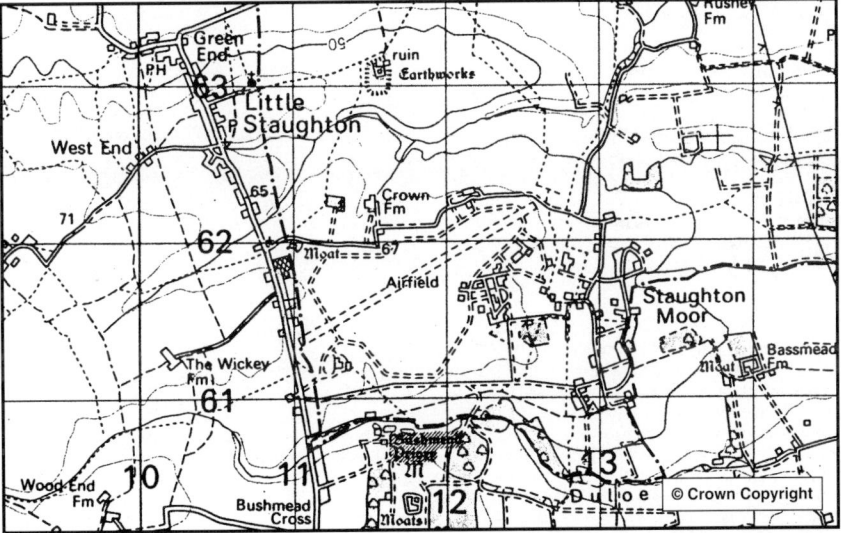

329

OAKINGTON

The tower of Oakington church can be seen on the extreme right of this photograph of No. 7 Squadron's Stirling MG-Y. At this time, early 1942, the T2 hangar that later stood in this area had yet to be erected.

Meadowland five miles north-west of the centre of Cambridge was selected as a site for an expansion scheme airfield in the 1930s and construction of Oakington began in the summer of 1939. However, the specification was changed after war was declared and, as a result, a limit was placed on the number of permanent buildings and more utility types were dispersed around the village of Long Stanton St Michael, which was adjacent to the camp site at the north-west side of the landing ground. The original plan called for a crescent of Type C hangars on the technical site but two Type J were erected instead.

The station came into use under No. 2 Group in July 1940 as a refuge for battered No. 218 Squadron, recently returned from France, and re-equipping with Blenheims and its first offensive operation from the station was made on August 19. In September, Oakington was passed to No. 3 Group and chosen as the base for the first Stirling squadron — No. 7 — which had been working up on the type at Leeming away from the air battles in the south. In November 1940, No. 218 Squadron left for Marham and re-equipment with Wellingtons and to give the expanding Stirling complement at Oakington more room. The squadron had lost two Blenheims while on operations from the airfield.

During that same month, a few Spitfires appeared in a corner of the station to take up the newly-formed No. 3 Photographic Reconnaissance Unit (PRU) with a mission to conduct high altitude camera work over Bomber Command's targets but due to poor surface conditions during winter months, the unit often operated from Alconbury. The following summer it was moved to Benson.

The choice of grass-surfaced Oakington to base Stirlings when hard-surfaced runways were available elsewhere in No. 3 Group is puzzling. Oakington's fen soil had under-drainage of the landing ground but it was no place for such a heavy aircraft in winter, and the soft surface put added strain on the Stirling's ungainly undercarriage resulting in a spate of landing and take-off accidents during the winter of 1940-41. Nevertheless, No. 7 Squadron sent out its first sorties on February 19, 1941 to attack Rotterdam docks. However, the airfield was so often unserviceable that the Stirlings had to take off light and bomb-up at drier Wyton to carry out operations. During 1940 a perimeter track and at least 26 pans and six square-shaped hard-

While bushes and wild flowers have invaded the greensward along the perimeter track, the church tower still prevails.

standings were put down, two of the former being lost when two T2 hangars were erected on the north-west side of the technical area. Bomb stores were off to the north.

Hard runway construction began at Oakington during the spring of 1941 but No. 7 Squadron remained in residence while work was in progress laying concrete parallel to the grass strips. The main runway 05-23, 1,700 yards long, was completed first but the other two were not finished until the spring of the following year, the 01-19 being 1,300 yards and 10-28 1,400 yards. Thirty pan hardstandings were provided.

This photograph of Oakington, taken by No. 1 Photographic Reconnaissance Unit on March 13, 1942, shows work still in progress on constructing runways 01-19 and 10-28. It is extraordinary that there should have been such a long delay in providing hard runways for the large aircraft on such a notoriously wet airfield. Eight Stirlings of No. 7 Squadron are parked on the west end of 10-28.

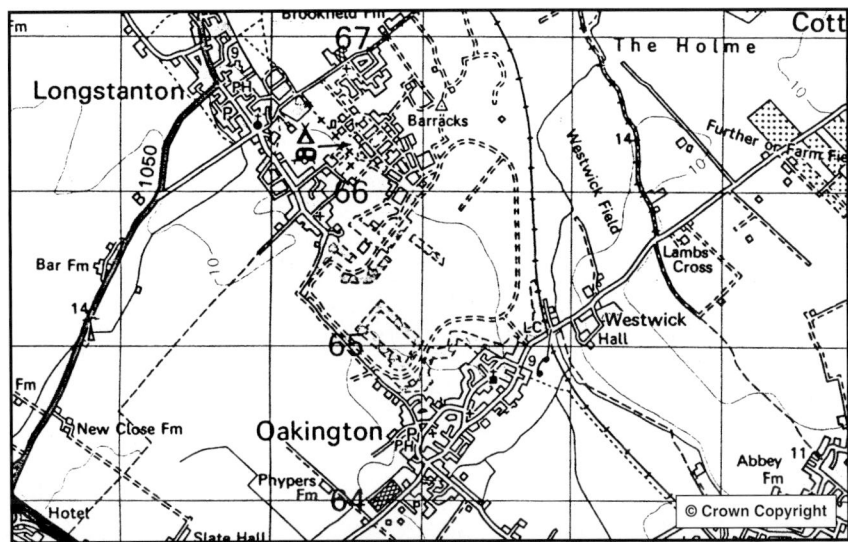

© Crown Copyright

Use was made of the 10-28 runway before it was fully completed to marshal No. 7 Squadron Stirlings before carrying out a raid. W7446 MG-B was lost on the Lübeck operation on March 28/29, 1942 when all the crew perished. No. 7 was the only squadron in Bomber Command that remained at the same airfield throughout its operational career.

In June 1941, No. 101 Squadron arrived from West Raynham to be re-established as a Wellington unit in No. 3 Group. In February 1942 No. 101 was moved to the new satellite at Bourn and in August No. 7 joined the Pathfinder Force as an original squadron.

Further work on the runways during the spring of 1942 saw 05-23 extended to 2,000 yards at its 23 end and 01-19 to 1,526 yards the north-eastern end. As a result of this work, the B1050 road had to be closed. Reworking the perimeter track to meet the extensions resulted in some loss of hardstandings, these being reduced to 28 to which eight loops were added. At a later date a B1 hangar was erected on the north-west side of the airfield near Long Stanton village. Expanded domestic accommodation allowed for a maximum of 1,591 males and 350 females.

In January 1943, the Pathfinder Force became No. 8 Group and, with the gradual withdrawal of the Stirling from main force bombing operations, an early move was made that summer to re-equip No. 7 with Lancasters. No. 8 Group had settled on a policy of two squadrons per airfield, one with

King Peter II of Yugoslavia fled his country in April 1941 when it was invaded by the Germans and Hungarians. He arrived in Britain via Greece, Egypt and Palestine in June to form a government in exile in London. He was already an enthusiastic pilot who had done a lot of amateur flying. The containers in the foreground would each carry up to 235 4lb incendiary bombs which were released in showers.

The deserted line of Type J hangars in 1999 . . . little changed from 1942 save for the fading of the camouflage paint and the later T2 hangar.

The middle of the airfield is now a wilderness and very water-logged with an army excavation known as Sapper Lake.

Sharp contrast to the trim conditions when the mighty Stirlings ruled the roost.

Lancasters and the other with Mosquitos and to this end No. 627 Squadron was formed at Oakington in November 1943 and became operational on the night of the 24th/25th. In April 1944 it went to No. 5 Group when that formation was developing its own target-marking techniques for precision attacks. A new squadron — No. 571 — was formed to replace No. 627, which started life at Downham Market, beginning operations from Graveley before moving into Oakington.

Total operational losses of bombers flying from the airfield, including those destroyed in crashes in the UK, amounted to 258. This was made up of 113 Stirlings, 93 Lancasters, 36 Mosquitos and 16 Wellingtons.

Post-war, No. 7 was moved to Mepal in July 1945 when Oakington was transferred to Transport Command, the squadron being unique in Bomber Command in having been based at the same station throughout its operational career. It was at Oakington for over four and a half years during which time it flew 546 raids — more than 5,000 sorties — with 78 Stirlings and 87 Lancasters failing to return from operations. The same month No. 571 Squadron was moved out to Warboys.

Ex-Coastal Command Liberators of Nos. 206 and 86 Squadrons then took up station at Oakington in July and August 1945 for long-range troop transport to the Far East but

these squadrons were disbanded the following April after which Yorks arrived. A succession of transport squadrons came and went until late in 1950 when Training Command inherited the station. Harvards, Meteors, Vampires and then Varsities and Jetstreams were the main types in succession through the next 25 years. The Army then took over the camp as a barracks but in 1999 the Royal Anglian Regiment moved from Oakington to North Luffenham. The runways have now been removed for hard-core but the perimeter track remains. In 2000, part of the former domestic area was earmarked for accomodating overseas applicants for asylum in Britain.

333

POLEBROOK

A Fortress I lifts off runway 26 bound for Brest on July 24, 1941. The J and T2 hangars can be seen on the far side of the airfield. Although No. 90 Squadron was part of No. 2 Group at the time, the airfield was later administered by the first No. 8 Group.

On September 1, 1941, Bomber Command formed No. 8 Group with headquarters at Brampton, near Huntingdon, to control squadrons to be formed to fly the American-made Fortress and Liberator heavy bombers on several new airfields in the Huntingdon/Northamptonshire area. However, the United States entry into hostilities, and the plan to base a USAAF heavy bomber force in the UK, saw this airfield grouping handed over to the Americans which led to the disbandment of No. 8 Group in January 1942. Nevertheless, one of the airfields earmarked for the original No. 8 Group did come into operational use during the summer of 1941 for the first Fortresses received by the RAF — Polebrook.

In May 1941, No. 90 Squadron was reformed at Watton under No. 2 Group, then some days later transferred to West Raynham to operate the Fortress I. As this airfield was found unsuitable for the aircraft, its satellite at Great Massingham was used for a few weeks but it was clear the type demanded a smoother and longer take-off run when fully loaded so in June the squadron moved to Polebrook.

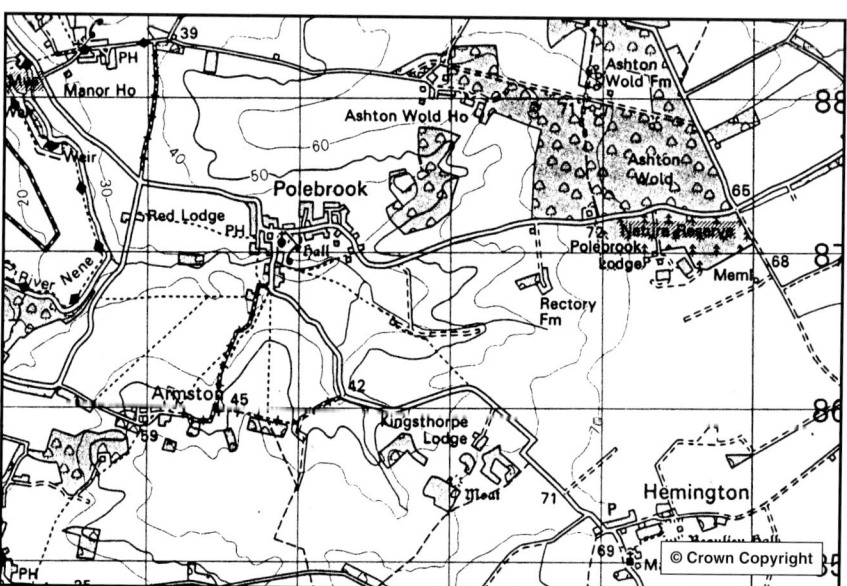

Arable set-aside has replaced the runway and the T2 was burnt down in 1979. The J hangar is now used for storage

Located 3½ miles east-south-east of Oundle, the airfield was built on Rothchild estate land from August 1940, George Wimpey & Co. Ltd being the main contractor. The concrete runway lengths were 08-26 at 1,280 yards, 14-32 at 1,200 yards and 02-20, 1,116 yards. Thirty square hardstandings, most on the eastern side, were reached by very long access tracks. The weapons store was unusual in that it lay within the perimeter track at the southern end. One Type J and two Type T2 hangars were erected on the technical site outside the northern perimeter with the domestic sites dispersed in woodland beyond. Several of the hardstandings and taxiways were still under construction when the squadron arrived.

No. 90's Fortress Is were used for very high-altitude attacks in daylight, the first operation from Polebrook being flown on July 8, 1941 when three Fortresses were despatched to a target at Wilhelmshaven. Their last raid launched from Polebrook was on September 2, 1941. While in residence No. 90 was then the sole operational squadron assigned to No. 8 Group and, before it was disbanded on February 12, 1942, its remaining aircraft and crews were only involved in experimentation and training. Although two Fortresses were missing from operations conducted from Kinloss, the only loss resulting from a raid flown from Polebrook involved a badly battle-damaged aircraft that crash-landed at a south-coast airfield.

With the departure of No. 90 Squadron work was put in hand to extend the runway lengths, increase the number of hardstandings and domestic accommodation for USAAF occupation. The first American units arrived in June 1942, and the station was subsequently occupied by the 97th Bomb Group from July to November 1942 and the 351st Bomb Group from May 1943 to June 1945, both formations being equipped with B-17 Fortresses.

Post-war the station came under No. 273 Maintenance Unit and the airfield was kept in useable state until October 1948 when it was closed. Agriculture returned to the flying field but in 1959 No. 130 Squadron was formed at Polebrook to operate three Thor missile emplacements constructed in the centre of the airfield. The rockets were removed and the unit disbanded in August 1963. Thereafter the land was repurchased by the Rothchild estate and the St Ives Sand and Gravel company broke up all concrete — apart from the ends of runways 02 and 32 — during the next decade. In 1999 the airfield has few reminders of its wartime past.

December 1948 saw the airfield abandoned although still retained by the Air Ministry against future requirements.

That need came in to being ten years later when Polebrook was selected as one of the 20 British airfields to be equipped with the American Thor ballistic missile (see page 63). Three launch pads were constructed close to the technical site, this photograph being taken in 1978, the missiles having been withdrawn in August 1963.

Today the last vestiges of concrete are being removed, the unusual triangle of the 02/32 runways having virtually disappeared.

UPWOOD

The Officers' Mess — the architecture being typical of that adopted during the expansion of the Royal Air Force in the 1930s. It became a training facility for American NCOs when Upwood was handed over to the USAF post-war.

Pasture at Upwood first came into use for an aeroplane landing ground in 1916 when the Royal Flying Corps established a training station there for night flying. A few huts and temporary aeroplane sheds were erected, only to be quickly removed when the RAF vacated the site in 1919. FE2b and BE2c/e were the aircraft types to be most commonly seen. However, the location was not forgotten and it was converted into a permanent RAF station in 1935-36.

Unchanged in over 60 years, only the motor cars indicate the passage of time. The building bears a sign over the entrance proclaiming 'Mathies NCO Academy, USAFE' named in honour of Sergeant Archie Mathies, the ball-turret gunner of a 351st Group Fortress who was posthumously awarded the Medal of Honor attempting to bring back a crippled B-17 from an operation to Leipzig on February 20, 1944 with wounded crewmen aboard.

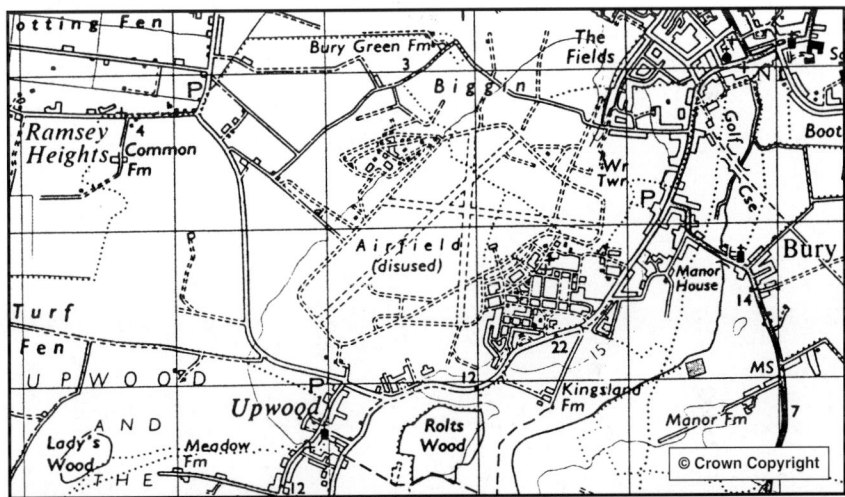

© Crown Copyright

This Fairey Battle, K7602, belonged to No. 52 Squadron in the spring of 1938. The hangar had yet to receive a disruptive pattern of camouflage paint.

Located a mile-and-a-half south west of Ramsey and in the north-east corner of Upwood parish, this expansion scheme airfield was grass-surfaced and comprised some 250 acres, the landing ground allowing runs of 1,000 yards in any direction. The camp of permanent buildings lay in the south-west corner adjacent to the village of Bury and consisted of the steel and brick flat-roofed buildings that were the hallmark of these expansion period stations. Three Type C hangars fronted the bombing circle in the usual arc arrangement, with a fourth situated behind that on the west side. The original bomb store was on the north-west side of the landing area.

Upwood was opened early in 1937 with Nos. 52 and 63 Squadrons arriving from Abingdon and Andover, respectively, in March. Both had Hinds as main equipment and during that year received the first Fairey Battles to reach Bomber Command. When

Upwood photographed from 10,000 feet on June 16, 1941 when No. 17 OTU was in residence. The perimeter track is still being laid.

Still intact . . . but for how long? How sad it is to see yet another piece of RAF history fade away.

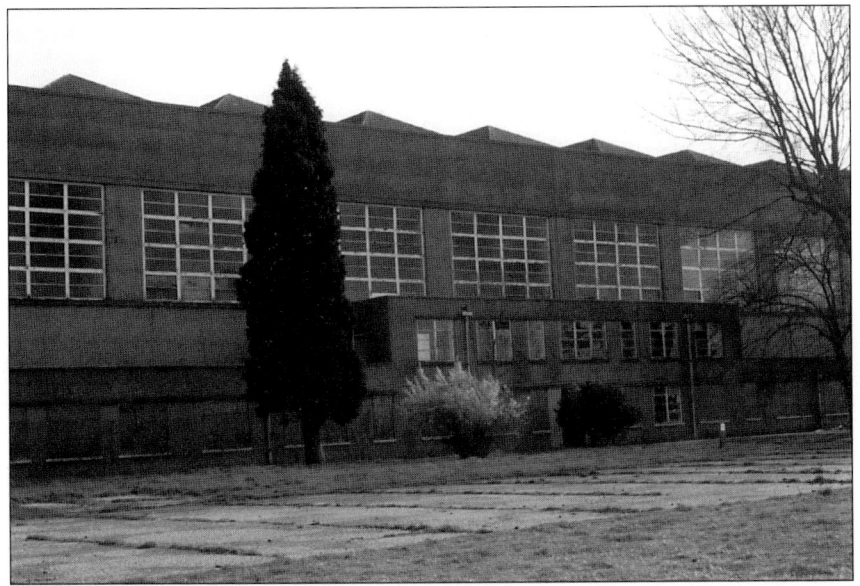

war was declared neither squadron was to see immediate action and they were soon moved to Benson to conduct operational training in No. 6 Group. Upwood remained a No. 6 Group station and became a training establishment for Blenheim crews with No. 90 Squadron arriving from West Raynham in September 1939 to replace the Battle units and No. 35 joining in February. In April 1940 both squadrons lost their identities when merged to form No. 17 Operational Training Unit.

During the following months tarmac hardstandings were put down round the airfield boundary together with a perimeter track. Until Blenheim usage was in decline Upwood hosted No. 17 OTU but the unit moved to Silverstone in April 1943, the reason being that the airfield was scheduled to receive hard runways. The main 06-24 was 2,000 yards long, 01-19 at 1,400 yards and 11-29 at 1,600 yards. These, constructed during the period May-October 1943, were linked by a compeletely new concrete perimeter track (the old one was broken up) to aircraft standings put down in the previous three years. Only six of the existing square hardstandings were considered still useable following this work and 30 of the loop type were added to bring the total to the required number. M. J. Speight & Partners Ltd were responsible for this construction work. Maximum accommodation at Upwood at this time was given as for 2,085 males and 336 females.

The station then came under No. 8 Group and in February 1944 No. 139 Squadron moved in with Mosquitos. The following month No. 156 Squadron joined them from Warboys to give Upwood an operational Lancaster unit and these two squadrons remained in residence for the rest of hostilities. Operational losses from Upwood totaled 66, half being Lancasters and half Mosquitos.

In June 1945, No. 156 was transferred to Wyton, the Mosquitos of No. 105 Squadron taking their place. This squadron was disbanded in February 1946 and moved to Hemswell in the same month. Upwood was then in the hands of Transport Command with Liberators of No. 53 Squadron present for three months.

The station reverted to Bomber Command in July 1946 with Lancasters of No. 7 Squadron being brought in from Mepal. Three more Lancaster squadrons arrived later in 1946, Nos. 49, 148 and 214, and in 1949 all Upwood squadrons re-equipped with Lincolns. Between 1954 and 1956 the Lincolns departed and their squadrons were disbanded to be replaced by four Canberra squadrons. New hardstandings were constructed by Mowlem in 1955. The Canberras endured until the end of the decade but were gone by late 1961.

In the 'sixties' Upwood ceased to be occupied by flying units and instead became an RAF ground station but in the following decade it was taken over by the USAF as a support base for Alconbury. For several years it housed a USAF NCO college and hospital until the former facility was wound up in 1995. The clinic hospital remains but the rest of the station has been sold for housing and light industry.

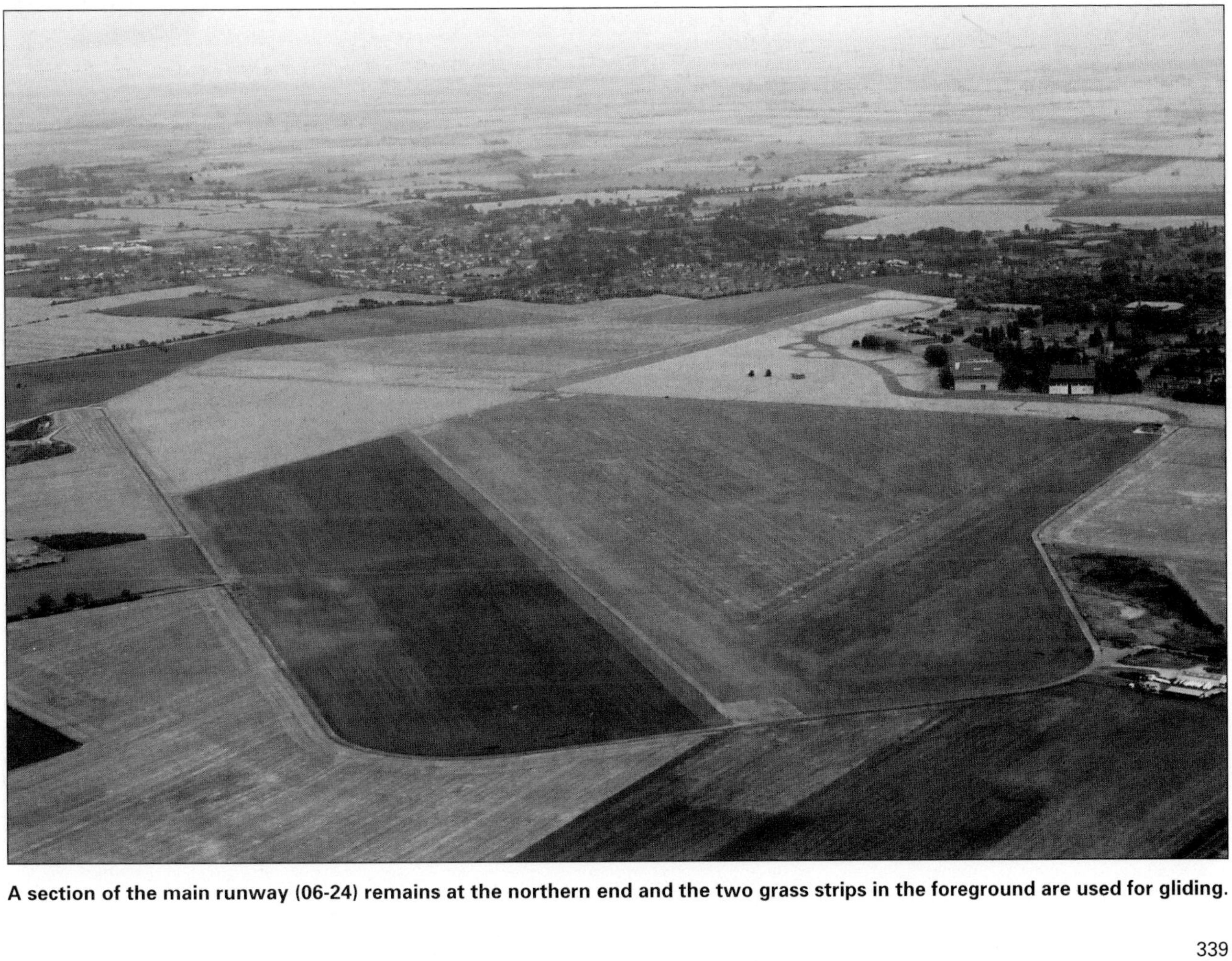

A section of the main runway (06-24) remains at the northern end and the two grass strips in the foreground are used for gliding.

WARBOYS

The King and Queen visited RAF Warboys on February 10, 1944. This picture was taken at the west end of the technical site T2 with a Pathfinder Lancaster of No. 156 Squadron in the background.

Located seven miles-south west of Chatteris and south of Warboys village, this airfield was constructed to the west of the A141 Huntingdon to Chatteris road in 1941-42. The runways were 12-30 at 1,250 yards, 07-25 at 1,100 yards and 18-36 at 1,100 yards. However, in early 1942, before the airfield was finished, the runways were extended. To achieve the required length for the 12-30 it was necessary to take it across the A141; consequently a new length of public road had to be built to bypass the airfield and the village. The final runway lengths were 12-30 at 2,097 yards, 07-25 at 1,447 yards and 18-36 at 1,350 yards. The perimeter track was reworked to connect the ends of the new runway. Twenty-four pan hardstandings had already been constructed but two of these were lost to hangar construction. With 18 loop type added, the total of aircraft standings was 39. The hangars were a T2 on the technical site on the south-east side near the start of the new bypass road with another on the north side and a B1 east of the 18 runway head. The bomb stores lay off the west side and eleven domestic, mess and communal sites dispersed either side of the A141 south to Old Hurst. Maximum accommodation was given as for 1,959 males and 291 females.

Allocated to No. 3 Group in August 1942, the Wellington's of No. 156 Squadron moved in from Alconbury which was then being turned over to the USAAF. The squadron's first operation from Warboys was on the night of August 9/10 and later in the month it became one of the original squadrons of the new Pathfinder Force. No. 156 converted to Lancasters in January 1943 being resident until March 1944 when it was moved to Upwood. Thereafter Warboys became an operational training station with No. 8

Group's Night Training Unit coming with Lancasters from Upwood and No. 1655 Mosquito Conversion Unit was re-formed to provide instruction on that type. This unit was absorbed by No. 16 OTU at Upper Heyford in December 1944 and the NTU continued part of the Mosquito instructional programme. A total of 99 aircraft were lost on wartime operations from Warboys: 16 Wellingtons and 83 Lancasters.

Following VE-Day, the training establishment was dissolved and in July No. 571

Squadron with its Mosquitos arrived from Oakington only to disband in September, the airfield closing to flying at the end of 1945. The flying field remained intact for many years although the B1040 was reinstated. In 1960 a Bloodhound unit, No. 257 Squadron, was set up on the western side beside runway 12-30, but these air-to-air missiles were removed in 1964 and the airfield sold. The technical site buildings were taken over by a transport firm and the airfield itself returned to agricultural use.

How are the mighty fallen! Hardly fit for a royal visit, the area at the back of the hangar has been reclaimed by nature.

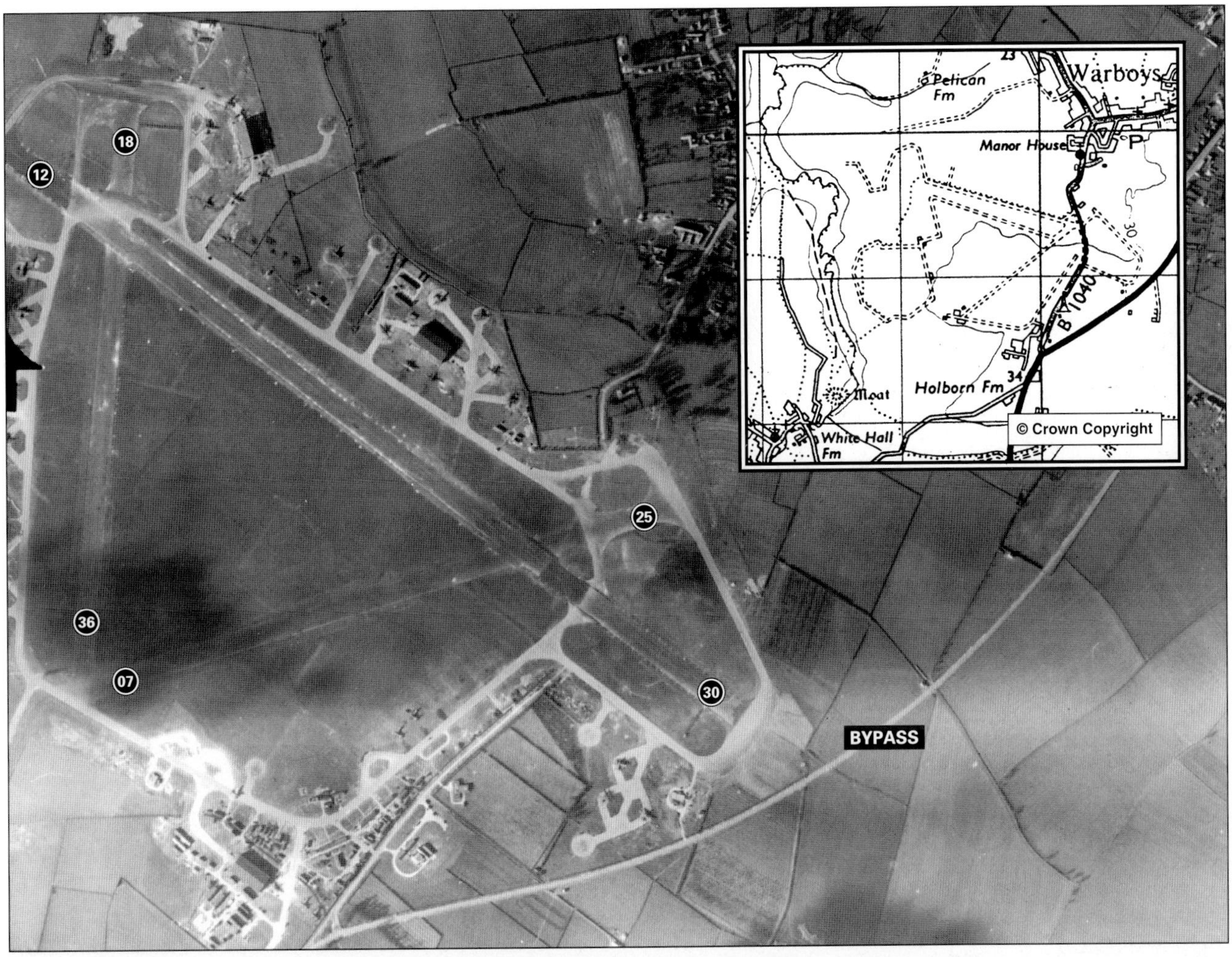

Covered by the US 7th Photo Group on March 2, 1944, the airfield appears well stocked with Lancasters.

Looking northwards in September 2000. The bypass built to allow the 12-30 runway to be extended can be seen lower right.

WYTON

As we have seen in these pages, airfields constantly change. They evolve and develop . . . have their moment of glory before they fade away. Wyton in July 1940 was a grass aerodrome. These Blenheims of No. 40 Squadron are in the north-western corner.

One of the oldest airfield sites in East Anglia three miles north-east of Huntingdon, a landing ground was established at Wyton in 1916 on meadowland at Hartford Hill on the eastern side of the crossroads. Developed as a training establishment, it survived until 1919 although it was occasionally used for private flying thereafter.

During the early expansion plans in the 1930s, the site was one of those approved for construction of a permanent RAF station, the camp being built on the south side of the landing ground adjacent to the B1090 road. The three Type C hangars were positioned in an arc fronting the usual bombing circle and a fourth Type C placed behind on the east side. Construction from 1935 took nearly two years to complete by the main contractors W & C French Co Ltd.

No. 139 Squadron was re-formed at the station in September 1936 and No. 114 in December, both to fly Hinds. No. 114 converted to Blenheims in March 1937 and No. 139 in July. Wyton was then the premier No. 2 Group station and these were its first Blenheim-equipped squadrons.

It was a No. 139 Squadron Blenheim that carried out the first Bomber Command sortie of the war — a photographic reconnaissance over the north-west German coast on September 3, 1939. In December 1939, both Wyton squadrons were sent to France and Nos. 15 and 40 Squadrons returned from the Continent to Wyton, the first step in converting Battle squadrons to Blenheims. Both squadrons flew their first bombing raids from Wyton on May 10, 1940 against targets in the Low Countries. The Blenheims of No. 57 Squadron were based briefly at Wyton in June before going south, returning for two weeks the following month before flying north only to appear again at Wyton in late October. Although Wyton was close to No. 2 Group Headquarters in Huntingdon, the airfield was far removed from the main grouping in Norfolk and Suffolk.

As Bomber Command was increasingly committed to building up its strength in medium and heavy bombers for operations in the hours of darkness, a decision was made to transfer Wyton to No. 3 Group, whose general area was spreading west, and to convert Blenheim squadrons to Wellingtons. However, as there was not room for three Wellington squadrons on one station, No. 57 was moved to Feltwell early in November while Nos. 15 and 40 were introduced to the Vickers type. Both became operational with the Wellington in December and in February 1941 No. 40 Squadron was moved to the satellite at Alconbury.

It was planned that No. 3 Group would ultimately become an all-Stirling formation and April 1941 saw No. 15 Squadron re-equipping with this giant. Hard runway construction was carried out at Wyton in the winter of 1941-42 with a main runway 09-27 at 2,000 yards and the subsidiaries, 06-24 and 16-34, both 1,400 yards. Thirty-seven irregular-shaped hardstandings had been put down on the airfield during the first two years of the war and these were now linked to a new perimeter track. At this time Wyton could accommodate a maximum of 2,293 males and 428 females. The bomb stores were located across the road to the north-west of the airfield.

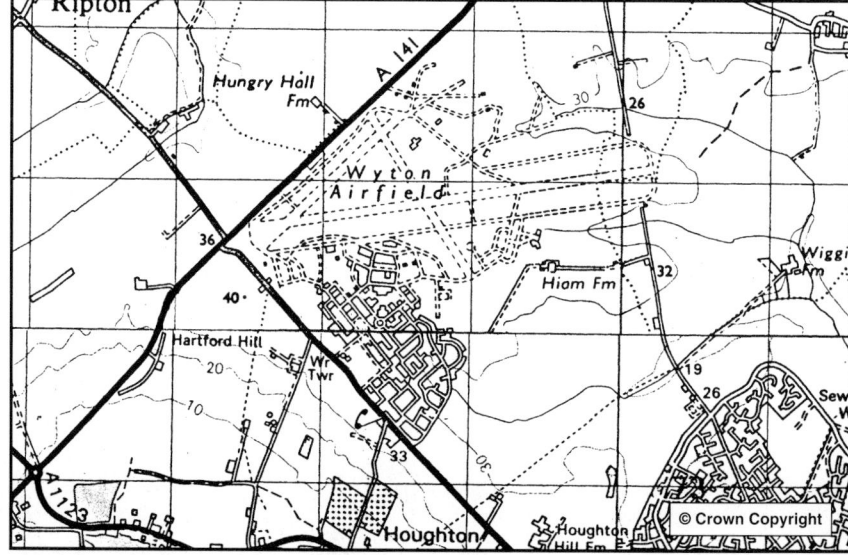

Sixty years later the airfield is dominated by its 2,750-yard asphalt-surfaced runway. Having expanded well beyond its 1940 boundaries even the minor road from St Ives to Oldhurst has been bisected by the eastern extension.

A141

16
24
09
06
27
34

Above: **Runways were laid down in the winter of 1941-42 this picture being taken on July 13, 1942. The facilities are already being expanded on the far side of the A141 and dispersals reach out like tentacles. There are ten Stirlings visible on the hardstandings and another six dotted around the airfield, all belonging to No. 15 Squadron.**

The formation of the Pathfinder Force in No. 3 Group — which became No. 8 Group in January 1943 — found Wyton its headquarters. No. 15 Squadron was one of the first assigned to the Pathfinder Force in August 1942 and it was moved to the satellite at Bourn (which had replaced Alconbury). Lancasters were considered the prime vehicle for heavy bomber pathfinder duties; consequently No. 83 Squadron was brought in from No. 5 Group at Scampton. In September 1942, No. 109 arrived from Stradishall to be organised as an Oboe Mosquito unit, carrying out its first operation from Wyton on

Right: **Unfortunately this print is undated but it has obviously been taken at a later date as the bomb storage has been fully developed west of the A141. During the first four years of war, there was ongoing development at every RAF Bomber Command airfield but little thereafter.**

Wizard Prang! This Stirling (LS-R) of No. 15 Squadron caught in a rather undignified position off the east side of runway 34. This incident occurred on June 2, 1942. More Stirlings can be seen parked in the distance.

December 20/21, 1942. No. 109 remained until July 1943 when it exchanged places with No. 139 Squadron at Marham where the Oboe-equipped Mosquitos were to be concentrated. No. 139 Squadron's Mosquitos performed pathfinder duties until being moved out to Upwood in February 1944 to make use of H2S equipment. No. 83 Squadron's Lancasters remained with No. 8 Group at Wyton until April 1944 when No. 5 Group set up its own pathfinder activities and reclaimed the squadron.

To further the Light Night Striking Force, No. 128 Squadron was re-formed at Wyton in September 1944 with Mosquitos, becoming operational on October 10/11, 1944. So successful was the LNSF that another squadron, No. 163, was re-formed in late January 1945, flying its first raid on 28/29th of the month.

During the war a total of 218 bombers were lost in operations from Wyton: 57 Blenheims, 5 Wellingtons, 48 Stirlings, 64 Lancasters and 47 Mosquitos.

After VE-Day No. 128 Squadron was moved to Warboys in June being replaced by No. 156 Squadron with Lancasters. No. 163 disbanded in August and No. 156 in September. After a year's lull, four Lancaster-equipped squadrons were based at Wyton, the Lancs eventually giving way to Lincolns.

In the early 'fifties the main runway was lengthened across a small public road in the east end and the airfield then became the main RAF centre for strategic reconnaissance with Mosquitos, later being replaced by Canberras and, later still, Valiants. Victors replaced the Valiants and endured through the 'seventies when Nimrods came on the scene. Canberras returned and were present during the next two decades. Wyton ceased to be a flying station in March 1995 when it was taken over by units of Logistics Command. The Cambridge University Air Squadron took up residence in 1999 and flying recommenced.

Left: **The same Hiam Farm still stands off the eastern perimeter and is visible behind the Stirlings and on the left of the comparison above.** *Below:* **Wyton, September 2000, now used for ab initio pilot training. The main runway is still designated 09-27 as it was during wartime.**

345

Some 125,000 aircrew served in RAF Bomber Command of whom more than 55,000 lost their lives. Of these, 38,462 were members of the Royal Air Force; 9,919 of the Royal Canadian Air Force; 4,050 the Royal Australian Air Force; 1,679 Royal New Zealand Air Force; 929 Polish Air Force; and 534 from other Allied and Dominion air forces. In total, nearly 60 per cent of air-crews of Bomber Command became casualties, either killed, missing or prisoners of war. The Halifax above, DT789, of No. 10 Squadron (coded ZA-B) was shot down on an operation to Dortmund on the night of May 23/24, 1943. All seven of the crew perished and today only the pilot, Sergeant John Rees, has a marked grave. His body was found on July 8 at Neufelderkoog. He was first buried at Brunsbüttel but was moved after the war to Kiel War Cemetery. The remainder of the crew — Sergeant Bill Oliver, Sergeant Fred Rose, Sergeant Sam Gaywood, Sergeant Denis Birkhead, Sergeant Evan David and Sergeant Frank Farnell — were never found and are now commemorated on the Air Forces Memorial at Runnymede.

The Men . . . and their Memorials

Eleven p.m. somewhere in the Ruhr. Overhead the drone of aircraft circling; on the ground guns and searchlights: hundreds of guns and searchlights, all of them quiet as death, but none the less guns and searchlights, and beside each of them soldiers at action stations, waiting. In all a mighty panorama; and surveying it, a new-born moon. A game worthy of the gods, and at the moment both sides jockeying for position. A stage, too, with players and audience waiting for the curtain to go up. But, before the curtain goes up and the act begins, stop for a while; stop and consider.

Overhead a few planes and in them a few bodies. On the ground a few guns, and beside them also a few bodies. The outcome, in essence, is certain. On the ground a few, very few, men and women will lose their lives, a few buildings will be destroyed. In the air, too, a few men will lose their lives, and a few machines be destroyed, possibly. A simple operation without great significance, but think for a while on all that has gone before.

To build the aircraft, there has been ship upon ship, bringing iron and steel across the seas. Factories working day after day

and year after year, converting raw materials into finished parts. Men and women, called away from their wives and their husbands, labouring at a task they hate and never were meant to perform. On the other side, too, the mighty structure of the Air Force. At the head, the Cabinet has issued a general order based on the dictates of their present policy. From them the order has passed through Air Ministry, the Ministry of Economic Warfare, Bomber Command, Group, the station, and finally to the Squadron itself. With each stage the orders have become more technical and more detailed, and to enable the first general declaration of policy to be interpreted into the orders given to the pilot, a countless staff of experts has had to be trained and fed and paid. An equally vast organization, too, has been created to provide a pilot capable of executing these orders, and equally a whole system of supply and maintenance of aircraft, and bombs, and guns, and petrol, and oil, and clothing and countless other tools. And this is but a vision, a small, fleeting vision, of the organization that has been created to enable one pilot to drop one bomb: and when this has been done there is not one member of the whole organization who can so much as lift one finger to influence where the bomb is actually going to fall.

At Melbourne today this fine memorial remembers those personnel of No. 10 Squadron who served . . . and those who died.

It stands beside the old main entrance through which so many passed never to return.

The memorials take all shapes and forms. *Left:* This well-tended monument, erected by the members of Nos. 35 and 635 Squadron Associations in 1991, stands at the roadside entrance to Cotton Farm at Graveley. *Right:* Nos. 109 and 582 Squadrons are remembered at Little Staughton. The T2 is the one on the western side of the airfield.

Then, and only then, when these mighty wheels have creaked into motion, is the stage set for the pawns to play their act. And behind the background of Air Vice-Marshals and Cabinet Ministers and blast furnaces and oil wells and ships and potentates of industry, these pawns are very small. Pilot Officers and Sergeants. Here and there a few Squadron Leaders and perhaps a Wing Commander or so, but mostly Sergeants and Pilot

Officers. Pawns, all of them; gone today and forgotten tomorrow, but, curiously, it is on them that the spotlights are turned.

The potentates of industry have built the stage, the Air Vice-Marshals have pulled the curtains apart and in front sit a whole host of reporters, with all the might of a worldwide news service behind them, waiting to flash the picture across the seven seas. The pawns should feel honoured, and, curiously enough, they do.

A small memorial stone for the personnel of RAF Gransden Lodge stands in a beautiful setting beside the preserved windmill on the road to Great Gransden, west of the airfield.

This bronze statue by Helen Granger Young is a half-size copy of the original in Winnipeg, Canada. Its erection at Croft was spearheaded by ex-431 Squadron aircrew member Jim Cable who wanted a memorial sited as close as possible to his old airfield. It was dedicated on September 26, 1987 at Dalton-on-Tees next to the Darlington to Northallerton road.

'To commemorate thirty-two years of service given in the cause of freedom by the men and women who were stationed at Royal Air Force Stradishall and honouring the sacrifices that were made.'

The advance formation of the attack has arrived. Overhead the air is full of the droning of aircraft, circling and twisting and diving: of dimmed lights so as better to be able to see the ground: of the rustling of maps and snatches of conversation: of gunners searching the sky for a warning of fighters. And everywhere, eyes. Dozens of pairs of eyes probing and straining, trying to pierce through the darkness to the clue for which they are looking. There is a moon of sorts and no clouds, but even then the ground is not clear.

From 8,000 feet prominent landmarks such as lakes and rivers and light-coloured roads stand out, but beyond that not much. The Rhine is the best of them all, but it is over to the west, and, anyway, it is hotly defended. So the eyes will only turn west as a last resort, or when the defences reveal themselves.

Back in England, too, there is a quiet air of action. From Air Ministry down to the squadron men are standing by, waiting for developments. Some of them have finished their work for the day: it was their responsibility to see the aircraft safely airborne, and now that is done it is their duty to be ready for tomorrow. Others are just getting up, preparing to take over from those who are finished. Others, too, are on duty at the present moment; for the last two hours probably sitting around killing time, but now zero hour is up. At any minute news will come through. Most of it will be 'Mission completed', but there will be other news as well. It may be anything: 'Task abandoned, bombs jettisoned, returning base' 'Pilot injured — require medical assistance on landing'; 'Fighter attack developing, will communicate results later.' There may be an SOS: 'Aircraft damaged by flak and unable to maintain height'. Perhaps someone will come down in the sea; his position will have to be fixed and the whole rescue organization put into action. If anyone is not awake or makes a mistake, five men who could have been saved may be lost.

To No. 115 Squadron at Witchford.

For No. 207 Squadron — motto 'Semper paratus' (Always prepared) — at Langar.

The Flight Sergeant Ken White memorial erected at Fulbeck in 1988 by the Bomber Airfield Society.

Binbrook's memorial to the Royal Australian Air Force squadron No. 460 (motto 'Strike and Return').

The matter is not a simple one: the aircraft's wireless may be damaged and the only clue of what has happened be a broken, incomplete message. The weather, too, has to be watched. There is a staff of experts who do nothing else but forecast the run of future conditions, but they cannot always be right. Fog may close in suddenly and the aircraft may have to be recalled or diverted to some other part of the country. If it is not done quickly, it may be too late. And in any case, whether an emergency arises or not, the organization has to be ready to receive the crews on their return. Half the task is to drop the bombs, the other half is to know where they have dropped and what are the latest movements of the enemy. Command wants news,

not history. And so, while the pawns are still jockeying for position, the brains behind them are stirring and watchful.

The defences are ready: they have work to do, and therefore there is not so much time to reflect. Predictors, sound-locators, shells, fuzes. A hundred-and-one things to be done and prepared, and all the time waiting for the order to fire. The night is dark — not very, but dark enough to make map-reading difficult — and it is not a foregone conclusion that the bombers will find their target. The defences are crafty; they are not going to give the position of targets away until they are sure the bombers know where they are. They do not always do that, but that is their policy tonight, and it is a good policy.

Left: **Oulton: 'Those who died for our freedom will live forever in our hearts'.** *Right:* **Burn: 'For all who served'.**

Memorials to Bomber Command are to be found in streets, on buildings and at abandoned airfields. *Above:* **Next to the entrance at North Killingholme.** *Below:* **On the control tower at Tholthorpe.** *Bottom:* **Beside the old runway at Fiskerton.**

In all there is an air of tension, both sides watching each other, like cats, for the first hostile move. Peace reigns over the world, but in the twinkling of an eye this peace may be transformed into a holocaust of steel and gunpowder and fire. The gunners have the drop. They can sit back and watch the movements of the bombers, but they do not know what exactly the bombers are looking for. At any moment one of the attackers may locate his target, and if the defences are not wide awake the boot may be on the other foot. He may drop his bombs undisturbed, and, because he is undisturbed, with accuracy: he may even break out without a single shot to impede him.

As soon as his bombs burst every gun will crash into action, but the sky is full of aircraft, all at different heights and speeds and courses. If the first bombs find their mark, every bomb-sight in the sky will converge overhead, because that is what the eyes behind the bomb-sights have been straining to see. As soon as they see it, the air of quiet tension will disappear. The crews will jump into action. 'Bomb-doors open. Bombs fuzed. Left, left; steady. Bombs gone.' It may all take a few seconds: it may even take five minutes, but in any case it will not take very long, and then overhead there will be silence until the next wave. . . .

At Strubby the Lincolnshire Military Preservation Society have set up a memorial next to the restored fire party hut by the main gate.

At East Kirkby where the airfield itself is also a memorial.

The last gun closed down, the last searchlight faded out, and overhead the drone of aircraft disappeared gradually into the distance. The play was over: the tension had come and risen and finally exploded in a fury of fire and steel, and now that too was gone. In its place was an air of relief and quiet.

Yes, now it was all over, it was funny to look back on, and a flood of memories swept through my mind. The crash of shells, the venom of the light tracer, the glare of the searchlights. They weren't particularly funny; it was our reactions and the expressions on our faces: the way we edged hopefully away each time a shower of splinters came rattling through the fuselage. Then our shouting and excitement against the noise from outside, until speech was almost unintelligible.

As the minutes ticked silently by we settled down to doze and to dream. The coast came, England came, and half an hour before dawn we landed.

GROUP CAPTAIN LEONARD CHESHIRE
VC, DSO, DFC
BOMBER PILOT, 1942

Memorials dedicated to fighting airmen are to be found at many of RAF Bomber Command's former airfields . . . like this one *(left)* at Holme-on-Spalding-Moor and on Elvington airfield *(right)*

. . . but wherever tributes in brick and stone have been erected, they all echo the empathy enshrined in the motto of the Royal Air Force: 'Through hardship to the stars'.

Memories fade with the passing of the years but Arthur Clarke *(above)* still recalls the names of some of his fellow crewmen on that last flght to Kiel. *Right:* Pictured on their return are (rear L-R) the rear gunner, Trevor Molloy; Jock Lawrence, the flight engineer; Jock Richie, wireless operator; unidentified; (front) unidentified; Sam Burley, their pilot, and Arthur, the navigator.

The Last Operational Aircrew over Europe

Adolf Hitler committed suicide in Berlin on April 30, 1945, and a surrender document (excluding Norway) was about to be signed. There had been no raids over Germany for several days and the war was generally thought to be over.

Aircrew of No. 199 Squadron, based at North Creake in Norfolk, breathed a sigh of relief for most were on a second tour of operations and, against all the odds, had survived.

Then, on May 2, there were reports of large columns of mechanised troops at Kiel where an armada of ships was assembled. It was thought that these troops would go as reinforcements to strengthen the German Army in Norway which, together with its Air Force, was still largely intact. The war might, therefore, continue for perhaps another year, with heavy casualties being expected as another invasion fought its way, mile by mile, across difficult, mountainous terrain favouring its defenders.

So, on May 2/3, 1945, six aircraft of No. 199 Squadron and two from No. 171 Squadron were detailed to carry out a radar counter-measures patrol to Schleswig, while 179 Mosquitos of Nos. 8 and 100 Groups and 89 Halifaxes of No. 100 Group attacked shipping and installations at Kiel. The final attack on red target indicators took place between 2325 and 2332 hours, the Kiel diarist, Detlef Boelck,

performing his duty to the end, reporting 18 casualties with a large column of military vehicles departing towards Flensburg in the early hours of the morning.

I was the navigator on Halifax 'N'-Nan (PN374) on the Schleswig patrol which was one of the very last to attack on this night, and our rear gunner (who had previously completed a first tour of operations with Squadron Leader Ian Bazalgette, VC) would, therefore, be one of the last — if not the very last — operational airman to enter and leave enemy German territory in the Second World War.

We set out on our RCM mission but one aircraft, 'A'-Able from No. 199 Squadron, returned early with its compass unserviceable and another, 'X'-X-Ray from No. 171, came back with a hydraulics failure. The rest completed their sorties successfully.

This was the last Bomber Command operation of the war on which our squadron suffered its last casualties, two aircraft 'R'-Roger and 'T'-Tare (RG375 and RG373) being lost with 13 of their crews killed, mostly second tour airmen. The aircraft crashed at Meimersdorf, just south of Kiel, the dead being buried in the Kiel War Cemetery.

FLIGHT LIEUTENANT ARTHUR CLARKE, DFC

199 SQUADRON. NORTH CREAKE. MAY 1945.						Time carried forward:—	186.55	414.35
Date	Hour	Aircraft Type and No.	Pilot	Duty	REMARKS (Including results of bombing, gunnery, exercises, etc.)		Day	Night
1/5/45.		P.N. 274 "N." HALIFAX III	F/LT. BURLEY.	NAVIGATOR.	CROSS COUNTRY +18 (KIEL) SCHLESWIC			2.55
2/5/45		P.N. 374 "N." HALIFAX III	F/LT. BURLEY.	NAVIGATOR.	(4 Y.) SPECIAL OPERATIONS. BOMBER SUPPORT. ESSEN			4.40
7/5/45.		R.G. 372 "P." HALIFAX III	F/LT. ARKINSTALL	NAVIGATOR.	RUHR AND RETURN. COLOGNE, DUSSELDORF,		5.10.	
							192.05	422.10
8/5/45.			V.E.	DAY.				

Arthur began his first tour in 1943 with No. 149 Squadron at Lakenheath (during which time he was awarded the DFC) and began his second at North Creake with No. 199 Squadron in February 1945. He was demobbed in January 1949.

INDEX

COMPILED BY PETER GUNN

No. 617 Squadron's memorial was built on the site of the Royal Hotel, destroyed by a German land-mine during WWII. Constructed of York stone and Cornish slate, the memorial takes the form of a breached dam. The centre panel, representing the water pouring through the breach, records the squadron's eight battle honours while the side panels list the names of 204 aircrew of the squadron who lost their lives.

Note: Page numbers in *italics* refer to illustrations. There may also be textual references on these pages.

IN MEMORIAM
RAF Bomber Command: *Strike Hard Strike Sure*